TEACHING MIDDLE SCHOOL PHYSICAL EDUCATION

Bonnie S. Mohnsen, PhD

Orange County (CA) Department of Education

Human Kinetics

This book is dedicated to Carolyn Thompson, 1994 National Secondary Physical Education Teacher of the Year, for her constant professional and personal support.

This book is also dedicated to the staffs at Montebello Intermediate (Karen Mendon, Harold Favilla, Virginia Rini, and Ray Rodriguez) and Ball Junior High School (Cheryl Mahlstedt, Gary Humphreys, Maggie Kelly, Jerry Thimgan and Debbie Willis) for their willingness to experiment with new ideas, risk failure, and accomplish the impossible. I have enjoyed being a part of their journeys. . . .

Library of Congress Cataloging-in-Publication Data

Mohnsen, Bonnie S., 1955-
    Teaching middle school physical education / Bonnie S. Mohnsen.
      p.   cm.
    Includes index.
    ISBN 0-88011-513-0
    1. Physical education and training--Study and teaching (Middle
school)--United States.   I. Title.
GV365.M65   1997
796'.071'2--dc20

                96-39066
                CIP

ISBN: 0-88011-513-0

Acquisitions Editor: Scott Wikgren; **Developmental Editor:** Kristine Enderle; **Assistant Editor:** Coree Schutter; **Copyeditor:** Bonnie Pettifor; **Proofreader:** Erin Cler; **Indexer:** Barbara E. Cohen; **Graphic Designer:** Stuart Cartwright; **Graphic Artist:** Denise Lowry; **Photo Editor:** Boyd LaFoon; **Cover Designer:** Keith Blomberg; **Photographer (cover):** Davis Barber; **Illustrators:** Patrick Griffin, line drawings; Tim Stiles, Mac art; **Printer:** United Graphics

Printed in the United States of America   10   9   8   7   6   5   4   3   2   1

Human Kinetics
Web site: http://www.humankinetics.com/

United States: Human Kinetics, P.O. Box 5076, Champaign, IL 61825-5076
1-800-747-4457
e-mail: humank@hkusa.com

Canada: Human Kinetics, Box 24040, Windsor, ON N8Y 4Y9
1-800-465-7301 (in Canada only)
e-mail: humank@hkcanada.com

Europe: Human Kinetics, P.O. Box IW14, Leeds LS16 6TR, United Kingdom
(44) 1132 781708
e-mail: humank@hkeurope.com

Australia: Human Kinetics, 57A Price Avenue, Lower Mitcham, South Australia 5062
(08) 277 1555
e-mail: humank@hkaustralia.com

New Zealand: Human Kinetics, P.O. Box 105-231, Auckland 1
(09) 523 3462
e-mail: humank@hknewz.com

CONTENTS

PREFACE

Teaching middle school students can be the most frustrating—and most rewarding—experience we can have as physical educators. Middle schoolers face significant physical, social, and emotional changes and challenges, and physical education class can amplify many of these factors. Yet when we are able to address the unique needs of middle school students, we can serve as a positive influence for transforming these children into adults.

Teaching Middle School Physical Education is the first comprehensive, practical resource for designing quality middle school physical education programs that both addresses the specific needs of middle school students and prepares them for our rapidly changing world. Indeed, this book is packed full of ideas and strategies to improve your program.

Developing a quality middle school physical education program is much like taking a journey, and this book will both prepare you for the journey and travel with you. In part I, "Prepare for Your Journey," we'll look at society, technology, health, and education changes and how these changes can shape middle school physical education programs for the better. We'll examine the development of middle schools, the current reform efforts, and examples of quality middle school physical education programs. I'll encourage you to buy your ticket by becoming equal partners in the entire education program of your school in order to gain equal funding, administrative support, and equitable class size and instructional time. In addition, I'll show you ways to increase respect for your program through developing extracurricular activities and coordinating an integrated, comprehensive school health program. To conclude part I, I'll discuss the physical and psychological components of a quality physical education environment.

In part II, "Map Out Your Journey," I'll guide you through the development of a physical education curriculum step by step, from start to finish. We'll discuss how to select a developmental committee and how to define a physically educated person. Then I'll show you how to translate this definition into exit standards and how to create grade level standards in alignment with the exit standards. Unlike other curriculum textbooks that may be collecting dust in your office, we'll go beyond ide-

als, as I show you how to select instructional units, how to integrate physical education with other subjects areas, and how to develop unit and lesson plans. But we won't stop there. We'll examine the benefits of authentic assessment and grading in physical education, including how to create rubrics and help students develop performance portfolios. We'll look at several alternative assessment tools that focus on student strengths and uncover student weaknesses in ways that are not demeaning or unfair, including structured observations, written tests, logs and journals, role-playing, reports, and projects.

In part III, "Travel Toward Your Destination," I'll share insights into the needs of middle school learners and the corresponding teaching behaviors, instructional styles and strategies, instructional materials, and new technologies that are especially effective at the middle school level. We'll discuss ways to motivate your students and reach all types of learners by engaging both your students and yourself. Specifically, we'll look closely at why and how to select a particular teaching style or strategy, based on the content standard you're teaching and the learning styles of your students. I'll conclude part III by encouraging you to continue to grow as a physical educator by attending in-services, conferences, or graduate school and by expanding your knowledge base through peer coaching, doing committee work, supervising a student teacher, or visiting other schools.

In part IV, "Discover Your Destination," I'll outline sample physical education programs for sixth, seventh, and eighth grades. In each unit, I'll include an overview, a list of unit standards linked directly to the grade level standards, and a day-by-day lesson outline. In addition, I'll suggest assessment tool ideas for each unit so that you can be sure that your students have accomplished the standards.

Designed with both you and your students in mind, *Teaching Middle School Physical Education* is a comprehensive yet flexible resource guide for creating a quality middle school physical education program at your school. It contains quality, up-to-date information that is practical and usable for both the veteran and new teacher. Now, let the journey begin. . .

Prepare for Your Journey

Physical education does not take place in isolation. In part I, we'll examine the middle school setting, the larger educational system, American society, and the global community. In chapter 1, we'll explore the many changes that are occurring in society, technology, health care, and education as well as their impact on quality physical education. In chapter 2, we'll examine the middle school reform movement's attempts to meet the special needs of middle school students, and we'll discuss the positive contributions that quality physical education programs can make as an equal partner in the middle school setting. In chapter 3, I'll define the role of physical education in the instructional setting, extracurricular program, and the comprehensive school health system. I'll also provide information on how to promote your program both in school and throughout the community. In chapter 4, I'll outline what makes an efficiently run physical education department that provides students with safe facilities and adequate equipment. And in chapter 5, we'll discuss the composition of physical education classes as well as how to create a psychologically safe environment in which all students are treated and disciplined respectfully.

CHAPTER 1

Physical Education in a Changing World

In times of change, learners inherit the earth, while the learned find themselves beautifully equipped to deal with a world that no longer exists.

—Eric Hoffer

Think for a moment about the physical education program you had in your middle or junior high school. Now, think about the physical education program at the school where you currently teach. How are the two programs similar and different? Are the differences for the better? Has physical education moved into the future with the same zest as the rest of the world?

Today's physical educator must keep pace with changes in technology, society, health, and education. Keeping pace can have an overwhelmingly positive influence on your physical education program. Through your updated physical education program, students will embrace technological, social, health, and educational advances and reforms.

In *Teaching Middle School Physical Education*, I examine the changes occurring around us and create a blueprint for quality physical education programs. I will not give you a lockstep approach to mindlessly follow, but rather a foundation upon which you and your middle school can build an ideal program. In this chapter, I will join you on your journey by first sharing some of the changes in technology, society, health, and education and their

implications for physical education as we approach the 21st century.

Our Changing Technology

By the first decade of the 21st century, a third of the world's population will be linked by computers (Cornish 1994). That's nearly 2 billion people! As of 1995, approximately 30 million people were already on the Internet. If you have ever surfed the net, you appreciate the abundance of information available at the click of a button. We already have more information than we could possibly read in one lifetime, and it's only a phone call away.

The dilemma is no longer how to find information, but how to sift through the information to find the most appropriate and accurate references. Eventually computers will be able to screen and discard all but the few items it thinks you want to use later (Negroponte 1995). You'll also be able to customize your computer as a personal reference librarian and secretary: The computer will select and store pieces of information you want to read or have read to you by the computer.

To accommodate such an enormous quantity of information, storage systems will become even more compact. Within the first quarter of the 21st century, information storage will be so compact that all the information a well-informed person could consume in a whole lifetime—all the books, manuals, magazine and newspaper articles, letters, memos, reports, greeting cards, notebooks, diaries, ledgers, bills, pamphlets, brochures, photographs, paintings, posters, movies, television shows, videos, radio programs, audio records, concerts, lectures, phone calls, whatever—will be able to be stored in an easily portable object, no bigger than a book and potentially as small as a fat fountain pen (Perelman 1992).

Moreover, computers will not only serve as reservoirs and links to information, they will continue to increase in ability and understanding. In Perelman (1992), Hans Moravec, Director of the Mobile Robot Laboratory at Carnegie Mellon University, anticipates big super computers with humanlike power by 2010 . . . and by the year 2030, compact, PC-like machines will be able to reason, perceive, and act upon their environment with full "human equivalence" (p. 29). These computers will take over numerous chores currently performed by humans, actually learning from their experiences. As a result even your toaster will "learn" whether you like your bread toasted dark or light, and will serve it up accordingly. Many of these computers will also look very different. Some futurists are suggesting that computers might be worn as belts around the waist and software will be stored on disks the size of credit cards so that information will be right at our fingertips at all times.

Other futurists predict that television will be more in the form of holography (Negroponte 1995). A hologram is a three-dimensional image made up of all possible views of a scene collected into a single plane of modulated light patterns. Imagine that instead of watching a football game on TV, your children or grandchildren will watch a football game by moving aside the coffee table and letting eight-inch-high players run around the living room passing a half-inch football back and forth! These holographic images will not only play football on our living room floor, they may also run around our desk organizing our work. They may, in fact, become the next generation of the computer interface. The holographic images will listen to our speech and implement our directions.

Programmers have already developed a technology that allows the user to transcend the barrier of keyboard and screen, and become immersed in an interactive experience generated by a computer. This is called virtual reality (VR). In 1985, a virtual reality system was developed by a programmer so he could learn to juggle. With virtual goggles over his eyes and virtual gloves on his hands, both connected to the computer, the programmer picked up the virtual balls and practiced juggling. The programmer created a new artificial world in which the balls moved downward in slow motion, altering physics to suit his needs. This allowed him more time to react accurately; indeed, each of his tosses and catches needed to be accurate since the computer responded to the force and release angle of each throw. The better the programmer juggled, the faster he had the virtual balls move until the speed matched that of reality. Eventually, the programmer removed the virtual equipment, and began juggling real balls.

Maybe you're thinking, "What does technology have to do with my classroom? These ideas would be too difficult and expensive to incorporate." Yet educators of every generation have learned to cope with new technologies. In the 19th century, teachers were given the chalkboard. Like many new things, it was at first rejected by teachers as being too

What they were saying . . .

Teacher's Conference, 1703: Students today can't prepare bark to calculate their problems. They depend on their slates which are more expensive. What will they do when the slate is dropped and it breaks? They will be unable to write!

Principal's Association, 1815: Students today depend on paper too much. They don't know how to write on a slate without getting chalk dust all over themselves. They can't clean a slate properly. What will they do when they run out of paper?

National Association of Teachers, 1907: Students today depend too much upon ink. They don't know how to use a pen knife to sharpen a pencil. Pen and ink will never replace the pencil.

Federal Teachers, 1950: Ballpoint pens will be the ruin of education in our country. Students use these devices and then throw them away. The American values of thrift and frugality are being discarded. Business and banks will never allow such expensive luxuries.

From the collection of Fr. Stanley Bezuska, reported in Thornburg, 1992.

difficult to use. After all, in 1850 classes contained students in several different grades, and teachers had little use for a board on which to write an assignment or lesson for all to see. It wasn't until schools began to divide students by grade level that the chalkboard became an important device.

Inherent in each of us is a fear of change and new technologies. We're not alone: Educators in previous generations were also wary of change. And society in general has been just as fearful of change. The questions you must ask yourself are: "What can I learn from these past fears?" and "How can the new technologies of this generation improve my physical education program?" After all, where would we be without stopwatches, ball pumps, and lockers?

Invention to Production

Fluorescent light—82 years

Ballpoint pen—50 years

Zipper—32 years

Helicopter—32 years

Television—29 years

Our Changing Society

In the late 1800s, society moved from an agrarian model to an industrial model. At that time, everything reflected the industrial model, including the schools. Indeed, students were moved in an assembly-line fashion from period one to period two without any attempt to pull the information together. During the late 1900s, our industrialized society developed into an information-based society, and now, with the impact of the "information superhighway," we are moving into a communication-based society. During the industrial age, we moved from the farm to the assembly line; in the information age, we moved from the assembly line to the office; during the communication age, we will go back home to work. Each of these changes in our society has changed the way in which we live and work; however, our schools—with their assembly-line approach—have essentially remained in the industrial age.

We must move all aspects of education, including physical education, into the information age. Con-sider that in terms of the ability to acquire and use information, knowledge is doubling every year, and, between the years 2010 and 2020, information experts predict that knowledge will double every 70 *days*. With this increasing knowledge base, the work we perform will change as well. Our students will hold several different jobs during their lifetimes. They will need to learn new and more demanding skills in order to work in globally competitive industries. These jobs will require more white collar workers as technologies replace many blue collar jobs. Businesses will need to create and implement on-the-job training strategies that will develop highly skilled workers who continuously upgrade their skills and retrain in response to new markets and technologies.

Concerned about the lack of significant change in schools, the Department of Labor's Secretary's Commission on Achieving Necessary Skills (SCANS) in 1991 identified five competencies businesses expect from students graduating from high school:

1. Identifies, organizes, plans, and allocates resources

2. Works with others

3. Acquires and uses information

4. Understands complex interrelationships

5. Works with a variety of technologies

Each of these competencies represents needs in our changing society. As financial resources become more difficult to secure, the ability to maximize their use through organizational and planning skills becomes more crucial. As societies become more multicultural, beliefs differ dramatically and norms of behavior are in constant conflict. An increase in child and spouse abuse, gang-related incidents, drive-by shootings, and neighborhood riots are contemporary examples of the violence surrounding us. We can easily see a greater need to learn to work better together. Yet ironically, we encourage competition in our society when most daily activities, including work, require cooperation.

When businesses want their upper level managers to work more efficiently together, one strategy they use is to put them through physical challenges like an Outward Bound experience to promote team building. During these experiences, participants must work together in groups, organize and allocate resources, use information, and analyze complex interrelationships in order to be successful with the physical challenge—like many of the experiences provided in physical education classes today.

Our Changing Health Issues

The current life expectancy in the United States is 77 years. However, the number of individuals living past 100 is increasing weekly and is currently around 30,000 Americans. Many futurists are predicting that children born today can expect to live into the 22nd century. Certainly, the quality of health care will continue to improve. Futurists predict that the development of ultra-thin "micromachines" may some day become small enough to travel in the blood vessels of the human body and do repair work. Current prototypes use motors that are thinner than a human hair with gears even smaller. But improvement in health care does not tell the entire story when we question the quality of life during the next century.

Who will benefit from improvements in health care? What is the responsibility of the individual for their health in terms of both prevention and intervention? The American Heart Association (1995) estimates that over 60 million Americans have one or more forms of heart or blood vessel disease, and that approximately one-third of the 1.5 million Americans who have a heart attack will die. While cardiovascular disease primarily affects the elderly, 5 percent of all heart attacks occur in individuals under 40 years of age and 45 percent occur in individuals under 65. Cardiovascular disease is also a significant contributor to physical disability, dramatically affecting the lives of many survivors. Yet, the American Heart Association notes that lifestyle choices, including smoking, alcohol abuse, poor nutrition, and physical inactivity, are leading causes of cardiovascular disease.

Adolescents and children are also at risk from poor lifestyle choices. Collins (1988) reports that one-fourth of all 14- to 17-year-olds have alcohol abuse problems. In the United States, more than 600,000 children already have some form of heart disease and have lifestyles characterized by poor nutrition and inadequate physical activity (Cornish 1994). One study (Bassin et al. 1989) of fifth through eighth grade students found that 13 percent of them had extremely high (200 mg/dl or higher) cholesterol levels. As for heart disease, the recommendations for lowering cholesterol level include a healthier diet and more exercise—both lifestyle choices.

Futurists predict, that along with current health issues, there will also be new health issues, due in part to the new technologies. For example: What effect will virtual reality experiences have on the personality of the individual who uses it? Will people become addicted to virtual reality in the same way that they are now addicted to drugs? Will people escape from their real lives by living in the artificial world of virtual reality? With the advances in medical technology, will humans one day become part biological, part mechanical, and part electronic? We already see examples of new health issues with the increase in carpal tunnel syndrome from computer keyboards, eye strain from computer monitors, and inactivity from video and computer games.

The cost of addressing health issues is taking its toll on the American economy. According to the United States Department of Health and Human Services (1990), health care costs have increased from $230 billion to $606 billion in the last decade and are expected to reach $1.5 trillion in the year 2000. The American Heart Association (1995) estimated the cost of cardiovascular disease at $151.3 billion for 1996, up from an estimated $56.9 billion in 1983. Quality physical education programs today can change harmful habits by promoting healthy lifestyles. If we put money into quality physical education programs today, we may be saving ourselves health care costs tomorrow.

The most recent guidelines from the Centers for Disease Control and Prevention and the American College of Sports Medicine (1995) recommend that every adult should accumulate 30 minutes or more of moderate-intensity physical activity on most, and preferably all, days. The Surgeon General's Report on Physical Activity and Health (1996) concurs with this recommendation, stating, "Significant health benefits can be obtained by including a moderate amount of physical activity on most, if not all, days of the week. Through a modest increase in daily activities, most Americans can improve their health and quality of life" (p. 4). Furthermore, to get future adults off to a good start, these organizations recommend that schools deliver comprehensive, developmentally appropriate health and physical education programs that promote physical activity, thinking skills, self-reliance, and enjoyment. The Surgeon General's report (1996) states, "Every effort should be made to encourage schools to require daily physical education in each grade and to promote physical activities that can be enjoyed throughout life" (p. 6). As a physical educator, you can use these recommendations from nationally recognized organizations to promote your programs.

In addition, the United States Department of Health and Human Services has developed *Healthy People 2000: National Health Promotion and Disease Prevention Objectives* (1990). These objectives promote the prevention of disease by increasing positive health practices. In an effort to meet these objectives, as well as to reduce absenteeism and health care costs and increase productivity, companies such as Ford Motor Company, Chrysler Corporation, and Campbell Soup have instituted company-wide wellness programs. Sentry Life Insurance has an on-site fitness center with a 25-meter pool, a gymnasium, racquetball and handball courts, an indoor golf driving range, and a weight training room. The program focuses on individualized fit-

ness goals for company people and their families. In addition, Sentry offers early glaucoma screening, low back clinics, hypertension screening, a program on dental health, and classes on healthful cooking. Sentry employs health professionals for weight control and nutritional counseling and fitness experts to teach skiing, slimnastics, first aid, self-defense, and cardiovascular fitness.

Naisbitt and Aburdene (1985) reported the following benefits from company-wide wellness programs:

Healthy People 2000 Physical Activity and Fitness Objectives

1. Reduce coronary heart disease deaths to no more than 100 per 100,000 people.

2. Reduce overweight to a prevalence of no more than 20 percent among people aged 20 and older and no more than 15 percent among adolescents aged 12 through 19.

3. Increase to at least 30 percent the proportion of people aged 6 and older who engage regularly, preferably daily, in light to moderate physical activity for at least 30 minutes per day.

4. Increase to at least 20 percent the proportion of people aged 18 and older and to at least 75 percent the proportion of children and adolescents aged 6 through 17 who engage in vigorous physical activity that promotes the development and maintenance of cardiorespiratory fitness 3 or more days per week for 20 or more minutes per occasion.

5. Reduce to no more than 15 percent the proportion of people aged 6 and older who engage in no leisure-time physical activity.

6. Increase to at least 40 percent the proportion of people aged 6 and older who regularly perform physical activities that enhance and maintain muscular strength, muscular endurance, and flexibility.

7. Increase to at least 50 percent the proportion of overweight people aged 12 and older who have adopted sound dietary practices combined with regular physical activity to attain an appropriate body weight.

8. Increase to at least 50 percent the proportion of children and adolescents in 1st through 12th grade who participate in daily school physical education.

9. Increase to at least 50 percent the proportion of school physical education class time that students spend being physically active, preferably engaged in lifetime physical activities.

10. Increase the proportion of work sites offering employer-sponsored physical activity and fitness programs as follows:

   –50-99 employees from 14 percent to 20 percent

   –100-249 employees from 23 percent to 35 percent

   –250-749 employees from 32 percent to 50 percent

   –More than 749 employees from 54 percent to 80 percent

11. Increase community availability and accessibility of physical activity and fitness facilities as follows:

   –Hiking, biking and fitness trail miles from 1 per 71,000 people to 1 per 10,000 people

   –Public swimming pools from 1 per 53,000 people to 1 per 25,000 people

   –Acres of park and recreation open space from 1.8 per 1,000 people to 4 per 1,000 people

12. Increase to at least 50 percent the proportion of primary care providers who routinely assess and counsel their patients regarding the frequency, duration, type, and intensity of each patient's physical activity practices.

Reprinted, by permission, from United States Department of Health and Human Services, Public Health Service, 1990, *Healthy People 2000*: National Health Promotion and Disease Prevention (Washington, D.C.: United States Department of Health and Human Services).

- New York Telephone Company saves at least $2.7 million annually in reduced absenteeism and insurance costs.
- Toronto's Canada Life Assurance recouped $37,000 in direct savings, $231,000 in decreased turnovers, and 22 percent in reduced absenteeism.
- Lockheed estimates $1 million annual savings on life insurance premiums directly related to employee participation in its wellness program.

As well-intentioned as *Healthy People 2000* may be or however inclusive the wellness program at a company, the responsibility for a healthy lifestyle still rests with the individual. Schools of the present and the future can help by becoming model health systems that provide smoke-free environments, healthy food, wellness centers for staff and community, counseling and other psychological services, opportunities for relaxation, and health services, alongside health education and physical education for all students. Seek to understand how the positive and negative changes in health and health care will impact your students' lives, then work to design physical education programs that will specifically meet their needs.

Our Changing Education System

The educational world is also changing, and often the physical educator, busy with coaching or other afterschool duties, is not involved or knowledgeable about these changes. More disturbing is the frequent exclusion of physical educators from staff development opportunities afforded to their colleagues in other subject areas because of misconceptions regarding physical education. Some physical educators meet only with other physical educators based on the assumption that their in-service programs should only directly relate to physical education. Worse yet are physical educators who may attend a staff-wide in-service but not see its relevance to physical education.

The time has come for us to see ourselves as an integral part of the education community. Join committees. Attend seemingly unrelated in-services and apply the information you gather to your physical education program. Seek out opportunities to learn from your colleagues in other subject areas. Perhaps most importantly, educate your colleagues and the school's administration about physical education.

To get started, first review the *Goals 2000: Educate America Act* (1994), designed to be the blueprint for educational reform in our nation. To address the need

Goals 2000: Educate America Act's National Education Goals

1. All children in America will start school ready to learn.
2. The high school graduation rate will increase to at least 90 percent.
3. All students will leave 4th, 8th, and 12th grades having demonstrated competency over challenging subject matter including English, mathematics, science, foreign languages, civics and government, economics, arts, history, and geography, and every school in America will ensure that all students learn to use their minds well, so they may be prepared for responsible citizenship, further learning, and productive employment in our Nation's modern economy.
3B(iv). All students will have access to physical education and health education to ensure they are healthy and fit.
4. The Nation's teaching force will have access to programs for the continued improvement of their professional skills and the opportunity to acquire the knowledge and skills needed to instruct and prepare all American students for the next century.
5. United States students will be first in the world in mathematics and science achievement.
6. Every adult American will be literate and will possess the knowledge and skills necessary to compete in a global economy and exercise the rights and responsibility of citizenship.
7. Every school in the United States will be free of drugs, violence, and the unauthorized presence of firearms and alcohol and will offer a disciplined environment conducive to learning.
8. Every school will promote partnerships that will increase parental involvement and participation in promoting the social, emotional, and academic growth of children.

for systemic change in the educational setting, *Goals 2000* takes what educators have learned over the past several decades about effective instructional strategies and combines it with the body of research on learning and success in school. Unlike previous school improvement endeavors, this reform effort (sometimes referred to as "restructuring") demands the redesign of the fundamental components of schools and sufficient time to adequately assess the effectiveness of the new design. The success of *Goals 2000* depends on the entire educational community as well as partners in the business community and society at large. The inclusion of physical education in this document has improved the standing of our profession in the educational community; therefore, strive to meet its goals.

Schools and teachers should be constantly responsive to the needs of all students. As we move into the communication age, our students must prepare for the future. On a national level, all subject areas have developed "world class" standards, which all students should achieve by high school graduation. In a world where knowledge is doubling rapidly, these standards are focusing on depth over breadth to prepare our students to compete in a global society.

Embedded in the standards are what Naisbitt and Aburdene (1985) coined the "three R's" of the new information society: thinking, learning, and creating, or learning how to think, learning how to learn, and learning how to create. The rapidly changing world has forced even the most reluctant of us into the role of lifelong learners; thus, schools must become communities of learners in which students and teachers alike must learn, think, and create in order to stay abreast of current topics. Teachers in this setting become facilitators of learning, rather than distributors of knowledge.

How can you demonstrate the accomplishment of the national standards? Authentic assessment—students applying their learning in real-life settings. One aspect of preparing your students for the work world is to provide them with opportunities to see the connections between different subject areas. You can connect one subject area to another by working in teams with other teachers. Through common planning periods, teachers share and plan lessons together, looking for natural connections between subject areas and creating projects or problems that students must solve using information from a variety of sources. Sources include not only different subjects but also information that must be found in the community. Restructuring schools are establishing partnerships with social and community agencies, parents, and businesses. Moreover, these schools are asking students to give something back to the community through community service. In some schools, this has even become a graduation requirement. By connecting student learning with these real world experiences, learning becomes more meaningful than it is when students study facts in isolation that they most likely will never use.

Students, as well as adults, learn in a variety of different ways, and schools are becoming more responsive to the individual needs of the students. The use of technology in education offers students the freedom to learn anything, anytime, anywhere, in the way that works best for them. Cooperative learning and constructivism (discussed in detail in chapter 11) are two other strategies that educators are using more often in schools, thereby helping students to learn to work together as they actively apply this wealth of information to new situations.

But keeping abreast of new ideas is not enough. You must also educate yourself as to possible changes in the near future. Some educational futurists are discussing classrooms that will be accessible to children, adolescents, and adults 24 hours a day. This access may be via the Internet, cable TV, satellite dish, or the old-fashioned way—attending on-site classes. Today, the largest growing segment of education is the home school. When you consider the potential of the Internet, you can readily see the possibility of students spending, at least part of their school day, learning from home. With this in mind, schools may become organized around clusters of ages and grades that provide students, when they do arrive at school, with cross-age and cross-grade tutoring and mentoring. Ironically, as physical educators begin to use student textbooks, futurists are predicting that we will see fewer and fewer textbooks in school. Replacing this media will be a variety of software, Internet access, and virtual reality systems.

Our Changing Physical Education Programs

As we enter the 21st century, each physical education program must have a written and articulated curriculum that is not only comprehensive in its physical educational scope but also addresses the competencies that businesses want from graduating seniors. We, as physical educators, must join with teachers of other subject areas to provide students with interdisciplinary instruction, and all teachers must align instruction with current research on how students learn.

If we take advantage of the technology that currently exists, such as using computer software, heart monitors, and other devices, we can provide students with the best possible physical education. Moreover, we must stay accountable by using a variety of authentic assessment tools to demonstrate student learning and to monitor program effectiveness. All of this needs to take place in a warm and supportive environment in which students learn to appreciate physical education and physical activity itself while they develop lifelong health habits that will ensure high qualities of life.

Summary

In this chapter, we have examined changes in technology, society, health, education, and physical education. We must continue to grow and change for the better or our physical education programs will surely die. Some programs are already being challenged by decreases in the time allocated to physical education and by specialists from the fitness and recreation industries who are attempting to replace physical educators. We are currently at a crossroads and the direction that we take now will determine the future of our profession. The time is now for us to reevaluate our existence and future as physical educators. We must look beyond our fear of change and accept the challenges that await us. *Teaching Middle School Physical Education* provides a specific vision, along with the necessary skills and techniques to bring about these changes. So pack your bags and start your journey!

Railroads: A Lesson for Change

In the late nineteenth century, the railroad magnates believed the purpose of their organizations was to move freight and passengers by rail. In brief, they viewed themselves as being in the railroad business, the rail freight business, and the rail passenger business. In the early part of the twentieth century, mass-produced automobiles and trucks, an improved highway system, and later, airplanes caused the railroads considerable trouble. In fact, competition from these sources, combined with other leadership failures, drove many rails into bankruptcy. If, as numerous management theorists contend, the leaders of the railroad industry had conceptualized the purpose of their business differently—if they had thought of their enterprises as the freight transportation business, for example—the results for railroads might have been quite different. If railroaders had thought of themselves as being in the transportation business, they would have viewed trucks and airplanes as new technologies for their business rather than as competition. They would have viewed an improved highway system as a subsidy (just as they view free land in the nineteenth century as a legitimate subsidy) and would have lobbied for improved highways rather than lobbying against them.

—Phil Schlechty

Reprinted from Thinking/Meaning-Centered Curriculum Module by the California School Leadership Academy, 1991.

Reform Efforts in the Middle School

No other grade span encompasses such a wide range of intellectual, physical, psychological, and social development, and educators must be sensitive to the entire spectrum of these young people's capabilities.

—Bill Honig, Caught in the Middle: Educational Reform for Young Adolescents in California Public Schools

You only have to spend a small amount of time in a middle school to realize that middle school students are unique. Throughout my years as a middle school teacher, I was constantly amazed by the heterogeneous mix of young adolescents. Each new class brought students as tall as I was who seemed mature and others who were half their peers' size, awkward, and immature. I saw fear in the eyes of some, extreme confidence in the eyes of others. Many of the students had already mastered the skills I planned to teach, while others weren't ready for the challenges. Indeed, middle school students are in transition from childhood to young adulthood—some closer to childhood and others closer to adulthood. This difficult transition makes most middle school students very self-absorbed and sometimes confused or depressed.

Does your physical education program meet the needs of this diverse group of students? Can you assess your current situation and determine the course you wish to pursue? In this chapter, I'll describe the characteristics of middle school students, explain the history and purpose of middle schools in the United States, and summarize the characteristics of quality middle schools. In addition, we'll discuss a document from the National Association for Sport and Physical Education (NASPE, 1995a) for program assessment and goal setting, so that you can create your own vision for your middle school physical education program.

Middle School Students

The most unique aspect of middle school students is their wide range of intellectual, physical, psychological, social, and ethical developmental levels. In appendix A, I have provided a detailed listing of common characteristics of this age group. Remember, however, that each middle school student has his own unique set of capabilities and needs.

It is important to recognize that middle school students are not miniature adults. The learning and playing opportunities you provide these individuals should reflect their developmental levels. Learning activities must be active—not passive. Make physical education more meaningful by connecting the activities you select to real-life experiences of adolescents. Certainly, middle school is the appropriate time to begin explaining the *why* behind everything that we do in physical education. These youngsters are moving from concrete to abstract thinkers and are capable of considering different viewpoints and of drawing their own conclusions. Physical activities that promote social interaction and provide many opportunities for hands-on learning in a variety of activities is most appropriate for young adolescents.

The Boston Middle School Leadership Initiative provides middle school students with social and physical challenges in situations relevant to their own lives. Through hands-on activities, students learn leadership, social, and cooperative skills. The introduction to the program, held at school, teaches the principles of leadership. The second part of the program, held on Thompson Island, involves students in activities of varying degrees of physical challenge. During the students' first visit, they participate in group activities designed to build self-confidence and trust in others. Common activities include figuring out how to pass each member of a group through a web of rope without touching the rope and walking the length of a balance beam suspended a few feet off the ground. During the second visit, students must experience the risks of leadership and stretch the limits of their courage when teachers ask them to climb a rope ladder, walk a cable 50 feet aboveground, and ride a harness down a zipline from a platform to the ground. In the final phase of the Leadership Initiative, students rock climb at a nearby quarry. Throughout the exercises, students learn to help and support one another.

Because of the many changes that middle school students are experiencing, they have a tendency to doubt themselves, often relying on peer approval for their identities. Yet these same students are also looking for a significant adult in their lives. They want someone they can talk to who will validate their feelings of confusion and frustration about the changes—someone to help them deal with their tension. This significant adult may be a parent, relative, or a teacher. If students are unable to deal with the tension associated with the changes they are experiencing, they are at risk of dropping out of school. Therefore, we must design middle schools—including physical education programs—to specifically meet their capabilities and needs.

History of Middle Schools in America

Many of us began our teaching careers in junior high schools, and some of you may still be in a junior high setting. Over the last 20 years, however, most junior highs have converted to the middle school model. Interestingly, the movement to provide a separate instructional setting for young adolescents dates back to 1913 when the National Committee on Economy of Time in Education (George, Stevenson, Thomason, and Beane 1992) first discussed a separate junior division of secondary education (7th through 12th grade).

This junior division led to the creation of many three-year junior high schools across the country. The purpose of this division was to meet the unique

Figure 2.1 Adventure-based activities are part of the middle school reform movement.

© Davis Barber

needs of young adolescents by focusing on learning skills while emphasizing guidance, exploration, independence, and responsibility. The junior high experience was supposed to provide students with a transition between elementary school and high school. You may recognize these reasons as the same ones given for the move from junior high schools to middle schools.

Unfortunately, over time, many junior high schools became more and more like little high schools. The elusive goals of junior high education included flexible scheduling, moderate class size, blocks-of-time instruction, and teachers prepared for and devoted to teaching young adolescents using new instructional strategies. The difficulty in attaining these goals led educators to issue a new call for the replacement of junior high schools with middle schools. By 1965, educators across the country were advocating schools that included fifth through eighth or sixth through eighth grades in order to achieve the 50-year-old goals of meeting the needs of young adolescents. Educators felt that without the ninth graders, these new schools could finally address the original reasons for establishing the junior high school model.

One of the first major documents to report on middle schools was Association for Supervision and Curriculum Development's (ASCD) *The Middle School We Need* (1975). This publication emphasizes the developmental characteristics of young adolescents and the need to respond appropriately to those characteristics. Unfortunately, the educational aims of middle school did not, in themselves, produce the necessary impetus for change. Instead, a decrease in the number of high school students and an increase in births primarily motivated administrators and boards of education to move ninth graders into high schools and sixth graders into middle schools.

By the late 1980s, states such as California were publishing their own educational agendas for middle school education in documents such as *Caught in the Middle: Educational Reform for Young Adolescents in California Public Schools* (1987). At the same time, the Carnegie Foundation published its vision of middle school education in *Turning Points: Preparing American Youth for the 21st Century* (1989). As more and more educators encountered positive experiences with the middle school concept, the total number of junior high schools (seventh through ninth grades) declined by approximately 53 percent, while the number of middle schools (fifth or sixth through eighth grades) increased by over 200 percent between 1970 and 1990 (George et al. 1992).

Quality Middle School Programs Today

Successful middle schools today provide students with strong academic programs that have personal meaning to them as well as the necessary health care, nutrition, counseling, and guidance services that help these students concentrate on their academic goals. Certainly, students who are sick, hungry, confused, or depressed cannot function well in school. Programs, such as Healthy Start in California, which address the whole child by placing comprehensive support services at or near schools, are effective at keeping students in school because they meet the physical, psychological, social, and emotional needs of the students and their families. Based on the community's assessment of their needs and resources, Healthy Start programs are able to reduce the fragmentation and cost of service delivery through interagency collaboration.

Turning Points: Preparing American Youth for the 21st Century by the Carnegie Council on Adolescent Development (1989) describes a 15-year-old who has graduated from a quality middle school program as an "intellectually reflective person, a person enroute to a lifetime of meaningful work, a good citizen, a caring and ethical individual, and a healthy person." The report focuses on eight characteristics to define quality middle school programs. Using these eight characteristics as a blueprint for middle school reform, the Carnegie Council has adopted a number of middle schools from across the United States, donating money to implement their vision. Although it is too early for definitive conclusions, educators involved in these schools have noticed improvements in the knowledge, attitudes, and behavior of their students.

Throughout the rest of this book you will see various references to the concepts embedded in these eight characteristics. For now, let's take a look at a few key points in order to better understand these characteristics and the role you and other physical educators can play in the middle school reform efforts.

You must establish your physical education program as an integral component of the total middle school program. Specifically, as middle schools begin to organize themselves as schools-within-schools or in houses, you must become involved. Currently, many schools have the mathematics, science, language arts, history, and social science teachers sharing a group of students as well as a common planning period. The teachers may, in fact, instruct these

Eight Characteristics of Quality Middle Schools

1. Create small communities for learning where stable, close, mutually respectful relationships with adults and peers are considered fundamental for intellectual development and person growth. The key elements of these communities are schools-within-schools or houses, students and teachers grouped together as teams, and small group advisories that ensure that every student is known well by at least one adult.

2. Teach a core academic program that results in students who are literate, including in the sciences, and who know how to think critically, lead a healthy life, behave ethically, and assume the responsibilities of citizenship in a pluralistic society. Youth service to promote values for citizenship is an essential part of the core academic program.

3. Ensure success for all students through elimination of tracking by achievement level and promotion of cooperative learning, flexibility in arranging instructional time, and adequate resources (time, space, equipment, and materials) for teachers.

4. Empower teachers and administrators to make decisions about the experiences of middle grade students through creative control by teachers over the instructional program linked to greater responsibilities for students' performance, governance committees that assist the principal in designing and coordinating school-wide programs, and autonomy and leadership within sub-schools or houses to create environments

tailored to enhance the intellectual and emotional development of all youth.

5. Staff middle grade schools with teachers who are expert at teaching young adolescents and who have been specially prepared for assignment to the middle grades.

6. Improve academic performance through fostering the health and fitness of young adolescents by providing a health coordinator in every middle grade school, access to health care and counseling services, and a health-promoting school environment.

7. Reengage families in the education of young adolescents by giving families meaningful roles in school governance, communicating with families about the school program and student's progress, and offering families opportunities to support the learning process at home and at the school.

8. Connect schools with communities, which together share responsibility for each middle grade student's success, through identifying service opportunities in the community, establishing partnerships and collaborations to ensure students' access to health and social services, and using community resources to enrich the instructional program and opportunities for constructive after-school activities.

same students throughout their middle school years in order to build a significant teacher-student relationship. If at your school, physical education is part of this kind of organization, you know how it facilitates teachers working together on thematic or interdisciplinary units of instruction. If your school excludes physical education from interdisciplinary teaming, speak up. You and your colleagues can easily and meaningfully include physical education across the curriculum. Participating on an interdisciplinary team demonstrates that you are an equal partner in the school and provides you with the opportunity to explain the physical, social, and intellectual benefits of physical education to your colleagues. In addition, many times there is the

added benefit of smaller class sizes, since every teacher on the team must have the same class size.

Everyone must view physical education as part of the core academic program. The Carnegie Council's second characteristic of a quality middle school notes that the ability to lead a healthy life is central to the middle school curriculum. Therefore, a few important content standards must be selected that prepare your students to become adults in the 21st century in meaningful ways. By focusing on a few key content standards from kindergarten through high school, you can expect students to master those skills and knowledge, which will, in turn, have a significant impact on their lives.

Over the last decade, society has held education

Over the past several years, we have been upgrading our content and delivery systems. We are always looking for some ways to improve. We aren't afraid to risk anything new. The things that seem to work we keep, the ones that don't, we drop. Nothing is sacred except for the overarching philosophy that physical education is an academic subject worthy of the same respect and accountability as other subject areas. We lobby hard and often that physical education belongs in the academic core. We constantly seek equity with our teaching peers in *all* phases of the education process. We are on school and district committees. We invite department chairs from other subjects to visit us and discuss our commonalities. We show that physical education can support what is going on in other subjects on the campus. In short, we demonstrate through our daily work that physical education is an integral part of the total education of students and that to think otherwise is a disservice to the students and community we serve.

At a faculty meeting, the administration presented a new teaming model for the school. It was based on a four subject interdisciplinary team: English, history, mathematics, and science. When the time came for questions and comments, the English department chair asked, "Where is physical education?" The administration responded, "It can't be done with physical education." The mathematics department chair stood up and said, "Without physical education, the mathematics department will not participate." The administration gave us one year to develop a way to include physical education on the teams. We did.

—Bill Silva, physical educator, Kenilworth Junior High, Petaluma, CA

Teaching heterogeneous classes certainly can be more challenging than working with homogeneous groups, but by offering a variety of developmentally appropriate activities and by using a variety of instructional strategies, you can accommodate and promote successful experiences for all your students. For example, through cooperative learning strategies, you can better meet the social needs of middle school students, which are essential to their success in school. Moreover, ensure a physically and psychologically safe environment in physical education. This alone may be the biggest factor in providing a quality, successful middle school physical education experience.

I didn't think that I played good enough to participate in after-school sports. Then my teacher told us that the three-on-three basketball games were for everybody. She also said that we were going to play basketball after school since that was what we were learning in physical education. Now, I am having a lot of fun playing with my friends, and I'm even getting better at basketball.

—Anonymous, eighth grade student

The Carnegie Council's sixth characteristic suggests that schools can improve the academic performance of young adolescents through fostering health and fitness. Many Japanese and Chinese schools, weave health and fitness into the class schedule. After every 40- to 50-minute academic period, students play vigorously during a recess. After formal classes have concluded for the day, all students spend an hour or more at school in extracurricular activities (Stevenson and Stigler 1992).

In the past, most sport programs in the United States have been reserved for the gifted athlete. In today's middle schools, however, we must design intramural programs to include all students. In so doing, we can extend the physical education instructional period into a practical application session, thereby extending the time allocated to physical education and, in turn, increasing student success in and out of physical education class.

To create a school environment in which all of the desired characteristics can flourish, the Carnegie Council insists that both the teachers and principal be specifically prepared to work with and take responsibility for the education of students in sixth, seventh, and eighth grades. Together, teachers and administrators must address the content areas of

accountable for student achievement and for documenting that achievement. Physical educators must also be accountable for student achievement and its documentation. Not only will you have proof that learning has occurred, you will also have proof that physical education is an equal partner with the other disciplines, putting physical educators on the same level of professionalism and accountability as other educators.

The Carnegie Council's third characteristic notes that the elimination of tracking and the promotion of success for all students is another key element in quality middle schools. Yet historically, many physical educators have grouped students by ability.

the core curriculum using a variety of instructional strategies and materials, emphasizing active learning, while also keeping in mind the developmental characteristics of young adolescents. Perhaps even more importantly, parents and community members become key players in the education of their youth instead of remaining on the sidelines.

Quality Middle School Physical Education

Now let's turn our attention specifically to our area of interest–quality middle school physical education programs. It is important to educate your colleagues as to the many major benefits of physical activity that your school should make available to your students. Do your colleagues know that physical activity

- enhances the function of the central nervous system by promoting healthier neuron function;

- aids cognitive development in these areas: learning strategies, decision making, problem solving, and acquiring, retrieving, and integrating information;

- improves aerobic fitness, muscle endurance, muscle power, and muscle strength;

- promotes a more positive attitude toward physical activity, leading to a more active lifestyle during unscheduled leisure time;

- enhances self-concept and self-esteem as indicated by increased self-confidence, assertiveness, emotional stability, independence, and self-control;

- creates a major force in the socializing of individuals during late childhood and adolescence; and

- effectively deters mental illness and alleviates mental stress?

In light of these benefits, physical education needs a more revered place in the school curriculum! More and more, educators in all subject areas are viewing physical education as an essential element in any school curriculum designed to educate the whole person. Indeed, today's quality middle school physical education program aligns itself with the characteristics of quality middle schools in general. Beyond this, you must address the specific needs of *your* middle school students.

According to the National Association for Sport and Physical Education (NASPE), a quality middle school physical education program should meet several conditions. Although not necessarily meant to be a list of the characteristics of a quality program, a program that aligns itself with all of the appropriate practices listed in this document is definitely a quality program.

Appropriate Practices for Middle School Physical Education

The first statement is the appropriate practice and the second statement is the inappropriate practice.

Curriculum

Curriculum Guidelines

The physical education program follows the same curriculum model as the rest of the school (e.g., thematic, integrated, multicultural).

The physical education program is isolated from the rest of the school in terms of content and methods.

Program Choices

Specific goals and objectives determine the selection of instructional units and learning experiences.

Instructional practices are based upon the teacher's interests and past experiences rather than the student's educational needs, personal progress, and goal attainment.

Refinement of Locomotor, Non-locomotor, and Manipulative Activities

Students participate in learning activities in which the major focus is to develop basic movement skills—locomotor, non-locomotor, and manipulative. Opportunities are provided to combine basic skills into sequences and to execute them under a variety of constraints and goals. All team and individual activities are used to assist students in increasing their skill proficiency (e.g., throwing, striking, catching, running, walking, etc.).

There is a lack of instructional time allocated to improving the fundamental skills. There is no instructional focus in the activity; participation is the only goal.

Physical Fitness Activities

Students participate in activities that are designed to help them understand and value physical fitness and its contribution toward a healthy lifestyle. Physical fitness development is an ongoing process and is incorporated into the daily lesson. Each component of physical fitness receives equal emphasis.

Students are required to participate in fitness activities without understanding the relevance to their lives. Programmatically, fitness is taught as a separate unit, is over or under emphasized, and scores on normative tests are used as the basis for grading.

Knowledge

Emphasis is placed on acquiring the knowledge necessary to develop critical thinking and problem solving skills within the context of physical activity. These knowledges include rules and strategies, fitness and skill level assessment, and the role of physical activity and sport within the culture and in their lives.

Sport skill acquisition and participation are the only objectives emphasized or valued. The program does not contribute to the student's knowledge of how to use physical activity in their life.

Cooperative Play

The program includes experiences which encourage students to learn the process of working and cooperating with others to achieve a common goal. Appropriate student behaviors which make goal attainment possible include communicating effectively, accepting individual differences, cooperative problem solving, and working within the framework of rules.

The focus of activities is based upon individual growth and dominance rather than on cooperation and group problem solving. Individuals, because of gender, skill level or race, are denied full benefits of the activity.

Integration with the Other Subject Areas

In the middle school, relevance of content and the interrelation of subject areas is a curriculum goal. The physical education program is planned in relation to and in conjunction with other subject areas to foster an integrated, multi-disciplinary curriculum.

Physical education stands alone from other curricular areas. Concepts and knowledges common to other subject areas are not taught or reinforced.

Variety

Depending on the school and community resources available, a wide range of activities are provided from the following areas: team and individual activities, gymnastics, rhythms and dance, outdoor and challenge pursuits, aquatics, and cooperative activities.

All school, community, and natural resources are not fully utilized to provide a variety of curricula offerings.

Variety

The students receive sequential instruction in a variety of activities based on their needs and interests. The types of activities are team and individual activities, rhythms and dance, cooperative activities, aquatics, gymnastics, outdoor and challenge pursuits. The need to provide variety is balanced with ample opportunities to achieve the skill, fitness, knowledge and social/emotional goals of the program.

There is an overabundance of one type of activity, with little consideration given to the wide range of developmental needs and interests of the early adolescent. Or, so many different activities are offered that sufficient time is not provided for the development of competence.

Team and Individual Activities

The program includes a wide variety of team and individual activities with ample practice time provided to ensure a sense of student accomplishment. Lead-up and modified versions of the game as well as the game itself are all used.

There is a predominance of free play and unstructured use of class time with no focus on skill or strategy. Selection of activities is based upon season of the year or teacher/student preference.

Rhythms and Dance

A variety of both artistic (creative) and recreational (square, folk, social, line, classical, ethnic) dance forms are taught representing a variety of cultures. Opportunities exist for students to develop an aesthetic appreciation for many dance forms. Dance represents a form of self-expression and communication.

The physical education program includes no rhythmical experience or only one dance form or one culture is represented. Dance or rhythmical expression may be excluded from the program because of teacher preference. Dance is not viewed as being related to other forms of sport and movement.

Aquatics

Basic skills are taught in a sequential manner by a certified instructor. Students develop competence in survival skills and water safety. Instruction is adapted to meet different ability levels.

"Free Swim," with no instructional focus, is a substitute for sequential, outcome based instruction. Instruction does not meet the needs of the individual learner.

Gymnastics

Activities are selected which encourage students to sequentially develop skills appropriate to their ability and confidence level in a non-competitive situation. Students are taught to design and perform a gymnastic routine that combines traveling, rolling, balancing, and weight transfer into a smooth, flowing sequence with intentional change in direction, speed, and flow.

All students are required to perform the same predetermined stunts and routines on and off apparatus, regardless of their skill level, body composition, and level of confidence. Routines are competitive, are the sole basis for a grade, and/or all students must perform for an audience.

Outdoor and Challenge Pursuits

The program provides a variety of adventure, challenge and outdoor education activities that are developmentally appropriate. Activities are selected that will enhance self-esteem and critical thinking skills, encourage cooperative learning and promote environmental awareness and appreciation. Hiking, camping, cycling, skiing, backpacking, and a ropes course may be included.

Activities are arbitrarily selected with little regard for student outcomes or sequential instruction. Students are forced to participate in activities in which they feel uncomfortable. All available internal and external resources are not used.

Instruction

Success

Instructional activities are designed to ensure individual success. A significant number of practice trials are provided as needed to develop motor skill competence. The activities are modified to provide an appropriate challenge for each individual.

The activities presented are too difficult, too simplistic, or developmentally inappropriate with no contribution to the lesson's focus or goal. There are single standards of performance for all students.

Learning Time

Students are given adequate time and sufficient practice attempts to acquire the concept or skill.

Excessive class time is spent in managerial tasks, teacher talk, waiting for turns, and/or with discipline procedures. Progression is based on schedule rather than student success.

Learning Environment

Verbal and nonverbal behavior of teachers and students promotes a positive climate. Teachers and students recognize effort, treat each other with respect, and acknowledge individual accomplishments. Discipline practices are fair and consistent, encourage students to be responsible for their own behavior, and provide a positive learning environment where students work cooperatively. Students have the opportunity to make decisions about their own learning. Both the physical and psychological atmosphere foster a feeling of safety and security. Students enjoy coming to physical education.

The atmosphere is unfriendly, apathetic, or punitive. Students experience indifference or ridicule from the teacher and classmates. All decisions are teacher directed.

Feedback

Each student receives specific instructional feedback that provides the student with information about his/her performance relative to instructional goals. For example, in catching a ground ball a student might be told, "Nice job of getting the glove down to the ground."

The student receives no feedback on performance, feedback is general or non-instructional, or feedback is directed only toward the entire class.

Inclusion

Selection of experiences and instructional strategies allow for the inclusion of all students regardless of level of capability, gender, racial, or ethnic group. Modifications are made to game rules and equipment to ensure a successful experience.

Individuals or groups of students are excluded from participating, competing, and being successful. There is a lack of individualization of instruction.

Practice

Students receive sufficient practice trials to achieve success. The scope of practice allows sufficient trials to accommodate students' varying abilities, experience, and skill levels.

Lack of equipment or space, allocated instructional time, or poor class management precludes the student receiving enough practice time to develop skill and competence. All students are provided with the same practice structure or given the same number of attempts regardless of their success rate or developmental level.

Forming Groups

Teams, squads, and learning groups are formed in ways that preserve the dignity and self-respect of every student. For example, the teacher privately forms teams by using knowledge of students' skills or the students form groups cooperatively.

Groups are formed by publicly selecting one student at a time, separating by gender, or in ways that alienate or embarrass individuals.

Teaching Styles

Instructors use both a teacher centered (direct) and student centered (indirect) teaching approach. A variety of teaching styles (command, peer, guided discovery, problem solving, and practice) are used. Choice of teaching style is determined by instructional goals and needs and attributes of the student.

There is a lack of variety in teaching style with only a lecture/demonstration or command style used. Students are given few opportunities to be self-directed.

Learning Styles

Information is presented in a variety of ways to accommodate the different modes that students use to learn best. Visual, auditory, kinesthetic, and tactile learners are all given optimal learning opportunities. In addition, multimedia are employed to enhance learning.

Information is presented through a single mode only with a narrow approach to learning.

Student Choices

Students are given choices in matters such as (a) equipment, (b) modification of rules, number of players, size of playing spaces, as well as (c) selection of activities to accommodate skill levels and interest, such as choosing between competitive games, cooperative games, or solitary skill practice.

Teacher always determines and controls the activity, game rules, equipment, and type of participation.

Individualization of Instruction

Instruction is individualized, by giving the students choices, providing additional necessary practice time or modifying the task difficulty depending on the student's achievement of prerequisite objective.

All students are doing the same thing at the same time regardless of their skill level, success at prerequisite objective, or developmental level.

Warm-Up

Warm-up is activity specific, conforms to guidelines for safe exercises, and accommodates different fitness levels.

A single warm-up routine is used regardless of the activity, ignores individual fitness levels, and is potentially unsafe.

Integration with Other Subject Areas

Physical education is integrated with the larger curriculum. The physical education staff member is part of an interdisciplinary team that plans, instructs, and evaluates in a cooperative manner. The curriculum reflects thematic teaching in which all instructional areas share a common concept.

Physical education is taught in an isolated manner. There is an absence of communication between physical education specialists and other academic instructors. There is no demonstration of common themes among subject areas.

Assessment

Role of Assessment

Teacher decisions and grades are based on continuous, formative (process) evaluation, as opposed to scores on a single test at the end of a unit. Evaluation is integrated into the instructional process. Students are involved in the selection and use of assessment measures.

Students are evaluated and graded on the basis of a score on a single fitness test, written test, or skill test. Students are graded on arbitrary measures that do not reflect the instructional objectives.

Achievement-Based Physical Education

Assessment is based upon clearly defined educational goals. There are distinctly defined criteria for determining student progress and achievement. Student achievement is based upon individual progress relative to goals and objectives.

Students are evaluated and graded using an arbitrary or subjective measure not reflecting the centrality of the instructional objectives. Single skill tests are given only one time as measure of performance instead of being integrated throughout the unit to measure student improvement.

Physical Fitness Testing

Scores on fitness tests are used to help students set personal goals and to determine individual progress.

Fitness tests are used for assigning grades

Class Atmosphere During Assessment

Students are tested in a supportive atmosphere which encourages optimal performance as opposed to one that exposes the student to undue pressure. Individual and group learning rates should determine time of testing rather than the class schedule. Test scores are reported in an individualized and private manner.

Students are assessed under the pressure of having to perform alone in front of the entire class or when not ready.

Techniques Available for Psychomotor, Cognitive, and Affective Assessment

Assessment covers all three domains of learning (psychomotor, cognitive, and affective) and uses a wide variety of assessment techniques which may include: skills tests, written tests, reflective journals, check lists, portfolios, case studies, videotape analyses, oral reports, peer or teacher observations, fitness appraisals, interviews, discussions, group projects, demonstrations, and student developed and/or selected techniques. Both standardized assessment (i.e., skill tests, fitness tests) as well as authentic assessment (i.e., interviews, journals, portfolios) are used.

Students are assessed in one domain using limited assessment techniques.

Outside of Class Activity Assessment

Students receive credit for engaging in instructionally related voluntary or assigned activities outside of class.

There is no value placed on activities which do not occur during regularly scheduled class time.

Curricular Decisions Based on Assessment

The results of student assessment may also be used for program and curriculum planning, including the development of daily and weekly objectives. Records of individual student progress are passed on from year to year. Instruction is modified as a result of assessment.

Assessment is not used in the curriculum planning process.

Interpretation of Program to Public

Assessment is used to evaluate the program's effectiveness and to communicate goals to faculty, administration, and parents.

Assessment is used solely for the purpose of determining grades.

Class Attire

Appropriate attire allows the student to participate in class activities safely and functionally, but has no bearing on progress or achievement grades.

Grading and participation are based on wearing prescribed clothing.

Support

Class Size

Physical education classes are assigned the same number of students as other content areas.

There are more students in physical education classes than sound educational and safety practices dictate.

Scheduling

Students are scheduled to attend physical education classes on a daily basis. The length of instructional time is comparable to other content areas.

Students do not receive daily instructional physical education of appropriate length.

Equipment

There is sufficient equipment to allow each student to benefit from maximum participation and optimal practice and learning time. A variety of developmentally appropriate equipment is utilized to meet varying student needs regarding age, body size, and skill level. The physical education budget is sufficient to support the number of students served.

The physical education program has inadequate equipment for the number of students or the equipment is not of the appropriate size for the developmental level of the student (e.g., junior size basketball for middle school students should be available along with regulation size).

Facilities

A variety of learning stations are available to accommodate the scope of the program and the number of students. Instructional areas provide a safe and healthy learning environment. Learning stations are reserved exclusively for the physical education program.

Physical education classes are scheduled in areas that restrict opportunities for students to move freely and safely. Physical education classes are routinely canceled or preempted to accommodate other school events.

Substitution of Credit

Physical education is viewed as having unique goals and objectives that cannot be achieved in other areas. There are no substitutions, exemptions, or waivers for physical education credit.

Physical education credit is regularly given for other activities such as intramural, inter-scholastic sports, band, ROTC, cheerleading, and private instruction.

Technology

The physical education department has access to sufficient technology and infuses it as part of the regular teaching-learning process.

The use of technology is viewed as separate from the content and instructional process in physical education.

Professional Development

The physical education faculty is encouraged to participate in professional development. Support may be in the form of release time for workshops and conventions, subscriptions to professional journals, local inservice, memberships in professional organizations, and opportunities to collaborate with colleagues.

Physical education faculty must assume full responsibility for their professional growth.

Administrative

Administrators support innovative ideas, provide adequate funding for physical education, enable teachers to attend workshops and conferences, and view the physical education program as an essential part of the total school curriculum.

Administrators view physical education as a nonessential or peripheral part of the school program.

Home-School Communication

Parents and the public are regularly informed about the goals and related activities of the physical education program through newsletters, parent nights, demonstrations, displays, parent conferences, etc.

There is a lack of communication between home and school. The physical education instructional program is not visible.

Reprinted from *Appropriate practices for middle school physical education* with permission of NASPE, 1900 Association Drive, Reston, VA 22091.

Take time now to review the appropriate and inappropriate practices of a middle school physical education program. For each component, make a note as to whether your middle school program is following the appropriate or inappropriate practice. If your program falls somewhere in between on some of the components, note that as well. By assessing your current middle school physical education program, you are taking the first step toward improving it.

Planning for Success

Now that you have determined where you are, you can decide where you want to go. Ideally, what do you want your physical education program to look like? How many changes can you address in the next three years? Using the information we've discussed so far and the results of your assessment, write a scenario describing your program three years from today.

Although the scenarios must be individualized, the following scenario provided by Kranz Middle School in El Monte, California provides you with one example. Remember, each program is at a different place on the change continuum, so your scenario or vision may look quite different.

Three years from today, our physical education department will have a fitness laboratory that utilizes technology and a project adventure component in the curriculum that addresses the social needs of our students. The fitness lab specifically will be fully equipped with exercise bikes, treadmills, steppers, rowers, and computers. Testing equipment, such as heart monitors, electronic blood pressure devices, and electronic skinfold calipers will be available to all physical educators. The project adventure component will include a low ropes course along with cooperative initiatives that stress social development. Project adventure will become a unit of instruction for our seventh graders as well as an ongoing program for our eighth graders.

Stanley Davis (1987), author of *Future Perfect*, says that we need to skip the present to a date well into the future, design a system that makes sense for that time, and then make changes now that work toward the long-term view. Thus, using the scenario you just created, begin to think about the steps you will take this year, next year, and the third year, so that by the end of the third year, your program will be on-target.

Summary

To align your physical education program with the current philosophy of middle school reform, be aware of both the specific needs of middle school students and the characteristics of quality middle school programs. In the last chapter, we discussed the general changes in society, technology, business, and education that you must consider as you design your middle school physical education program. In this chapter, I have taken this concept one step further to include monitoring the changes in the middle school reform efforts so that your middle school physical education program progresses in alignment with the other middle school changes designed to meet the needs of students.

The next fourteen chapters will help you clarify your vision of a quality middle school program by providing you with additional information and a blueprint for the future. I'll also give you information on the knowledge and skills necessary to implement your program. Keep the answers that you have written in response to the questions posed in this chapter and revisit them after completing the book. Then modify your plan based on your newfound knowledge, thereby creating your own personal blueprint for change.

CHAPTER 3

The Role of Physical Education in Middle School

The middle school principal began his back-to-school address to the teachers and classified staff at his new middle school. As he explained his vision, he announced that all departments would be treated equally and receive the same amount of funding for instructional materials. In addition, the class size for all classes would be the same. The physical education teachers looked at one another, smiled, and realized that they finally had attained the respect and endorsement of a school administrator.

Does this story sound like a dream? It could happen at your school if you remember that physical education does not take place in a vacuum. It is part of a larger world both within the middle school reform effort and the middle school site where it exists. Thus, to achieve the dream, your colleagues and community need to see the physical education program as part of the overall school environment. As a physical educator, you need to be seen as an equal partner in the educational program, you need equitable class size and instructional time, and you want sufficient funding to provide a quality program for your students. In order for you to receive what you want and need, however, we must first examine what the profession of physical education owes.

Participation in various school-wide programs can earn your physical education department the respect and endorsement it needs from administrators, other teachers, community members, parents, and students—those individuals who already have a vested interest and say in what goes on in the school. Gaining the respect of these stakeholders can give you the access to get what you want and need. In this chapter, I will address the role of physical education in the school environment, specifically related to the instructional program, the extracurricular program, and the comprehensive school health program. I'll give you ideas on how to continually promote positive public relations for your physical education program.

Physical Education and the Instructional Setting

Physical education is one of several subject areas required in most middle school curricula. As described in the opening scenario, schools should include physical education in all school-wide reform projects, allocating it equitable instructional time, class size, funding, and interdisciplinary participation. In other words, your school should allow and encourage students to apply knowledge and skill they have gained in physical education across the curriculum. For example, some middle schools

require the students to complete an eighth grade research project. If teachers expect the eighth graders to take an interdisciplinary approach this should certainly include both the physical educator and physical education content.

Instructional Time

Students in middle school should take physical education every semester or quarter for a total time equal to that allocated to other subject areas. If students spend 50 minutes a day in language arts, science, mathematics, and social science, then they should spend 50 minutes a day in physical education. If the school is on block scheduling and students spend 100 minutes every other day in language arts, science, mathematics, and social science, then they should spend 100 minutes every other

---

Sample Letter to Your State Legislator

June 15, 1992

The Honorable John Seymour
United States Senator
11111 Santa Monica Blvd.
West Los Angeles, CA 90025

Dear Senator:

I would like to express my concern over the lack of inclusion of physical education and health education in the list of educational goals for the year 2000. During a time when the fitness scores of youth are at an all-time low, the health of all Americans is threatened by HIV/AIDS, a large number of individuals are addicted to illegal substances, and our society is being threatened by gangs, poverty, and unemployment, I ask you, how can these critical subject areas be omitted from the list of educational goals for the year 2000?

A Comprehensive Health Education program provides youngsters with information regarding substance abuse, family life, personal health, nutrition, mental/emotional factors, diseases and disorders, consumerism, accident prevention and emergency procedures, community health, and environment health. At the same time, a Comprehensive Health Education Program provides students with self-awareness, coping, and decision-making skills.

A Comprehensive Physical Education program provides students with improved levels of physical fitness, improved self-confidence and self-esteem, a method for reducing stress and depression, improved coordination and motor skills, an understanding of human movement, and the opportunity to lead healthier lifestyles.

I certainly hope you will reconsider and include both physical education and health education in the list of educational goals for the year 2000!

Thank you for your time, and I look forward to hearing your response.

Sincerely,

Bonnie Mohnsen, PhD
18832 Stefani Avenue
Cerritos, CA 90703

day in physical education. Many states mandate the number of minutes students must spend in physical education or the number of courses that they must take. Work with your state professional association to change state laws that mandate time spent on physical education. And take advantage of any trend in your state that gives local school sites more freedom to make decisions regarding curriculum and instruction. As your school becomes involved with local (or site-based) decision making, seek to increase the instructional time allocated to physical education beyond state mandates.

Class Size

The class size and the grouping of students in physical education classes should also be the same as other content areas. In some schools, guidance counselors or computers first assign students to other classes and then put them into whatever physical education class fits into their schedules. As a result, you may have sixth, seventh, and eighth graders in the same class or very small classes in the morning and larger classes in the afternoon. A better approach is to determine the number of courses for each grade level that will be offered in physical education and then spread the students equally throughout the day. Next, determine the current class size average for physical education, add 5 to 10 percent to that number, and make that the limit for the number of students in each class. Now, it's up to the counselor or computer program to assign students to their appropriate classes, staying within the class size limits.

Funding

Does your school spend the same amount of money on instructional materials for physical education as it does for other subject areas? Probably not. The instructional materials for physical education include equipment and supplies as well as the same types of instructional materials used in other classes, such as textbooks and technology. Equitable funding is evidence that your school and the community at large see physical education as a full member of the instructional program.

Administrative Support

Physical educators must gain the respect of their administrators and colleagues in other subject areas before physical education will be fully included in the instructional setting. Butler and Mergardt (1994) found that gaining administrative support was the most significant factor in creating and maintaining effective physical education programs. Naturally, in schools in which administrators and colleagues respect the physical educators and physical education, the physical education program benefits from more equitable treatment. Goodlad (1984) noted a direct correlation between the amount of time allotted for a subject and the respect it received from society as a whole and, specifically, from the educational community.

What's the secret to gaining administrative support? First, provide a quality physical education program, including an articulated kindergarten through high school curriculum, such as the one I'll outline in this book, taught by qualified physical education teachers in a supportive environment. Continually assess your program and your own and student performance. In turn, use the data from these assessments to improve the instructional program.

The second step is to share your program and its benefits with the school's stakeholders. You must educate them as to the positive influence of physical education on the lives of the students. The public relations information at the end of this chapter will assist you with promoting your program and educating your stakeholders.

The third step is to represent your department's interests on school-wide committees. Representation on funding, staff development, restructuring, and curriculum committees ensures equal access to the resources and—sometimes more importantly—information. By actively participating on decision-making committees as a representative of the physical education department and your students, you can play a vital role in the restructuring of your school. For example, if allocation of instructional time is a committee issue, work to ensure that the committee allocates equal instructional time to physical education. Otherwise, you'll have no guarantees and little chance for equitable treatment.

Another example of the importance of representation on school-wide committees involves a curriculum committee that was given the task of creating additional electives for the eighth graders. In this school, a physical educator on the committee was able to add physical education electives in addition to the required eighth grade physical education class. One elective class the committee added to this program was the "Junior Physical Education Teacher Class," in which the students learned the basics of teaching physical education. Part of the requirement for the class was to assist with the teaching of a sixth or seventh grade class—of great value to everyone involved. Would this committee have thought to include electives related to physical education without a physical educator's input? Maybe not.

Other key committees at your school may require physical education representation as well. But how do you find time and energy for them all? Distribute the responsibility of serving on committees throughout the department, thereby reducing the pressure and time commitment on any one person as well as educating all staff members about the issues facing the school.

Committee membership provides two other benefits you may not have considered: You can more easily get to know your colleagues in other subject areas and you can increase the opportunities you have to educate other stakeholders as to the positive attributes of your physical education program. Likewise, your colleagues and other stakeholders will have a better chance to come to know and respect you personally. In short, committee membership creates valuable networking opportunities that may lead to more equitable treatment of your physical education program.

Physical Education and the Extracurricular Setting

Caught in the Middle: Educational Reform for Young Adolescents in California Public Schools (California State Department of Education 1989) identifies extracurricular and intramural programs as being essential for every middle school student, stating that these programs, ". . . develop a sense of personal connectedness to school through activities that promote participation, interaction, and service" (p. 85). Physical education has a significant role to play in the offering of these extracurricular activities, including providing intramural programs, participating or organizing fund-raising programs that involve physical activity, and creating fitness-wellness programs.

Intramural Programs

The purpose of the physical education program is to provide instruction to all students so that they can accomplish the standards I'll describe in part II. Intramural programs, on the other hand, provide students with opportunities to apply the motor skills they have learned in physical education. His-

torically many extracurricular programs were exclusive, working only with the most elite athletes on campus, but a model intramural program is open to and enjoyable for the average and below average motor skill ability students as well.

The ideal intramural program is run by an intramural council comprised of students and a faculty advisor. The council sets the schedule, decides on the activities and form of competition, and assigns the personnel—equipment monitors, officials, scorekeepers, and organizers who provide students with information as to where and when they are playing. You must train these individuals to understand and implement their roles in order to create and deliver an effective intramural program.

Figure 3.1 Boys and girls, including students with disabilities, benefit from a well-organized intramural program.

As you start to set up an intramural program, make decisions regarding the level of competition. We often think that competition promotes sportsmanship. Yet competition often impedes both learning and performance and can encourage negative attitudes and behaviors. Individuals who have had extended experiences in organized sport as children tend to display poorer attitudes of sportsmanship than nonparticipants (Seefeldt and Vogel 1986). The sport participants tend to be more concerned with winning, while the nonparticipants are more concerned with fair play. Looking for an alternative? Rotate players from team to team during a game so that no group can actually be declared the winners. This type of intramural program emphasizes participation instead of competition. If you have ever watched students playing a sport during recess or lunch, you've seen that they are, indeed, more interested in participation than competition. Students rarely maintain win-loss records beyond the immediate game, and yet back they come the very next day to play again. Ultimately, greater participation equals greater benefits.

Intramural programs can function at various times throughout the school day. In some schools, students have a free period during which they can select from alternative recreational activities, including intramural activities. Other schools create time during advisory periods, recess, nutrition, lunch, or before or after school, including evenings, to ensure opportunities for all students to participate. When setting up the intramural program, however, make sure it does not compete with physical education for the use of facilities and equipment.

Intramural Activities

Yo-yo events

Frisbee golf

Over-the-Line

Two-on-Two Basketball

Juggling events

Modified soccer

Pickleball

Miniature golf

Orienteering

Modified team handball

Select activities for the intramural program based on the activities you have recently covered in physical education or use novel activities. Note, however, that the physical education program drives the intramural program—not vice versa. For example, because the instructional units should be different for each grade level in a middle school, it makes sense to have separate intramural programs for the various grade levels as well.

Fund-raisers

Physical education is in a unique position when it comes to fund-raising. Today, walk- and jog-a-thons are popular fund-raising activities. Or you may think of something more creative and unique. In any case, your physical education department can promote physical activity while simultaneously raising funds for your community, school, or physical education program. Although you'll probably use or adapt activities you've taught during physical education for the fund-raising events, the actual events need to take place outside of the school day so they do not interfere with the instructional program.

The Jump Rope for Heart Program was developed by the American Heart Association and the American Alliance for Health, Physical Education, Recreation and Dance. It is a fitness education and fund-raising activity as well as a positive physical activity. Most physical educators hold this event as the culmination of a fitness or jump rope unit. It consists of six-member jump teams. Team members take turns jumping during a three-hour period. Students solicit pledges for the amount of time they jump.

Goals of the Jump Rope for Heart Program

Promote the lifelong benefits of regular exercise.

Provide an opportunity for students and parents to work together toward a common goal.

Reinforce the merits of the physical education curriculum as well as provide visibility for physical education professionals in the community.

Encourage teamwork by involving participants in working toward a common goal and instilling school pride.

Emphasize to participants and the community the importance of a healthy lifestyle, including proper nutrition, not smoking, and controlling high blood pressure.

For more information about the Jump Rope for Heart Program, contact your local American Heart Association, or call 1-800-242-8721.

School-wide jog-a-thons (or walk-a-thons, bike-a-thons, and the like) have the potential of bringing financial resources to the school and physical education program. Unlike candy drives, this form of fund-raising both promotes positive health habits and develops in the students a sense of responsibility for their school. Students secure and collect pledges that can be a certain monetary amount for each mile completed or a flat rate for participation in the event. The school or its physical education program receives the money.

Fitness-Wellness Programs

In addition to providing intramural programs and fund-raising events outside the instructional program, your physical education program can also promote fitness and wellness by creating a fitness center to be available for student (and perhaps school and community) use during noninstructional times. Students who would like to improve their cardiorespiratory endurance, muscular strength and endurance, muscular flexibility, or body composition can drop into the fitness center during recess, nutrition, lunch, or before or after school and participate in a personal fitness program that they have developed in consultation with a physical educator. Some schools include the fitness-wellness program as part of an optional student fee that allows participants to attend school events and, in this case, the fitness center. Other schools either charge a fee for participation in this optional activity or provide it free-of-charge to their students. Those schools that provide the program free-of-charge often use money secured from grants to support the program or funds from jog-a-thons or other fund-raisers.

Physical Education and the Comprehensive School Health System Setting

Another way physical education can give and receive support to the school community is through a comprehensive school health program located on-site. This is a coordinated approach to addressing the health status of students so that they are better prepared to learn in school. It's not intended to simply tell students what constitutes a healthy lifestyle, but rather to encourage them to practice good health habits that will remain with them for a lifetime. This approach consists of eight components designed to reinforce and build on one another.

Eight Components of a Comprehensive School Health Program

Health education
Physical education
Health services
Nutrition services
Counseling and psychological services
Parent and community involvement
Health promotion for staff
Safe and healthy school environment

In order to address the health status of each student, schools and districts need to establish comprehensive school health committees comprised of physical educators, health educators, school nurses, risk managers, principals, food service personnel, school counselors, custodial staff, and other teachers as well as parents and community members. Then the committee proceeds through the next five steps of institutionalizing a comprehensive school health program.

Steps for Institutionalizing Comprehensive School Health Programs

Establish a committee.
Create a vision.
Conduct a needs assessment.
Develop a three-year plan.
Implement a three-year plan.

The committee begins by creating a vision for their comprehensive school health system. Next, they assess the current status of the eight components of comprehensive health and set goals for improving each of these areas to realize their vision. This step provides an opportunity for each group of professionals to learn to respect the other areas related to school health. Then, the committee develops a three-year plan for implementing their vision. Finally, the committee begins to implement the three-year plan. It is important for committee members to recognize, however, that they will need to update and modify their plan as they progress through the implementation stage.

Many strategies that help to raise the awareness level of other faculty and community members to the issues surrounding comprehensive school health exist. Staff development workshops and wellness fairs are two of the most helpful practices. A holistic approach to staff and student health also helps—from the creation of a smoke-free work place to screening for high blood pressure to serving healthy food in the cafeteria to teaching relaxation techniques for stress reduction. In order to have a strong comprehensive school health system, however, each of the eight components must deliver top-quality service.

Physical Education

How fit are your students? A high-quality physical education program contributes to the comprehensive school health system by seeking to improve the fitness level of the middle school students. How? A fitness center is an exciting and effective approach to fitness. It becomes a source of pride for the middle school with a strong focus on comprehensive school health. Furthermore, it demonstrates your interest in the health of your students.

Physical educators at some schools also promote the inclusion of one or more fitness breaks during the school day for which the classroom teacher conducts stretching exercises, takes the class for a walk or jog, or provides some other type of aerobic activity. The physical educators in these schools serve as a resource for the type of activities that the classroom teacher may wish to provide. Periods of increased aerobic activity increase blood and oxygen flow to the brain and have proven to be effective in increasing student learning (Caine and Caine 1990; Jensen 1994). (See chapter 9 for more details.)

Health Education

A quality health education program is similar to a quality physical education program in the sense that a sequential kindergarten through 12th grade curriculum exists taught by qualified health education teachers. A health education curriculum committee establishes both local exit standards (based on the National Health Standards) and grade level standards. The committee uses information from

the following areas to set the standards: community health, consumer health, environmental health, family life, mental and emotional health, injury prevention and safety, nutrition, personal health, prevention and control of disease, and substance use and abuse. As in physical education and other subject areas, health education instructors must establish a positive learning environment, develop a sequential curriculum, use effective instructional approaches and materials, and set up performance-based assessments. It is also crucial that health education programs promote active student learning, critical thinking, and the development of positive health behaviors. Physical educators and health educators also must work together to integrate concepts addressed in both curricula.

National Health Education Standards

1. Students will comprehend concepts related to health promotion and disease prevention.

2. Students will demonstrate the ability to access valid health information and health-promoting products and services.

3. Students will demonstrate the ability to practice health-enhancing behaviors and reduce health risks.

4. Students will analyze the influence of culture, media, technology, and other factors on health.

5. Students will demonstrate the ability to use interpersonal communication skills to enhance health.

6. Students will demonstrate the ability to use goal-setting and decision-making skills to enhance health.

7. Students will demonstrate the ability to advocate for personal, family, and community health.

This represents the work of the joint Committee on National Health Education Standards. Copies of *National Health Education Standards: Achieving Health Literacy* can be obtained through the American School Health Association, Association for the Advancement of Health Education, or the American Cancer Society.

Health Services

In addition to providing information regarding health issues, a comprehensive school health system provides students with health service support. Every school has established procedures for dealing with emergency health care situations as well as health care maintenance. Schools maintain accurate records of student immunizations and routine screenings. The health service program takes these services one step further and seeks to identify health problems that may interfere with student learning. Health service workers regularly administer hearing, dental, vision, height and weight, posture, and blood pressure screening to determine those students having difficulties.

One recent innovation that has proven to be highly effective in reducing student health problems is the school-based health clinic or school-linked health center. These health clinics or centers are located on or near school campuses and are often cosponsored by county health departments or private foundations. The advantages of health clinics include convenience for students, ease of follow-up care, integration with health education activities, and opportunities to address health issues specific to the adolescent population.

Nutrition Services

Nutrition services also reinforce the information students receive in the health education and physical education classes. Cafeterias are, in fact, the laboratory for students to see good eating habits in practice. The school cafeteria provides students with nutritionally balanced meals that follow the United States Dietary Association guidelines for foods high in fiber and low in fat, sugar, and salt. Certainly, proper nutrition plays an important role in preparing students for maximum learning during the school day.

Even schools that have nutrition-conscious cafeteria staffs must contend with the selling of unhealthy foods by outside vendors, the student store, and candy- and soda-selling fund-raisers. Developing policies banning the sale of unhealthy foods on school property and substituting healthy fund-raising activities helps to improve school-wide nutrition.

Counseling and Psychological Services

The counseling and psychological staffs promote the mental, emotional, and social health of both students and staff. By working in partnership with teachers, these specialized staff members develop plans for helping students cope with difficult situations. They also provide staff development for all teachers on the warning signs of emotional stress, on staying sensitive to student well-being, and on knowing the appropriate steps to take when students are under emotional stress.

Students learn best in a psychologically safe environment (see chapter 5). They need to sense that the school supports their needs not only for academic achievement but also for self-esteem and relationships. Students who have a forum for discussing concerns and a system through which they may receive assistance in making healthy decisions, dealing with depression, coping with crises, and setting goals, will be more ready to learn. In addition, the counseling and psychological staffs can provide support for students and their families after disasters or violence occurs at or near the school.

Parent and Community Involvement

Often physical educators complain that parents don't support their children's education in physical education class. By involving parents and other community members in the school's comprehensive health program, they will understand our goals and needs better and, in turn, support the physical education and health programs more. Parents and community members make excellent guest speakers or volunteers in the physical education program. Invite them to your class to share their experiences, assist with activities, and learn more about your program. In addition, involving parents in the educational process increases student motivation (Henderson 1987), thereby presenting both parents and teachers with fewer discipline problems.

Sound great? Unfortunately, many adults will be unable to participate due to work schedules. Include them by assigning homework that requires your students to work with their parents or community members to extend the scope and depth of the physical education and comprehensive health programs. For example, ask students to calculate target heart rate ranges for their entire families based on each individual's age and resting heart rate. This type of activity not only promotes positive health behaviors in your students but also educates the entire family and community about fitness concepts. You do, however, need to be sensitive to the role of the family as the student's primary caretaker. Understanding different family structures and the differences between various cultural and ethnic groups will ensure that you don't overstep your boundaries when assigning family homework. For example, many students come from single parent families, so be careful not to require the simultaneous participation of both mother and father.

Two other ways to involve others in your physical education program are physical activity nights or health fairs through which you bring students, parents, and community members together for wellness and physical activities at the school. In addition to physical activities, provide learning experiences so that all participants leave the evening with a greater understanding of the concepts related to improving fitness. One alternative to your leading this activity is to have the students lead their parents through the physical activities and learning experiences. When students must do the teaching, they must assimilate what they have learned well enough to pass it on to someone else—a highly effective teaching approach and assessment tool.

The school and community must work together to ensure a complementary recreation program for students and adults. In schools without recreational programs, the community recreation department provides activities for students during appropriate times of the day. Communities and schools also share facilities for the benefit of both programs. For example, fitness courses and swimming pools are often built on park and recreation facilities. These specialized facilities are often unavailable to students in school, but provide opportunities for practice in the evenings, on weekends, and during vacations. Assign homework and extra credit that encourages the use of these community facilities; students can report to the entire class about the benefits.

Community service is a new area in the educational arena. In physical education, ask your students to work with younger students in recreation programs, provide exercise breaks for the elderly, or assist at community health fairs. Each of these activities extends students' physical education learning while giving something back to the community.

Safe and Healthy School Environment

Naturally, it is difficult to learn in an environment where fear and unsanitary conditions prevail. A healthy school environment provides students with a clean and safe (physically and psychologically) environment in which to learn. In such schools, maintenance of every area, including the school grounds, parking area, playground and its equipment, floor areas, stairs, classrooms, and physical education facilities, is a priority. Schools with healthy environments keep rest rooms, which are especially vulnerable to vandalism, clean and supplied with soap and towels, eliminating graffiti and maintaining doors on individual stalls for student privacy. They check all facilities for asbestos dust, radon, and lead-contaminated water. They adhere to legal regulations regarding lighting, heating, and ventilation.

Health Promotion for Staff

The last area of comprehensive school health focuses on health promotion for the staff. A model wellness program meets the needs of staff, too, incorporating fitness, stress management, health screening, weight control, and nutrition. Often, if the school has a student fitness center, the staff uses it during noninstructional times. Model programs offer classes on weight management, smoking cessation, personal goal setting, aerobic workouts, and strength building. All participants new to the program undergo medical tests, receive appraisals of health and fitness status, set goals, and follow individually prescribed exercise routines. The benefits of a staff wellness center include reductions in absenteeism and health insurance costs. In schools with wellness centers, school morale often increases. An often unrecognized benefit is that teachers who are involved in fitness programs become models for the students within their care.

Public Relations

A strong public relations program communicates to all stakeholders the quality features of the school's physical education program; its relationship to the instructional program, extracurricular program, and comprehensive school health program; and the positive benefits that students are getting from physical education. Public relations is more than a one-time announcement or participation in a special activity like National Physical Education Week; instead, it must be an ongoing program to gain support for physical education from the various stakeholders.

Community members are an especially important group in which to instill a strong commitment to the physical education program. School administrators and teachers are often influenced by the community's beliefs, and parents, as part of a community, internalize many of the beliefs held by that community. Historically, the Olympics has—at least temporarily—heightened awareness of the efforts of physical education programs. More significantly, society has given more or less respect to physical education programs during times of war when a physically fit military is valued by society. Every day, however, opportunities for you to communicate with parents, teachers, business leaders, community members, and legislators about physical education arise.

Physical educators who put forth quality physical education programs and tell others about it are protecting their programs before any threat against them can occur. Placek's (1983) famous study of physical education teachers found that many teachers and administrators think of a successful physical education lesson as one in which students are on-task, enjoying themselves, and not presenting discipline problems. Often summarized as "busy, happy, and good," this study demonstrates the need to refocus physical education on the business at hand—that of educating students through a quality middle school physical education program. Let others know how physical education programs have changed. Share with the community that physical educators no longer "throw out the ball." Let parents know how physical education promotes the health, physical fitness, and psychosocial growth of their children.

To get started, follow these three steps to develop a public relations program. First, determine your message, including information on your current program and your future needs. Second, use a variety of media—print, video, audio, and displays—to present your message. Third, don't give up—no matter what happens or doesn't happen. Keep delivering your message.

To determine and fine-tune your message, start with a public service announcement for your local newspaper. Make your public service announcement specific to your program. Tell your students' parents, "See what your kids are learning in physical education!"

Your public service announcement is only one way to communicate your message. Many more ways to promote your physical education program exist. Write or call the National Association for Sport and Physical Education (NASPE) for more information. NASPE publishes a notebook entitled *Sport and Physical Education Advocacy Kit* (NASPE 1994), which provides you with a complete public relations package.

Crash Course in Public Relations: 10 Ways to Promote Physical Education

Create displays of student work for exhibition at special community and school events.

Make presentations at school board meetings, including student demonstrations.

Visit local state legislators to solicit their support.

Create a physical education newsletter that goes home to parents and out to local businesses and community members describing your program.

Present adventure-based or other workshops for businesses, parents, and community members.

Put on student demonstrations at a local shopping center.

Make and send a fitness fact sheet to community members.

Speak at your local civic organization luncheon meeting about your quality physical education program and its benefits to students.

Arrange for messages about quality physical education to be printed on grocery bags.

Write short public service announcements for local radio and television stations to make.

Sample Public Service Announcement

Did you know America's school children are not "Fit to Achieve?" Often, schools overlook the need for physical education. Our children are missing out on very important benefits—such as improvement of physical fitness, physical competence, and positive attitudes that accompany a healthy, active lifestyle. Get involved. Learn about your children's physical education programs. Make sure your children are getting the complete education they deserve (NASPE 1994).

Summary

Imagine every school in the United States with a supportive principal like the one I described at the beginning of this chapter. Make that scenario a reality by aligning your physical education program with the total school environment, including the instructional setting, the extracurricular setting, and the comprehensive school health program. You can earn respect and support in a number of ways. Above all, provide quality physical education for all your students. Beyond this, work with other subject area teachers, administrators, and community mem-bers on numerous projects and committees through which you can share and augment your program. Finally, publicize your program through physical education newsletters, public service announce-ments, and school board presentations.

CHAPTER 4

The Physical Education Environment

Through fund-raising, we have developed our fitness lab using an empty woodshop room. The lab has been painted by the district, carpeted by fund-raising, and outfitted with a cardiovascular exercise circuit, a classroom area, and a computer area by grants. The lab is used by the seventh and eighth grade students and is open to the staff and community after school hours.

—*Physical Educator Karen Mendon, Montebello Intermediate, Montebello, California*

To learn in physical education, students need access to a quality physical education environment consisting of adequate and safe facilities, equipment, and supplies. Some physical educators are fortunate enough to already work in schools with excellent facilities. For example, Punahou School is a kindergarten through 12th grade private school on the island of Oahu in Honolulu, Hawaii. The physical education facilities include a four-story building, outdoor swimming pool, 440-meter track, court space, and all the open field space you could ever want. The building contains the teachers' offices; locker rooms; laundry room; trainer's room; storage rooms filled with equipment and supplies; dance, weight training, gymnastics, and wrestling rooms; handball courts; classrooms; student health center; and gymnasium.

Unfortunately, we don't all work under these conditions. Yet many of your colleagues have created better physical education environments for their students under less than ideal circumstances. While individual teachers can create quality physical education environments, when all members of the physical education department (also known as the physical education team) work together, the task is much easier. In this chapter, I'll discuss improving your physical education environment as well as successful strategies for organizing your department.

Facilities

The actual need for specific facilities is directly linked to the curriculum. For example, if the

Figure 4.1 Swimming pool at Funahou School.

Figure 4.2 Gymnastics room at Punahou School.

curriculum calls for aquatics, then you need a pool. Be creative in your choices as well. You'll probably think of many standard facilities, but have you ever considered adding a ropes course? A ropes course is a collection of challenges (or elements) that students, working in small groups, must solve. These challenges require the group to overcome anxiety and fear and learn to function together under stress in order to arrive at a solution. For more information on how to build a ropes course and for the different types of challenges, contact Project Adventure, P.O. Box 100, Hamilton, MA 01936, 508-468-7981.

Although most departments have little opportu-

nity to change their facilities except during the construction of a new school or renovation projects, you can expand your facilities by exploring alternative locations, converting other school buildings, and using portable facilities. Alternative locations you should consider include nearby elementary or high schools, community recreation centers, and state parks. Typically, field space, swimming pools, tennis courts, and gymnasiums are the most-prized facilities. Some schools have also initiated rollerblading, hiking, and bicycling programs using trails in local or state parks. Other school agencies have worked effectively with local community gov-

Figure 4.3 Students on a ropes course prepare to step onto the swinging log, which is suspended six inches off the ground.

Figure 4.4 Students attempt to balance themselves on the swinging log.

ernments to build new diamonds, gymnasiums, or pools, which are available for school use during the day and community recreation at night and on the weekends. Physical educators have secured free or low-cost services from businesses such as golf courses, bowling alleys, skating rinks, and climbing centers for physical education classes during the school day. These businesses understand that students taught on their facilities are more likely to return with their families to use these facilities during their free time. Be open-minded and creative and see what's available in your area.

Another approach to increasing facilities is to appropriate empty buildings on campus and con-

vert them into physical education facilities. The practice of converting wood shops into fitness labs, as described at the beginning of this chapter, is becoming very popular at many middle schools. Likewise, schools have successfully converted unused classrooms into physical education classrooms, dance rooms, or storage rooms.

Can't find what you need anywhere? Bring it in on wheels! An excellent example of this is the Los Angeles Unified School District summer swimming program for which portable pools are moved from site to site in order to bring aquatics to students who otherwise would have limited access to swimming. But portable *pools*? It took an innovative, creative,

Suggested Facilities

Hard Surface Area

Basketball courts with standards

Handball courts

Racquet sports courts

Running lanes

Track, 400-meter (if located not in dirt area)

Volleyball courts

Dirt and Turf Area

High jump area

Long jump and triple jump area

Running track

Shot put and discus area

Softball diamond with 250-foot batting radius

Gymnasium or Multipurpose Room

Swimming Pool

Ropes Course

Fitness Center

Locker Rooms

Dryer

Lockers with built-in locks that can be programmed with five different combinations*

Showers

Washing machine

Classroom

Storage Rooms

Teachers' Offices

* Lockers with built-in locks and five combinations are specified for several reasons: You won't have to handle locks separately; combinations can be changed quickly when students check out; they facilitate inputting of locker data in a computer.

and determined physical educator to make it happen.

You don't have to wait for new facilities, however, to improve your physical education learning environment. Start today by making your current facilities more attractive: Make the most of those bulletin boards. Retire those drab posters your predecessor put up and use your bulletin boards to communicate important messages to students. Make the messages and presentations informative, exciting, and relevant to your current physical education content. Don't forget to use student work to help

Figure 4.5 "Fitness Lab" at Montebello Intermediate School.

convey your message. If you include any pictures, however, ensure that they represent boys and girls of various ethnicities.

Bulletin Board Themes

Back-to-school information
Student fitness projects
Athletes with physical challenges
History of a sport
Myths about diets
Olympics
Social skills
Physical fitness testing information
Water safety
Analysis of a skill

Equipment and Supplies

Typically, we can classify "equipment" as items that cost over two or three hundred dollars (as determined by the local educational agency) and "supplies" as items that cost less than that amount. Many times the administration or local committee allocates funds specifically for equipment or supplies, limiting departments as to the amount they can spend in each category. In this section, we'll specifically discuss sport equipment and supplies. We'll explore other instructional materials, such as textbooks, technological devices, and videos, in chapter 12.

As with facilities, the curriculum defines the need for various pieces of equipment and supplies. If the curriculum calls for a unit on softball, then you need backstops, gloves, softballs, bats, and catcher protective equipment. Ensure, however, that when you are purchasing or receiving donations of equipment and supplies that they are appropriate for middle school students. For example, sporting good companies are beginning to produce softer balls, pucks, and projectiles of various sizes that are safer and facilitate more success for middle school students, making them more educationally sound for middle school physical education settings.

Increase the amount of equipment and supplies you have access to by sharing materials with other schools, community recreation programs, and local

Suggested Equipment for Programs in Chapters 14 Through 16

Aerobic equipment (treadmill, bicycles, ergometers, climbers, stair steppers)
Backboard for basketball, tennis, and handball
Balance beam
Body bags for self-defense
Cassette or compact disc player
Climbing poles or ropes, 12 feet high
Floor hockey goals with nets
Goal uprights for field sports
Graduated horizontal bars, 5, 6, 7, 8, and 9 feet high
Hair dryers
High bar
High jump standards and crossbars
Horizontal ladder, 7 feet high
Hurdles, low and high
Mats for tumbling
Parallel bars
Ropes course elements
Scales
Side horse
Softball backstop and bases
Springboard
Stationary traveling rings
Table tennis tables
Team handball goals
Uneven bars
Unicycles
Vaulting box
Weight training equipment

businesses. Lobby to have your district purchase items that you usually use only once or twice a year, such as golf clubs or gymnastics equipment, to be shared by a number of different schools. This system maximizes the use of materials, frees storage space, and, perhaps most importantly, frees funds for other materials. However, either the central

Recommended Supplies for Programs in Chapters 14 Through 16

Air pump

Badminton rackets and shuttlecocks

Ball and bat bags

Basketballs (junior and regular size)

Beanbags

Bowling balls and pin sets

Cage ball

Chalkboards or easels

Discus

Field markers (cones)

Flags for flag football

Floor hockey balls or pucks, sticks, and shin guards

Footbags

Footballs (junior and regular size including Nerf)

Golf balls, plastic and regular

Golf clubs, woods, irons, and putters

Golf tees

Handballs

Juggling balls

Juggling scarves

Jump ropes, individual and long

Kickboards

Kicking tees

Lane markers

Measuring tape, 50 and 100 feet long

Nerf balls, a variety

Paddle balls and rackets

Pinnies

Racquetballs and rackets

Rope

Rubber batting tees

Shot puts

Snorkeling masks, fins, and air pipe

Soccer balls

Softball bats

Softball catcher's protective equipment, including chest protector and mask

Softball gloves

Softballs

Spinning balls

Spotting belts, hand and overhead

Starting gun and blanks

Stopwatches

Table tennis sets—paddles, balls, and nets

Team handballs

Tennis balls and racquets

Track batons

Volleyball nets

Volleyballs (extra soft and light)

Whistles

office administrator or one physical educator needs to take responsibility for organizing and overseeing the program to make sure everyone has a fair chance to use the equipment and to reduce the potential for loss or theft.

Don't forget free materials. Many agencies, such as the United States Tennis Association and the Young American Bowling Alliance provide free supplies to schools in order to promote their sport. Local agencies, such as golf courses, bowling centers, and the American Heart Association, also have free supplies for the asking. Some physical educators have experienced great success writing letters to various companies such as health clubs or fitness equipment companies and requesting donations of new or used equipment. Explore all of these gold mines to augment your supplies and equipment.

Creating a Safe Environment

Providing students with a safe environment in which to learn is your moral and legal responsibility. You certainly don't want your students physically hurt in the process of learning new skills. You have legal obligations as well. In a litigious society, it becomes the responsibility of professionals, including you and your colleagues, to protect yourselves and your school from being sued.

You are not responsible for student injuries if you

Sample Letter to Fitness Equipment Company

September 10, 1996

Holiday Spa
11234 Sepulveda Blvd.
Culver City, CA 90230

To Whom It May Concern:

I am the physical education department chairperson at James Middle School in Culver City. My department is in the process of creating a fitness lab for our students on campus. We envision a room equipped with exercise machines, computers, and fitness testing devices. In order to make our vision a reality, we are requesting a donation of any used equipment that you may be replacing at this time or in the near future. Specifically, we are interested in treadmills, ergometers, and rowers.

As you are well aware, healthy behaviors are established at a young age. My department and I are eager to teach our students to participate regularly in a fitness program, so that as adults they will participate in health clubs such as yours and lead more quality lives. We anticipate posting the names of our benefactors on one of the walls of our new fitness center to show our appreciation for their support. We hope that we can include your name in the listing.

Thank you for your time and I look forward to hearing from you soon.

Sincerely,

Mark Allen

have acted as a reasonable, prudent person would have acted during a similar situation. The basis for legal suits against a teacher is almost always negligence—the failure to exercise the care that a reasonable, prudent person would have taken. The law requires four elements to be present in order for negligence to be declared:

1. The teacher must have a responsibility to ensure the safety of the participant; this is implied in the teacher-student relationship.
2. The teacher must have violated this responsibility by either failing to perform a required duty (act of omission) or doing something that they should not have done (act of commission).
3. An injury must have occurred while the student was under the care of the teacher.
4. The injury must be the result of the teacher violating the responsibility for the safety of the student.

Students also have a responsibility to exercise care for their own welfare. In fact, courts many times attribute an injury to both parties (teacher and student) and make an award based on comparative negligence. To protect the institution from being sued, however, you must take active steps by (1) providing adequate supervision, (2) anticipating foreseeable risks and warning students of any inherent risks, (3) making sure the activity is suitable for the participants, and (4) by ensuring that the activity takes place in a safe learning environment. While it is impossible to completely eliminate the risk of being sued, by following certain procedures, you can reduce that risk.

Adequate Supervision

Failure to provide adequate supervision is the most common allegation of negligence (van der Smissen 1990). Adequate supervision includes the ratio of teachers to students, the teacher's training, the physical distance between the teacher and the students, and the establishment and implementation of safety rules. You and your department can use the issue of teacher to student ratio as you work to lower class size, since large classes can result in claims of inadequate supervision. Typically, courts look at the age, maturity, and skill level of the students before determining the appropriate ratio.

You can reduce the risk of a successful lawsuit against yourself and your school district by following certain supervision principles. But how do you prove you have adequately supervised your students? Document any injuries in writing, along with standard operating procedures; and make sure all the physical educators in your department are trained by the American Red Cross in first aid and cardiopulmonary resuscitation and have current certification cards. Documentation and certification are strong defenses against accusations of negligence pertaining to inadequate supervision and the handling of medical emergencies.

Selection and Conduct of Activities

Another common area for allegation of negligence is the selection and conduct of activities. If you

Typical Questions Examined by Expert Witnesses in Negligence Actions

Did the activity or drill in progress at the time of the injury have a legitimate educational objective or purpose?

Is the activity or drill inherently dangerous?

Are the participants appropriately grouped or matched?

Is the activity or drill appropriate for the readiness level (i.e., the age, ability, maturity, mentality, and so on) of the injured participant?

Did the teacher appropriately warn all the students about the inherent risks of the activity, telling them how to guard against injury as a result of those risks?

Did the teacher provide the participant with appropriate feedback related to proper skill or activity execution so as to prevent injury?

Did the teacher provide correct instruction?

Were all necessary physical skills covered prior to the student's participation in the activity?

Were all necessary progressions covered so that the participant could master essential simple skills before attempting complex skills?

Did the teacher develop, communicate, and consistently enforce all necessary safety rules?

Did the teacher adequately anticipate the hazards involved in the activity and take the necessary steps to provide reasonably for the participant's safety?

Was the participant properly supervised at the time of the injury?

Did the equipment play a role in the injury sustained by the participant?

Did the facility contribute to the injury because of improper design or condition?

Did the potential likelihood and potential severity of injury outweigh the teacher's reasons for conducting the activity in the way he or she did?

Adapted from G. R. Gray, 1995, "Safety tips from the expert witness," *Journal of Physical Education, Recreation & Dance.*

Supervision Principles

Always be in the immediate vicinity (within sight and sound) of the students.

Secure an adequate replacement (not a paraprofessional, student teacher, or custodian) in place before leaving the area.

Obtain ongoing training on how to handle emergency situations.

Create written supervision procedures that designate the responsible teacher (e.g., locker room, before class, after class).

Develop written procedures for what to do if a problem or emergency arises.

Have access to a phone or other communication device and post emergency phone numbers in a handy location.

of grade level standards, however, you can demonstrate that the activities are based on the age, size, physical condition, and ability of the students. If physical educators in your district develop and implement a curriculum for kindergarten through 12th grade that progressively and appropriately develops skills, then your defense against negligence is even stronger. (See chapters 6 and 7 for more information on how to develop a progressive, developmentally appropriate curriculum for your district.)

Although a written curriculum can provide a good defense in terms of what physical educators should be teaching, the defense for *how* you provide instruction rests with you, the individual. Daily written lesson plans, including suitable activities, documentation of any injuries that occur, and adequate supervision provide you with a more than adequate defense against a law suit.

Safety Issues

Beyond providing adequate facilities and materials (both equipment and supplies) for your students to use, it is also important to maintain the facilities and materials, ensuring that they are clean, safe, and used appropriately. Specifically, you must establish, teach, and enforce safety rules. Create safety rules specific to your site, then include rules that state that students must use materials for their intended purpose only and that students must always use safety

select units of instruction merely according to your own preference, you have little defense against charges of negligence when a student is injured. If you select units of instruction based on the sequence

Checklist for Providing Suitable Activities

☑ Are the skills properly sequenced so all prerequisite skills have been taught before a new skill is introduced?

☑ For strenuous activities, are the students in sufficient condition before the introduction of the skill?

☑ Did you properly demonstrate and explain the skill's technique?

☑ Did you explain the safety rules related to the skill, activity, or game?

☑ Did you demonstrate and discuss incorrect techniques that might result in injury?

☑ Did you warn the students of any inherent risk involved in the skill?

☑ Did you provide proper equipment, including safety equipment, to the students?

☑ Did you provide a series of developmental drills for practicing the skill?

☑ Did you provide adequate feedback for students regarding their execution of the skill?

Inspection Checklist

☑ Playground layout has been planned so that there are appropriate traffic patterns.

☑ Signs are posted informing users of any inherent risks involved with using the facility or material.

☑ Area is free of glass, vandalism, trash, gravel, and broken or lost equipment.

☑ At least 12 inches of sand lies under outdoor equipment.

☑ Top of all concrete footers are below the playing surface.

☑ Poles for volleyball and badminton are secured.

☑ No broken or worn-out parts exist.

☑ No cracks or splintered wood exist.

☑ Paint is not rusted or peeling.

☑ Bearings are not worn.

☑ Locking devices are provided for all bolts.

☑ Exposed ends of bolts do not exceed one-half the diameter of the bolt.

☑ No open-ended "S" hooks.

☑ Bolts and nuts are screwed tightly.

☑ All connecting and covering devices are secured.

☑ No sharp edges or points exist.

For more information, read the United States Consumer Product Safety Commission's *Handbook for Public Playground Safety*, 1991.

materials, such as catcher's protective equipment and eye goggles for handball.

Inspect facilities and materials weekly with a checklist in hand. After completing the safety inspection, date the checklist and save it as written documentation. Report any defects in materials or facilities in writing to the appropriate administrator so that they can be corrected as soon as possible. Keep a copy of such reports for yourself. If the defect is severe enough, don't allow anyone to use the material or facility until the defect is corrected.

Probably the most frustrating situation for physical education staffs located in areas prone to crime is leaving a clean facility on Friday only to return to a littered, graffiti-covered, or otherwise vandalized facility on Monday. Many schools facing this issue have instituted community watch programs asking neighbors whose properties overlook the school facilities to keep an eye on them during the evenings or over the weekends. Other schools have taken an additional step by hiring a custodian or watch person to live on the school campus and be responsible for maintaining and watching the facilities. Still others use cleanup crews that clean up early Monday morning before most of the staff and students arrive.

Organizing the Program

Both teachers and students benefit when teachers work together instead of operating independently or at odds with one another. You'll discover that the more your department works as a team, the more you'll be able to accomplish, the more smoothly your program will run, and the more rewarding your work will be. In addition, students will respond more appropriately when consistency from one teacher to another exists. How can you and your colleagues work better together to support one another as you strive to provide an organized physical education program for your students?

The Physical Education Department

The physical education department should be one department, including both male and female physical education teachers, with one teacher acting as chairperson or lead teacher. The chairperson should assume the role of facilitator or leader as opposed to commander or manager. The chairperson should not, as a manager or commander would, focus exclusively on the tasks at-hand while ignoring the long-range goal of developing and maintaining a quality physical education program. Instead, such a leader must possess a clear vision of where the department is going and must work with the other physical educators to realize the vision.

One helpful way to work together is for department members to share responsibilities, thereby more efficiently using everyone's time. These managerial functions include organizing equipment for the upcoming instructional units, maintaining facilities, inventorying and ordering new equipment, laundering and maintaining loaner uniforms, issuing and maintaining the locker system, conducting safety inspections, organizing the public relations campaign, serving on school-wide committees, and completing paperwork required by the school administration. Department members can select the task they would like to perform for the year and then rotate from year to year, so that everyone is aware of all the operational procedures required to run a physical education program. And what about the daily chores, such as locker room duty, yard duty, checking out loaner clothes, and issuing forgotten locker combinations? Some schools are fortunate enough to have classified personnel who handle many of these responsibilities. If your school is not so lucky, the physical educators in your department should share them equally.

Naturally, department members must share facilities as well. A yearly schedule designating who will have what facility based on the curriculum prevents conflicts during the year. Departments must also work together to maintain programs during special days, including rain, snow, smog, and minimum schedule days, retaining as much consistency with the regular program as possible. In some schools, all classes must share a common facility on a special day; however, with a little creativity many schools find alternative meeting areas, minimizing disruption of the learning process. Try using multi-purpose rooms, classrooms not in use during certain class periods due to teacher preparation time, weight training rooms, locker rooms, libraries, and hallways. If it is not possible to continue with the current instructional unit, then prepare a special day series of lessons ahead of time. Base this series on a cognitive standard, such as developing a fitness plan, or on a particular set of motor skills, such as dancing, or create any other lesson that you can conduct indoors.

Another way to create a positive working atmosphere is, as members of the department retire or leave for other positions, to bring in new staff members who are qualified and hold a philosophy of physical education consistent with the department. Lobby your administration to make sure that new staff members possess a college degree in physical education and have updated their skills through continual staff development. If allowed by local policies, the department chair or lead teacher should sit in on the interviews with the administrative staff. Along with being knowledgeable about physical education and instructional strategies, new staff members should possess the ability to work with others and share your department's vision for implementing a quality physical education program.

Student Handbook

Creating a student handbook as a department is evidence of working together as educators. It sends a clear message to students and other stakeholders that your department knows what it is trying to accomplish and that it will consistently apply standard procedures. Your students are, in effect, the customers for your physical education program. They are the end-users of the product (information) that you provide. A student handbook can introduce your students to the what and the why of the physical education program so that they may fully understand and participate in your department's vision.

Distribute the student handbook during the first few days of school and use it for a number of lessons introducing the students to the physical education program. One homework assignment should involve taking the handbook home and reviewing it with parents or guardians. In addition, give the handbook to each new student who arrives after the school year is under way. Keep in mind, too, that the student handbook is further documentation that your department is actively seeking to provide adequate supervision and instruction.

Your department will need to allocate sufficient time to the creation of the student handbook. First, however, determine department policies, curriculum, and extracurricular events. Many times the student handbook makes for an excellent summer or off-track project. The specifics for many of these items need to be based on your own program (I discuss suggestions for many of them in detail throughout this book). But let's take a moment to discuss the items in Roman numerals six through eight, since they relate to the physical education environment and are common issues for physical educators.

It is reasonable to require students to change their clothing for physical education due to sanitary and safety conditions. The most common concerns related to uniforms is what to do with students who forget their uniforms or refuse to wear their uniforms. The first step is to require attractive and suitable clothing, so that the students are not embarrassed to change into their physical education uniform. Many physical education departments have changed their required uniform for this reason. For example, most programs now provide longer shorts and a plain T-shirt with the option of sweats for inclement weather. One creative department had the name of the school along with the words "Health Center" printed on the front of each T-shirt. This simple act created positive feelings in the students about their physical education uniforms. In my county, we are promoting physical education by putting "Everyone Can Through Quality Physical Education" on the back of physical education T-

shirts. The second step is to require that everyone dress everyday with no exceptions. The third step is to provide "loaner clothes" for those students who forget their uniforms. These loaners will need to be laundered after each use, which is why you need a washer and dryer in the locker room or some other nearby area. This three-step process may sound too simple to work—especially for students who refuse to wear their uniforms—but it does. Simply treat refusing to wear the uniform as an act of defiance and deal with it like all other defiance issues that occur at school (e.g., students throwing textbooks on the floor, students refusing to follow directions). In schools throughout the country that adamantly follow these three steps, very few problems with students changing clothes for physical education occur. But if students find a loophole in this process and one or two students start to not change clothes for physical education, then the three-step process will fail.

It is important to provide showers in the middle school setting and encourage students to use them after physical activity. You, however, should not require showers; instead, promote the use of showers by explaining the reasons for taking a shower after physical activity. Then take a look at your showering facilities. Would you want to shower there? Can you do anything to make the shower environment more inviting? Can you increase privacy within the showering facilities? Many middle school students are embarrassed by their bodies, and the more privacy you can provide, the more comfortable they'll be with changing clothes and showering.

You, as a physical educator must address medical excuses that your regular classroom colleagues get to ignore. A typical policy that seems to work well for many departments is the requirement of a parent signature for a one- to three-day excuse, and then a nurse (including the school nurse) or doctor's signature for longer medical excuses. Students should still be required to put on their uniforms (unless the medical situation prohibits the changing of clothes), participate in those activities that don't interfere with their medical situation, and complete alternative tasks when injury prohibits the class activity.

Summary

A quality physical education environment provides the physical surroundings that promote student learning and enjoyment during physical education. Many times you inherit your facilities and equipment, but with a little creativity, your program can share facilities with other schools, community centers, or businesses. Businesses and community groups can help by purchasing, loaning, or donating adequate equipment and supplies. Work together as a department to accomplish the seemingly impossible in order to provide your students with an outstanding physical education setting.

CHAPTER 5

The Psychological Environment

Our program stresses cooperation, integration of other subject areas, and motivation to succeed regardless of gender, age, size, and current level of ability or interest. This approach ensures that all students experience personal success and enjoyment from physical activities such as team sports, lifetime and leisure activities, physical conditioning, body management, safety skills, and circus arts.

—*Physical Educator Jerry Ronk, Meany Middle School, Seattle, Washington*

At least once a year a letter is written to a newspaper columnist describing how, when the writer was a child, he was always picked last when teams were picked. The letter writer goes on to describe how this experience shattered his self-esteem and how he has always associated physical activity with this negative experience. Having personally observed classes where this practice continues, I often include a segment in my presentations on not picking teams. After one presentation, a young professional came up to me and asked, "If teams should not be picked, then how should they be selected?" She couldn't imagine any other way. This reinforced for me that picking teams and other detrimental activities, such as elimination games and using exercise as punishment, are still going on in our middle schools.

As opposed to the experience of the letter writer, in a psychologically safe environment, you must treat every student with the utmost respect and dignity, including learning and using students' names, taking students' needs into consideration, listening to students, helping students feel valued and recognized for who they are and what they are capable of doing, and setting up a positive, warm, and cooperative climate. Never use sarcasm, choose teams with methods that lower student self-esteem, or assign exercise as a form of punishment. Most importantly, be sincere about wanting to establish a positive relationship with each of your students. Make these simple adjustments in your approach to conducting classes to invite more students into the physical education learning environment as well as improve the image of physical education in society.

Ensuring psychological support in your classes

not only benefits the students on an affective level, it also increases the potential for learning. In this chapter, we'll take a look at promoting a psychologically safe environment through the total inclusion of all students in your classes, the teaching of prosocial skills, and the development of class management strategies that promote the positive self-esteem in students. We'll examine the type of environment in which all students experience success and demonstrate a willingness to risk participating in new activities and skills.

Physical Education Code of Ethics

I promise to

always provide quality instruction;

assign appropriate and safe exercises to my students;

respect the diversity of my students including gender, sexual orientation, race, culture, and language dominance;

include all my students (highly skilled, poorly skilled) in the learning process;

never sell candy or sodas or give them as rewards;

assign teams, never allowing students to pick teams;

have and maintain a vision and implementation plan for a quality curriculum; and

never use exercise as punishment.

Inclusion

If you don't even allow students access to your classes, you can't say to them that you are providing them with a psychologically safe environment. According to a number of legal mandates, the composition of classes must include students with disabilities, boys and girls, and students representing different ethnicities and cultures. Simply placing students in a well-balanced class is, however, only the first step toward inclusion and the meeting of each student's needs.

If psychological safety refers to respect for students, then it must include respect for all students—boys and girls, black and white, Christian and Jew, homosexual and heterosexual, low income and high income, and low skill and high skill. Students who are valued and who value one another are more

Public Law 94-142, Education for All Handicapped Children Act of 1975

To the maximum extent appropriate, children with disabilities, including children in public and private institutions or other care facilities, are educated with children without disabilities, and that special classes, separate schooling, or other removal of children with disabilities from regular educational environments occur only when the nature or severity of the disability is such that education in regular classes with the use of supplementary aids and services cannot be achieved.

Section 504 of the Rehabilitation Act of 1973, Reauthorized Public Law 99-057 of 1986

No otherwise qualified handicapped individual shall, solely by reason of his handicap, be excluded from participation in, be denied the benefits of, or be subject to discrimination under any program or activity receiving federal financial assistance.

Educational Amendment Act of 1972 (Title IX)

No person in the United States shall, on the basis of sex, be excluded from participation in, be denied the benefits of, or be subjected to discrimination under any education program or activity receiving federal financial assistance.

likely to reach their academic and physical potentials (Williamson 1993). Therefore, the respect and psychological support must not only come from you, the teacher, but also from fellow students. You can use a number of strategies to ensure total inclusion of students from all groups in your classes, including establishing class norms that support the rights of all students, providing direct instruction on social skills, sharing information on the contributions of various groups of people, and ensuring that instructional materials are inclusive of various groups.

Class norms need to focus on students treating one another with respect, including not allowing "put downs" or comments based on stereotypes. One junior high in a Chicago suburb expanded on this concept and established their own "Bill of Rights," outlining specifically what students are entitled to and how students should be treated. As you think about developing your own class norms, why not include some of these rights or, better yet, let your students establish their own set of class norms?

Student Bill of Rights

1. The right to develop one's own personality (so long as it does not interfere with the rights of others) without disrespectful criticism or pressure from cliques.

2. Freedom from physical abuse and mental abuse such as name calling, intimidation, or harassment.

3. Freedom from being set apart or mocked because of race, sex, religion, physical strength, size, features, friendship groups, age, culture, disability, financial status, clothing, classroom performance, etc.

4. The right of privacy and freedom from being harassed in the classroom; the right to be treated respectfully.

5. The right to an education, which means that the teacher should be free to teach and students free to learn without being interrupted by inconsiderate students.

6. The right to have personal and school property respected. Our school should be a safe place for property as well as people.

Reprinted from Williamson, 1993, "Is your inequity showing? Ideas and strategies for creating a more equitable learning environment," *Journal of Physical Education, Recreation & Dance*, 20.

Along with establishing class norms, you must actively teach social skills. Just as motor skills do not develop on their own, prosocial skills will not occur by chance. I'll discuss specific strategies for teaching social skills later in this chapter in a separate section. And in chapter 11, I'll discuss cooperative learning, which provides an opportunity for students to not only master content but also improve their social skills.

Including instruction on the contributions of different groups of people, including women, ethnic minorities, and people with disabilities in physical education, sport, and other areas will help your students recognize that all individuals have something to offer. Weave this instruction throughout the instructional process or create separate units that focus on one or more groups. The common practice of designating time periods as opportunities to focus on a group, like Black History Month (February), Women's History Month (March), or the Special Olympics, ensures that the contributions of these groups are highlighted. Relate this information to ongoing instruction and make an even more significant impact on your students.

Portraying positive images of individuals from all groups along with descriptions of their unique contributions is especially important when it comes to instructional materials. This practice will heighten your students' awareness of the significant contributions of these various groups and provide the students with models of inclusion. Moreover, when students see pictures of men and women participating in sport activities together, they learn that a particular sport is not the exclusive domain of one gender. Remember, bulletin board displays are an excellent forum for setting an inclusive atmosphere. You must also be willing to provide students with time for discussion when issues of race, gender, and other differences arise.

It's vital to commit yourself to making all students feel included and valued in the physical education class. So let's look at special considerations for including students representing different ethnic groups, genders, special needs, skill levels, and at-risk groups.

Inclusion of Ethnic Groups

As our culture becomes more diverse, the need arises for all of us to be more tolerant of individual differences. To adequately address the ethnic and cultural diversity in your classes, you must look first at your own cultural background and understand how your own biases affect your interactions with students. Then, you must examine the backgrounds and needs of your students as well as *their* cultural biases.

Sometimes the cultural backgrounds of our students may run counter to what you're trying to accomplish in physical education. This type of situation can either result in a conflict between the school and family or a compromise that meets the needs of both the physical education program and the culture. For example, some cultures do not allow girls to wear shorts. Physical educators in this situation have allowed these girls to wear culottes (a divided skirt) instead of the required shorts. The culottes met the needs of the culture as well as the safety and hygiene requirements of the physical education program.

Ethnocentrism to Multiculturalism

Isolate Stage—identify with one's group.

Inquiry Stage—acknowledge the existence of difference and recognize the complex process of culture.

Contact Stage—accept the validity of differences and put into perspective strengths and weaknesses of culture.

Integration—master knowledge and skills to feel comfortable and to communicate effectively with people of any culture in cross-cultural situations.

Reprinted from Williamson, 1993, "Is your inequity showing? Ideas and strategies for creating a more equitable learning environment," *Journal of Physical Education, Recreation & Dance.*

Williamson (1993) has identified four stages that individuals experience on the way to accepting a multicultural environment. In order to assist students with advancing from the isolate stage to the integration stage, you must provide students with critical thinking skills, which help them challenge social inequalities and promote cultural diversity. By becoming aware of how students within various cultures perceive physical education, physical activity, and interpersonal relationships, you can integrate issues related to social change into the physical education program.

Inclusion of Boys and Girls

One of the most widely debated areas of equity in physical education is coeducational classes. In today's society, most teachers would never think of segregating students by different ethnic groups, but some still have a hard time accepting students from different gender groups in the same classes. Segregated classes prevent boys and girls from interacting with one another and learning how to work and play together. Segregation by gender limits opportunities for boys and girls to reconsider their stereotypical assumptions in the physical domain.

Placing boys and girls in the same physical education class is only the first step toward providing students with the opportunity to examine their preconceived ideas about the opposite gender. Figure 5.2 lists six steps to equity. Not every teacher needs to pass through all six steps; however, you

Figure 5.1   Boys and girls participate on an equal basis in a quality middle school physical education program.

should be able to identify the step you currently occupy. Step six is complete equity, including opportunities for both genders to demonstrate skills, answer questions, receive feedback, and feel respect from the teacher and other students. It also includes an environment in which the teacher uses inclusive language (referring to the class as "students" instead of "you guys") and omits stereotypical phrases (e.g., "You throw like a girl").

Reaching step six does not occur haphazardly. To arrive at step six, first write down your concerns about coeducational physical education so you can examine and deal with each concern one at a time. Second, visit programs where coeducational physical education has become the norm. During the visit, observe the type of strategies and curricula that works in middle school coeducational settings. Ask questions about how they were able to make the transition.

As you progress through steps two through five, continually reflect on your own teaching behaviors. When boys and girls appear to not be working well together, examine the learning environment and determine what might be causing the problem. Often, I hear physical educators state that the boys won't let the girls touch the ball. Sometimes, the physical educator shares that she has even made a rule that a girl must touch the ball before the team can score. When I question the teacher as to whether or not all the boys in her class refuse to share, she typically responds, "No, it is a few aggressive boys." This tells me that the situation has little to do with coeducational physical education, since these same boys are also preventing the other boys from touching the ball. The remedy is either to make a rule that everyone must touch the ball, or better yet, reduce the size of the teams so that everyone on the team must be involved for the team to be successful. Requiring that a girl must touch the ball before scoring sends the message that girls need special

> I have found coeducational physical education to be highly successful, both for girls and boys. Certainly the skill levels of girls have improved . . . . The boys, too, have benefited from exposure to a greater diversity of activities, experienced more opportunities to be successful, and learned more social skills—with no decline in their learning of movement skills.
>
> —Jean Flemion, 1990 NASPE Secondary Physical Education Teacher of the Year

treatment, which only serves to reinforce the stereotype that the girls are not as competent as the boys.

Inclusion of Students With Disabilities

The term inclusion, as it relates to students with disabilities, means placing these students in regular education classes at the school they would attend if they did not have a special need. Special education and other services are brought to the student, rather than having the student go to these services in separate classes or schools. Considerable evidence from the past 15 years suggests that segregation of these students can be harmful to their academic performance and social adjustment. Indeed, all students have a legal right to placement in a regular physical education class, even if they have special needs and require extra support to be successful. Support for the student can come from a special educator, adapted physical educator, parent, peer tutor, volunteer, or teacher assistant.

The first step toward inclusion requires that you develop a positive attitude and a willingness to work with students with disabilities. Many times the students with disabilities may take longer to learn skills, drills, and routines; however, if you

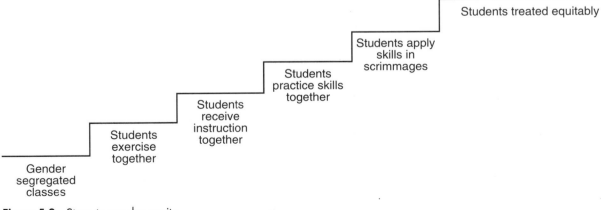

Figure 5.2 Steps to gender equity.

Figure 5.3   All students have a right to placement in a regular physical education class—even if they have special needs and require extra support to be successful.

I feel like having differently abled students be a part of the class, socializing, and trying the activities is very important. My student aides usually take these students and do the class activity with them. I enjoy watching while these students blend in with the rest of the class. The regular education students tell them where to stand, give them the ball for a chance, and really work hard at including them. The regular education students also really get on someone that does not include or tries to bully them. It has taken us a couple of years to get to this place. I have had to change the way I think. I now see how meaningful it is to include these students.

—Physical Educator, Marcia Troutfetter, South Middle School, Salina, Kansas

believe that all students can learn given enough time, then the situation will be less stressful for both you and the student. In addition, you can visit other schools and classes where inclusion is working. Don't hesitate to join the Individualized Education Program (I.E.P.) team so that you can give input as to what level of placement you think the student is ready for.

The second step is to gain an understanding of the characteristics of the disabilities your special needs students have. By understanding the nature of each disability, you will have a better understanding of the instructional styles and strategies that will work best with each student and of any appropriate modifications. Base modifications on the lifelong needs of each student with disabilities, always ensuring that the modifications do not embarrass the stu-

dent. These modifications can include adaptations to equipment, rules, and instructional strategies as well as additional prompts and cues. Block (1994) suggests that you ask yourself four questions regarding any modification:

- Does the change allow the student with disabilities to participate successfully yet still be challenged?

- Does the modification make the setting unsafe for the student with a disability as well as for students without disabilities?

- Does the change affect students without disabilities?

- Does the change cause an undue burden on the regular physical education teacher?

While most students with disabilities should have a chance to try regular physical education classes, it's possible that regular physical education may not be appropriate for all students. If a student is not receiving any benefit from regular physical education, is disruptive to other students, or poses a severe threat to the safety of the other students, then the I.E.P. team, with input from you, should consider an alternative placement (Block 1994). One alternative short of segregating the student completely is to allow the student limited time in regular physical education with support from an adapted physical educator or another individual.

Skill Level

In all areas of the curriculum, educators are debating the concepts of tracking (assigning students to classes based on ability) and ability grouping within a class. So it's not surprising that these concepts are also an issue in physical education. As a physical educator, you may very well come from a background of athletics where you were the most highly skilled, in which you participated and competed against others who were also highly skilled, perhaps predisposing you to a philosophy that leans toward homogeneous groupings. Little evidence, however, supports this philosophy or the claim that tracking or grouping by ability produces greater overall achievement than heterogeneous grouping (Berliner and Casanova 1993; Gamoran 1992; Kuykendall 1992; Slavin 1990). In fact, the research shows that tracking and ability grouping are detrimental practices to low ability students.

Another related issue, which I described in the opening scenario for this chapter, is the practice of having captains stand in front of the class to pick teams. Even though the end result is heterogeneous teams, the emotional impact on the last student picked and the amount of instructional time spent on the process does not justify its existence in the educational world. I am often asked about various alternatives to picking teams, such as having captains pick teams in private or having captains pick two or three players while the rest of the students get to choose their teams themselves. I believe these are, in fact, variations on the same theme, and even if they shelter the dignity of the last student, we can never be sure that a captain will not share with a student that he or she was picked last. My second concern is the amount of time invested in these activities when we already have such limited time for instruction. Instead, save time and feelings and choose from a variety of appropriate methods for assigning groups, including randomly assigning students to teams prior to class, lining students up by birth month or favorite ice cream flavor, or assigning students to teams so that each team consists of high-, medium-, and low-skilled students.

At-Risk Students

At-risk students are the fastest growing special need student. These students are more likely to experiment with drugs and participate in gangs and

Risk Factors

Peer Factors

Early antisocial behavior

Alienation and rebelliousness

Antisocial behavior in late childhood and early adolescence

Favorable attitudes toward drug use

Early first use [of drugs]

Greater influence by and reliance on peers rather than on parents

Friends who use tobacco, alcohol, or other drugs or sanction their use

School Factors

Lack of a clear school policy regarding the use of tobacco, alcohol, or other drugs

Availability of tobacco, alcohol, or other drugs

School transitions

Academic failure

Lack of involvement in school activities

Little commitment to school

Community Factors

Economic and social deprivation

Low neighborhood attachment and high community disorganization

Community norms and laws favorable to the use of tobacco, alcohol, or other drugs

Availability of tobacco, alcohol, or other drugs

Family Factors

Family management problems (lack of clear expectations of children's behavior, lack of monitoring, inconsistent or excessively severe discipline, lack of caring)

Use of tobacco, alcohol, and other drugs by parents or parents' positive attitudes toward use

Low expectations of children's success

Family history of alcoholism

less likely to put effort into their school work. Research has identified several factors which predispose students to becoming at-risk. The greater the number of these risk factors present within a student's life, the greater likelihood that the student will be at-risk.

Protective Factors

Effectiveness in Work, Play, and Relationships
They establish healthy friendships.
They are goal-oriented.

Healthy Expectancies and Positive Outlooks
They believe that effort and initiative will pay off.
They are oriented to success rather than to failure.

Self-Esteem and Internal Locus of Control
They feel competent, have a sense of personal power, and believe that they can control events in their environment rather than being passive victims.

Self-Discipline
They have the ability to delay gratification and control impulsive drives.
They maintain an orientation to the future.

Problem-Solving and Critical Thinking Skills
They have the ability to think abstractly, reflectively, and flexibly.
They are able to define alternative solutions to problems.

Humor
They can laugh at themselves and situations.

Reprinted, by permission, from *Not schools alone: Guidelines for schools and communities,* copyright 1991, California Department of Education, 515 L Street #250, Sacramento, CA 95814.

More important than the risk factors are the protective factors. If present, these factors help students develop individual resiliency and strength, making them less likely to participate in at-risk activities. The more protective factors present in a student the less likely that student will be at-risk. You can help

your students develop resiliency by creating opportunities for all students to be successful, by helping students set realistic and manageable goals, by helping them problem solve in difficult situations, by creating a trusting atmosphere in which to learn, by reducing stress, and by helping students develop positive self-esteem. Interestingly, these are many of the same strategies that the major middle school reform documents have identified as being important for *all* middle school students.

Developing Social Skills

Naturally, the teaching of prosocial skills is an effective strategy for helping students deal with inclusion issues. Students who demonstrate prosocial skills are better able to communicate and work with a variety of peers. The establishment of a psychologically safe environment, including the modeling of prosocial skills by you is the first step to introducing students to prosocial skills.

Prosocial Skills

Compliments	Helpful
Compromises	Kind
Courteous	Listens
Disagrees positively	Shares
Encourages	

Often, students do not know the prosocial skills that we expect them to demonstrate. Therefore, you must teach them to students much like you teach motor skills. When teaching motor skills, you probably recognize that each student goes through stages: describes the skill, forms a mental image of the skill, practices the skill, executes the skill correctly, and applies the skill in a variety of settings. The same process is true for the development of social skills:

- Self-conscious—student feels awkward because the skill is new.

- Phony—student applies the skill because they are being monitored.

T-Chart for Encouragement	
Looks like	**Sounds like**
Smiles	Good job!
Thumbs-up	Way to go!
Light tap on the shoulder	Good try!
Nods	Clapping

- Habitual—student internalizes skill for use in certain situations.
- Natural—student exhibits skill appropriately in a wide variety of situations.

In the past, we have simply put students into situations and told them to play fair. We now recognize that this is not enough. For students to develop prosocial skills so that eventually they use them naturally, you can (1) introduce the social skill, (2) ask students to identify what it looks like and sounds like (T-Chart), (3) instruct students to demonstrate the social skill as they are practicing the motor skill in a drill or activity, and (4) provide feedback to the students as they attempt to use the social skill.

Once students have begun to develop their prosocial skills, they are ready to learn how to negotiate and resolve conflicts instead of getting into fights or ignoring issues. Johnson and Johnson (1991) have identified a two-step negotiation process for students. In the first step, each student describes what she wants out of the negotiation and then together the students involved specifically define their conflict. In the second step, each student presents her reasons for what she wants and then they clarify their differences before exploring possible solutions that are in the mutual interest of both parties. Once a solution is agreed upon, both parties must agree to stick to it. After the solution is implemented, you can ask the students, "Is the solution working?" If not, students can reexamine possible solutions.

Possible solutions to the conflict, especially minor conflicts, can be that the parties take turns or share the resources, compromise, or resolve the conflict by chance. Chance may involve flipping a coin or playing "Rock, Scissors, Paper." In "Rock, Scissors, Paper," students pound a fist into the palm of the other hand two times and then form a rock (fist), scissors (extended index and middle fingers), or paper (hand flat). The winner is based on the following order: rock beats scissors, scissors beats paper, and paper beats rock.

Positive Class Management

Waiting in lines, feeling afraid of being made fun of, and suffering from being put down by others often lead to severe disruptions. Few disruptions occur, however, when you create a learning environment that makes students feel psychologically safe, that provides intellectual and physical challenges, that includes interesting and relevant activities, that fosters prosocial skills, that employs a variety of instructional strategies, and that allows students to contribute to the class. Yet often when we think about effective class managers, the image of the military-style instructor who demands the attention of the students comes to mind. You, as a physical educator, however, should be a teacher who commands the attention of the students through high expectations and firmness combined with attitudes and actions that demonstrate concern for the students as individuals.

Because of large class sizes and the early adolescent predisposition to challenging authority, however, a few precautions in the form of routines, rules, and a plan for handling discipline problems can ensure an effective learning environment. Research supports actively teaching students routines, rules, and consequences during the first several days of the school year. Although this may seem to waste instructional time, in fact, it saves class time in the long run by reducing the likelihood of disruptive behavior. So invest early and reap the dividends throughout the school year.

Routines

Establish class routines to effectively organize your classes. Most teachers have routines that they use, and students eventually learn them. More effective teachers, however, take the time at the beginning of the year to teach their routines.

Another effective technique for class order is the use of routine or leadership groups. To use this strategy, assign every student in the class to a group. Each group is then responsible for handling one of the classroom routines. Sample assignments include

- exercise leaders who lead their groups in warm-up exercises,

Suggestions for Effective Routines

Starting Class

Students sit down on their numbers as the teacher approaches the class, so the teacher can readily see which students are absent.

Students write in their journals in response to a prompt (e.g., describe a social skill that you demonstrated during the last 24 hours) while the teacher takes attendance.

Students write a summary of the previous day's activities in their journals as the teacher takes attendance.

Students read directions (task analysis of a skill or rules for an activity) on a chalkboard or task card while the teacher takes attendance.

Students begin exercising, while the teacher goes from group to group checking attendance.

Warm-Up Exercises

Students get into small groups; each group forms a circle around their exercise leader, who takes them through their warm-up exercises.

Students rotate through exercise stations set up around the physical education area.

Getting and Putting Away Equipment

Ask one student from each group to hand out and collect equipment.

Equipment monitors hand out and collect equipment for all the groups.

Gaining Student Attention

Slap a tambourine once to indicate to students that you have additional directions. The students stop what they are doing, put down their equipment, and listen.

Blow a whistle once to indicate to students that you have additional directions. The students stop what they are doing, put down their equipment, and listen.

Ending Class

Students sit down on their numbers for the closure of the lesson.

Students sit down in their practice groups for the closure of the lesson.

- junior teachers who learn a skill from the teacher and then teach it to their groups,

- greeters who are responsible for welcoming and answering questions posed by visitors,

- equipment managers who are responsible for distributing and collecting equipment,

- conflict resolution managers who assist with disputes,

- homework checkers who monitor homework completion, and

- assistants to substitute teachers who welcome substitutes and help them learn the class rules and routines.

Rotate membership in these groups frequently so that students have the opportunity to learn a variety of necessary organizational tasks.

Establishing Rules

In addition to class routines, state a few specific rules in a positive way. In order to be effective, however, make sure your rules are fair and enforceable. Some teachers have had great success with

guiding their students in creating their own rules. Other departments have created rules for the entire physical education department, so that consistency between the physical educators exists.

Classroom Rules

1. Arrive on time.
2. Dress appropriately for participation.
3. Listen when the teacher or another student is talking.
4. Respect yourself and others.
5. Treat equipment and facilities with care.

Regardless of who creates the rules, they must be communicated to both the students and their parents. First, remember that the rules should be the focus of each lesson for the first several days of the school year. Post the rules where students can see them and send copies home so that parents also become familiar with them. Teach the rules and their reasons. Next, check to make sure students understand the rules. Then enforce the rules, having students practice rules throughout the instructional period, reminding and reinforcing as needed.

Reinforcing the rules is important throughout the year, but especially during the first several weeks of school, since rules that are not mentioned are quickly forgotten. I believe that one of the main reasons that many physical educators, as well as other teachers, have more discipline problems in their afternoon classes is that they are too tired to follow up on minor rule infractions. If you really want your students to obey the rules, you must *consistently* identify *all* rule violations. When pointing out misbehavior, however, it is important to preserve students' dignity and to show the students that they are responsible for their own actions. In addition, you must follow through, so that the student ends up following the rule.

Remember Your Students' Dignity!

Sara and Jose are whispering while the teacher Ms. Smith is giving directions for the next activity.

Ms. Smith: *"Sara and Jose, what are you doing?"*

Jose: *"Why are you picking on us?"*

Ms. Smith: *"I would like to know if there has been a violation of one of our rules."*

Sara: *"Rule number three: 'Listen when the teacher or another student is talking.'"*

Ms. Smith: *"Jose, why do we have this rule?"*

Jose: *"So that we know what to do in the next activity."*

Sara: *"Also, so that other people can hear you and know what to do in the next activity."*

Dealing With Disruptions

Although planning and establishing rules and routines will reduce the number of discipline problems in the class, nothing can be done to completely eliminate all disruptions. There will always be one or two students in your classes who want to constantly challenge the system no matter what. The question has always been, "How should the teacher handle these situations?"

In the past, many thought that punishing misbehavior and rule violations was the answer. Punishment refers to any action that embarrasses, threat-

---

Remember to Follow Through!

Mr. Garcia: *"John, where is your physical education uniform?"*

John: *"I forgot it at home."*

Mr. Garcia: *"What are you supposed to do when you forget your uniform?"*

John: *"Borrow from the office."*

Mr. Garcia: *"So, why didn't you borrow today?"*

John: *"Because I was late getting to the locker room."*

Mr. Garcia: *"What can you do tomorrow so you are not late?"*

John: *"Not stop by my locker on the way to physical education."*

Mr. Garcia: *"Okay, for now go get dressed so that you can participate in class today."*

---

ens, physically hurts (including using exercise as punishment), or otherwise reduces self-esteem. Punishment, however, does not work. If it did work, then teachers who use it would not continue to experience disruptive events in their classes.

What is often less obvious to many teachers is that rewards can also be detrimental to students. Lepper and Green (1978) have shown that using rewards and praise to motivate learning increases the student's dependency on others for learning, instead of helping him find the learning inherently satisfying. As Kohn (1993) describes, "No behavioral manipulation ever helped a child develop a commitment to becoming a caring and responsible person" (p. 161).

So what can you do when a student is disruptive or violates a rule? The first step is to double-check and make sure that you are implementing the suggestions for teaching prosocial skills, providing a psychologically safe environment, using effective instructional strategies, and establishing rules and routines. Second, be prepared for disruptions so you are not caught off guard. Third, constantly monitor student behavior. And finally, deal directly with the student who is being disruptive.

When monitoring student activity during the class period, position yourself where you can constantly watch and be aware of the activities of all students, even when working with an individual or small group. This is sometimes referred to as "back to the wall," since you must position yourself around the perimeter of the activity area instead of in the center of the class in order to see *all* students. In addition, if you constantly move around the instructional area in unpredictable patterns, you can spot and stop inappropriate behavior more quickly. Many times, simply calling out the student's name respectfully or moving closer to the student who is misbehaving will put an end to the misbehavior.

When the student does not immediately stop the misbehavior, walk quietly over to the student to either remind the student of the rule and the reasons for it (e.g., "What is the rule about respecting equipment? Does hanging on the volleyball net violate this rule? What damage occurs when someone hangs on the net?"). This encourages the student to examine her own behavior and the consequences of her behavior. If the misbehavior continues, provide a time-out for the student and ask the student to think about how she can change her behavior (e.g., "What will help you to remember not to hang on the volleyball net? How can you better spend your time?"). This provides students with an opportunity to find possible solutions for themselves. Initially, time-outs should last no more than five to ten minutes, then give the student the opportunity to share how she is going to change her behavior. If the misbehavior continues after the time-out, then a phone call home to the parents to solicit their involvement is in order. It is important for you to remember to keep your sense of humor and not to let your ego become involved in a confrontation with the student.

The student who constantly challenges your authority is probably challenging authority in all her classes. In this situation, look for underlying reasons. Check to see if the student is having a problem in learning the material, with other students in the class, or in her family. It may become necessary in these cases to temporarily remove such a student from the class while you investigate and work on the underlying problems. The need to remove more than one or two students on a continuous basis, however, should cause you to reflect on what is occurring in the class and to concentrate more on preventing problems.

Summary

A psychologically safe environment sets the stage for learning. When all students—regardless of their group affiliation—have the opportunity for success, they are more willing to risk trying new skills and the potential for learning increases. When you provide instruction on social skills and related social issues, you not only eliminate many behavior problems, you also prepare your students to live in a multicultural society. Social skills instruction along with routines, rules, and consequences consistently enforced reduces the amount of class time you spend on student misbehavior and creates an environment in which learning is the focus.

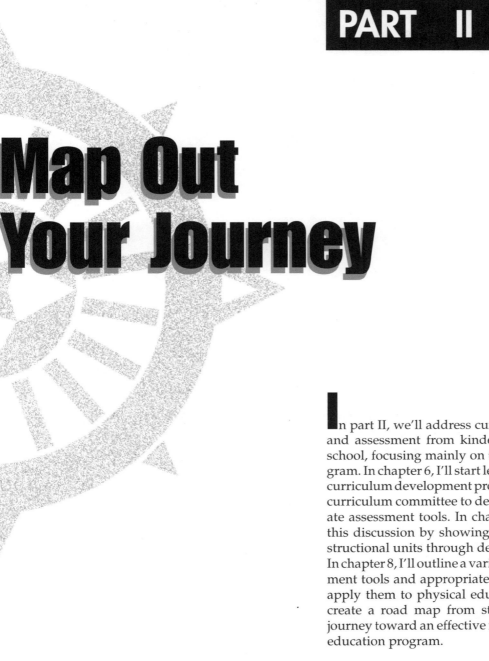

PART II

Map Out Your Journey

In part II, we'll address curriculum development and assessment from kindergarten through high school, focusing mainly on the middle school program. In chapter 6, I'll start leading you through the curriculum development process from selecting the curriculum committee to developing the appropriate assessment tools. In chapter 7, we'll complete this discussion by showing you how to select instructional units through developing lesson plans. In chapter 8, I'll outline a variety of authentic assessment tools and appropriate grading practices and apply them to physical education. In effect, we'll create a road map from start to finish for your journey toward an effective middle school physical education program.

CHAPTER 6

Benefiting From Quality Physical Education

"Will you please tell me which way I ought to go from here?"

"That depends a great deal on where you want to get to," said the Cat.

"I don't care much where," said Alice.

"Then it doesn't much matter which way you go," said the Cat.

—Lewis Carroll, Alice in Wonderland, 1865

As you begin your journey toward quality middle school physical education, you must first create a map of where you want to go. The map is your curriculum; it identifies what you will teach. As you create your map, you must take into consideration the future in which your students will live and the needs that they will have as they become adults in the 21st century.

Historically, many have criticized most physical education curricula for problems such as a lack of sequential progressions; for including too many objectives and too much or too little content; for redundant instruction, units that were too long or too short, and activities unrelated to the objectives; and for placing too much emphasis on teacher preference. To provide effective instruction, you must establish a curriculum foundation that can stand up to these criticisms. You must provide middle school students with activities that progressively increase their competence, improve their feelings about themselves, and that have relevance to their lives. Challenging? Yes, but a well-planned curriculum is well worth the effort.

The development of a curriculum is typically prompted by one of several events: a new state framework, a curriculum reform movement, or a group of teachers who are interested in improving their program. Regardless of the catalyst, the development of a district or county physical education curriculum instead of an individual school curriculum is in the best interest of your students. A curriculum that encompasses several elementary, middle, and high schools allows for articulation (sharing of information) and a variety of opinions while still allowing local control. If your district or county is not interested but your school wants to create a new curriculum, then you should still follow the curriculum development process I'll outline here.

Curriculum Development Process

Select a committee.

Prepare a committee.

Define a physically educated person.

Review NASPE's definition of a physically educated person.

Develop exit standards.

Develop grade level standards and determine grade level content (task analyses).

Select instructional units.

Develop unit standards.

Integrate with other subject areas.

Determine the yearly plan.

Develop unit plans and lesson plans.

To develop a curriculum ask yourself these questions: "What do students need to know? To feel? To be able to do?" Beginning at the end forces you to take a broader look at the entire educational process. Then, after choosing your goals, work backward to develop a program that focuses on what students need and what is relevant and meaningful, prioritizing components in order to make the most of the short time set aside for physical education. In so doing, your program will produce physically educated individuals rather than physically trained individuals. Individuals who understand movement and move efficiently, instead of individuals who leave school fit, but have no understanding of how to maintain their fitness. Let's take a look now at the first six steps in the curriculum development process.

Select a Committee

The central office either appoints the committee or asks for volunteers. Either way, the committee should be comprised of elementary teachers (elementary physical education teachers if they are available), middle school physical education teachers, high school physical education teachers, adapted physical education teachers, site and central office administrators, parents, community members, and students. Why do you need elementary and high school teachers if you're developing a middle school

curriculum? Ideally, the committee is responsible for developing a kindergarten through 12th grade curriculum; however, even if you are only developing a middle school curriculum, still include representatives from the elementary schools and high schools so that during the initial steps of the curriculum development process, you can develop a kindergarten through 12th grade perspective. Then shift your focus to the specifics of the middle school curriculum in the later stages of the process, creating a curriculum that both builds on what your students learned in elementary school and prepares them for high school.

The administration usually selects members for the curriculum committee in one of two ways. The first is to select only those individuals who are knowledgeable about educational reform and who agree with the direction that the leadership wishes to take in the development of the physical education curriculum. This choice eliminates most of the potential for dissension as the committee moves forward with its work. The second option seeks out individuals with a variety of opinions. This will create a very diverse group and the possibility of many heated debates during the developmental process. This second option, however, is more likely to produce results that the district or individual school will implement. Thus, I recommend this second option. To further facilitate the implementation of a new curriculum, I recommend that, whenever feasible, the committee includes a representative from each school. The representative makes a report to the school staff after each committee meeting and solicits any concerns or questions so that everyone is both well-informed and heard from during the developmental process.

Prepare a Committee

Now that you have selected your committee, spend some time on preparing and educating them for the task at-hand. The amount of time you devote to this step will reap dividends in the steps to follow. The committee needs to understand the curriculum development process, current educational reform issues related to curriculum development, the central office's holistic goals, and the current body of physical education knowledge (research). Depending on the general knowledge level of your committee, you may complete this step relatively quickly or you may have to educate committee members throughout the entire curriculum development process.

Current Educational Reform Issues

To assist you with preparing the committee, a variety of materials are available on educational reform, technology, and the future of education, such as those I covered in chapters 1 and 2. In addition, the Association for Supervision and Curriculum Development (see appendix D for address) has many excellent resources on these topics.

One key concept that committee members will definitely need to understand is what a "thinking-meaning centered curriculum" is. This concept encompasses many of the educational reform concepts related to curriculum development. A thinking-meaning centered curriculum gives students interactive learning experiences in which they can construct their own meanings by considering and processing ideas and concepts. The components of a thinking-meaning centered curriculum include (1) allowing students to form their own meaning out of the information presented, instead of telling them what they should think, (2) asking students to make their own connections between the information presented and their current and future out-of-school endeavors, (3) having students apply the new information to meaningful projects, (4) helping students connect the new information to what they already know, and (5) encouraging students to take responsibility for their own learning.

Applying this concept to physical education results in a standard that you might write as, "Applies movement concepts and principles to the learning and development of motor skills," instead of, "Identifies the critical features in 10 movement patterns." Stated the first way, the objective expects students to take the information learned from movement concepts and principles and create their *own* learning plans. The ability to create learning plans has significance both now and in the future. For example, suppose, at 40, a former student wants to take up golf. Given what the student has learned as a result of this standard, the student (now an adult) should be able to create a practice plan for learning golf, or at least, be able to select a competent golf instructor and know whether the information that the golf instructor is conveying is accurate. Stated the second way, the objective simply expects students to reiterate the key elements of a throw, kick, catch, or the like—not to use that information to make meaning out of it for themselves.

Holistic Goals

If your state, district, or county has a description of an educated person stated in holistic terms, the committee will need to see this document so that the physical education curriculum can support it. For example, as a result of the Kentucky Education Reform Act (KERA) of 1990, the state of Kentucky established six goals for learning, which the writers stated holistically, based on an open-ended survey of citizens, businesses, and industry. These goals represent what they believe to be most important for an educated person to know and be able to do when exiting high school. KERA states that upon exiting high school, a student should be able to do each of the following:

1. Use basic communication and math skills
2. Understand core concepts and principles: math, science, social studies, practical living, arts and humanities, and vocational education
3. Become a self-sufficient individual
4. Become a responsible group member
5. Use thinking and problem solving skills
6. Integrate knowledge

The second goal addresses the content standards for health, physical education, and home economics. However, you can relate many of the national physical education standards (NASPE 1995b) to the other goals. Certainly, the more links you can make between physical education and such holistic goals, the more established the position of physical education in the overall kindergarten through 12th grade educational program will be.

Physical Education Content

The committee must have a solid base of understanding about physical education. I have listed textbooks in the bibliography that will help broaden committee members' understanding of the various subdisciplines of physical education. In addition, NASPE has plans to release a new book in 1997 that essentially updates the *Basic Stuff Series I* and *II* from the American Alliance for Health, Physical Education, Recreation and Dance (Dodds 1987), with the new national standards for physical education (NASPE 1995b). By reading this book, committee members will bring themselves up-to-date on important physical education information.

Although it is tempting to do so at this point, refrain from providing any official definition of a physically educated person or any exit content standards for physical education to the committee. It is important for the committee to first determine what they value and believe about a physically educated person themselves before you give them another group's work.

Define a Physically Educated Person

Once the committee begins to understand the curriculum development process, understands the educational reform issues related to curriculum, has read the holistic goals for your educational system, and has completed some readings and discussions on the current content of physical education, it's time to begin writing. The committee must first define for themselves what it believes a physically educated person should look like. In other words, the committee should ask, "What should students on graduation day from high school know, feel, and be able to do as a result of their physical education experience?"

> ## A Definition of a Physically Educated Person
>
> Students graduating from high school are individuals who can plan their own lifelong fitness and wellness programs, develop their own learning plans for acquiring new motor skills, and analyze their own movement performances by applying biomechanical principles. These individuals can also explain the purpose of physical education and give an historical perspective; they understand and appreciate skillful movement from both a personal and social perspective. As adults, they will be able to apply their understanding of developmentally appropriate activities for the children within their care.

The committee needs sufficient time to brainstorm their definition, since they will base all other decisions on it. Interestingly, the more than 100 groups I have worked with have developed results very similar to each other and to the national standards.

Review NASPE's Definition of a Physically Educated Person

After the committee members have had a chance to share and reflect on their definition, they should study NASPE's definition of a physically educated person, using it to stimulate further thought as they work to refine and complete their definition. The formatting, either lists or paragraphs, should match the formatting used by the central office for other curricular areas. Keep in mind that it's the strength of the committee members' belief in their definition that counts the most—not the format.

Develop Exit Standards

The next step involves taking the definition of a physically educated person and turning this statement into a list of exit, or high school graduation, content standards. These standards should be broad-based, challenging, demonstrable, and relevant. Indeed, the standards must be set at a "world-class" level so that your students will be successful in the global society of the 21st century, a time when knowledge will be doubling very quickly. Therefore, the standards need to focus on securing and applying new information and on learning a few central concepts instead of memorizing facts,

> ## Content Standards for Physical Education
>
> ### A physically educated student:
>
> 1. Demonstrates competency in many and proficiency in a few movement forms.
> 2. Applies movement concepts and principles to the learning and development of motor skills.
> 3. Exhibits a physically active lifestyle.
> 4. Achieves and maintains a health-enhancing level of physical fitness.
> 5. Demonstrates responsible personal and social behavior in physical activity settings.
> 6. Demonstrates understanding and respect for differences among people in physical activity settings.
> 7. Understands that physical activity provides opportunities for enjoyment, challenge, self-expression, and social interaction.
>
> Reprinted from *National Physical Education Standards: A Guide to Content and Assessment* with permission of the National Association for Sport and Physical Education, 1900 Association Drive, Reston, VA 22091.

Definition of a Physically Educated Person

A physically educated person:

HAS Learned Skills Necessary to Perform a Variety of Physical Activities

1. moves using concepts of body awareness, space awareness, effort, and relationships.

2. demonstrates competence in a variety of manipulative, locomotor, and nonlocomotor skills.

3. demonstrates competence in combinations of manipulative, locomotor, and nonlocomotor skills performed individually and with others.

4. demonstrates competence in many different forms of physical activity.

5. demonstrates proficiency in a few forms of physical activity.

6. has learned how to learn new skills.

IS Physically Fit

7. assesses, achieves, and maintains physical fitness.

8. designs safe personal fitness programs in accordance with principles of training and conditioning.

DOES Participate Regularly in Physical Activity

9. participates in health-enhancing physical activity at least three times a week.

10. selects and regularly participates in lifetime physical activities.

KNOWS the Implications of and the Benefits from Involvement in Physical Activities

11. identifies the benefits, costs, and obligations associated with regular participation in physical activity.

12. recognizes the risk and safety factors associated with regular participation in physical activity.

13. applies concepts and principles to the development of motor skills.

14. understands that wellness involves more than being physically fit.

15. knows the rules, strategies, and appropriate behaviors for selected physical activities.

16. recognizes that participation in physical activity can lead to multicultural and international understanding.

17. understands that physical activity provides the opportunity for enjoyment, self-expression, and communication.

VALUES Physical Activity and its Contributions to a Healthful Life-style

18. appreciates the relationships with others that result from participation in physical activity.

19. respects the role that regular physical activity plays in the pursuit of lifelong health and well-being.

20. cherishes the feelings that result from regular participation in physical activity.

Reprinted from *Definition of the physically educated person: Outcomes of quality physical education* with permission of National Association for Sport and Physical Education, 1900 Association Drive, Reston, VA 22091.

such as the rules of games, that may soon be outdated.

It is just as important for your committee to establish their own exit standards based on their definition of a physically educated person as it is for them to establish that definition. After the committee has had an opportunity to brainstorm their ideas, however, they should study the seven content standards identified by NASPE. These standards can stimulate further thought as the committee works to refine and complete their list of exit content standards. Take a moment now and compare the national standards with the concepts discussed in chapter 1; you'll see that they align well with the Department of Labor's Secretary's Commission on Achieving Necessary Skills (SCANS) 1991 report and many of the other future trends discussed in chapter 1, such as lifelong learning. So for the purpose of discussion, I'll use the national standards as the exit standards.

After reviewing the NASPE standards, your committee's exit content standards should reflect or align with NASPE's *Moving Into the Future National Physical Education Standards* (1995b) document as well. Yet, if the goal is for your committee to develop standards similar to NASPE, then why not simply adopt the national standards? It is valuable for your committee to recognize that, in fact, their beliefs are similar to those expressed in the national standards. The process of going through each of the steps in the curriculum development process will increase the possibility of the curriculum being implemented, rather than left on shelves collecting dust. For this reason, as often as possible, the committee should share their work with as many other teachers in the district or county as possible. In fact, the greater the number of teachers that go through these last three steps (defining a physically educated person, reviewing NASPE's definition of a physically educated person, and developing the exit standards), the greater the possibility of implementation. This is where having teacher representatives from every school in the district on the committee comes in handy. If it's not possible to have noncommittee members go through the process, then at least solicit their reactions along the way.

Develop Grade Level Standards

Once the committee identifies and agrees on exit standards, the next step—developing grade level standards and determining grade level content (task analyses)—falls easily into place. Simply put, for each exit standard, the committee must determine how much of it can be learned at each grade level where physical education is taught. The grade level standards must be performance-based, developmentally appropriate, relevant to the students' lives, and directly related to corresponding exit standards.

Let's look at an example of the development of kindergarten through 12th grade level standards for national standard five, "Demonstrates responsible personal and social behavior in physical activity settings." The progression develops from simple to complex issues: working alone, sharing space, working with a partner, working in a small group, working cooperatively with a group, solving problems, and leadership and personal responsibility. Each grade level standard builds upon the previous grade level standard and all of the grade level standards align with the exit standard. Moreover, this progression is developmentally appropriate because it parallels the social development of the student. For example, at the middle school level, this progression takes into consideration the students' capacity for abstract thought.

I consulted the *Moving Into the Future National Physical Education Standards: A Guide to Content and*

Standards Related to National Standard Five

5.0

12th – Initiates independent and responsible personal behavior in physical activity settings.

11th – Accepts the responsibility for taking a leadership role and willingly follows as appropriate in order to accomplish group goals in physical activity settings.

10th – Keeps the importance of winning and losing in perspective relative to other established goals of participation.

9th – Demonstrates the use of conflict resolution in physical activity settings.

8th – Collaboratively solves problems by analyzing causes and potential solutions in physical activity settings.

7th – Applies problem solving techniques in physical activity settings.

6th – Works cooperatively and productively in a group to accomplish goals in physical activity settings.

5th – Works cooperatively and productively with a small group in physical activity settings.

4th – Respects the rights of others and their property in physical activity settings.

3rd – Supports and encourages a partner, both male and female, in physical activity settings.

2nd – Works cooperatively with another to complete an assigned task in physical activity settings.

1st – Shares space and equipment with others in physical activity settings.

Kindergarten – Plays alone in personal space without interfering with others.

Adapted from Region 9's *Physical Education Curriculum*, 1994 and NASPE's *National Physical Education Standards: A Guide to Content and Assessment*, 1995.

Assessment and *Basic Stuff Series I* to develop my sample. Your committee's progression may be different for the fifth standard; simply make sure that it is logical, meets the criteria for grade level standards, and works for your situation.

The strategy I recommend you follow to complete this task is to start with the exit standard and work

Standards Related to National Standard One

1.0

6th – Applies the correct technique for locomotor, nonlocomotor, and manipulative skills in a variety of cooperative activities.

7th – Applies the correct technique for locomotor, nonlocomotor, and manipulative skills to appropriate risk-taking activities.

8th – Applies the correct technique for locomotor, nonlocomotor, and manipulative skills to sport-specific skills in a variety of team-related activities.

Adapted from Region 9's Physical Education Curriculum, 1994 *and NASPE's* National Physical Education Standards: A Guide to Content and Assessment, 1995.

Standards Related to National Standard Three

3.0

6th – Participates daily in some form of physical activity based on personal interests and capabilities.

7th – Participates daily in some form of physical activity, including new and appropriate risk-taking activities.

8th – Sets personal goals for participating in physical activities, then participates and monitors progress.

Adapted from Region 9's Physical Education Curriculum, 1994 *and NASPE's* National Physical Education Standards: A Guide to Content and Assessment, 1995.

---

backward, answering the following questions in succession: What does this look like in 12th grade? 11th grade? 10th grade? . . . Kindergarten?

Remember for each exit standard, your committee must also write kindergarten through 5th and 9th through 12th grade level standards; however, I am only including the standards directly related to the middle school program. Notice that exit standards 2 and 6 include three (2.1, 2.2, and 2.3) and two (6.1 and 6.2) standards at each grade level, respectively, because, in my opinion, these exit standards embody more than one major concept. Included in exit standard 2 are the concepts of motor learning (learning how to learn); scientific or biomechanical principles; and game strategy. Included in exit standard 6 are the concepts of motor development and

---

Standards Related to National Standard Two

2.1

6th – Applies appropriate feedback to a partner while developing or improving movement skills.

7th – Sets goals and monitors change in the development of movement skills in order to improve performance.

8th – Applies the principle of transfer of learning in order to facilitate the learning of a new skill.

2.2

6th – Analyzes movement performance using Newton's Third Law in order to learn or improve a movement skill.

7th – Analyzes movement performance using rotational principles in order to learn or improve a movement skill.

8th – Analyzes movement performance using spin and rebound principles in order to learn or improve a movement skill.

2.3

6th – Creates a cooperative game by combining a variety of locomotor, nonlocomotor, and manipulative skills.

7th – Creates an individual or dual game with scoring options.

8th – Creates a team game with scoring options.

Adapted from Region 9's Physical Education Curriculum, 1994 *and NASPE's* National Physical Education Standards: A Guide to Content and Assessment, 1995.

Standards Related to National Standard Four

6th – Assesses personal fitness, compares scores to health-related standards, sets goals for improvement or maintenance, and develops a one-day personal fitness plan.

7th – Assesses personal fitness, compares scores to health-related standards, sets goals for improvement or maintenance, and designs a one-week personal fitness plan.

8th – Assesses personal fitness, compares scores to health-related standards, sets goals for improvement or maintenance, refines one-week personal fitness plan, and implements the plan.

Adapted from Region 9's *Physical Education Curriculum*, 1994 and NASPE's *National Physical Education Standards: A Guide to Content and Assessment*, 1995.

Standards Related to National Standard Seven

6th – Analyzes patterns in physical activities to determine the influence that the qualities of movement have on the aesthetic impact of these activities.

7th – Appreciates the aesthetic features or stylistic differences of one's own approach to movement activities.

8th – Appreciates the aesthetic features or stylistic differences of someone else's approach to movement activities.

Adapted from Region 9's *Physical Education Curriculum*, 1994 and NASPE's *National Physical Education Standards: A Guide to Content and Assessment*, 1995.

historical perspectives. Every committee must decide how to divide the standards for their curriculum. Your group may decide to have only one grade level standard for each exit standard.

The grade level standards presented here are based on the premise that the elementary feeder school or schools are focusing their physical education pro-grams on kindergarten through fifth grade level standards, which cover basic locomotor skills, nonlocomotor skills, basic manipulation, qualities of movement, learning speed and accuracy in movement, appropriate practice of skills, aesthetic features of movement, origin of activities in the local community, enjoyment and participation in movement, physical changes occurring in the child, and scientific principles of movement. If this is not occurring at your feeder schools, then this is one reason why your grade level standards may need to

Standards Related to National Standard Six

6th – Analyzes the variables of physical development within his peer group and the effect on movement performance, as he works cooperatively with both more- and less-skilled peers.

7th – Explains the growth rates of her body segments and the relationship to movement-related experiences.

8th – Analyzes how growth in height and weight alters the mechanical nature of performance and how it affects the selection of developmentally appropriate activities.

6th – Describes the development and role of movement-related activities and physical education in the ancient world and their influences on physical activities today.

7th – Describes the development and role of movement-related activities and physical education during Medieval times and their influences on physical activities today.

8th – Describes the development and role of movement-related activities and physical education in the United States during the 19th and 20th centuries and their influences on physical activities today.

Adapted from Region 9's *Physical Education Curriculum*, 1994 and NASPE's *National Physical Education Standards: A Guide to Content and Assessment*, 1995.

Sequencing of Scientific Principles Related to National Standard Two

10th – Application of levers

9th – Principles of resistance

8th – Spin and rebound principles

7th – Rotational principles

6th – Newton's Third Law (equal and opposite reaction)

5th – Newton's Second Law (force is a result of mass times acceleration)

4th – Projection principles

3rd – Newton's First Law (object at rest remains at rest until acted upon by an outside force)

2nd – Speed, velocity, and acceleration

1st – Dynamic stability

Kindergarten – Static stability

be different from the ones I am presenting. For example, the K-12 grade level standards (2.2) related to exit standard 2.2, are based on the sequencing of scientific principles of movement from simple to complex and aligned with the type of physical activity taught at each grade level. If elementary teachers are not teaching the simpler scientific concepts (standard 2.2) at the elementary school, then you, a middle school physical educator, must adjust the sixth, seventh, and eighth grade level standards for exit standard 2.2 accordingly. In addition, the committee may instead choose to cover the biomechanical principles in a different sequence altogether or choose to cover all of them each year in increasing complexity.

Consider, also, other variables that may warrant the creation of different grade level standards, including the types of local recreation, the amount of instructional time set aside for physical education, and the content taught in other subject areas. For example, for exit standard 6.2, I have chosen to have students learn about movement-related activities in the ancient world in sixth grade, Medieval times in seventh, and United States (19th and 20th century) in the eighth, paralleling the content that students in my area are studying in their history and social science classes; however, your history and social science classes may be different, and I recommend you adjust your standards accordingly. Furthermore, the sample standards for 6.2 also line up with

the motor skills identified in standard 1 for sixth, seventh, and eighth grade. For example, many of the team sports we play in the United States either became popular or were invented during the late 1800s. Thus, we have a match: United States history (19th and 20th century) and team sports in the eighth grade. (I'll discuss aligning with other subject areas in more detail in chapter 7.) Certainly, it is possible to show meaningful connections between physical education and other subject areas while still maintaining the integrity of your physical education curriculum, thereby integrating physical education across the curriculum and, in so doing, make the entire school curriculum more relevant and interesting.

Once the committee finishes writing the grade level standards, they must review each one to ensure that it is performance-based (can be assessed), developmentally appropriate, important, and relates to the exit standard. They must also double-check the sequencing of grade level standards for each exit standard to ensure that it is logical and works for your situation. In addition, it is important for the curriculum committee to begin to address assessment at this point in the process (see chapter 8 for more on assessment). At this point, the committee must ask the key question, "Can teachers assess the grade level standard?" For example, standard four for seventh grade states, "Students design a one-week personal fitness plan." Can this be assessed? Yes, each student can create a calendar, videotape, or an essay outlining the fitness plan so that the teacher can assess each student's understanding. The committee must rewrite any standard that is not performance-based, important, and related to the exit standard.

For each approved grade level standard, the committee needs to determine what information (content or task analysis) is necessary for the student to demonstrate learning in a real life situation. For example, grade level standard 2.1 for sixth grade states, "Applies appropriate feedback to a partner while developing or improving movement skills." In order for students to accomplish this standard, they must understand information outlined on page 70. Appendix B gives sample content for all the grade level standards I've discussed in this chapter. Yes, this step is very tedious, but it helps make it possible for everyone to implement the new curriculum by adding clarity to the grade level standard and by providing information necessary to developing student assessment (see chapter 8).

Now that you have the grade level standards and their related content identified (the sequence), sort the standards so that everyone can look at them by

Sixth Grade: Standard 2.1

Applies Appropriate Feedback to a Partner While Developing or Improving Movement Skills

Feedback improves the learning of motor skills by providing error detection and motivation for the learner.

Feedback is based on the critical elements for each skill.

Only one or two corrections should be identified for feedback after each performance.

Feedback is delayed for a few seconds after the performance to give the performer an opportunity to reflect on his or her own performance.

Feedback is given when the performer cannot see the result of the performance (e.g., technique).

Feedback is not given when the performer can see the result of the performance (e.g., accuracy, speed, or distance).

Feedback is most helpful when it is specific and meaningful.

Feedback should be given frequently in the early stages of learning and then tapered off.

---

grade level (the scope). The committee must now consider the reality of physical education time constraints. For example, I created the sample grade level standards identified in this chapter for daily physical education classes, 30 to 40 minutes long. Ask, "Is there sufficient time in our program to accomplish the listed standards?" By implementing the reform concept of "less is more" (better to focus on a few important standards) in defining the exit standards, by working backward when developing curriculum, and by being aware of your time constraints throughout the curriculum development process, the answer to this question should be, "Yes." If by chance, however, the answer is, "No," then the committee must determine their priorities and either eliminate those standards (exit and grade level) of lower priority or rewrite the exit or grade level standards, narrowing their focus.

The work done during this step is definitely committee work and does not require the participation of all teachers in the district. It is important, however, for all teachers to give input to the committee before the committee members make final decisions about the grade level standards and content. Therefore, near the end of this step—as throughout the development process—the committee should share their work with as many teachers as possible.

Summary

In this chapter, we have begun to map out our curriculum journey from kindergarten through high school with special emphasis on the middle school program. This process took us from selecting and educating the physical education curriculum development committee, defining a physically educated person, and translating the definition into exit (graduation) standards to creating grade level standards in alignment with the exit standards. In the next chapter, we'll continue our journey by adding checkpoints along the way to our destination. We'll select instructional units, look at integrating with other subject areas, and outline the yearly plan. As we have throughout this process, we'll focus on the major concepts or "big ideas" that will prepare students for the skills they will need as adults in the 21st century.

CHAPTER 7

Planning a Course of Study

I am really proud of the work we've been doing in tying physical education to other subjects. We always begin with our physical education curriculum outcomes, but we have the other subject area teachers tell us about their program, so that we can try to support them as well. We have found that physical education is a natural medium for interdisciplinary learning and the kids often have that "aha!" look in their eyes.

—Physical Educator Cindy Kuhrasch, Barneveld Schools, Barneveld, Wisconsin

Once the curriculum development committee completes the exit and grade level standards, you have a map that shows the route to be followed during each year of middle school. This prepares you to look for interdisciplinary links with other subject areas. In this chapter, we'll examine the remaining steps of the curriculum process. We'll look at selecting instructional units, developing unit standards, integrating with other subject areas, determining the yearly plan, and developing unit and lesson plans.

Select Instructional Units

Unfortunately, when committee members begin to determine the units of instruction for each grade level, they often completely forget about the exit and grade level standards. Everyone must remember that the purpose of the units is to deliver the standards. For example, in language arts, the purpose of language arts is not to read *Moby Dick*, but rather to develop competent readers and writers. *Moby Dick* is simply one book that assists in the development of competent readers and writers. Likewise, in physical education, our purpose is not to teach basketball, but rather to develop competent and knowledgeable movers. We use basketball as a vehicle with which to reach certain standards.

Beyond selecting units that teach the content that will help students reach the standards, provide the students with a variety of movement experiences. Just as language arts teachers don't have students read *Moby Dick* every year, you don't need to teach basketball every year. Indeed, some students will be successful in some activities and some in others. By providing a wide variety of activities, including a balance between the different types of activities (dance; combatives; individual, dual, and team sports; cooperative games; aquatics; tumbling; and adventure), you provide opportunities for all students to experience success while still stretching their skills in weaker areas. Moreover, when selecting instructional units, take into consideration which instructional units the feeder elementary schools have covered. As with developing grade level standards, build on what students already know. Then include a variety of activities to create more interest and greater chances for success.

> At Sacramento Country Day School, we strive to provide our middle school students with a wide variety of activities and units. We hope that this will allow each student the opportunity to find their niche and areas of interest, so that success is experienced and lifetime participation is encouraged . . . . Activities from different countries and cultures are encouraged as well as new American cultural activities, such as country line dancing.
>
> —Bill Stainbrook, Sacramento Country Day School, Sacramento, California

Finally, when selecting instructional units, ask yourself, "What type of units (sometimes referred to as organizing centers) do I want to offer?" You can organize your instructional units with many different approaches, including skills theme, process,

Skills Theme Approach Examples

Physical fitness	Throwing and catching
Body management	Striking with body parts
Locomotor skills	Striking with objects

Process Approach Examples

Making choices	Developing strategies
Problem solving	Decision making
Conflict resolution	

Social Approach Examples

Adventure and risk	Socialization through sports
Cultural preservation	New games
Games in the city	

Activity Approach Examples

Volleyball	Square dancing
Golf	Soccer
Track and field	Swimming

Fundamentals of Movement Approach Examples

Buoyancy	Spin
Force	Stability
Laws of motion	Velocity

Standards Approach Examples

Movement skills

Movement concepts

Daily physical activity

Fitness development

Personal and social behavior in physical activity

Respect for others in a physical activity setting

Enjoyment, challenge, and self-expression

social, activity, fundamentals of movement, or standards (which includes one instructional unit on each grade level standard) approaches.

You might think that the standards approach is the way to go since it emphasizes the standards, making it easy for you to see if you are meeting them. You can, however, deliver the standards through one of the other approaches. In figure 7.1a, each unit of instruction addresses one standard, so that during the sixth grade personal and social responsibility unit, you use a variety of social initiatives and new games as the physical activities addressing sixth grade standard five, "Works cooperatively and productively in a group to accomplish goals in physical activity settings." In figure 7.1b, each unit of instruction is an activity through which you address each of the standards—at least to some extent. For example, during volleyball, teach the skills and the movement concepts and cover fitness development, individual differences, social skills, and so on. As illustrated by figure 7.1c, the skill theme approach uses thematic instructional units to address each of the standards (to some extent) in each skill area. For example, during the striking with objects unit, you address all seven (or more) standards through skills and activities that involve striking with a racquet, bat, and club. You can also select units combining approaches.

When selecting the type of instructional units and then the specific instructional units, I have found it helpful to first identify grade level themes, tying the grade level standards together under ﹍ umbrella. Several other sources have als﹍ do this as well. For example, in the Kend﹍ Publishing Series *Essentials of Physical E﹍* (Spindt 1992a, b, c), the 6th grade book is ﹍ ﹍﹍ *Moving With Confidence*, the 7th grade book is entitled *Moving With Skill*, and the 8th grade book is entitled *Moving as a Team*. The *Physical Education Framework for California Public Schools* (California Department of Education 1994b) identifies grade level themes for kindergarten through 12th grade. The theme for 6th grade is "Working Cooperatively to Achieve a Common Goal," the 7th grade theme is "Meeting Challenges and Making Decisions," and the 8th grade theme is "Working as a Team to Solve Problems."

For my sample curriculum, I have selected "Learning Skills Through Cooperation" as the sixth grade theme, "Taking Acceptable Risks Through Problem Solving" as the seventh grade theme, and "Working as a Team to Develop Strategies for Success" as the eighth grade theme. Or you may wish to choose

a. Standards delivered through the standards approach

	Standard 1	Standard 2	Standard 3	Standard 4	Standard 5	Standard 6	Standard 7
Movement skills (Standard 1)	X						
Movement concepts (Standard 2)		X					
Daily physical activity (Standard 3)			X				
Fitness development (Standard 4)				X			
Personal and social behavior in physical activity (Standard 5)					X		
Respect for others in a physical activity setting (Standard 6)						X	
Enjoyment, challenge, and self-expression (Standard 7)							X

b. Standards delivered through the activity approach

	Standard 1	Standard 2	Standard 3	Standard 4	Standard 5	Standard 6	Standard 7
Volleyball							→
Golf							→
Track and field							→
Square dancing							→
Soccer							→
Swimming							→

c. Standards delivered through the skill theme approach

	Standard 1	Standard 2	Standard 3	Standard 4	Standard 5	Standard 6	Standard 7
Physical fitness							→
Body management							→
Locomotor skills							→
Throwing and catching							→
Striking with body parts							→
Striking with objects							→

Figure 7.1 Standards delivered through various approaches.

three different grade level themes, even if you are using the same exit and grade level standards that I selected. As long as you select grade level themes thoughtfully and logically, aligning them with the grade level standards, thereby setting the stage for the selection of the specific instructional units, then you have many options for the specific grade level themes. First, however, I'll explain my rationale for the grade level themes that I selected.

My sixth grade theme, "Learning Skills Through Cooperation," emphasizes sixth grade standard 1, which includes basic skill practice, such as the refinement of basic locomotor, nonlocomotor, and manipulative skills, and the many sixth grade standards that require cooperation. For example, notice that even standards 2.1 and 2.2 focus on cooperation as the students learn to provide appropriate feedback to a partner. Likewise, students must cooperate to apply Newton's Third Law as they explore the concept of for every action there must be an equal and opposite reaction. Most importantly, however, an emphasis on social interaction early in the middle school experience can make both the physical education *and* school climate a positive experience for all throughout the middle school years.

"Taking Acceptable Risks Through Problem Solving" suits seventh graders especially well because they like to experiment with new challenges and, unless the school curriculum provides challenging activities in a safe environment, they are likely to take unacceptable risks on their own. This theme teaches students the difference between appropriate and inappropriate risk-taking activities. Furthermore, this theme encompasses the seventh grade standards that emphasize problem solving through setting and monitoring goals, analyzing rotation, creating new games with various options, participating in challenging activities, and looking for relationships between growth rates and success in movement experiences. Concerned about interdisciplinary aspects? The risk-taking theme works well with seventh grade's history and social science emphasis on Medieval times and the adventurous activities that predominated in that era.

My eighth grade theme, "Working as a Team to Develop Strategies for Success," helps students combine their motor skills into more complex patterns and strategies as they use the skills in team situations. By the eighth grade, students have the capacity for the abstract thought that effective offensive and defensive strategies require—especially necessary in team sports. During this stage of mental development, students are able to consider various aspects of a situation simultaneously. For example,

an offensive player in speed-a-way who is approaching the goal line must assess the situation in order to determine whether to run across the goal line or drop the ball and go for the higher score. By delaying introducing students to the content of team sports until this point, they are less likely to experience the frustration felt by younger students who are not capable of mentally dealing with the number of variables involved with team activities. The link to the grade level standards is found in the transfer of learning, since there are many similarities in skills and strategies between different team sports, the emphasis on collaborative problem solving, the creation of new team games, and the growth of team sports during the 19th and 20th centuries—the period that the students are studying in their United States history and social science classes.

Sixth Grade Units of Instruction (Skills Theme Approach)

Learning Skills Through Cooperation

I. Introduction and Fitness Pretesting (three weeks)

II. Cooperative Activities (three weeks)

III. Body Management (three weeks)

IV. Locomotor Skills (six weeks)

V. Underhand and Sidearm Throwing and Catching (three weeks)

VI. Overhand Throwing and Catching (three weeks)

VII. Striking With Body Parts (three weeks)

VIII. Striking With Objects (three weeks)

IX. Circus Skills (three weeks)

X. Creating New Games (three weeks)

XI. Closing and Fitness Posttesting (three weeks)

Each year includes an introductory unit that focuses on learning class rules and routines including exercises and includes participating in the fitness pretest while encouraging students to get to know one another. A "Closing" unit concludes each grade and includes fitness posttesting and the completion of class projects to assess student understanding of the grade level standards.

I selected a skills theme approach for sixth grade because my grade level theme focuses on learning skills and because my feeder elementary schools don't have an exceptionally strong program. The

Seventh Grade Units of Instruction (Activity Approach)

Taking Acceptable Risks Through Problem Solving

I. Introductory Unit and Fitness Pretesting (three weeks)

II. Tumbling and Gymnastics (five weeks)

III. Outdoor Education (Orienteering) (four weeks)

IV. Racket Sports (four weeks)

V. Aquatics (four weeks)

VI. Golf (four weeks)

VII. Self-Defense (five weeks)

VIII. Medieval Times Activities (four weeks)

IX. Closing and Fitness Posttesting (three weeks)

Eighth Grade Units of Instruction (Activity Approach)

Working as a Team to Develop Strategies for Success

I. Introductory Unit and Fitness Pretesting (three weeks)

II. Project Adventure (four weeks)

III. Invasion Team Sports (eleven weeks)

IV. Team Net Sports (five weeks)

V. Team Field Sports (five weeks)

VI. Square Dancing (five weeks)

VII. Closing and Fitness Posttesting (three weeks)

first instructional unit after the introductory unit targets social skills acquisition to get sixth graders off to a good start on personal interactions skills. Then for the next six units, students work on six different skills theme approaches. Unit 9 reviews all the skill units and challenges the students to increase proficiency in an especially fun way, as they work on circus skills. Unit 10 gives students practice in selecting and applying a number of skills refined during earlier units as they create new cooperative games in small groups.

I have applied an activity approach for unit selection in the seventh grade because many of the traditional activities that involve risk taking are new to *my* students. Instructional units such as racquet sports, golf, self-defense, outdoor education, tumbling and gymnastics, swimming, and Medieval games provide my students with the challenges that they need while simultaneously preparing them for a variety of lifetime activities from which to choose. In addition, swimming, outdoor education, and self-defense involve life skills that every individual must possess. Individual and dual sports also help students learn to set goals and monitor their own progress, while activities such as tumbling and gymnastics and self-defense help students learn to apply the biomechanical principles of rotation. Even the Medieval times activities unit brings together all of the seventh grade standards, as you'll see as I begin to develop unit standards. Yet, we could categorize the Medieval times activities unit as a standards approach instructional unit, because it specifically addresses standard 6.2. From this perspective, my selection of seventh grade instructional units mixes approaches.

Because the eighth grade level theme focuses on team strategies, I have selected an activity approach with an emphasis on team sport units, along with a unit on Project Adventure, which involves problem solving activities for teams and square dancing which requires a group approach to dancing. Through these instructional units, students learn team strategies and how to apply basic skills to sport-specific skills in a variety of everyday team sports and activities that they can enjoy throughout their lives. More importantly, these activities highlight the same major movement concepts, encouraging students to transfer learning from one activity to another. Team sports, Project Adventure activities, and square dancing, all teach spin and rebound principles, the effect of height and weight on the mechanical nature of performance, and the appreciation of aesthetic features in someone else's performance. Thus, the activity approach in eighth grade creates a program that meets all the grade level standards.

Remember, however, that even if you choose the same exit standards, grade level standards, and grade level themes that I have selected, you must base your specific instructional units on your own situation. Take into account the type of elementary school program feeding your program, local interests, local geography and climate (e.g., snow, water, and so on), whether you are on a traditional or year-round calendar, whether your school is in a rural or urban area, and your philosophy regarding the type of instructional units better-suited for middle school. Perhaps, philosophically, you choose the skills theme approach for every grade level. Teachers in Florida base most of the instructional units in middle school on skills theme units such as throwing and catching, striking with objects, and striking with body parts. This helps students develop competence in motor skills while applying them to a wide variety of movement forms. Or, let's say you choose the same themes and types of units I did for my sample curriculum, but, depending on your geographic location, you select rollerblading, sailing, downhill skiing, or water skiing as a seventh grade unit. Depending on community interests, you select an eighth grade unit on cricket, lacrosse, or ice hockey. If you choose to include grade level themes, as your standards committee work proceeds, you will probably find yourself jumping back and forth between selecting units of instruction, finalizing your grade level themes, and refining your grade level standards.

No matter what grade level themes (if you use them), what types of instructional units, or what specific units you select, you must ask, "Can we deliver the grade level standards through the units we select?" For example, if class A learns the standards through the skills theme approach and class B in the same grade learns the standards through the activity approach, then that is what is important. Interestingly, some schools are conducting "action research" projects to see what really works best with students. Wouldn't it be interesting to teach the sixth grade class this year with the skills theme approach and the sixth grade class next year with the activity approach, then compare the results?

As you finalize your selection of instructional units, you will also need to determine the optimal length of time required to complete a unit. First consider how often and how long your physical education classes meet. My instructional units assume 30- to 40-minute classes. Yet no definitive answer to the question, "What is the ideal length of an instructional unit?" exists. Ensure, however, that the unit is long enough so that most of the students can accomplish the unit standards (see the next section). As a rule of thumb, most instructional units at the middle school level will last from three to six weeks, allowing enough time to develop new skills. The average length of the units will become progressively longer from grade to grade as the students' attention spans and depth of understanding increase.

Depth or Breadth?

A colleague of mine went to visit a local school district. The first day he visited the middle school. The teachers showed him their program, which consisted of new activities every week. When my colleague asked why they changed units so frequently, the teachers responded that they wanted to "expose" the students to a wide variety of activities. The next day, he visited the high school. Again, the teachers showed him their program, which, in the high school's case, consisted of new activities every other week. When he asked why they changed units so frequently, the teachers responded that they wanted to "expose" the students to a wide variety of activities. After his second visit, he called me to ask if anyone in this school district actually "taught anything" or did they all spend all of their time "exposing" students to the curriculum.

Develop Unit Standards

Once the committee has determined the units of instruction, they must determine how to address each of the grade level standards within each unit. The strategy for determining unit standards from grade level standards is similar to the strategy used to determine the grade level standards from the exit standards. Obviously, if the committee has selected the type of units based on the standards approach, then each unit addresses one grade level standard. For example, if I include a fitness unit, which could occur in either the standards approach or mixed approach, then I could deal exclusively with standard four during that unit.

But because most middle schools do not use the standards approach for their unit selection, let's discuss how to determine how much of each grade level standard you can teach in each unit. By the end of the school year, the majority of your students should be able to demonstrate all the standards. But don't be concerned that some units focus primarily on one or two grade level standards; you can cover the other standards in other units. During this process, it may become obvious that certain units of instruction need to come before others. Make a note of this, so that when you get to the interdisciplinary and yearly plan steps you can refer to it.

As when we examined the exit standards, certain patterns emerge as we begin to determine which part of a grade level standard belongs in each unit.

Sample Unit Standards for Seventh Grade Related to Grade Level Standard Four

Assesses personal fitness, compares scores to a health-related standard, sets goals for improvement or maintenance, and designs a one-week personal health-related fitness plan (warm-up, flexibility, muscle strength, muscle endurance, body composition, cardiorespiratory endurance, and cooldown).

Introduction and Fitness Pretesting

Assesses personal fitness, compares scores to health standards, and sets personal goals.

Tumbling and Gymnastics

Participates in a variety of exercises for all five areas of health-related fitness and describes the frequency, intensity, time, and type concepts related to flexibility development.

Outdoor Education

Participates in a variety of exercises for all five areas of health-related fitness and describes the frequency, intensity, time, and type concepts related to warm-up and cooldown.

Racket Sports

Calculates caloric input and output for an entire week and performs exercises for all five areas of health-related fitness.

Aquatics

Participates in a variety of exercises for all five areas of health-related fitness and describes the frequency, intensity, time, and type concepts related to cardiorespiratory development.

Golf

Participates in a variety of exercises for all five areas of health-related fitness and describes the frequency, intensity, time, and type concepts related to muscular endurance development.

Self-Defense

Participates in a variety of exercises in all five areas of health-related fitness and describes the frequency, intensity, time, and type concepts related to muscular strength.

Medieval Times Activities

Performs exercises for all five areas of health-related fitness and designs a one-week fitness plan.

Closing and Fitness Posttesting

Reassesses personal fitness and compares scores to pretest scores, health standards, and personal goals, and finalizes one-week fitness plan.

See the "Sample Unit Standards for Seventh Grade Related to Grade Level Standard Four." In this example, each unit addresses a different part (flexibility, muscular endurance, muscular strength, cardiorespiratory endurance, and body composition) of health-related fitness. In so doing, I have taken into consideration the parts of health-related fitness that are most improved through each of the activities. For example, swimming requires cardiorespiratory endurance; tumbling and gymnastics require flexibility; and self-defense requires strength. Just as easily, I could have addressed all five parts of fitness in each instructional unit, beginning with simple ideas and progressing to more advanced ideas through the year. Either way works.

As you can see, many options exist for each stage of curriculum development. Choose those that work best for your situation.

For seventh grade for grade level standard five, students could build social skills from the simple to the complex by first learning each other's names, then describing the problem solving strategy, using it in mock situations with a partner, in real situations with a partner, in mock situations with a small group, and in real situations with a small group, then by applying it to life-threatening activities in which self-defense may help, and, finally, by analyzing how people in other times did or did not use problem solving techniques. In this situation, the order of the units is important, because each unit builds on previously covered problem solving skills. In contrast, for standard number four, the order was not as important. We will take this issue into consideration when we develop our yearly plan. Check the content (see appendix B) or task analysis of each standard, for a breakdown of the grade level

Sample Unit Standards for Seventh Grade Related to Grade Level Standard Five

Displays problem solving techniques in physical activity settings.

Introduction and Fitness Pretesting

Knows other students' names.

Tumbling and Gymnastics

Describes problem solving techniques.

Outdoor Education

Uses problem solving techniques with a partner when solving outdoor education challenges.

Racket Sports

Applies problem solving techniques with a partner for situations that arise during racket activities.

Aquatics

Uses problem solving techniques with a small group when solving swimming challenges.

Golf

Applies problem solving techniques with a small group during situations that arise during golf.

Self-Defense

Applies problem solving techniques to real-life self-defense scenarios.

Medieval Times Activities

Discusses the use of problem solving techniques during Medieval times.

Closing and Fitness Posttesting

Applies problem solving techniques in physical activity settings.

Seventh Grade Self-Defense Unit Standards

1.0 – Applies the correct technique for locomotor and nonlocomotor skills in self-defense.

2.1 – Sets goals and monitors change in self-defense skills.

2.2 – Describes how the scientific principle of rotation applies to self-defense skills in order to learn skills or improve performance.

2.3 – Creates a combative-type game.

3.0 – Participates in appropriate self-defense activities outside of physical education.

4.0 – Participates in a variety of exercises in all five areas of health-related fitness and describes the frequency, intensity, time, and type concepts related to muscular strength.

5.0 – Applies problem solving techniques to real-life self-defense scenarios.

6.1 – Explains the growth rates of body segments and their relationship to activities in self-defense.

6.2 – Describes combat activities from Medieval times and the Renaissance period.

7.0 – Appreciates the stylistic differences of own approach to self-defense.

standards, which you can then assign to appropriate units of instruction.

Once you complete the process of establishing unit standards for each grade level standard and each unit, you can reorganize the information to see what needs to be accomplished in each unit. You will find all the specific unit standards in chapters 14, 15, and 16 as well as sample unit plans. The committee should not finalize the units of instruction until they have completed the unit standards and can therefore verify the validity of the selection of the instructional units against the unit standards. Now is also the time for the committee to make sure that they have allocated sufficient time to each unit, enabling the majority of students to attain the unit standards.

Integrate With Other Subject Areas

Now that your committee has identified the units of instruction based on unit standards, it's time to ask, "How can we integrate physical education with other disciplines?" Before finalizing the sequence of units in the yearly plan, you and your physical education colleagues should meet with teachers from other subject areas to identify interdisciplinary possibilities. Caine and Caine (1991) have identified several reasons why interdisciplinary teaching is important:

- The brain searches for common patterns and connections.

- Every experience actually contains within it the seeds of many, and possibly all, subject areas, and one of the keys to understanding is what is technically known as *redundancy*, or revisiting information through different experiences.

Ultimately, interdisciplinary teaching adds more meaning to learning while, at the same time, approaching learning from a real-life perspective. When your students go out into the world as adults, they don't apply their science knowledge for an hour, then apply their language arts skills for an hour, and then their understanding of human movement for an hour. Rather, real world situations integrate disciplines. Interdisciplinary instruction is the wave of the future, and we must join in. Yet, let's not engage in interdisciplinary activities for the sake of engaging in interdisciplinary activities. To avoid this pitfall, keep focused on your physical education exit, grade level, and unit standards while looking for meaningful links to other subject areas.

Let's examine four models (sequenced, shared, integrated, and webbed) for connecting subject areas. (*Note*: Consider interdisciplinary connections using any one of the first three models at this point in the process; however, when using the fourth model, the webbed model, the interdisciplinary step should occur just before selecting instructional units.)

Sequenced Model

The sequenced model (figure 7.2) encourages teachers from various disciplines to rearrange the order of topics so that similar units coincide with each other, synchronizing the content of two related subject areas. In this way, the content and activities in each class enhance the learning in both. This model is an easy way to initiate an interdisciplinary approach because it requires little articulation between teachers.

Let's examine some examples of how to apply the sequenced model to physical education. You could coordinate your teaching of body composition with the health educator's teaching of nutrition. Of course, the connections between health and physical education are easy to see, but what about connections between physical education and other subject areas? Try timing a Medieval times activities unit to occur when the history teacher is covering Medieval times. By learning two units simultaneously, students will begin to see relationships between concepts, helping them make more sense out of the content of both classes. Keep it simple when

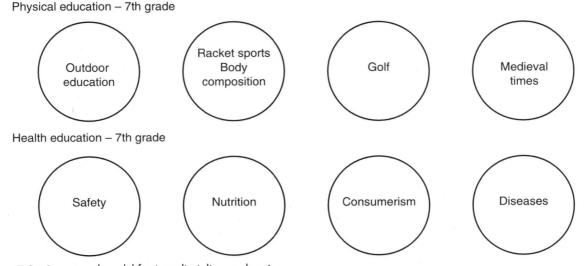

Figure 7.2   Sequenced model for interdisciplinary planning.

planning, though; you don't necessarily have to go into the details of how each of you will approach the unit using this model—simply offer the units at the same time.

Shared Model

The shared model (figure 7.3) encourages two teachers to look for overlaps in subject matter content. This approach is most appropriate when subject content is clustered into broad themes, such as humanities or practical arts. Each subject area in the shared model relates its curriculum to the common theme. For example, physical educators provide instruction on dance while music educators provide instruction on theater music to create a thematic unit on the performing arts. In another example, physical educators provide instruction on health-related fitness and health educators provide instruction on personal health to create a unit on wellness. The two teachers involved in this model

plan their instruction together, so that their lessons complement each another. Although the shared model takes more effort to plan than the sequenced model, the benefits are greater as students see more connections between the content taught in the two classes. This approach is an appropriate intermediary step between the sequenced model and the integrated model.

Integrated Model

The integrated model (figure 7.4) involves interdisciplinary sharing among four or more subject areas. To follow this model, each subject area must first set its own priorities. Then, all participating teachers look for the skills, attitudes, and concepts that overlap between those subject areas. One example of this model is a thematic unit on "Life Under Water."

In this unit, the physical education instruction focuses on swimming and skin diving, the science instruction is on the laws of physics below sea level,

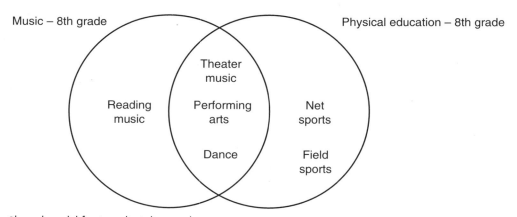

Figure 7.3 Shared model for interdisciplinary planning.

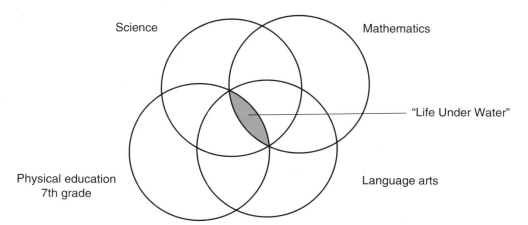

Figure 7.4 Integrated model for interdisciplinary planning.

the mathematics instruction is on performing calculations on the laws of physics below sea level, and the language arts instruction is on the writing process through which students describe what it would be like to live under water. Because this approach is very time consuming and requires the total commitment of all teachers involved, I recommend that you start small with a three- to four-week unit before attempting to develop a semester- or year-long plan. As you continue to work together and learn more about each other's subject areas, you can then plan longer instructional units.

Webbed Model

The webbed model is a thematic approach that integrates subject content from several disciplines, beginning with a theme such as "inventions" or "consumer ideas." The theme becomes the overlay for the other subject areas. This approach is also very time consuming; you should start with one unit of instruction before attempting a semester- or year-long plan. Common themes that work well when including physical education include transi-

tions, change, social skills, and taking acceptable risks. Figure 7.5 illustrates a webbed model focusing on taking acceptable risks.

The webbed model differs from the others in that the theme does not necessarily come from within one or more of the other subject areas; instead, the theme is simply a common area of interest for teachers or

Caught in a Web!

To coincide with our "Heart Adventures Challenge Course" (see chapter 12), the music department developed a unit where all music heard, sung, or played related to the heart, with additional emphasis on the beat (relating to the heartbeat). Social studies classes studied countries that have high rates of heart disease. Home economics students studied healthy foods, and math students learned how to calculate heart level percentages in the target zone.

Reprinted from B. Kirkpatrick and M.M. Buck, 1995, "Heart Adventures Challenge Course: A lifestyle education activity," *Journal of Physical Education, Recreation & Dance*, 17.

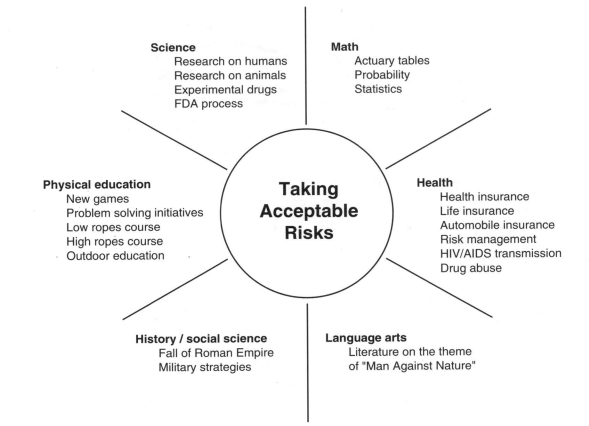

Figure 7.5 Webbed model for interdisciplinary planning.

students. And unlike the other three models, you must design your web before—not after—choosing instructional units. As with the first three models, physical educators must remember to stay devoted to their own grade level standards, joining a web only when participating in it helps students meet the physical education standards.

Determine the Yearly Plan

Next, you must decide the order in which you'll teach the units of instruction you have chosen. Consider the following aspects when determining the yearly plan: sequencing of instructional units, interdisciplinary possibilities, and use of facilities. Make sequencing issues your top priority when designing your yearly plan. Ask, "Why should one unit come before another?" Look back at any notes you made regarding sequencing issues while writing unit standards. For example, in seventh grade, the fifth standard clearly presented sequencing issues, since the unit standards moved from simple to complex. For units for which sequencing can be more flexible, look closer at the interdisciplinary possibilities. By choosing and sequencing your units before looking at interdisciplinary possibilities, you ensure that the goals of physical education receive top priority.

After sequencing your units, you must set up a yearly schedule for sharing facilities and equipment within the physical education department. Unfortunately, this often becomes a limiting factor when planning sequencing and interdisciplinary units. Sometimes, limited facilities and equipment make ideal sequencing of units impossible. For example, if the seventh grade class needs the gymnasium during the second unit for gymnastics and the eighth grade class needs the gymnasium during the second unit for dance, and only one class at a time can use the gymnasium, then either one of the grade levels will have to change the unit sequence or one of the grade levels will need to find an alternative location for the unit of instruction. Some sequences are more easily accommodated than others, such as introductory units, which you can teach in a variety of locations and don't require a specific facility. Be creative and work out facility sharing and rotation, keeping students' needs at the forefront.

One helpful hint is to not lock yourselves into teaching units of instruction during the corresponding sport season. Not only does this approach tie you down to an activity-based approach, it also tends to ignore important educational considerations, such as appropriate sequencing. Although this traditional approach can have some positive benefits, such as students watching the activity on television to better understand the game concept, let them enjoy the flexibility created by videotaping instead. Focus on educational considerations and, if you're able to teach basketball skills during the NCAA finals in March, great, but don't let that restrict your yearly plan to the detriment of students' overall skill acquisition.

In many counties and districts, the development of yearly plans as well as the development of unit plans and lesson plans is left to the individual teacher. Yet, regardless of who develops the yearly, unit, and lesson plans, all three must occur. As the saying goes, "What is not planned for is not taught and what is not taught is not learned."

Develop Unit Plans and Lesson Plans

Congratulations—you've made it this far in the curriculum development process! Now it's time to put all your hard work into developing the actual unit plans. Chapters 14, 15, and 16 contain sample unit plans for each of the suggested units of instruction. Remember, when developing the grade level standards, we worked backward from the exit standard. When developing the unit standards, we worked backward from the grade level standards. Now, as we develop unit plans, we again work backward from the unit standards.

When I provide direct assistance for a physical education department, I always recommend that they work cooperatively to develop unit plans, since unit plans can take a long time to develop well. When creating a unit plan, be sure to list the unit standards on the first page to keep them foremost in your mind as you plan. Next, begin to create a day-by-day unit outline showing the unit standards and concepts you'll address and the skills and activities you'll include. Constantly go back and forth between the skills, activities, concepts, and unit standards to ensure that you are, in fact, addressing each standard so that your students will be able to demonstrate their understanding of it by the end of the unit. Once you have your outline, complete a task analysis for each skill and activity. The task analysis for each skill describes in detail how to execute it and identifies its critical features, or the key points that you will want to communicate to your students. The task analysis for each activity lists the directions and desired outcomes for the activity. In addition, note the type of facility, equipment, media, and other resources you'll need for the unit. Finally, determine how you will assess student learning at the end of the unit (see chapter 8).

Task Analysis: Rolling a Ball

Squares shoulders to direction of roll.

Swings arm in pendulum action on preferred side of body.

Faces palm of rolling hand in direction of roll.

Steps forward on opposite foot.

Bends at knees and waist to roll ball.

Once you complete a unit plan, ask, "Do the concepts, skills, and activities match the unit standards?" Double-check to make sure the unit content lines up with the exit, grade level, and unit standards. But you're not quite ready to teach yet. If curriculum is the map (or the what), then instruction is the vehicle of transportation (or the how); before entering the classroom, you must create lesson plans, the delivery vehicles of the curriculum. We'll discuss lesson planning in part III.

Summary

In chapters 6 and 7, we have discussed an 11-step process for curriculum development in a linear fashion. You, however, will probably find that as you begin to work through these steps that you'll have a tendency to jump back and forth between grade level standards, selecting instructional units, and integrating with other subject areas. Each of these areas has an influence on the other, so avoid a lockstep approach. Yes, the task of curriculum development is arduous; however, the benefits for you and your students are many. Now, with our map laid out, we can see our destination. But before we begin our journey, let's make sure we clearly understand our destination. Thus, in the next chapter, we'll examine student assessment.

CHAPTER 8

Assessing and Grading Your Students

When I began to try self- and partner assessments in class, kids learned more. I believe that it helped to make clearer for them the specifics of what I was asking them to learn, and it touched every area a learner might be more proficient in.

—*Physical Educator Francesca Zavacky, Clark School, Charlottesville, Virginia*

In many physical education programs, we have forgotten the intended purpose of grading and have begun to use it as a means of punishment or reward. Grading of this kind shortchanges the students, whereas a well thought out assessment plan is likely to cultivate higher-order thinking and problem solving capacities in your students. You may put a lot of energy into your teaching, but only assessment can tell you if the students are learning. In this chapter, we'll look at the alternative assessment movement and the role of grading in physical education.

We can readily see that the purpose of curriculum is to determine where we are going, or to create a plan to elicit changes in student behavior (knowledge, skills, and beliefs). The purpose of assessment is to determine whether students have reached the curriculum goals. You must hold yourself accountable by asking and answering the question, "Have I accomplished what I set out to accomplish?" If not, reevaluate your instruction and reteach those concepts. If problems persist, reevaluate your

Tilford Middle School's Accountability System

During the fitness unit students enter personal data (lifestyle information, wellness tests, food intake) into a computer and get a detailed analysis of their current lifestyle and future lifestyle choices. At the end of the week, students complete a personal lifestyle prescription based on their experiences. In keeping with the accountability aspect of educational reform, Tilford Middle School had Ball State University assess the data on over 3000 students. Their analysis revealed that almost all the physical variables examined showed significant improvement between pre- and post-test results.

From B. Kirkpatrick and M.M. Buck, 1995, "Heart Adventures Challenge Course: A lifestyle education activity," *Journal of Physical Education, Recreation & Dance* 66(2): 17-24.

curriculum to determine if the goal in question is developmentally appropriate.

So why discuss assessment now before discussing instruction itself? After all, assessment follows instruction. First, you must identify for students, up front, what you expect from them and how you will assess their learning. Let's say, for example, that you are grading a student on a headstand at the end of your seventh grade tumbling and gymnastics unit. The student performs a tripod (inverted position with knees resting on elbows) and remains balanced for five seconds. What grade would you give this student? I have asked this question often in workshops, and I get answers ranging from a "B" (very good) to an "F" (failing). But if I provide you with my headstand criteria for an "A," "B," "C," "D," and "F," then you can readily see that the grade for the student is a "C." Sharing this information with students at the beginning of a unit motivates them by giving them something to work toward. In addition, when you announce the student's grade, the student will understand why she received that grade, eliminating unnecessary conflict.

Sample Headstand Grade Criteria

A: Performs a headstand and balances on own for at least three seconds.

B: Performs a headstand, but receives support from a partner in order to remain balanced.

C: Performs a tripod and balances on own for at least three seconds.

D: Initiates a tripod, but is unable to balance on own.

F: Fails to initiate a tripod.

Another reason I'm addressing assessment now is that part of the restructuring of assessment, or *alternative* assessment, involves what is called *embedded* assessment. This means assessing students while they are involved in the learning process. You can record students' grades periodically throughout the unit as they are practicing. Perhaps a student is initially unable to perform a headstand, and you record an "F." Then, during the first two weeks of practice, you observe the student in a balanced tripod, and you record a "C." Finally, during the last week of practice, you observe the student extending her legs over her head with her partner assisting, and you record a "B." This type of documentation

provides evidence of student growth over the instructional unit. In addition, the "B" (the end result) becomes the final grade for the headstand, instead of making the student nervous by telling her you're assessing her. We'll discuss later in this chapter a better approach to documenting skill growth by using rubrics instead of grades.

Assessment

Traditionally, physical educators have based assessment and grading on standardized motor skill tests for accuracy and distance; on written tests of rules, history, and strategy; and on physical fitness tests. With the move toward standards-based curriculums, physical educators have begun to use alternative assessment tools, including observations, written tests with an emphasis on open-ended questions, student logs and journals, role playing and simulations, research and reports, and projects.

Authentic assessment goes one step further requiring students to use alternative assessment tools in challenges for which they must apply skills, knowledge, and attitudes to "real world" situations that reflect the ambiguities of life. It is important that the assessment, regardless of type, provides students with relevant and timely feedback focusing on strengths and aspects of their performance that may need improvement. Moreover, authentic assessment tasks are more likely to motivate students because the value of the work goes beyond the demonstration of competence in school and relates to their lives and futures.

The exit, grade level, and unit standards I identify in chapters 6, 7, 14, 15, and 16 set the stage for assessment. Indeed, if your curriculum committee writes the standards so that they are observable, measurable, and require evidence of students' ability to create new knowledge or apply motor skills in new situations, then it'll be relatively easy to construct assessment tools. In fact, the tools should be self-evident. Even if they aren't, at the very least, there must be a match between an assessment tool and each standard. Be accountable—be able to clearly show how students are progressing toward each of the grade level standards.

Alternative Assessment Tools

Let's turn now to specific alternative assessment tools appropriate for physical education. While one or more types of assessment can be effective, you must ensure that your choices match one or more grade level standards. In fact, you may opt to allow students with different primary intelligences (see chapter 9) to select different assessment tools in order to utilize their strengths. The products created by students are then assessed using a rubric and placed in the student's portfolio—but more on rubrics and portfolios later.

Sample Seventh Grade Assessment Ideas for Standard Four

Assesses personal fitness, compares scores to a health-related standard, sets goals for improvement or maintenance, and designs a one-week personal fitness plan. After assessing personal fitness, comparing scores to health-related standards, and setting goals for improving or maintenance, the student:

1. designs a chart showing his one-week fitness plan,
2. writes an essay describing her one-week fitness plan,
3. creates a multimedia project showing his one-week fitness plan,
4. creates a video project showing her one-week fitness plan, and
5. creates a rap describing his one-week fitness plan.

Structured observations. In a subject area such as physical education in which you can see so much of what students learn, structured observations provide a key assessment tool. Teachers, peers, or students themselves can observe and assess performance of motor skills, exercises, and demonstrations of appropriate social interaction skills, including helping a peer learn a new skill. When assessing performance based on an observation, use a checklist, a rubric (see later section), or a simple counting system, such as number of encouragements or number of curl-ups. In some situations it's appropriate to use several assessment tools. For example, students may first assess themselves, then have a peer validate their observations, and only then is the teacher brought in to make a final assessment.

Assessments from observations are sometimes difficult to justify because there is no concrete product for both you and the student to review. Once the observation period is over, no way to replay the performance to verify the observer's assessment exists. Or is there? Videotaping the performance provides a permanent record of the incident. You can save video clips either on videotape or digitized (see electronic portfolios later in this chapter) for use on a computer. Either way, you can document growth over time, saving the information for future review.

Observations work especially well with grade level standards one and five. For example, taking sixth grade standard one, "Applies the correct technique for locomotor, nonlocomotor, and manipulative skills to a variety of cooperative activities," and specifically targeting an overhand throw, a checklist of critical features is used by a peer and/or teacher to assess performance. Looking at the checklist after his performance, the student will see his throwing strengths and weaknesses. In keeping with the embedded assessment concept, many of these assessment tools work well not only as assessment tools but also as instructional activities.

An Observation Checklist for an Overhand Throw

☑ Keeps nonthrowing side and arm toward target.

☑ Places weight on back foot.

☑ Swings throwing arm backward in preparation.

☑ Steps forward with foot on opposite side of body from throwing arm.

☑ Makes forward body rotation occur through lower body, then upper body, then shoulders.

☑ Transfers weight to foot on opposite side of body from throwing arm.

☑ Leads the way with the elbow for the arm movement, followed by forearm extension, ending with a wrist-snap.

☑ Follows through in the direction of the target.

Written tests. In order to assess cognitive understanding, written tests are still appropriate tools. A shift has taken place, however, from emphasizing true and false, multiple choice, matching, and fill-in-the-blanks to essay and open-ended questions. Other subject area educators often refer to this change as "beyond the bubble," meaning going beyond filling in a scantron sheet to using higher-order thinking skills to answer questions. Although true and false, multiple choice, matching, and fill-in-the-blank questions will sometimes still be appropriate, we must shift our emphasis to essay and open-ended questions.

Through answering essay questions, students can demonstrate deeper understanding of the content. For example, instead of answering a series of true and false or multiple choice questions on strategies related to volleyball, ask students to, "Describe the game of volleyball and explain how different offensive and defensive strategies are used to gain an advantage in the game." Or, instead of answering matching or fill-in-the-blank questions on the FITT (frequency, intensity, time, and type) concepts, ask students, "How would you go about improving your flexibility?" Remember when writing essay questions, be very specific both about the information you're requesting and how extensive you expect answers to be.

Sample Open-Ended Questions

1. Name three similarities between soccer and speed-a-way skills. How can these similarities help you learn speed-a-way if you already know how to play soccer?

2. Name one of the movement-related activities in the ancient world. What influence has this activity had on modern-day games and sports?

3. What is one difference between approaching a problem solving situation as an individual and as a member of a group?

4. In tennis, your serve constantly veers to the left. What is one reason why this may be occurring and how can you use that information to help you improve?

Open-ended questions differ from essay questions in that they ask students for their opinions on an issue. Thus, many different, yet valid, answers should result. When creating an open-ended question, be sure to ask the question in such a way that the students are able to approach it from many different angles. For example, asking students why the ball may be veering left in tennis gives them an opportunity to share different reasons why including the effect of spin. In addition, ask questions in such a way that students can be confident that they have provided a complete answer either by specifying the amount of information you're

requesting (e.g., "Name one . . . .") or by including this information in the grading rubric (see later in chapter).

Keep in mind that you're using each assessment item to collect data for one or more grade level (or unit level) standards. Thus, you must ensure that your questions originate from the standards themselves. Don't simply think up open-ended questions to fill a category; to authentically assess student understanding, you must specially design questions to match certain standards.

Sample Log Entry Prompts

Maintain a record of your health-related fitness test scores along with the physical activities you perform out of school over [a designated period of time].

Maintain a record of your improvement for [a given skill] along with your practice schedule.

Maintain a record of your resting heart rate, training heart rate, and recovery heart rate for [a designated period of time].

Participate in a variety of lab situations involving [manipulatives (e.g., release the ball at various angles, release the ball after involving various body segments, or the like)] and record your results.

Sample Journal Entry Prompts

How do you feel when you participate in a physical activity after a stressful event in your life?

Describe a situation where you encouraged another person during a physical activity. How did it make you feel?

Describe a class situation where someone was excluded. Describe how you would feel if you were that person.

Describe examples of your behavior in which you displayed cooperative skills and examples in which you did not display cooperative skills during a physical activity. Describe how each event made you feel.

Student logs and journals. Use student logs and journals to document the accomplishment of standards that relate to a performance of a physical activity and feelings surrounding that experience.

Logs and journals differ from open-ended and essay questions in that students record their feelings or data, instead of answering a single question. Often in situations where logs and journals are kept, students take notebooks or steno pads along with a pencil or pen out to class with them or the teacher stores the notebooks rather than relying on students to keep track of them.

Specifically, students can maintain a log of the various kinds of physical activity that they perform outside the school day. The log can show the frequency, intensity, time, and type of exercise. In some cases, students record and verify their own involvement. In other situations, you may wish to ask parents or guardians to verify student participation. After several weeks of record keeping, students can evaluate their improvement and compare the results to their out-of-school participation in physical activity. This type of data can demonstrate growth over time, specifically as it relates to standards 2.1, 3, and 4.

Students can also maintain a journal where they describe events and their feelings. Journal writing is especially effective after a cooperative learning or social skill activity, aligning well with standard five. Students can describe their abilities to demonstrate certain social skills as well as the feelings participation as an active team member aroused. Through the journal writing process, students can document their own growth over time as well as develop goals for future growth.

Role-playing and simulations. In chapter 12, I'll discuss virtual reality technology in which students experience "semi-realistic" situations controlled by a computer. Once in these situations, students respond as if they were in the real situation. Putting students into virtual reality situations where they must demonstrate skills and apply knowledge is truly an authentic assessment. Short of having the software and hardware for virtual reality, we can ask students to role-play or perform in simulations that we create. For example, some students are confined to a chair and requested to play the role of persons who are mobility-impaired while the other students find ways to include these students into the sport or activity.

Other role-playing assessment activities include asking students to

- resolve simulated conflicts,
- create performances for simulated gymnastic meets,
- practice dances for simulated recitals,
- participate in a simulated on-campus orienteering experience, and

- participate in a stimulated round of golf by using hula hoops for the holes, long jump pits for sand traps, and benches for obstacles.

Authentic assessment asks students to demonstrate their learning in real-life situations; however, this is not always possible, so role-playing and participating in simulations may be the next best option. This type of assessment is especially effective for determining if students are meeting standards one and five.

Reports. A common element of real-life work is the ability to research a topic and write a summary. Student reports have been a feature of education for the last century; however, it is becoming increasingly important for students to be able to search through a variety of resources (e.g., CD-ROMs, books, the Internet) and find the most accurate, up-to-date information on a topic. Another important report resource is the interview. In this case, students interview someone who is considered an expert on a particular issue as a means of research. Because information is doubling yearly, the availability of information is not the issue; the issue is selecting the most appropriate and accurate information.

NASPE (1995b) provides several examples of research topics:

- Critical elements of a motor skill (e.g., overhand throw, instep kick)
- Practice ideas (e.g., amount of feedback, whole or partial skill practice) for improvement of a motor skill
- Physiological responses (e.g., strength improvements, lactic acid production) of the body to exercise
- History of a sport or dance
- Why people exercise

Research is a viable option related to every standard that has a cognitive component. As a physical educator, however, you must be sure that students possess the necessary skills to conduct the research. Student reports provide an ideal arena for interdisciplinary efforts, since the language arts teacher can ensure that students learn to search the Internet, find information on CD-ROMs and in books, and conduct interviews. You, in turn, can provide students with specific resources and guidance to complete their research. Students then produce documents to share with the rest of the class. Including additional subject areas also encourages students to look at a topic from many perspectives.

For example, students can explore the topic "Why People Exercise" from a financial and health insurance perspective (mathematics), a health perspective (science, health, and physical education), and the meeting of social needs perspective (history and social science). Students can produce these reports as individuals or in a cooperative group.

Projects.   Take student reports one step further and assign projects that ask students (working alone or in small groups) to create products from their research other than a written report. These products can take the form of a video, multimedia presentation (using a computer), chart, speech, demonstration, publication, or lesson. One example of a project is a movement pattern video presentation with an introduction to the movement pattern followed by video clips of different sport skills that utilize that pattern. When assigned the task, one group of students chose the overhand throw and, after an introduction to that pattern, videotaped the volleyball overhand serve, the football forward pass, the softball throw, and the team handball pass. Projects motivate students because they can select their own topics for study, use skills associated with their primary intelligences (see chapter 9), and use their creativity.

Both research reports and projects require a great deal of time. Yet, through them, students not only learn information regarding their selected topics in depth, they also learn time and resource management, social skills, technological skills, proper telephone use (for conducting interviews), and how to conduct original research—the process skills that students need to know in the next century.

Ideas for different projects are limited only by your imagination. Simply make sure they relate to specific standards. Notice that project one relates to

standard 4; project two, to standard 2.2; project three, to standard 2.3; project four, to standard 1; and project five, to standard 3. Projects are far-reaching in that you can use them to address most, if not all, standards. Remember, that even though the sample projects specify the media (e.g., video, multimedia, paper), you may prefer to have students select their own media or rotate students through the various media. For example, if you only have one video camera, then for one project, group A has access to it, and in the next project, group B has access to it, and so on.

A new area for projects is community service. Although more common at the high school level, middle school students can benefit from giving something back to the community as well. Keeping in mind the desired outcomes of physical education, students provide one of the following services to demonstrate their learning of one or more of the grade level standards. Students could

- teach a new motor skill to elementary school students,
- visit nursing homes and take the residents through simple stretching exercises,
- help out at a park and recreation center by teaching younger participants new games,
- invite a parent or another adult who does not regularly exercise to participate in an aerobic activity, or
- work as conflict managers on the middle school playground during recess and lunch.

In some middle schools, students must complete an eighth grade project. The school sets the parameters for the projects, then allows students to choose the specific problem they wish to investigate. Typically, students must follow six steps to complete their projects:

1. Identify a problem to investigate (e.g., "Is there a difference between the type of physical activities that girls and boys prefer?").

2. Outline procedures to follow while doing project (e.g., research the topic, interview a local college professor, develop a survey, conduct the survey, and draw conclusions).

3. Conduct the research (e.g., access the Internet, review books, interview experts, and administer the survey).

4. Revisit the expert to discuss conclusions.

5. Prepare the project (the report and presentation).

Sample Projects

1. Develop a week-long health-related personal fitness plan and present it by developing a chart.

2. Conduct a biomechanical analysis of an individual performing a motor skill and present the results through a multimedia presentation.

3. Create a new game and teach it to a small group of peers.

4. Develop a 60-second tumbling routine and demonstrate it to a small group of peers.

5. Design a brochure on the physical activity opportunities in the community.

6. Present the project to an audience of peers, parents, or community members.

Students, working alone or, preferably, in groups, complete their projects, including developing all or most of the following: oral presentations, written documentation, visual aids, audio aids, and multimedia presentations. Many schools require students to present their projects to the entire community or at least to outside evaluators. This last step helps add a more realistic dimension to the project. Unfortunately, all too often these projects omit the physical education angle. If your school has eighth grade projects, make sure that the parameters of the project allow students to investigate issues related to physical education. And of course, projects are not just for eighth graders.

Rubrics

Now that you're using authentic tools and reviewing the products they produce, how do you grade or assess the quality of the products? As educational reform has moved forward in the area of alternative and authentic assessment, rubrics, or scoring guides, have emerged as a consistent and fair method that explicitly states what you expect students to achieve.

Rubric Scoring Guidelines

6: Fully achieves purposes of the task.

5: Accomplishes the purposes of the task.

4: Completes the purposes of the task substantially.

3: Purposes of the task not fully achieved.

2: Omits important purposes of the task.

1: Fails to achieve purposes of the task.

A rubric is similar to a score awarded by a diving or gymnastics judge in that it provides a description of various qualitative levels of performance on a specific task or product. A well-written rubric presents a picture of what the final product looks like. Although you can define any number of qualitative levels, a range of one through six, with six being ideal, is most common. Typically, teachers consider scores of four, five, and six as meeting the minimum standard criteria. Rubrics not only inform teachers, they answer for students, "How good is good enough?"

Steps for Creating a Rubric

1. Identify the grade level standards (see chapter 6).

2. Choose the alternative assessment tool that allows students to demonstrate each standard (see assessment tools in previous sections of this chapter).

3. Make a list of the critical elements involved in each standard.

4. Identify critical attributes of a representative performance for each element of the task.

5. Describe levels of quality starting with a six, then a four, then a three, and then the others—one, two, and five.

Creating rubrics is not easy. Initially, you'll probably feel more comfortable developing rubrics by yourself. But as your confidence and experience grow, you may wish to include students in the process. See pages 92 and 93 for sample rubrics.

Ideally, once you have created the rubric, you should provide samples of student work that illustrate each rubric level. In physical education, this may be products at each level or video clips that illustrate each level if the rubric relates to the demonstration of a skill. By providing examples, you show students and other stakeholders what you expect.

What score should you assign if a student's performance falls between two levels? Most teachers give the lower score. Perhaps in the future, we'll eliminate the actual rating number and this problem by simply providing a descriptive analysis of the product that merely lists those elements of the critical features that the student can demonstrate, thereby giving a more accurate picture of the student's progress.

Portfolios

How do you keep track of student work? How do you assess the total learning of each student? The authentic assessment movement brings us another new concept: the student portfolio. A portfolio is a permanent collection, similar to an artist's portfolio, of a student's best work showing her progress toward the grade level standards. It can contain a wide range of assessment tools.

Sample Rubric for an Overhand Throw

6: Performs the correct technique for an overhand throw in game-like situations.

5: Performs the correct technique for an accurate overhand throw at a variety of distances.

4: Performs the correct technique for the overhand throw:

____ Keeps nonthrowing side and arm toward target.

____ Places weight on back foot.

____ Swings throwing arm backward in preparation.

____ Steps forward with foot on opposite side of body from throwing arm.

____ Makes forward body rotation occur through lower body, then upper body, then shoulders.

____ Transfers weight to foot on opposite side of body from throwing arm.

____ Leads the way with the elbow for the arm movement, followed by forearm extension, ending with a wrist-snap.

____ Follows through in the direction of the target.

3: Moving toward the correct technique for the overhand throw:

____ Flexes elbow by swinging throwing arm upward, sideways, and backward.

____ Rotates trunk and shoulder back.

____ Steps forward with foot on opposite side of body from throwing arm.

____ Rotates body forward very little.

____ Leads way with elbow in the arm movement.

____ Follows through in the direction of the target very little.

2: Performs an incorrect overhand throw when requested to do so by the teacher:

____ Stands facing the target.

____ Generates action mainly from the elbow.

____ Employs little or no rotation.

____ Keeps feet stationary.

1: Attempts an overhand throw:

____ Stands erect, facing the target.

____ Throws with little or no body rotation.

____ Throws with very little arm action.

____ Employs action that resembles a push more than a throw.

Sample Rubric for Encouragement

6: Encourages others at and away from school during physical activities.

5: Encourages teammates and friends during physical activities.

4: Rarely puts down others and usually encourages friends during physical activities.

3: Limited interactions—mixes encouragement and put downs during physical activities.

2: Does not ever encourage others and sometimes puts down others during physical activities.

1: Regularly puts down classmates during physical activities.

To get started, have students create a "working" portfolio, which will temporarily hold everything the student completes. Selecting from their working portfolios, have students develop a "performance" portfolio, your ultimate goal. These portfolios are purposeful collections of work that demonstrate student effort, learning, emerging insights, progress, and achievement in physical education over time. Most teachers who use portfolios suggest including 6 to 10 pieces of work in each student's performance portfolio—some from earlier and some from later in the year. In addition, a portfolio should include a reflective essay in which the student comments on his portfolio.

But what exactly should go into a performance portfolio? Typically, the student does the selecting; however, you may wish to select one particular project that you want included in all student portfolios and then leave the rest of the selecting to the

Rubric for a One-Week Personal Fitness Plan

6: Bases plan on personal assessment of own fitness, includes all five areas of health-related fitness, and correctly applies the FITT (frequency, intensity, time, type) concepts to each area of fitness.

5: Bases plan on personal assessment of own fitness and includes all five areas of health-related fitness, but makes minor errors in the application of the FITT principles to each area of fitness.

4: Does not base plan on personal assessment of own fitness but includes all five areas of health-related fitness with minor errors in the application of the FITT concepts to each area of fitness.

3: Does not base plan on personal assessment of own fitness; plan includes four areas of health-related fitness and applies the FITT concepts to these four areas of fitness with only minor errors.

2: Does not base plan on personal assessment of own fitness; plan includes three areas of health-related fitness, attempts to apply FITT concepts but makes major errors.

1: Does not base plan on personal assessment of own fitness; plan includes only one or two areas of health-related fitness and contains major errors in the application of FITT concepts.

students. A performance portfolio for sixth grade may include the following:

- Rubric scores for several different motor skills as assessed by the teacher
- A copy of a checklist showing feedback given to a peer
- A video of one motor skill accompanied by an oral description of how the application of Newton's Third Law can help improve performance
- A group project, created out of paper, that illustrates a new cooperative game
- A log showing participation in out-of-school activities
- A chart showing a one-day fitness development plan for all five areas of health-related fitness

- A reflective essay describing participation in a cooperative activity
- Rubric scores for how well the student, when working in a small group, was able to assess others' strengths and weaknesses based on physical development, and was able to use this information to solve a physical challenge
- A report on one game from ancient times that has had an influence on a physical activity played today
- A description of an aesthetically pleasing movement activity accompanied by a description of the qualities of movement in that activity in response to an open-ended question

Note that these items collectively document student progress through all of the sixth grade standards. Therefore, it is imperative that students be informed about the grade level standards at the beginning of the school year.

At the end of the year, the portfolio provides the teacher and students with a springboard to discuss student progress and set goals for the next year. During this end-of-the-year conference, ask students to explain the connection between the grade level standards and the pieces they selected to demonstrate their learning. This process will help students understand how learning occurs. You may also wish to ask students to share their work with their parents during end-of-the-year parent conferences. In many schools, the teacher takes a secondary role during these conferences, while the student explains her own progress to her parents. This is also an opportunity for students to reflect on their own work. It also presents students with a "real-world" experience, since students must explain (and perhaps justify and defend) their performances as they will as adult employees.

Time and Storage Management

The storage of portfolios for every student in all your classes and the school can become an overwhelming task. Then there's the time students need to create projects and the time you need to assess student projects and performances. If you are currently assessing your students exclusively on motor skills and fitness, you will notice a significant increase in the amount of work you face when you start using portfolios. How can you manage the storage of portfolios? More importantly, how can you handle the additional workload?

In terms of the time it takes for students to complete some of the projects and reports, we must examine two issues. The first, which I introduced in chapter 1, is the need for depth over breadth, while the second issue is the use of homework in physical education. If you believe, as you look to the next century, that students need to develop the ability to investigate problems so that they can understand a few things well, then the amount of time needed to complete projects and reports is justified. Everything related to the projects does not have to be produced during class time. Students can work on these projects and reports as homework.

Reduce the time needed for assessment in a number of ways. First, you can ask students to self-assess, then peer-assess, and, finally, have you assess their performances. This alone should reduce the amount of your time spent on the assessment process. Embedded assessment, which allows for instruction and assessment to occur simultaneously, will also reduce the time you spend on assessment. In chapter 12, we'll also discuss the use of handheld data collection devices that can reduce the amount of teacher time spent collecting and storing rubric levels. Lastly, all too often when teachers begin to focus on cognitive development in physical education, they hand out one assignment after another and then are frustrated by the amount of paperwork. Instead, choose your assignments carefully, remembering to focus on depth over breadth. A few well-chosen large projects in which students look for connections themselves are better for both you and your students than a large quantity of shorter assignments for which you must create the connections.

To store portfolios, schools tend to follow one of three paths. The first requires students to take full responsibility for their own portfolios. They keep their portfolios in a locker or at home and bring it to class as requested by the teacher. Naturally, the drawback to this approach is students forgetting their portfolios. The second approach puts the responsibility for the portfolios completely on the teacher, who stores portfolios in large boxes or crates by class period. Then, when the students need their portfolios, the teacher brings the box or crate out to class. Still others have moved to electronic portfolios. In an electronic portfolio, you and your students store everything on a computer floppy disk or hard drive. Electronic portfolios can include text, drawings, pictures, audio recordings, video clips, rubrics, and projects—all available at the click of the mouse (see chapter 12). The appropriate choice among these three options depends on your

situation and your students' general level of responsibility.

The Role of Grading in Assessment

Don't, however, confuse grading with alternative assessment. Grading requires the selection and display of a final symbol to communicate the results of assessment. But if you base your grading on standards, identify and use alternative assessment tools, and set clear criteria for each letter grade, then you can move toward alternative assessment—even if you are required to assign a single grade representing student learning.

Grading on Dressing?

A friend of mine, who is a college professor, and I were discussing the issue of universities not including the grade from high school physical education in the grade point average used for admissions. At the same time, a number of high school physical educators were sitting nearby and were engaged in their own conversation about grading. As I challenged my colleague as to why she didn't approach her dean on this matter, the high school teachers were discussing the number of "non-suits" that should result in an "F" in physical education. My colleague turned to me and said, "That's why!"

Dressing Policy and Grading

Students are expected to dress out daily in their physical education uniform, which is available for purchase from the teaching staff. If a student's uniform is unavailable, a loan uniform will be issued for that day. Dressing out is not included in the student's grade, but instead is an expectation of all students.

—Ball Junior High School, Anaheim, California

Unfortunately, some physical educators are still giving grades based on variables other than grade level standards. These variables, including attendance, tardiness, showering, and dressing out still account for a major portion of a student's grade in some physical education programs. Although you need to address these issues, you should not consider them when calculating the physical education grade. Some schools and districts do give a "work habits" grade and, perhaps, a "cooperation" grade as well as a physical education grade. Use this type of forum to grade issues not directly related to attaining set standards. Certainly, as you begin to understand the many different methods and tools available for assessment, you'll also begin to recognize the limitations of calculating the physical education grade based on attendance and dressing out.

Sample Grading Policy From Ball Junior High School, Anaheim, California

30% Motor learning: development of motor skills and movement knowledge; rules and history of sports and games; transfer and application of skills

30% Social skills: sociology, psychology, self-esteem, cooperative problem solving, personal responsibility

30% Exercise physiology: fitness concepts, nutrition and wellness, biomechanics, personal assessment, setting and monitoring fitness goals

10% Extended project: student choice of outside project to be completed quarterly

Sample Grading Policy From Montebello Intermediate School, Montebello, California

20% Motor skill: related to standard one

20% Fitness: related to standard four

20% Social skill: related to standard five

20% Outside physical activity: related to standard three

20% Other: related to standards two, six, and seven

When basing grades on standards, you must first decide whether all standards are created equal. If your philosophy holds that all standards are, in fact, created equal and there are 10 standards, then each standard contributes 10 percent to the total grade. If, however, you believe that standard one is significantly more important than the other standards, then perhaps standard one contributes 28 percent and the other 9 standards contribute 8 percent each. This is strictly a philosophical issue, since once you calculate the final grade, it will either equally reflect all the standards or be biased by one or more standards, depending on the weight given to the standards. This is the inherent weakness in grading: to determine an appropriate final grade that represents an individual's wide range of abilities in 10 different areas. Let's look at a student who receives a "C" in physical education. This particular student excels in motor skill ("A"), has minimal understanding of movement concepts ("D"), participates daily in physical activity ("A"), and has the worst social skills ("F") in the class, so you average out these abilities and report to the parents that the student is a "C." This, in reality, tells the parents nothing about their child's strengths or weaknesses related to physical education.

Once you decide whether or not all standards are created equal, your second major decision is whether or not to give unit grades. If you decide to, you may wish to assign a grade for each unit standard. Then, at the end of the year, average all unit grades into a final grade. Other options include giving one grade for each grade level standard—perhaps assigning one major project for each standard regardless of the number or type of instructional units you've covered during the year. Or assign one grade per unit or every other unit related to each standard. If you give more than one grade for a grade level standard, then you must average those grades to find the final grade for each standard. Then you calculate the grading period's final grade based on the standard grades.

Use one or more assessment tools to collect data on student progress for each standard. For example, when determining the grade for standard 3, you may simply require that students turn in logs that chronicle participation in daily activities. When determining the grade for standard 1, however, you might take into consideration a wide variety of grades (or rubrics) on various motor or sport skills. Of course, one project or other assessment tool may provide data for more than one standard.

Grading on Units

	Unit 1	Unit 2	Unit 3	Unit 4	Unit 5
Standard 1	A	B	B	C	A
Standard 2.1	A	B	C	B	A
Standard 2.2	A	B	B	C	A
Standard 2.3	A	B	C	B	A
Standard 3	B	C	B	C	A
Standard 4	A	B	B	C	B
Standard 5	B	C	A	A	B
Standard 6.1	A	B	C	B	A
Standard 6.2	A	C	A	B	A
Standard 7	A	B	B	B	B
Final unit grade	A	B	B	B	A

Final grade = B

Grading on Standards

Standard 1	A	Standard 4	A
Standard 2.1	B	Standard 5	A
Standard 2.2	B	Standard 6.1	B
Standard 2.3	B	Standard 6.2	B
Standard 3	A	Standard 7	C

Final grade = B

Grading on a Combination of Unit and Grade Standards

	Unit 1	Unit 2	Unit 3	Unit 4	Standard Final
Standard 1	A	A	B	A	A
Standard 2.1	A	B	B	B	B
Standard 2.2	A	B	B	B	B
Standard 2.3					C
Standard 3					A
Standard 4	B	A		A	A
Standard 5	B	B	B	B	B
Standard 6.1	C		C		C
Standard 6.2					B
Standard 7	A		C		B

Final grade = B

Grading on Use of Feedback

Applies appropriate feedback to a partner when developing or improving circus skills.

The teacher observes the student during the lesson.

A: Provides continual corrective feedback using only one or two cues for each performance and delaying feedback until the performer has had time to think about the performance.

B: Provides corrective feedback on most trials using only one or two cues each time and delaying feedback until the performer has had time to think about the performance.

C: Provides corrective feedback on many trials using only one or two cues each time.

D: Provides feedback occasionally.

E: Provides no feedback to any partner at any time.

For example, you might assign students a project for which you assess how well they perform a motor skill (standard 1). They, in turn, analyze their own performances, and then develop ideas for improvement based on biomechanical principles (standard 2.2).

Grading based on the achievement of clearly stated grade level standards informs parents and students of what you expect and what progress students are making. Furthermore, giving students feedback on their projects and performances as soon as possible motivates students to perform well on the next assessment. Ultimately, use authentic assessment and appropriate grading to prove you're accountable. At a time when accountability in education is at a premium, take this responsibility seriously.

Summary

Alternative assessment tools such as observations, written tests, logs and journals, role-playing, reports, and projects benefit your students greatly by focusing on their strengths and uncovering their weaknesses in ways that are not demeaning to them. No matter how much or how well you teach, you must demonstrate that the students have learned or you have accomplished very little. Positive and relevant feedback, which flows naturally from a well-planned assessment system, develops skills in young adolescents. Moreover, helpful feedback may motivate students to work hard to successfully complete the task, skill, or exercise. Ultimately, they will apply the techniques they learn in physical education to real-life situations, thereby preparing them for the future.

Travel Toward Your Destination

Now that you know your destination and the checkpoints along the way, let's determine the mode of transportation. In part III, we'll look at the various factors that influence the instructional process. In chapter 9, we'll examine the learning styles of middle school students. In chapter 10, we'll discuss the behaviors of an effective teacher. In chapter 11, we'll look at a variety of teaching styles and strategies that you can use to reach all your students. In chapter 12, we'll examine effective instructional materials. And in chapter 13, we'll discuss the necessity for change in physical education, steps for change, and how effective staff development can assist with this change as you and your staff continue along on your journey.

CHAPTER 9

Understanding Today's Learner

Middle schoolers are very self-centered. I decided to use that to their advantage—focusing on personal best scores in fitness testing and asking them to meet or beat their best score. The shift eradicated the "competition" within the fitness testing scenario, and changed it to a goal-setting mode, resulting in enthusiasm for reaching an achievable goal as opposed to embarrassment because one couldn't beat the athlete of the class.

—*Physical Educator Francesca Zavacky, Clark School, Charlottesville, Virginia*

You have just finished teaching what you consider to be one of your finest lessons. You gave great demonstrations, used exciting drills and activities, and you equitably distributed effective teaching behaviors throughout the lesson to all your students (see chapter 10). But are you sure your students have learned the material? How can you be sure that what you teach is actually being learned by all of your students? In this chapter, we'll examine what motivates students, how students learn, and how students may learn differently from one another.

Motivating Students

I often hear teachers ask, "How can I motivate my students?" or, "How can I get the apathetic learner turned-on to what I am teaching?" The reality is that you can't motivate students—you can only influence how they motivate themselves. Some students are intrinsically motivated and do not need your influence. These are the self-confident students in your class who are willing to try new and challenging activities. They are also the ones who are the first to volunteer for an extra responsibility (e.g., equipment monitor) or answer a question.

For other students, ensure that certain elements are present in your classes to help motivate them. I have found that five key elements associated with motivated students exist. These elements include providing learning experiences that (1) are safe, (2) are interesting and meaningful, (3) are more cooperative and less competitive in nature, (4) allow students to set their own goals and monitor their own progress, and (5) promote success for all students. Interestingly, many of these elements also help prevent discipline problems. Base your units and lessons on student needs, and high motivation and good discipline follow naturally. Let's take a closer look at how you can set up student-centered classes using these five elements.

Safe Learning Experiences

We have discussed providing a physically safe environment (chapter 4) and helping students to feel psychologically safe (chapter 5). Certainly, students who feel physically and psychologically safe are also more motivated to learn. Remember, too, that both verbal and nonverbal interactions with you affect the student's feelings and attitudes about learning. Review the concepts in chapters 4 and 5 for more information on providing safe learning experiences.

Interesting and Meaningful Learning Experiences

Students are more motivated to learn when the content and activities you present are interesting and meaningful. When you explain the purpose of the lesson, relate the lesson to the overall outcome of the unit, and connect the material to students' current knowledge, skills, and experiences, the material becomes more meaningful. For example, in a self-defense unit, you could start the first lesson by asking students, "What do you know about protecting yourself?" You could chart the students' responses in one of two categories: preventive measures and protective measures. Then explain that throughout the self-defense unit, students will be increasing their understanding and skills related to both of these areas; however, the first several lessons will focus on prevention since it can eliminate the need for protective measures.

Teachers can deliver more interesting lessons by

- connecting the material to students' existing interests,
- setting up a variety of drills or activities for practicing the same skill,
- using a variety of teaching styles,
- engaging a variety of intelligences (see multiple intelligences later in this chapter),
- setting up stations or learning centers so that students can review different skills at each station,
- holding students accountable for the completion of the task through the use of worksheets where students must record their participation or success in the activity, and
- introducing topics in a problematic fashion and asking students to resolve the issues.

The last suggestion refers to the involvement you experience when trying to solve a puzzle or riddle. Your challenge is to set up learning situations that elicit from students the same intensity and involvement they feel when trying to solve a mystery. For example, give each group of students a fitness scenario for a fictitious person. Then the group must create a fitness plan for this person so that he can increase his life expectancy by 10 years.

More Cooperative and Less Competitive Learning Experiences

Many teachers share with me how much their classes enjoy a competitive situation. The teachers convey that they see a high level of enthusiasm and motivation whenever they incorporate competitive activities. But when I ask them to take a closer look at their classes and to chart the students who are displaying enthusiasm and motivation, it becomes clear that what was perceived as a class full of enthusiasm is, in fact, the enthusiasm of a few boisterous students. Pitting students against one another can actually significantly lower student motivation and the quality of student work. Remember, peer approval is very important to middle school students and competition tends to promote conflicts instead of approval.

As you review your grade level standards and recognize that students experience many situations in society where competition is the norm (e.g., promotions, awards, elections), you may see the need to spend more instructional time providing ways for students to learn to work together. You may also remember from chapter 1, that businesses want students who can work together cooperatively, since more and more work situations require cooperation rather than competition. Furthermore, the social aspect of working and discussing with others motivates many middle school students. So look for more ways to include cooperative learning experiences. For example, instead of a culminating tournament at the end of a unit, have students participate in lead-up activities and scrimmages for which you continually rotate the opponent and don't keep score.

Opportunies for Students to Set Goals

What else motivates students? Let them assume more responsibility for their own learning. One way to do this is to teach them how to create appropriate personal goals that are concrete and specific and that have a deadline. For example, "By May 1, I will increase the number of curl-ups I can perform by five." Not surprisingly, setting goals also improves performances.

In conjunction with setting goals, make students accountable for monitoring their own improvements. They can graph fitness scores, chart motor skill performances, or write their reflections on skill technique improvements. Recently, I visited a middle school physical education class where each student brought a steno pad and pencil out to class with them. The students put their pads and pencils in a designated area when not using them. As the students began station practice for volleyball, they picked up their pads and pencils, and, after completing each station, they recorded their personal scores. At the end of the class period, after an additional activity, the teacher asked the students to reflect on their growth over the past several weeks. Once again, the students got their pads and quickly made notes regarding their progress.

In order to properly monitor progress, students require knowledge or information about their performances. Sharing assessment duties and information in the form of self-, peer-, and teacher assessment helps students determine how well they are doing so they can periodically readjust unrealistic goals.

Successful Learning Opportunities for All Students

Success leads to success. Students who are successful want to continue to be successful. To help your students be and feel successful, you must first believe that all students can succeed. Otherwise, it'll be nearly impossible to convince students that they have the potential for success. Adopt the philosophy that while not every student will be successful to the same degree on the same day, each student can succeed.

Using an inclusive style of teaching (see chapter 11) can help to ensure that all students experience success. In addition, eliminate certain practices from your program that tend to promote failure: elimination games, choosing up sides, and playing sports by adult rules. Finally, putting students in small practice groups with sufficient equipment promotes many practice opportunities, which also leads to success.

Rewarding Students

Often teachers believe that to motivate students they need to offer rewards. Rewards in this context refer to any tangible (pizza, gift certificates, patches, other small gifts) or intangible (praise, compliments, public approval) item. Current research, however, indicates that rewards do not have a lasting effect on learner motivation; instead, they offer quick fixes that disregard the ultimate impact on students (Kohn 1993).

Taking Away Extrinsic Rewards

I once heard a speaker tell the following story: There once was an elderly man who lived in a rickety house on the corner of two streets. Every day after school the neighborhood children would walk by his house and taunt him. He tried everything to get them to stop. He yelled at them and he tried calling the police, but nothing worked. Finally one day, he walked out to the children and he gave each of them a one dollar bill explaining that if they came back the next day he would pay them again. The next day, the children were back taunting the man. He came out of his house, thanked them, and handed them each 50 cents. This continued for several days as the old man paid the children less and less for taunting him. One day, the man came out of his house, thanked the children again, and handed them each a nickel. The man explained that if they came back the next day he would pay them each a penny. The children responded that, "It wasn't worth it!" and they never returned.

Several research studies have found that incentives have a detrimental effect on performance. In one study among artists, creativity dropped once they had signed a contract to sell their work upon completion (Amabile 1989). The fact that they knew they were going to be paid for their work lessened their artistic expression. Other researchers have found that incentives have a detrimental effect on performance when the task meets two conditions: It is already interesting for subjects and it is open-ended so that the steps leading to a solution are not immediately obvious.

How do students feel about rewards as motivators? First, rewards communicate to students that the information must not be very interesting, since the teacher feels the need to entice them to learn it. Second, students feel manipulated. All in all, rewards are not the answer to motivating students.

For those middle school teachers trying to wean their students off six years of rewards received in elementary school, it's often a difficult task. However, as Kohn (1993) explains, "The more difficult it is to wean students off gold stars and candy bars, the more urgent it is to do so" (p. 200). As a middle school physical educator, you have two options. You can work within the current structure while minimizing the use of rewards or you can work with other teachers to change the structure. Regardless of which approach you take, lean away from the use of rewards and focus your efforts on the five key elements that increase motivation: a safe learning environment, interesting and meaningful learning experiences, cooperative learning situations, goal setting, and success.

How Students Learn

Now let's take a look at the current research on how students learn and at practical ways to apply this research. We can approach the topic of "How Students Learn" from many perspectives, including behaviorist and constructivist theories. Behaviorists believe that students learn best when the teacher breaks down content into small pieces and feeds them to students one piece at a time. Constructivists believe that learning is an interactive process through which students construct personal meaning from information available to them, then integrate that information with their previous learning. Often referred to as "active learning," this interactive process involves all the students' senses, places emphasis on developing students' learning and problem solving skills, engages students in activities that require higher-order thinking skills, and allows students to explore their own ideas.

The constructivists believe that holistic problem solving activities engage student interest the most, making it more likely that students will learn requisite information and skills. Let's take, for example, the learning outcome of students creating their own week-long fitness plans. From the constructivist perspective, you ask students to create their own week-long fitness plan, providing them with the materials to accomplish the project. Then, to complete their projects, the students seek out information by asking questions of the teacher and other experts, and searching through books and other data sources, about the various components of fitness and how to improve fitness. From a behaviorist perspective, you introduce students to each component of fitness one at a time until they have learned all the parts, then ask them to complete a related project.

Many researchers and educators question whether these two perspectives can coexist. I believe that they can. Students learn best in certain situations when you break the information down for them as in the behaviorist perspective. Yet, with the increase in the amount of information in our communications-oriented society, the constructivist approach is sometimes more appropriate. Let's discuss the variables that lend themselves to one perspective or the other, depending on the situation (see chapter 11 as well).

First, what are some specific ideas for how to improve student learning? Let's explore the current brain-based research on how students learn best, in general, and the motor learning research on how students learn motor skills best. This information will not only help you to become a better teacher, it will also give you additional evidence for proving to others the importance of a quality physical education program in every middle school. Share the research with your students as well to help them become lifelong learners.

What the Brain-Based Research Says

Naturally, improved discipline and motivation increase learning. So the same attitudes and actions that lead to better discipline and higher motivation lead to more effective learning: Creating a physically and psychologically safe environment, presenting concepts in an interesting and meaningful way, allowing students to set goals and monitor their own progress, and showing how new information links to previous information or interests all make learning easier. Over the last decade, we have learned much about how the brain learns. By using this information to teach more effectively, you can increase your students' understanding.

Organizing Information

Students learn best when they can organize information in a meaningful way. This is why it is so important to link new information to what students already know: It gives them a hook on which to hang new information. I recently observed a teacher who was giving a lesson on the parts of the golf club. Before she labeled the parts, she asked the students for the names of the parts of the tennis racket (the unit they had just completed). She then compared the common labels for the tennis racket's components with the parts of the golf club, giving students a linking place to store and remember the new information.

People remember information best when it is chunked into groups of seven or fewer pieces. Remembering a list of 10 items is very difficult. However, if you break the list into two parts, the students can memorize 5 items—a more realistic amount to recall. For example, for the parts of fitness, you might separate the list into health-related items (cardiorespiratory endurance, muscular endurance, muscular strength, body composition, and flexibility) and skill-related items (agility, balance, coordination, power, reaction time, and speed). Making an acrostic (first letter of each key word forms a new word) out of new information is a good mnemonic (memory) device. The acrostic FIT (frequency, in-

tensity, and time) has been very effective in helping students to remember the concepts related to health-related fitness development.

Mapping is still another strategy for helping students organize information. The mapping concept refers to organizing material into a graphic that clarifies the relationship of the member information bits or concepts. Try asking students to brainstorm about some subject and then chart their ideas in the form of a graphic organizer. Figure 9.1 shows a comparative graphic, also called a Venn diagram, that one teacher created as the students brainstormed the similarities and differences between basketball and team handball. You can use mapping to present new information as well.

Active Learning Strategies

Actively using information helps students digest concepts and move the information into long-term memory. Have students apply new information as soon as possible. The more realistic the application, the better. For example, teach students how to calculate their target heart rate zones, then for homework, require students to teach their parents how to calculate their target heart rate zones.

Group projects not only encourage students to apply new information, they also call for students to discuss and sort out conflicting ideas to solve problems. And we all know how much middle school students like to talk! So give them a productive social outlet: Try asking each small group to create a new game so they can apply their understanding of game concepts, including the use of equipment, skills, players, rules, and strategies.

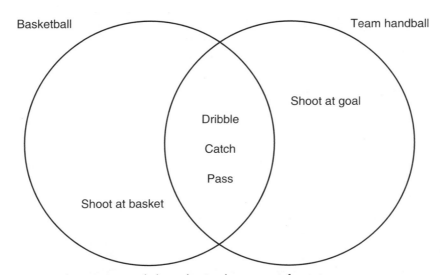

Figure 9.1 Mapping, or graphic organizers, help students to learn new information.

Choose from a variety of active learning strategies, including having students create a concrete reminder of information, such as putting the information on large colorful pictures or posters and posting them around the room, having students act out the information (see simulations in chapter 12), and letting students test new information, such as asking, "Does the ball travel farther when released at an angle greater than or less than 45 degrees?" Engage as many of the students' five senses in the learning process as possible.

Use of Music

Many physical educators use music during exercising or other instructional times. When asked why they use music, they often state that the students enjoy music and are motivated by it. Music also increases learning. It helps students (and teachers!) relax, reduces stress, fosters creativity by activating more brain waves, invigorates imagination and higher-order thinking, promotes motor skill development, stimulates speech and vocabulary development, reduces discipline problems, and increases concentration (Halpern 1985). Specifically, classical music (circa 1750-1825) and romantic music (circa 1820-1900) are useful while introducing new information and Baroque music (circa 1600-1750) is helpful while reviewing information at the end of a lesson (Jensen 1994).

Music for Physical Education Class

Baroque Period

Mass in B Minor by Johann Sebastian Bach

Messiah by George Frederik Handel

Classical Period

Minuet from "Surprise" Symphony by Josef Hayden

Minuet from Symphony No. 40 by Wolfgang Amadeus Mozart

Romantic Period

Romeo and Juliet by Peter Tchaikovsky

"Träumerei" by Robert Schumann

Scherzo from "Midsummer Night's Dream" by Felix Mendelssohn

"Lohengrin" by Richard Wagner

Exercise

Of course, as physical educators, we've always been advocates for the physical, psychological, and cognitive benefits of exercise. Finally, research supports our contention that physical exercise has a positive effect on memory and learning. Indeed, vigorous physical activity improves blood and oxygen flow to the brain increasing the number of synaptic connections (Jensen 1995). This helps improve reasoning, short-term memory, reaction times, and creativity (Jensen 1994). Simply changing from sitting to standing increases the heart rate by 10 extra beats per minute sending more blood to the brain, thereby telling the central nervous system to increase neural firing (Jensen 1995). So students really do need quality physical education in schools as well as stand-and-stretch breaks every 20 minutes in other classes (Jensen 1994).

Proper Nutrition

The foods we consume fall into three categories: carbohydrates, proteins, and fats. Carbohydrates tend to have a relaxing effect on the body while protein aides alertness, quick thinking, and fast reactions. The best foods to consume for protein are eggs, fish, turkey, tofu, pork, chicken, and yogurt.

Minerals and water help the brain function efficiently as well. Foods high in folic acid (dark leafy greens) and selenium (seafood, whole grain breads, nuts, and meats) reduce depression and boost learning (Jensen 1994 and Jensen 1995). Boron (broccoli, apples, pears, peaches, grapes, nuts, and dried beans), zinc (fish, beans, whole grains, and dark turkey meat), and iron are also associated with improved mental activity. Drink 8 to 15 eight-ounce glasses of water per day, depending on the weather and level of physical activity. Don't depend on thirst to dictate when to drink because the thirst-signaling mechanism lags behind your actual need for fluids. If you find that some of your students are easily bored, listless, drowsy, or that they lack concentration, they may be suffering from dehydration. Try suggesting that they increase their water intake. If this doesn't help or a student is experiencing other mental deficiencies, such as a reduction in cognitive or physical performance, then review the student's diet to try to determine what she is lacking.

In addition to what you eat, your brain prefers a nibbling diet over large meals. Nibblers maintain insulin levels better, have lower cortisol levels, and better glucose tolerance. This results in better cognitive functioning, fewer discipline problems, and an enhanced sense of well-being. Give students this nutritional information so they can take the first steps toward improving their eating habits and toward increasing their thinking and learning capacities. Engage the cooperation of your comprehensive school health system committee for even better results (see chapter 3).

Motor Learning Research

Now that their brains are working better, you must help students become more proficient in their motor skills. We have learned much about motor learning over the last decade and can use this information to develop more effective learning experiences. Share this information with your students as well so they can use it throughout their lives.

Stages of Motor Learning

Students progress through three stages to learn a new skill: cognitive, associative, and automatic. During the first stage, the cognitive stage, students need an accurate model of the skill. As you provide a demonstration of the skill, identify its most critical features. Cognitive processes are heavily involved at this stage as the learner develops a mental picture of the skill and sequencing pattern. At this stage, however, the learner can't manage small details of the movement or adapt the movement to different environmental conditions.

Students usually spend most of their time in the second stage, the associative stage. Here, students concentrate on refining the mechanics of the skill. As consistency increases during this stage, students begin to be able to adjust to environmental conditions.

At the third stage, the automatic stage, the learner has mastered the skill and no longer has to concentrate on how to perform the skill. At this point, he shifts his attention from the cognitive aspects of the performance to the environmental.

Mental Practice

Forming a mental picture of the motor skill before practicing it enhances learning. Continuing mental practice after the initial learning enhances long-term retention. If the student visualizes herself as a noted performer, identifying as completely as possible with that role model, she will develop and improve her performance further. If she gives herself a pep talk while visualizing, she'll enhance her performance even more. So you don't take away

from physical practice time during class, assign or encourage mental practice during rest intervals or as part of a homework assignment.

Improving Speed and Accuracy

When introducing students to new skills, emphasize generating speed or force without pressuring them to be accurate. In other words, don't emphasize accuracy until students demonstrate that they can generate sufficient force, otherwise they, as beginners, may never develop the force necessary for success in many sport skills. For example, when a student is working on the correct technique for an overhand throw, emphasizing accuracy causes the student to throw with a "dart throwing" technique. By focusing on force, the student learns to bring the arm back, rotate the body, and transfer body weight to project the ball a greater distance. As the learner progresses to the associative and automatic stages, he can begin to focus more on accuracy. The student will always need to make some trade-off between speed and accuracy, but over time, he can continue to work on improving both.

Practice Schedules

Spacing of practice sessions, often referred to as "distributed" practice, generally leads to more effective (but not necessarily more efficient) learning, especially in the early stages. To apply this finding to physical education classes, consider changing unit plans that focus on one skill each day. You can use instructional time more effectively if you have students practice a number of skills during each class period (Schmidt 1991).

I've noticed that teachers tend to be behaviorists, breaking each task down into the smallest units possible. Whenever possible, however, introduce new skills in their entirety—especially when breaking down the skill changes it significantly (Magill 1993). For example, breaking the skill of batting into its parts to practice those parts does not teach batting since the parts are significantly different when practiced alone and when applied to the entire skill. But for a very complex skill that has difficult—yet relatively independent—parts, still demonstrate the whole skill first, next demonstrate and have students practice the parts, then as quickly as possible, have the students put the parts together and practice the skill as a whole. This approach is often referred to as "whole-part-whole" approach.

When putting the skill back together, use forward or backward chaining. In the triple jump, for example, forward chaining involves practicing the run, then practicing the run into a hop, then practicing the run into a hop into a skip, and finally practicing the run into a hop into a skip into a jump. In backward chaining, students begin practice with a standing jump, then add the skip, then the hop, and finally, the run. Backward chaining may be more effective perhaps because students see it as being more logical and meaningful than forward chaining, or beginning with the first part of the skill (Magill 1993).

"Variable practice" refers to setting up practice with changing conditions. Change the speed (fast, slow), distance (far, near), and organization (number of shots per turn) of the practice drills and activities to enhance learning during the associative and automatic stages of learning an open skill, or skills that students must perform in changing environments. In contrast, students perform closed skills under constant conditions. For example, dribbling and layups are open skills in basketball, whereas the free throw is a closed skill. Practicing open skills in unchanging environments after the cognitive stage does little to prepare the learner for the real-life application of the skill to a game setting. So to have students practice the layup during the associative and automatic stages of learning, ask them to approach the basket from different angles while defenders try to block their shots. To benefit the most, students must practice skills under conditions that match as closely as possible actual game settings. It follows, then, that students should practice closed skills in game-like settings as well, that is, in a constant or unchanging practice situation.

Feedback

Feedback benefits the learner especially during the associative and automatic stages of learning. The learner needs either corrective (e.g., "Forming a wider triangle with your hands and head gives you a wider base of support, making it easier for you to perform the headstand.") or positive specific (e.g., "Good job—you stepped forward on your opposite foot.") feedback. In this situation, "Good job!" is used to draw the student's attention to the correct aspect of his performance, which is helpful, as opposed to praise which is used to manipulate students. Delay feedback until about five seconds after the student completes the skill so that she has time to process the kinesthetic feelings associated with the performance before hearing external feedback. Teach students to delay feedback when assessing peers as well.

Restrict feedback to commenting on features not readily apparent to the learner. For example, feedback on throwing accuracy does not give the learner any additional information, since he can clearly see the outcome of the throw. But information about the technique of his throw is important because he cannot get that information for himself.

Limit feedback further by concentrating on only one or two critical features at a time. Making too many points at once will overwhelm the learner. Select for feedback only the critical features you highlighted while explaining and demonstrating the skill. If you introduce a skill by only pointing out its main features, you are also less likely to overwhelm the learner. For example, when teaching the basketball dribble, I initially focus on the use of the finger pads and on pushing the ball as opposed to slapping the ball. Therefore, during practice I only comment on these critical features. As we progress through the striking or basketball unit, I highlight other critical features of the basketball dribble so that I can help students refine their skills.

Transfer of Learning

It is important, especially in learning motor skills, to point out the ways in which many skills share similarities with other skills, showing students how to transfer learning appropriately from one situation to another (a positive transfer of learning). For example, we use the underhand movement pattern in the underhand volleyball serve, badminton serve, and softball pitch. Although differences between these patterns can cause negative transfer, highlighting the similarities between skills has a positive effect on learning.

How Students Learn Differently

Throughout this chapter we have looked at enhancing learning for students in general. But students are individuals and what works with one student may not work with another. Over the years, researchers have developed many different methods of and theories for looking at how individual students learn. This disjointed approach reminds me of the story about the blind men and the elephant. Each man held a different part of the elephant (trunk, leg, tail), and when asked to describe what they were holding, they each gave a different description. Likewise, each learning theory looks at learning from a different perspective. Let's discuss two of the more popular theories, Bandler-Grinder and multiple intelligences.

Bandler-Grinder

The Bandler-Grinder approach looks at which modality a student prefers to learn through—auditory, visual, or kinesthetic. A quick method to determine students' preferred learning modality is to ask them a question that they must think about. As the students are pondering their answers, watch their eyes. Visual learners tend to look up, auditory learners, sideways, and kinesthetic learners, down.

Teachers tend to teach using their own modality preferences. It is interesting to note that the majority of educators are visual learners, but the majority of physical educators are kinesthetic learners. The students who often have difficulty in the classroom setting, also tend to be kinesthetic learners. They perform well in physical education because they learn best through doing. The challenge in physical education is to engage the visual and auditory learners. By including pictures, graphics, readings, and video clips, the visual learners become engaged in the learning situation. Add audio recordings, music, and discussions to engage auditory learners. Provide a wide variety of learning activities so all your students learn.

Multiple Intelligences

Another way we are all different is in the area or areas in which we excel. Howard Gardner (1983) has defined seven different areas in which we can view intelligence. Gardner says that each of us has varying levels of ability in each of these intelligences. Typically, however, most people find that they excel in one or two intelligences. Students can usually identify their strongest intelligences themselves. Interestingly, watching how students misbehave will give you insights into those students' most highly developed intelligences as well.

Since most classes are made up of individuals with different primary intelligences, utilize a broad range of teaching strategies in each class (see chapter 11). A station approach can address a different intelligence at each station. While it's not necessary to include every intelligence in every lesson, the greater the number of intelligences addressed in a lesson, the greater the number of students who will be highly engaged in learning. In addition, if you are having particular difficulty with one or two stu-

---

Sample Station Activities for Golf Based on the Multiple Intelligences

1. Use SyberVision video (spatial).
2. Play one hole of golf wearing a heart monitor (bodily-kinesthetic).
3. Link heart monitor to computer; graph printout of heart rate during one hole of golf (logical-mathematical).
4. Practice with long iron (bodily-kinesthetic).
5. Videotape swing (spatial).
6. Practice putting (bodily-kinesthetic).
7. Practice golf swing to music (musical).
8. Write answer to the question: "Why does golf tend to be more popular with the forty plus age group?" (Linguistic.)
9. Practice putting with a partner. Provide partner with feedback (interpersonal).
10. Perform shadow golf drill in order to provide feedback on own golf swing (intrapersonal).

---

dents, you may want to make a special effort to reach them through their primary intelligences.

Linguistic intelligence. Students whose primary intelligence is linguistic in nature have a capacity to use words effectively. They prefer to learn through lectures, large and small group discussions, reading, storytelling, brainstorming, debate, tape recording their thoughts, and writing activities. The types of instructional materials that work best with these students are books, worksheets, manuals, talking books and cassettes, and word games. When you ask these students to develop a project, they will more than likely develop an oral or written report. When misbehaving, these students tend to talk, interrupt, and argue with the teacher and other students.

Logical-mathematical intelligence. Students whose primary intelligence is logical-mathematical in nature have a capacity to use numbers and reason effectively. They prefer to learn through mathematical problems, scientific demonstrations, logical-sequential presentation of subject matter, classifications and categorizations, critical thinking, and logical problem solving exercises. They prefer to work with logic puzzles and games, computer programming languages, and mathematical problems on the chalkboard. When you ask these students to develop a project, they will typically include statistics, cause and effect charts, and formulas to prove and convey their points of view. When misbehaving, these students tend to daydream or challenge the logic of the teacher.

Spatial intelligence. Students whose primary intelligence is spatial in nature have the capacity to perceive the visual-spatial world accurately. They prefer to learn through visualizations, picture metaphors, sketching of ideas, charts, graphs, diagrams, maps, slides, photographs, and mind-maps. They prefer to work with building models, hands-on projects, videos, graphics software, visual puzzles and mazes, and microscopes. These students typically develop projects that include maps, flow charts, sketches, and diagrams. When misbehaving, these students take things apart to see how they work or they doodle on their papers.

Musical intelligence. Students whose primary intelligence is musical in nature have the capacity to perceive, discriminate, transform, and express musical forms. They prefer to learn through rhythms, songs, raps, chants, memory music, mood music, and musical concepts. They prefer to work with music software, musical instruments, and recorded music. When you ask these students to develop a project, they will include music, chants, and raps. I know that I always had one of these students in each of my classes, because whenever I handed out pencils there was a student who insisted upon drumming with it. These students also misbehave by humming and by tapping their feet.

Interpersonal intelligence. Students whose primary intelligence is interpersonal in nature have the capacity to perceive and make distinctions in the moods, intentions, motivations, and feelings of other people. They prefer to learn through cooperative learning, group brainstorming activities, community-based activities, peer sharing, conflict mediation activities, cross-age tutoring, interpersonal interactions, and simulations. They prefer to work with interactive software, simulations, and board games. When you ask these students to develop projects, they will more than likely include their own simulations, demonstrations, and discussions. They tend to misbehave by exerting negative leadership, writing notes, and talking to friends.

Intrapersonal intelligence. Students whose primary intelligence is intrapersonal in nature have the capacity to understand themselves. They prefer to learn through reflection, personal connections, interest centers, goal setting, self-paced instruction, and self-esteem activities. They prefer to work with programmed instruction materials, individualized projects and games, and journals. When you ask these students to develop a project, they will more than likely include scrapbooks, their own feelings, and their own interpretation of events. They exhibit misbehavior through daydreaming and tuning out the teacher.

Bodily-kinesthetic intelligence. Students whose primary intelligence is bodily-kinesthetic in nature have the capacity to use their whole bodies to express ideas and feelings. They prefer to learn through creative movement, physical education activities, mime, crafts, theater, and hands-on activities. They prefer to work with virtual reality software, field trips, hands-on materials, crafts, cooking, gardening, and tactile hands-on materials. These students typically develop projects that include three-dimensional representations of events, a demonstration, or a performance. Their misbehaviors include being out of their seat in the classroom as well as pushing, shoving, and fighting with others. Similar to the kinesthetic learner in the Bandler-Grinder model, these students often do well in physical education while getting into trouble in their other classes. You can help these students by sharing strategies for relating to them with their other teachers.

Summary

For learning to occur in the middle school, you must first motivate students to learn. Next, you must align instruction with what we know about learning—especially motor learning. Finally, you must take individual learning needs into consideration, introducing new information through each student's preferred learning style, then reviewing it through as many other avenues as possible. By setting up a positive and safe learning environment, providing interesting instruction, and ensuring success for all, your students will learn. In the next chapter, I'll look specifically at how you can change your teaching behaviors to further ensure success for all your students.

CHAPTER 10

Improving Your Teaching Effectiveness

My students experience much more quality learning and activity time when I have prepared a well-thought-out and organized lesson. For example, when using a fitness circuit, I set up stations ahead of time with equipment and task cards. The task cards give students clear, concise instructions, along with pictures to illustrate the activity, so I am free to assist students who need me during the lesson.

—Physical Educator Joan Van Blom, Hill Middle School, Long Beach, California

To a large extent, how much students learn in physical education is directly related to the quality and effectiveness of the physical educator. Teachers who pay little attention to the individual needs of their students and the current research on teaching and learning often see little improvement in their students throughout the school year. However, teachers who are enthusiastic, have high expectations for all students, and use effective teaching behaviors see their students gain motor, cognitive, and affective skills. Have you ever wondered what you can do to improve your teaching? In this chapter, we'll examine those teaching behaviors that can lead to instructional success in middle school. As you read this chapter, answer the questions I pose at the beginning of each section to see how well you are currently implementing each behavior.

Staying Current

Have you attended a college or university graduate course recently? When was the last time you attended a professional conference? How long has it been since you picked up a professional journal and read all the way through it?

So far in *Teaching Middle School Physical Education*, we have discussed a wealth of information that you need to know in order to be effective. You may remember some helpful information from your college preparation program as well. But have you kept up with the current research? Few of us have all the knowledge we need of what it takes to form a complete physical education program appropriate for middle schoolers. Without up-to-date knowledge and understanding of curriculum development, content, student needs and learning styles, instruction, and assessment, it'll be difficult—if not impossible—to deliver a quality physical education experience. In chapter 13, I'll provide additional information on staff development opportunities to help you maintain and improve your skills, but first, let's discuss effective classroom management skills.

Planning

Do you have a unit plan for every unit you teach? Do you always have a lesson plan in hand as you walk into class? Does your lesson plan include written objectives? Have you taken into consideration the individual needs of each student in each of your classes? Are the activities you planned directly related to the objectives?

As a young teacher, I made the decision to never go to class without a lesson plan. I often pretended that the class was full of adults who would otherwise quickly discern that I was unprepared for the lesson. I thought that if I couldn't stand in front of a group of adults without knowing exactly what I was going to do, then why should I try to teach a group of children without being as well-prepared?

Unfortunately, many teachers believe that they can walk into class and deliver a lesson on any topic without planning. But the fact is, many decisions go into a lesson, and not planning simply means that the teacher is unable or unwilling to make those decisions. Teachers who plan for organization, management, and task appropriateness promote learning better, because their students present fewer behavior problems, spend less time waiting, and have more practice time during the lesson (Maryland State Department of Education 1989). By developing unit and lesson plans, you can also see and demonstrate the links among the exit, grade level, and unit standards and the instruction itself.

Using Time Effectively

Do you spend your instructional time effectively? Do your students spend most of the instructional period engaged in active, hands-on learning? Do you keep the time you spend on management to a minimum?

Typically, state guidelines mandate the number of minutes per day or week allocated to physical education. For example, California's guidelines allocate 200 minutes of physical education every 10 school days to students in sixth grade and a minimum of 400 minutes to students in seventh and eighth grades every 10 school days. New Jersey's guidelines allocate all grades 150 minutes of physical education per week. How much time do you have to teach? How well do you use it?

Physical educators tend to divide their class time into three categories:

- Student engagement time: the amount of time in which students are actively involved in physical education content (but not necessarily at the appropriate level for success)

- Lecture time: the amount of time for which students sit and listen while the teacher provides information

- Management time: the amount of time spent on noninstructional activities, such as roll call, disciplining students, and handing out equipment

Reducing Management Time

Begin and end class on time.

Establish routines.

Reduce the transition time between activities.

Give brief but precise instructions.

Use short demonstrations followed by immediate practice.

Provide students with sufficient equipment so they are not waiting in line for a turn.

Use prompts (verbal cues or task cards) to keep students on task.

Change practice activities to keep students interested and involved.

I recently visited a class that was working on golf putting. Each group of four students was assigned to a carpet square with a tin can as the target. The teacher instructed the students to practice the putting stroke while trying to get the ball into the can. Initially, all the students were actively engaged taking turns and watching each other try to get the ball into the container. After about fifteen minutes, however, the students lost interest in the activity and began to entertain themselves by hitting the ball across the instructional area and, at times, toward me. Sometimes teachers ask, "How do you know when it's time to change an activity?" I respond, "The students will let you know—one way or another."

Students should spend at least 70 percent of class time engaged in active learning and no more than 15 percent in lectures and 15 percent in management activities (Batesky 1988), depending on the teacher's style and strategy as well as on the nature of the information. In general, make it your goal to decrease managerial time and increase engaged learning time whenever possible. How? Some of the most helpful ways to do so are to establish and follow routines, give brief but precise directions and demonstrations followed immediately by practice time, use enough equipment to keep lines short and groups small, and move on to a new activity when interest wanes. To further reduce the time you spend on management, review the management tips in chapter 5 and motivational strategies in chapter 9.

Using Students' Names

When you address a student, do you use her name? When giving feedback to a student do you use her name? Do you know the names of all your students?

Everyone likes to hear his or her own name. More importantly, a student likes to know that the person teaching him knows his name. Effective teachers take the time to learn their students' names and how to pronounce them correctly. Then they use the students' names during class. One teacher I work with took a picture of each of his students using the Connectix Camera (digital camera for the computer) and created a visual seating chart on the computer to help him remember the names of his 250 students.

Knowing students' names promotes not only learning but also class management. As I discussed in chapter 5, calling out a student's name in a respectful manner is a very effective strategy to putting a stop to misbehavior. Several activities, such as the name games in appendix C, help both students and teachers learn each other's names.

Providing Model Demonstrations and Explanations

Are you able to correctly demonstrate each motor skill that you teach? If there is a skill that you can't demonstrate, do you have video clip of that skill? When you aren't able to demonstrate a skill, are you willing to use a student as a model? Do you know the critical features for every motor skill that you teach? Do you clearly explain and demonstrate those critical features to your students?

Providing a model performance for the learner during the first stage of learning is critical to their success. Effective models are accurate; they highlight the critical features of the skill and provide visual information that students can use to form a mental image of the action. Effective teachers accompany the demonstration with an explanation that focuses on the same critical features highlighted in the demonstration.

You should only demonstrate the skill yourself if you can provide an accurate model. Otherwise, use videos to provide effective demonstrations. Interestingly, students benefit from seeing the demonstration of a task from the performer's viewpoint, which is only possible through the use of video. Or if a video is unavailable, use students who are proficient at the skill as models. Be sure to use student models of both genders and various ethnicities.

Checking for Understanding

Are you sure that your students understand the directions that you have given for an activity? The critical features of a new skill after your presentation?

When teaching, check for understanding before sending students out to practice the skill. Many teachers are unaware that students do not understand their directions until the students try to demonstrate the skill or implement the activity. Check understanding through a variety of techniques: signaled answers, choral responses, or sampling individual responses. Signaled answers refer to asking students true or false questions and requesting a thumbs up or thumbs down response to indicate their understanding. For a choral response, students call out the answer to a question in unison. Both the signaled answer and choral response are quick ways to check for understanding, saving time and frustration later in the class period.

You can also call on individual students to check understanding of the task and skill and then generalize the understanding of a few students to the entire class. One alternative to sampling individual responses is a cooperative learning technique in which you ask the question, give partners time to discuss the answer, and then call on a sampling of students to ascertain the level of understanding. This approach gives all students an opportunity to discuss the question and learn from one another.

Follow these effective questioning steps when asking for individual student responses:

1. Ask the question.

2. Wait at least five seconds (some students require more time to process).

3. Call on one student.

4. Affirm or correct the student's answer (this indicates to the students that you are interested in the response).

5. Follow up with a second or third question when you receive an incorrect answer to clarify student understanding and to lead students to the correct answer (often times a student's incorrect response may indicate a partial understanding of the concept).

Asking Questions

Mr. Chan: "Today, we are going to see how many curl-ups each of you can perform. Which part of health-related fitness do we test with curl-ups?"

[Teacher waits five seconds.]

Mr. Chan: "Temika?"

Temika: "Cardiorespiratory endurance!"

Mr. Chan: "Why do you think the correct answer is cardiorespiratory endurance?"

Temika: "Because my heart beats faster when I do curl-ups."

Mr. Chan: "How long can you do curl-ups?"

Temika: "Three or four minutes."

Mr. Chan: "How long do we need to perform an exercise to work on cardiorespiratory endurance?"

Temika: "Twenty to thirty minutes. Oh, I guess the answer can't be cardiorespiratory endurance—it must be *muscular* endurance!"

If you immediately call on a student after asking a question, the other students have no reason to even think about the answer. By waiting five seconds and then calling on a student, the other students also have time to think about their answers. This keeps the entire class involved in the learning process—not just the student answering the question.

Providing Effective Practice

Do your students get enough practice opportunities during the class period? Are your students practicing at the appropriate level of difficulty? Are your students using the correct technique when they practice?

Even after you have limited your managerial and lecture time so that most of your class time is left for students to engage in the activity, how do you know that the students are getting enough *appropriate* practice? Providing effective practice (also known as Academic Learning Time in Physical Education or ALT-PE) involves engaging students in a maximum amount of practice at the appropriate level of difficulty using the correct technique so that learning can occur. The appropriate level of difficulty is typically defined as an 80 percent success rate, although some set the success rate closer to 50 percent for target activities, especially with beginning learners (Rink 1993a). Unfortunately, research has found that students typically spend under 15 percent of their class time in ALT-PE (Lemaster and Lacy 1993).

One day I was observing an in-school bowling class and decided to count the number of opportunities that students had to practice their bowling technique. The class was well-organized into practice stations with four students, one bowling ball, and a set of pins at each station. The students rotated from bowler to pin setter as they practiced their bowling skills. Still, at the end of the practice time (approximately 20 minutes), each student had received only three or four chances to roll the ball.

To increase the amount of ALT-PE, you must first increase student engagement time, thereby making more time for practice as we have already discussed. Second, set up the instructional environment so that students get as many opportunities as possible to practice the skill. Increasing the amount of equipment and limiting the size of practice groups are two of the most effective strategies for increasing the number of practice trials per student. For example, in the previous bowling scenario, the number of students per bowling set up should have been reduced in order to increase ALT-PE. Finally, ensure that the tasks and drills are at the appropriate level of difficulty for each student. The inclusion style of teaching effectively creates the appropriate levels of difficulty for all students through the use of alternative activities (see chapter 11). For example, when students are working on the volleyball serve, you can let them choose how far from the net they will stand instead of requiring all of them to practice from behind the end line.

Actively Supervising

Do you move around the instructional area as your students are practicing? Do you spend an equal amount of time in each quadrant of the instructional area? Do you know where all your students are all the time?

Actively monitoring students during practice helps to keep them on-task. Often, misbehavior or off-task (doing something other than the assignment) behavior occurs in the quadrant of the instructional area that the teacher has not visited. You should move around the instructional area in an unpredictable pattern spending an equitable amount of time focusing on each student or group of students while staying aware of the other students in the class. I often find that beginning teachers have a tendency to focus exclusively on the group they are working with and, as a result, off-task behavior tends to occur in the other groups. This ability to focus on the students you are working with and simultaneously stay aware of the other students is called "overlapping" (Rink 1993a). Awareness and experience improve the skill of overlapping.

Providing Feedback

Do you provide your students with positive, specific feedback as they are practicing their motor skills? Do you provide your students with corrective feedback?

Students want to know how they are doing, so effective teachers provide them with feedback on their performances. Base feedback on the critical features you introduced during the demonstration and explanation of the skill so that the student knows what you are looking for in her performance. Be careful to comment on only one or two features at a time when correcting a student so as not to overwhelm her. For example, when introducing the soccer dribble, I initially focus on contacting the ball with the instep of the foot and keeping the ball within one to two feet. Then I limit my feedback to comments related to these two critical features. At this point, I don't comment on other aspects, such as being aware of what is going on around the student. Feedback can be general ("Way to go!") or specific ("Way to bend your knees!"). Specific feedback,

however, is much more effective (Siedentop 1983). In fact, effective teachers provide their students with two to three specific feedback comments per minute during practice periods. In addition, feedback can be positive ("Great job!"), negative ("Not that way."), or corrective ("Try bending your knees more."). Effective teachers stay away from negative feedback and focus their energies on positive, specific, and corrective comments, often at a ratio of three or four positive to every corrective (Batesky 1988).

Treating Students Equitably

Do you provide all students with the same amount of feedback? Do you have the same expectations for all your students? Do you provide all students with the opportunity to respond to questions and demonstrate activities?

Effective teachers have high expectations of *all* students and are enthusiastic and use effective teaching behaviors with *all* students. Teachers are more likely to call on high-achievers than low-achievers when asking questions (Kerman 1979). They tend to provide boys with more feedback; however, it tends to be more negative in nature. I know I used to find myself typically asking boys to demonstrate a new skill, even though I had girls who were equally capable of being models. And, many teachers tend to give high-achievers up to five seconds to respond to a question whereas they give low-achievers only one or two seconds (Kerman 1979).

Students tend to "live up to" or "down to" your expectations (Martinek, Crowe, and Rejeski 1982). When you provide some students with more opportunities to demonstrate, practice, receive feedback, and answer questions, it communicates to the other students that you either don't care as much about them or that they are not as good as the other students. Moreover, many students will pick up on your expectations even through nonverbal communication.

So what can you do to improve your use of effective teaching behaviors and ensure that all students are on the receiving end? First, become aware of effective teaching behaviors (reading this chapter is a good start). Second, determine to what extent you are currently using these behaviors by doing one of the following:

1. Audiotaping one of your lessons
2. Videotaping one of your lessons

	Use of name	Positive feedback	Corrective feedback	Positive specific feedback	Negative feedback
John Adams	✓✓			✓	✓
Sue Brown		✓		✓✓	
Ann Chan			✓		
Jose Garcia					
Ann Hernandez	✓	✓			
Tony Nguyen			✓✓		
Juan Ortega				✓✓	
Tom Smith	✓				
Mary Washington		✓			
Tanya Washington	✓		✓✓		

3. Having a colleague observe one of your lessons

When using one of the first two examples, you will collect data by listening to or watching the tape of the lesson, whereas in the third example your colleague will collect the data. Regardless of which method you use, list your students' names on a piece of paper, determine which behaviors (e.g., use of names, amount of feedback, types of feedback) you are going to chart and make them column headings, then simply check off (or have your colleague check off) each time you use the behavior with a student. Sometimes, depending on class size, it's easier to collect data on a few students rather than on the entire class. In addition, be aware that when collecting data from an audiotape, it's often difficult to determine which student is the recipient of the effective teaching behavior unless you use the student's name. Once you see how you're doing, focus your attention on increasing the use of one or two effective teaching behaviors at a time and equitably distributing the behavior to all students. Collecting data on a regular basis provides you with the feedback you need to continue to increase your use of effective teaching behaviors.

Summary

Effective teachers have high expectations of all students and are enthusiastic and use effective teaching behaviors with all students. They are constantly looking for ways to improve their effectiveness. You can increase your effectiveness as a physical educator by increasing your knowledge base; by spending more time on planning; by increasing the time your students spend in active learning; by learning students' names; by improving your ability to demonstrate and explain new skills, always checking for understanding before students practice; by actively supervising the instructional area; by providing more effective practice; and by increasing the amount of positive, specific, and corrective feedback that you give.

CHAPTER 11

Teaching Styles and Strategies to Meet Learners' Needs

I am very excited about the new teaching strategy I am using in physical education called GeoGym. GeoGym utilizes computer technology (GeoSafari computer game) and core curriculum in various fitness and game activities allowing students to focus on their individual self-paced needs. In addition, it creates socialization through cooperative learning, encourages peer tutoring, and allows for a variety of student learning styles to be met in the learning environment of the gym.

—Physical Educator Kathleen Engle, Central District Middle School Teacher of the Year 1995, New Castle, New York

Although Mosston and Ashworth had identified a variety of teaching styles, which they called the "Spectrum of Teaching Styles," in *Teaching Physical Education* (1st ed., 1968), my own teacher training in the 1970s primarily taught me simply to explain and demonstrate motor skills to students. I learned to follow this with having everyone practice the same skill simultaneously in the same way and to give students feedback afterward. As I visit classes across the United States today, this is the same strategy I still observe in the majority of classes. This style of teaching, often referred to as direct instruction, or the behaviorist approach, saves instructional time and leads to significant learning when the content can be learned in a strictly sequential, progressive manner. Direct instruction, however, is not appropriate for teaching skills requiring higher-order thinking and unstructured organization. These situations require a more indirect, or constructivist, approach. In this chapter, we'll look at different ways you can vary your teaching styles and instructional strategies as well as at how you can incorporate specific methods that work well with limited-English proficient (LEP) students.

Teaching Styles

In "Spectrum of Teaching Styles," Mosston and Ashworth categorize instruction according to the types of instructional decisions made by both the teacher and the students, including the decisions made before, during, and immediately after a lesson. In their most recent edition of their popular textbook (published in 1994), they identify 11 teaching styles: command, practice, reciprocal, self-check, inclusion, guided discovery, convergent discovery, divergent production, individual program-learner's design, learner-initiated, and self-teaching. The styles are on a continuum from the command style, for which the teacher makes all of the decisions, to the self-teaching style, for which the students make virtually all of their own decisions about the learning process.

When the "Spectrum of Teaching Styles" was first published, many teachers thought they should make it their goal to move their instruction from the command style to the self-teaching style. In their 1994 edition of *Teaching Physical Education*, however, Mosston and Ashworth clarified their position, explaining that every style has a place, depending on the particular situation (time and environment), students, teacher, and content. So let's examine each of these styles and identify when each may be appropriate. Although my examples are of lessons that focus exclusively on one style, feel free to mix styles as appropriate in any lesson you teach.

Command

In the command style of teaching, you make all the decisions. You give step-by-step instructions, for example, demonstrating a dance sequence or skill, and the students copy each step. In other words, all students perform the same task at the same time as directed by you. This style is often appropriate for the initial stage of learning, especially for situations in which safety is a concern, such as for beginning swimming and archery. The command style is also appropriate when instructional time is limited or student behavior dictates a highly structured class routine.

Command Style Sample Lesson: Grapevine Dance Step

Objective

Students demonstrate the correct technique for the grapevine dance step.

Activities

1. Demonstrate the starting position with your feet together, facing the front of the room with your back to the students.
2. Have the students face the front of the room with their feet together and give them feedback.
3. Say "Step right" and take one step to the right.
4. Have the students step right and give them feedback.
5. Say "Step left behind right" and perform the step.
6. Have the students step left behind right and give them feedback.
7. Say "Step right" and perform the step.
8. Have the students step right and give them feedback.
9. Say "Close left" and perform the step.
10. Have the students close left and give them feedback.

Practice

The practice style is the most commonly used style in physical education. In the practice style, you determine what you'll teach, introducing the skills and tasks through demonstration or the use of task cards (see chapter 12 for sample task cards). Then the students determine the number of practice trials and often the order in which they will practice the tasks (if there is more than one) within the time you allocate. During the practice time, you circulate throughout class, giving feedback and answering questions initiated by the students.

Like the command style, the practice style is also most appropriate for the initial stage of learning and when you don't have much instructional time. Unlike the command style, however, the practice style does give students more time to master motor skills and concepts as well as more responsibility for their own learning. But if like most physical educators you do the majority of your teaching in this style, it may be helpful to reevaluate your lessons and determine which ones you might be able to teach more effectively using another style.

Reciprocal

In the reciprocal style, students give each other feedback. You, however, determine the task they'll practice and identify the critical features for them. Before starting the activity phase of the lesson, you

---

Practice Style Sample Lesson: Soccer Skills

Objectives

Students demonstrate the correct technique for dribbling.

Students demonstrate the correct technique for passing.

Students demonstrate the correct technique for trapping.

Students demonstrate the correct technique for dribbling, passing, and trapping while combining the three skills.

Students demonstrate the correct technique for shooting and guarding the goal.

Students demonstrate the correct technique for all skills during a four-on-four game.

Activities

After you review each skill, have students rotate through the following stations in groups of four. At each station, place a task card describing that station's activity. I have written the instructions as a model of how to word your own task cards so that students can easily follow them. The information in the parentheses is for you only, however. Keep in mind that a lesson can be longer than one instructional period.

1. (Set up two lines of five cones—the distance between the cones depends on how much space is available.) Divide your group of four into two pairs. Each pair of players takes turns dribbling around one line of cones.

2. (Set up two goal areas, marking each area with two cones.) Divide your group of four into two pairs, one pair for each goal area. One partner shoots while the other partner guards the goal area. Switch positions after five attempts.

3. On the computer, research the history of soccer, noting how the game has changed throughout the years.

4. In pairs, dribble the ball up and down the field, passing the ball every five yards.

5. Play a Four-on-Four Minisoccer game against the group at station six.

6. Play a Four-on-Four Minisoccer game against the group at station five.

7. (Mark two areas with four boundary cones for each pair to play in.) Divide your group into two pairs. Each pair plays One-on-One Keep-Away, staying within the marked area. The player without the ball tries to steal the ball away. If the ball goes out of bounds, the ball is given to the player who did not kick it out of bounds.

8. Play a Two-on-Two Keep-Away game. The team with the ball can dribble and pass anywhere in the marked area. The other team tries to steal the ball. If the ball goes out of bounds, the ball is given to the team that didn't kick it out of bounds.

9. (Provide students with a checklist of critical features for each skill.) Watch the video to review the skills of passing, trapping, dribbling, shooting, and defending the goal, and check the critical elements you observe.

10. Divide your group into two pairs. Each pair passes the ball back and forth, trapping the ball to bring it under control.

11. Divide your group into two pairs. Each pair takes turns shooting the ball at a target on the wall.

12. (Provide appropriate reading and writing materials.) Read about the biomechanical principle of absorption of force and write a paragraph explaining how it relates to soccer.

You circulate from station to station, providing feedback and indicating when students must rotate to the next station.

Adapted, by permission, from B. Mohnsen, 1995, Building a Quality Physical Education Program (Grades 6-12) (Medina, WA: Institute for Educational Development), 67.

check for student understanding by providing a number of demonstrations that include common errors, asking students to identify the errors and give you appropriate feedback. Then have students work in pairs. While one student (the doer) performs the task, the second student (the observer) gives feedback, reversing roles as appropriate. For this style, it is helpful to provide students with a checklist or criteria sheet with pictures (if possible) to remind them of the critical features they are looking for in the performance.

You circulate from pair to pair, communicating only with the observer who is providing the feedback. If the observer correctly identifies the error and gives the appropriate feedback, then you give positive, specific feedback to the observer. If, however, the observer incorrectly identifies the error or provides inappropriate feedback, then you give corrective feedback to the observer. Refrain from speaking directly to the doer so as not to disrupt the student-to-student relationship this style fosters.

Because the reciprocal style does emphasize social relationships, it can help students learn social as well as motor skills, making it especially effective with middle school students. Limit its use, however, to the review of previously learned skills. This is because the learning of a new skill requires accurate feedback and coverage of safety rules, which often cannot be delivered by someone who is just learning the new skill themselves.

Self-Check

In the self-checking style, the feedback comes from the learners themselves. You still determine the task the students will practice and identify its critical features. For this style, however, you must select a

---

Reciprocal Style Sample Lesson: Front Crawl Stroke

Objectives

Students identify the critical features of the crawl stroke.

Students demonstrate cooperation by helping partners learn the crawl stroke.

Students demonstrate the correct technique for the crawl stroke.

Activities

1. Review the crawl stroke.

2. Identify the critical features of the crawl stroke.

3. Demonstrate the crawl stroke incorrectly, requesting feedback from several students.

4. Have students practice the crawl stroke in pairs. Ask one student to perform the stroke while the other student gives feedback. Have the student giving feedback focus first on the arms, then on the breathing, and then on the kick. Have students use the following criteria sheet to guide their feedback. Laminate forms so they stand up to the deck and pool environment and can be used for many years.

Arms

- Places hand of one arm in water in line with the shoulder.

- Bends elbow slightly as hand pushes water down the center of the body toward the feet.

- Stops hand at the thigh and, without hesitating, lifts the arm out of the water with the shoulder and elbow.

- While pushing one arm underwater, recovers the other arm over the water.

Breathing and arms

- Turns head to one side, angling the chin slightly up.

- Inhales (breathes in) quickly through the mouth.

- Turns head back down and exhales (breathes out) from mouth.

Kick

- Begins up and down flutter kick at hip.

- Bends knee downward slightly at the start of the kick.

- Straightens knee on the up beat.

- Barely breaks the surface of the water with the heel on the up kick.

You give feedback to the student observers.

Adapted, by permission, from B. Mohnsen, 1995, *Building a Quality Physical Education Program (Grades 6-12)* (Medina, WA: Institute for Educational Development), 68.

task that students can evaluate for themselves. Typically, activities such as throwing and shooting for accuracy are appropriate because students can clearly see for themselves the results of their efforts. On the continuum of teaching styles, this style gives students opportunities to become more self-reliant as they determine how to address their own limitations and how to use their practice time effectively. Unfortunately, however, this style does limit the interaction between you and your students and between students. Therefore, I don't recommend that you use it much in middle school physical education.

Inclusion

Because the inclusion style gives middle school students the feeling of success so important to them, it is especially well-suited to the middle school physical education setting. In the inclusion style, you still determine the task your students will practice and identify its critical features, but you also give students a choice of performance levels for the task from which they may select the level of practice they think is right for them. Factors that alter the performance level of the task include the size and weight of an object; size, distance, and height of a target; body position; and quantity or quality of performance. For example, when performing push-ups, let students choose from wall push-ups (the easiest form), chair push-ups, modified push-ups, regular push-ups, and elevated feet push-ups (the hardest form).

In the inclusion style, it is the students' responsibility to determine when they are ready to move to a more difficult performance level. This style is ideal for middle school heterogeneous classes, because it accommodates all learners at their levels of readiness. This style also takes the students one step closer to taking full responsibility for their own learning.

Self-Checking Style Sample Lesson: Full Golf Swing

Objectives

Students demonstrate the correct technique for the full golf swing, using an iron club.

Students demonstrate responsibility by assessing their own performances.

Students develop a practice plan for improving their golf swings.

Activities

1. Review the full golf swing.

2. Introduce and demonstrate the concept of shadow golf.

3. Have students line up with their backs to the sun, each with iron club and five tees in-hand.

4. Have students place tees on their own shadows as follows:

   First—top of head

   Second—back hip line

   Third—back knee line

   Fourth—three inches forward of shadow of front hip line

   Fifth—forward of head toward target

5. Have students practice three steps of golf swing, checking their own body positions as follows:

   Stance—shadow line in contact with first through third tees

   Backswing—shadow line remains in contact with first through third tees

   Follow-through—maintain shadow line with first tee and move shadow forward to fourth tee and hands to fifth tee

6. Have students gradually increase the distance of their fourth tees from their shadows to four, five, then six inches while maintaining shadow contact with the first tee.

Homework

Have students develop a practice plan for improving their golf swing technique. Encourage students to use their understanding of developing and improving the performance of closed skills, performed in a stable environment (learned in previous lessons), to write their practice plans.

Adapted, by permission, from B. Mohnsen, 1995, *Building a Quality Physical Education Program (Grades 6-12)* (Medina, WA: Institute for Educational Development), 70.

Inclusion Style Sample Lesson: Clear Stroke, Using Badminton Equipment

Objectives

Students improve the accuracy of the forehand underhand clear, the forehand overhead clear, the backhand underhand clear, and the backhand overhead clear.

Students demonstrate responsibility for selecting the appropriate practice setting.

Activities

1. Set up each court in the gymnasium or outside area for clear stroke practice. Mark one side of the court in three places down the center of the court at different distances from the net. Mark the other side of the court with a large rectangular area and a smaller rectangular area.

2. Have students select one of the three distances from the net to begin practicing. Allow students to make 10 attempts to hit the shuttlecock into the large target area, using one of the four clear strokes. Based on their success, allow students to choose to aim either for the large target area again or to try for the smaller target area. After successfully hitting the shuttlecock into the smaller area, allow students to decide whether they want to move farther from the net or try a different clear stroke.

Adapted, by permission, from B. Mohnsen, 1995, *Building a Quality Physical Education Program (Grades 6-12)* (Medina, WA: Institute for Educational Development), 73.

Guided Discovery

In the guided discovery style, you determine the task and then arrange a sequence of problems or questions that, when solved by the students, leads to the one correct response. The students must give a verbal or motor response to each of your prompts. Thus, the students improve their motor performances by using their higher-order thinking skills to discover the correct technique for a particular skill.

When using the guided discovery style, you must give students sufficient time to think through each

Guided Discovery Style Sample Lesson: Long Jump

Objectives

Students demonstrate the correct technique for the long jump.

Students explain how to increase their jumps, using the biomechanical principles of projectiles.

Students use higher-order thinking skills to discover the correct technique for the long jump.

Activities

1. Ask students a series of questions in order to help them understand the correct technique for the long jump and to increase the distances of their jumps.

   • Is it better to start the long jump from a running or standing position?

     (Anticipated answer: Running.)

   • Is it better to run fast or slow?

     (Anticipated answer: Fast.)

   • Is it better to take off from one or two feet?

     (Anticipated answer: One.)

   • Is it better to land with knees bent or straight?

     (Anticipated answer: Bent.)

   • Is it better to fall forward or backward on landing?

     (Anticipated answer: Forward.)

2. If some students respond incorrectly to a question, you can ask the students with the correct answer to explain the reason for the correct answer. If most or all students respond incorrectly to the question, ask them to experiment with the skill in order to determine why the other choice is correct.

Homework

Have students write an essay describing or draw a picture illustrating the correct technique for the running long jump.

Adapted, by permission, from B. Mohnsen, 1995, *Building a Quality Physical Education Program (Grades 6-12)* (Medina, WA: Institute for Educational Development), 74.

question or problem. And be prepared to adjust your questions or problems, depending on the students' responses. If all or most students respond incorrectly to the prompt or question, you will need to present an activity through which students can test their answers.

When using this style, your role is not simply to ask questions, but to logically guide students to the correct solution. Indeed, students' success will depend on your ability to ask the appropriate questions at the right time. The strength of this style is that, although it takes more time and you are leading students to the *one* correct answer, students are more likely to remember the information than if you had simply told them the answer.

Convergent Discovery

Extending the guided discovery style, the convergent discovery style is new to the "Spectrum of Teaching Styles." In the convergent discovery style, the learner proceeds through the discovery process without any guiding clues from you. In addition to the benefits of the guided discovery style, this style encourages students to take on even more responsibility for their own learning. I recommend using this style after your students have demonstrated success with the guided discovery approach. Both the guided discovery and convergent discovery styles are useful in the middle school setting as long as you select learning activities through which the students are able to discover the correct answer—either through your use of questions or problems or through student trial and error.

Divergent Production

I prefer to think of the divergent production style as the problem solving style. You select the task and design a problem that can be solved in a variety of ways. Then you ask students to discover different solutions to the problem and evaluate the effectiveness of each solution. This style improves student motor performances by showing students that many possibilities for skillful and efficient movement exist.

Problem solving conditions are best for learning tasks similar to tasks students have already mastered. I have found this style effective in team building activities in which small groups of students must work together to find a solution to a physical

---

Convergent Discovery Style Sample Lesson: Generating Force

Objectives

Students demonstrate the correct technique for the overhand throw.

Students use higher-order thinking skills to discover the relationship between throwing a ball farther and the size of the ball, weight of the ball, and approach before releasing the ball.

Activities

1. Ask students to experiment with throwing several balls of different sizes and weights. Present the students with the following problem: What relationships exist between throwing the ball farther and

   • the size of the ball?

   • the weight of the ball?

   • the length of the approach before releasing the ball?

2. Have students record their findings on a worksheet or in their notebooks.

Homework

Ask students to draw pictures or create charts depicting the relationships between the size and weight of the ball, length of the approach before releasing the ball, and the distance the ball travels.

---

challenge. Indeed, this style is especially effective for developing social skills.

Individual Program-Learner's Design

In this style, the responsibility for designing the task, question, or problem shifts from you to the learner. You still choose the general subject material, but you allow the learner to choose the specific question and determine possible solutions. This style provides learners with opportunities to develop their own learning programs, based on their capabilities, intelligences, and learning styles. Other than for assigning the development of special projects, middle school physical educators

Divergent Style Sample Lesson: Game Design

Objectives

Students demonstrate their understanding of rules, boundaries, and strategies by developing their own games.

Students use higher-order thinking skills in the creation of their new games.

Students collaborate to develop their new games.

Activities

1. Explain to students the five important elements of a game are as follows:

   - Boundaries—large areas, small areas, specific dimensions
   - Equipment—bats, balls, gloves, beanbags
   - Players—numbers, positions
   - Scoring—how to score, scoring options, point value
   - Penalties—illegal events and penalties for those events

2. Have groups of four students each develop a game. Once developed, have each group teach their game to another group.

Adapted, by permission, from B. Mohnsen, 1995, *Building a Quality Physical Education Program (Grades 6-12)* (Medina, WA: Institute for Educational Development), 77.

Individual Program-Learner's Design Style Sample Lesson: Exercise Physiology and Health-Related Fitness

Objectives

Students improve their personal fitness.

Students develop personalized fitness plans, based on their own fitness levels.

Activities

1. Introduce the exercise physiology and health-related fitness unit to be sure students have a basic understanding of the principles and concepts related to health-related fitness.

2. Have students select their own questions or problems related to improving their personal fitness.

3. Have students each research an area of interest and share the information with one other student.

Adapted, by permission, from B. Mohnsen, 1995, *Building a Quality Physical Education Program (Grades 6-12)* (Medina, WA: Institute for Educational Development), 78.

rarely use this style. As schools restructure for the 21st century and instruction becomes more individualized, however, we should use this style more often.

Learner-Initiated

The learner-initiated style is similar to the individual program-learner's design style, except that learners initiate the style for themselves. The students approach you and state their willingness to initiate and conduct learning activities. For students who are ready, this style allows them to initiate their own learning projects. Like the individual program-learner's design style, we don't use this style very often at present, yet we should strive to include it more as we move into the 21st century.

Self-Teaching

The self-teaching style is at the opposite end of the spectrum from the command style. In this style, learners make virtually all the decisions on their own without any input or assistance from the teacher. If able to implement this style, individuals truly become lifelong learners, capable of creating their own learning experiences. This style does not currently exist in the classroom; however, it does exist in real life. To this end, encourage students to pursue their own educational interests, based on their own capabilities and needs both outside the school setting as well as, when possible, within the school setting.

Instructional Strategies

Whereas teaching styles address the question of who is making the decisions about instruction, in-

Learner-Initiated Style Sample Lesson: Motor Learning

Objectives

Students improve their motor skills in activities of their own choosing.

Students develop personalized learning plans for activities of their own choosing, based on their current performance levels.

Activities

1. Encourage students to approach you with ideas on how to teach themselves a skill or activity.

2. Have students plan the entire learning process as well as the criteria they'll use in the evaluation process.

3. Have students explain their learning plans while you listen, ask questions, and point out when they have omitted important decisions.

4. Have students implement their learning plans.

5. Learners produce final projects, demonstrating their learning.

Adapted, by permission, from B. Mohnsen, 1995, *Building a Quality Physical Education Program (Grades 6-12)* (Medina, WA: Institute for Educational Development), 79.

structional strategies refer to the arrangement of the teacher, learner, and environment. You can choose from many instructional strategies; however, I have found two that are especially effective with middle school students: station teaching and cooperative learning.

Station Teaching

The station teaching strategy in which students in small groups rotate from learning center to learning center effectively and efficiently provides students with a variety of drills or tasks (see figure 11.1). This strategy works especially well when your equipment or space is limited because—although some stations may require a great deal of equipment and space—many stations require very little or different equipment or space. The station approach can also give students opportunities to practice and apply the same skill to different situations—crucial to mastering open skills.

To employ the station approach, set up different activities around the gymnasium, room, or outdoor area. Divide the class into an equal number of groups and assign each group to a different starting station. To keep students focused at each station, place a task card describing what you want them to perform or accomplish there. Make sure that the time required to complete each task is about the same so that students at one station are not waiting

Figure 11.1 Middle school students enjoy using a variety of equipment to improve cardiorespiratory endurance.

for other students to finish their tasks before rotating. Many teachers have found it effective to have students complete a data collection sheet at each station, making students accountable for completing the work.

Planning for the stations requires a great deal of thought. Will the stations focus on a variety of activities (e.g., different gymnastics equipment or track and field events), a review of several skills (e.g., forearm pass, set, spike, serve, and block for volleyball) for a given sport, or on the application of one skill (e.g., overhand movement pattern) in a variety of activities or sports? Whatever your plan, it is best at first to introduce only three or four types of stations, setting up more than one of each type as necessary to keep groups small. In most cases, you'll need to give students some instruction regarding each station before allowing them to try them. So by limiting the number of initial stations, you limit the amount of lecture time. Then, you can gradually add three or four more stations every day or two until every station is unique. Later, you can change or alter stations as necessary.

You can use this strategy with a variety of teaching styles, including reciprocal, self-check, and inclusion. Either you, a peer, or the student himself gives feedback, depending on the teaching style you choose. Be careful, however, to keep the tasks fairly simple so that students can work independently as you circulate, offering feedback and noting special needs.

Cooperative Learning

Cooperative learning is a unique strategy that promotes the development of social skills while augmenting learning. Numerous studies have shown that cooperative learning results in greater achievement gains, improved cross-cultural friendships, increased social skills, enhanced self-esteem, greater interdependence (teamwork), increased cognitive and affective abilities, and an improved classroom climate (Johnson and Johnson 1991). Thus, it's an effective strategy for middle school students.

Be aware, however, that putting students into groups is not in and of itself cooperative learning. True cooperative learning requires (1) the formation of heterogeneous teams, (2) the establishment of positive interdependence and individual accountability, (3) the opportunity for team members to get acquainted with one another and establish a team identity, (4) the use of an established structure, and (5) the opportunity to debrief the situation. When teachers first started using this strategy, they used extrinsic rewards (including grades) to motivate students to work cooperatively to achieve a common goal. As we discussed in chapter 9, however, extrinsic rewards are not necessary if you make sure that the learning tasks are challenging and meaningful, if you allow students to make some key decisions about what they are doing, and if you emphasize students helping one another to learn.

Form heterogeneous teams.   To get started using cooperative learning, form teams that include a balance of gender, ethnicity, ability, and other aspects. You can randomly assign students to teams and then check to ensure that each team is heterogeneous or rank students according to ability and then assign students to teams by selecting one student from the top, one from the bottom, and several from the middle. Usually, cooperative groups range in size from four to six; however, partners work well, too.

Establish positive interdependence and individual accountability.   For the second step of cooperative learning, set up one task to be accomplished by each group. Ensure that the task (e.g., report, project, skill development) can only be completed if the students cooperate. This establishes positive interdependence among team members. For example, assign a group the task of developing a report on the modern Olympics or of analyzing the overhand movement pattern. Each group turns in one report or project.

Sometimes, a group may tend to lean on the most able or most committed member, expecting this member to accomplish the task alone. In order to eliminate this possibility, establish individual accountability, making sure each member has a specific task (e.g., striking with hand, striking with short object, striking with long object), role (e.g., facilitator, arbitrator, encourager, equipment manager), or resource (e.g., textbooks, videos, software), ensuring that she must contribute to the successful completion of the task. In this way, group success will depend on the individual learning of all group members. Remember, to create an effective cooperative learning structure, you must address both positive interdependence and individual accountability.

Team building.   Think about the last time you joined a committee or group. Did the group immediately begin to work on the topic or did the committee members spend some time getting to know each other? The Tuckman's team development model looks at four stages of development: forming, storming, norming, and performing. At the forming stage of team building, members become acquainted by learning each other's names, backgrounds, and interests. At the storming stage of development, the group determines who in the group will have the most power to make the decisions. This is a good time to introduce social initiatives (physical or mental challenges that groups must work together to solve) or physical challenges in which group members must support one another in order to be successful, increasing the level of trust among team members (see Project Adventure unit in chapter 16). At the norming stage, members determine roles and make decisions through consensus. Asking the group members to establish a team name and determine the outcome of their work together is appropriate for this stage. Finally, at the performing stage, group members see the value of working together and are ready for you to tell them (or for the group to select) the specific structure that they will use to complete their task.

Although this model is typically used with adult work groups, the steps are just as important for middle school cooperative learning groups. Indeed, students need time to get to know one another and develop trust before being presented with a task. Therefore, use cooperative games, social initiatives, and physical challenges with middle school students, helping them establish their group or team identities whenever new groups are formed.

Structures.   The structure or format determines how students will work together in cooperative learning groups. Although quite a few structures exist, we'll limit our discussion to four of the more popular ones appropriate for middle school physical education: think, pair, share; numbered heads; STAD (student teams achievement divisions); and jigsawing (Kagan 1989).

For think, pair, share, you ask students to work in partners. Pose a question and give students time to think about their answers. For example, you might ask "Which area of health-related fitness is most important?" After students have time to think about their answers, have them share their responses (e.g., "cardiorespiratory endurance") with their partners. The partners then question one another about their answers in order to help one another refine their thinking (e.g., "Why do you think cardiorespiratory endurance is the most important?").

For numbered heads, you also ask students to work in partners. Pose a question, such as, "What are the five areas of health-related fitness?" Then ask students to discuss their answers with their partners to ensure that both of them will be able to name the five areas if called on. Then you call on one student in one pair to share the answer.

For STAD, assign the students to four-member groups. Present the lesson and supply instructional materials, such as information sheets and checklists of critical features for motor skills. Then have groups ensure that all team members master the information. You should usually assess students (written test, motor skills test) on an individual basis; however, some teachers on some occasions assess group members together. Your lesson material can be a cognitive concept or a motor skill. For example, team members can work together to master juggling. Using the reciprocal style from the "Spectrum of Teaching Styles," have students give each other feedback so that each member learns to juggle.

For jigsawing, assign students to home teams of four to six members. Then let each member of the home team select a different piece of the material to learn. For example, if students are learning the rules of softball, then the four-member teams divide up the pitching, baserunning, batting, and miscellaneous rules. Next have students from different teams, who have similar pieces of information, form expert groups to discuss their information and to develop a presentation for their home teams. Expert groups should be no larger than six members, so you may need to form double or triple expert groups covering the same material. Finally, have the students return to their home teams to share their information. Ask all students to take a quiz or complete a project on an individual or group basis to assess their learning of *all* the softball rules.

Debriefing.   Unfortunately, teachers often omit this last, but not least, step either due to lack of time or to feeling uncomfortable with the facilitator role. Like anything else in teaching, practice and experience can help you feel more comfortable with completing this task. Mercier (1992) suggests several processing questions that you should have students answer to debrief an activity:

- Was the task completed?

- If not, why?

- How did it feel to have someone accept your suggestion?

- How did it feel to have someone compliment you?

- What can you do next time to make your group work more successfully?

- What were some encouraging things you saw or heard?

By allowing students time to process their learning, this step ensures that they practice social skills as well as learn what you planned.

Cooperative Learning Sample Lesson: Jigsawing

Objective

Students increase knowledge about wilderness survival.

Preparation

1. Assign students to one of eight heterogeneous groups of five (six if necessary). These groups are their home teams.

2. After several preliminary team building activities (see Project Adventure unit in chapter 16), give a short introduction to wilderness survival and the jigsawing activity.

3. Give each group time to decide who will specialize in each of the following areas: navigating and traveling, setting up camp, obtaining food and water, maintaining health and giving first aid, and dealing with wildlife (in groups with six members, two will specialize in the same area).

4. Once each student has selected a role, form expert groups for each area of specialization. If necessary, form more than one group for each area, keeping expert group size to no more than six members.

Expert Activity

Have each expert group read through the chapter or material on their area, noting important points. Have other resources available so that students who finish early can use the extra time to find additional information. If students have difficulty reading the material, the group can read through it together. Once all group members have read and taken notes on the chapter, have each group prepare a presentation for their home group.

Home Group Activity

Have each team member return to her home group to present her findings. At this point, the students will be very dependent on one another for the knowledge their teammates gained in their expert groups.

Concluding Group Activity

After each expert has had a chance to present their information, use the last day of the unit, to present each group with a different outdoor education survival scenario that they must resolve using the information they have learned throughout the unit.

Adapted, by permission, from B. Mohnsen, 1994, *Using Technology in Physical Education* (Champaign, IL: Human Kinetics).

Working With Limited-English Proficient Students

Working with limited-English proficient (LEP) students calls for the use of additional teaching methods (often referred to as sheltered instruction or SDAIE—specially designed academic instruction in English) in order for these students to understand the information you're presenting in English. Specifically, employ the following four methods to ensure the LEP student's success:

1. Create a supportive environment.

2. Use a variety of instructional strategies, including cooperative learning.

3. Make sure information is comprehensible to the students.

4. Include a technique referred to as "total physical response" (TPR).

It is interesting to note that these methods also work well with English proficient students and should therefore be included by effective teachers in all classes. In this section, let's look closely at each element that contributes to the LEP student's success.

Supportive Environment

We discussed the importance of developing a supportive learning environment in chapters 5 and 9. It is important, however, to ensure that all students are benefiting equally from the supportive learning environment that you have established. Naturally, if either you or other students target non-English or limited-English speaking students for ridicule, these students will begin to feel isolated and rejected, becoming less likely to risk either verbal or motor participation. In contrast, if you model respect for these students by asking them to share their unique experiences for the educational benefit of all students in the class, they will develop stronger self-esteem and take more responsibility for their own learning, thereby living up to the expectations you communicate to them.

It also helps if you become more informed about your students' cultures. Then you'll be able to acknowledge and incorporate various aspects of these cultures into the learning experiences of all your students. This will also help the non-English or limited-English speaking students feel more comfortable in your class. To further help these students, establish consistent patterns and routines so that they will have a better idea of what is coming next in the lesson.

Moreover, I encourage you to establish an environment in which these students not only grow in terms of physical education but also in terms of English language acquisition. Within the context of a supportive environment, two techniques that you can use to help them learn English work well. First, avoid forcing these students to speak. Keep in mind that it often takes non-English speaking students six months to a year before they have mastered enough English to communicate. Second, when the students begin to speak English, correct their errors *only* through "verbal mirroring." For example, if a student says "My clothes home," you should respond, "I see. You left your clothes at home."

Variety of Strategies, Including Cooperative Learning

The English speaking students in your class represent various levels of motor skill ability, divergent learning styles, and different primary intelligences. So too do the limited- and non-English speaking students in your classes. Therefore, both groups need a variety of interactive strategies and teaching styles in order to be successful. The use of technology (see chapter 12) and cooperative learning strategies have proven especially effective with non- or limited-English speaking students. If possible, when setting up cooperative learning groups, make sure that you place a bilingual student (who speaks the same language) in every group that has a limited- or non-English speaking student. In this way, the limited- or non-English speaking student will have someone to share ideas and information with in her dominant language.

Comprehensible Input

During a sheltered-English workshop that I attended, the instructor gave a lesson in German. She stood in one place and without using any facial features whatsoever rambled on in German for 20 minutes. Not one person in the room had any idea what she was saying. Then, she began the lesson again. This time she began to hold up prompts, such as toy people, small balls, and plastic horses. She pointed to pictures and ran around the room acting out various parts of her presentation. Although, we still did not understand a word of German, this time we understood that she was reenacting a polo match.

Providing information to students in both languages simultaneously only causes confusion to the learner (Wong-Fillmore 1980). Therefore, if you have classes that include both English and limited-English speaking students, convey the information in English and use a number of sheltered strategies to ensure that the information is comprehensible to the limited-English speaking students. It is also important that you deliver the information within the appropriate context because isolated pieces of information lack relevance and connection, making it even more difficult for limited-English speaking students to understand new words. Finally, if at all possible, use a translator when conveying new information to non-English speaking students.

Sheltered Strategies

Reinforce key concepts over and over again.

Check often for student understanding.

Slow down speech pattern.

Pause frequently.

Enunciate clearly.

Emphasize key words or phrases.

Use visual aids, gestures, organizers, and other realia.

Demonstrate concepts.

Simplify information.

Expand on student's ideas by asking additional questions.

Provide definitions.

Make comparisons.

Total Physical Response

Asher (1977), the developer of total physical response (TPR), was a pioneer in second language learning. He maintains that learning on the immediate, physical, and gut levels actually speeds language acquisition dramatically. TPR is actually an English language development (ELD) method used with non-English speakers; however, since physical education classes contain both non- and limited-English proficient students, this method is appropriate for physical education.

All physical educators and second language acquisition teachers must recognize the link between physical activity and language acquisition. Indeed, the teaching of new vocabulary words in English, English as a second language (ESL), and physical education classes, must include physical involvement. For example, the best way to teach words such as over, under, behind, walk, skip, jump, fast, and slow is through a physical demonstration by you, followed by a physical response on the part of the student. Certainly, some words may require creativity on your part in order to convey their meanings to students. For example, the term "cardiorespiratory" does not easily translate into the physical. Creative teachers, however, have developed heart-lung models that students physically move through in order to better understand the cardiorespiratory system and its function, a boon to all students—not only those who are struggling with English. Fortunately in physical education you can communicate most of the motor skill vocabulary to students by demonstrating the skill, repeating the appropriate vocabulary, and having the students practice the skill.

Summary

As a physical educator, you'll often work with 20 to 60 different learning styles during one instructional period. Taking into consideration recent research on "brain-based" learning, you must ensure that learning is hands-on, relevant, and student-centered. You must base your selection of the specific teaching style or strategy on both the content and the learning styles of the students. By employing a wide variety of instructional styles and strategies, you will engage and promote learning for all. In the next chapter, we'll examine various types of instructional materials that can help you teach even better.

CHAPTER 12

Selecting Instructional Materials

The relationship between exercise and good nutrition is strong. In order for our students to make healthy choices about the foods they eat, they must first know what is in the foods they are choosing. The *DINE Healthy* software package allows the students to do a complete nutritional analysis of their diet and provides information for adjusting their diet and personal exercise plan according to the dietary information [see appendix D]. Analysis results can be printed out in chart, graph, and message form. We have found *DINE Healthy* to be one of the most user-friendly, yet comprehensive, software packages available.

—Physical Educator Susan Sellers, Einstein Middle School, Seattle, Washington

We know that some of our students are kinesthetic learners, some are visual learners, and some are auditory learners. They come to us with strengths in one or more of the multiple intelligences as well. Because we emphasize movement in physical education, we tend to do an excellent job of engaging bodily-kinesthetic learners. Even the auditory learner may fare well through oral communication. But what about the visual learners and those students with strengths in the other intelligences? Are we reaching all of our students through movement and oral communication, or do we need to provide them with other avenues to the information we're trying to teach?

By using a wide variety of visual and auditory aids, task cards, worksheets, textbooks, simulations, videos, laser discs, camcorders, software for data management, other technological devices, telecommunications, instructional software, and virtual reality hardware and software, you can increase the involvement of all your students in the instructional process. Perhaps as importantly, you'll be preparing them to use the tools of the 21st century. In this chapter, I'll describe many types of instructional materials and provide samples of appropriate materials for a middle school program.

Visual and Auditory Aids

Visual aids can provide visual learners with the additional information they need in order to better understand the concepts you're explaining. Pictures, charts, graphs, and diagrams are fairly common in physical education, but have you ever used models? Models are three-dimensional representations of real-life events. They can be made out of boards that depict playing fields and toy people for you to demonstrate how players move during a real game. But don't forget pictures, charts, graphs, and diagrams: Display them on chalkboards and posters or with overhead projectors or slides.

Naturally, auditory aids are especially effective with

Visual Aids

Pictures: still images of sport skill techniques

Chart: calendar showing frequency, intensity, time, and type of exercise over a week

Graph: showing average heart rate before, during, and after aerobic exercise

Diagrams: offensive basketball plays

Models: soccer players demonstrating offensive and defensive situations

auditory learners. These aids include classical music for relaxation, a variety of music to accompany different movement experiences (e.g., exercising, tumbling routines), or recordings that explain specific concepts.

Task Cards for Golf Unit

Station 1: Chip, Pitch, and Catch

Pair off and face each other at a starting distance of 20 feet. Chip the practice ball back and forth to each other. Gradually move farther apart until reaching pitching distance (30 yards). Continue activity using pitching stroke. Give your partner feedback on their stroke.

Station 2: Line Putting

Take turns with a partner putting 10 balls toward a line 24 feet away. If you come within 18 inches of the line, you score 5 points; within 36 inches you score 3 points; and within 4 feet you score 1 point. Give each other feedback and count scores for each other.

Station 3: Bull's-Eye Golf for Driving

[The target area is concentric circles expanding in size and decreasing in point values (high to low) from the center.] Find a partner and take turns driving 10 balls toward a target. Count your partner's score and give them feedback.

Station 4: Golf Bocci for Short Irons

To begin, have one of your group toss the target ball (colored tennis ball) in any direction and distance within the station area. Use a short iron to hit a golf ball at the tennis ball. The player coming the closest gets to toss the target ball for the next round.

Station 5: Obstacle Shot

Take turns with a partner hitting the ball over the crossbar on the goalposts into the scoring zones located just beyond the goalposts. There are three scoring zones (5, 3, 1) with the highest zone located closest to the goalposts. You only score points if the ball clears the crossbar.

Station 6: Ball Bounce

Take turns bouncing a golf ball off the face of a short iron. The other players count the number of times in a row contact is made before the ball touches the ground. Player bouncing the ball must keep some part of their hand on the grip at all times.

Station 7: Tee Track

Count the number of strokes it takes you to complete the track from start to finish. Count a penalty stroke whenever a ball goes out of bounds.

Station 8: Tee to Target

Complete one official hole of golf, practicing the correct etiquette.

Adapted from Professional Golfers' Association of America Junior Golf Foundation, 1987, *First Swing*.

SyberVision is one company that publishes auditory cassettes that explain various concepts related to athletic performance. When using auditory aids, it is important to have a good stereo system. Be sure to purchase or select one with a cassette player, a compact disc player, and good speakers so all students can hear clearly. In addition, a remote microphone can save your voice when you must give oral instructions to large groups or over music.

Task Cards

Task cards are typically used in station teaching. You can either purchase preprinted cards or create your own by hand or on a computer. Print each task on a separate card and post one card per station. Then have students in groups of four to six follow the directions on the task cards as they rotate through

---

Task Cards for Circus Skills Unit

Station 1: Instep Kick for Footbag Skills

Place a check mark next to every statement that accurately describes your partner's performance:

_____ Flexes support leg, placing weight on ball of foot.

_____ Brings kicking foot up to about knee height of support leg.

_____ Turns ankle to create a flat surface.

_____ Leans slightly from waist.

_____ Contacts ball on "flat" instep of foot.

Station 2: One- or Two-Scarf Cascade

Place a check mark next to every statement that accurately describes your partner's performance:

One-Scarf Cascade

_____ Holds scarf in center.

_____ Lifts arm high across chest.

_____ Tosses scarf with palm out.

_____ Reaches up with catching hand and catches straight down, clawing the scarf.

Two-Scarf Cascade

_____ Holds center of a scarf in each hand.

_____ Tosses first scarf high across chest with palm out.

_____ Throws second scarf as first scarf reaches peak.

_____ Claws first scarf.

_____ Claws second scarf.

Station 3: Ball Spinning—Inside Spin (counterclockwise)

Place a check mark next to every statement that accurately describes your partner's performance:

_____ Begins with ball at eye level in front of the shoulder.

_____ Keeps elbow out and palm up with the dot of ball on palm.

_____ Points thumb toward body.

_____ Spins ball counterclockwise, using wrist and forearm.

_____ Makes ball rise into air 6 to 12 inches.

_____ Catches ball with both hands.

Station 4: One-Ball Juggling

Place a check mark next to every statement that accurately describes your partner's performance:

_____ Throws ball from hand to hand in figure-eight pattern.

_____ Both hands use underhand throws.

_____ Releases ball toward midline of body.

_____ Catches toward outside of body.

_____ Keeps figure-eight pattern in a "box" below the top of the head.

Station 5: Ball Spinning—Outside Spin (clockwise)

Place a check mark next to every statement that accurately describes your partner's performance:

_____ Begins with ball at eye level in front of the shoulder.

_____ Keeps elbow out and palm up with the dot of ball on palm.

_____ Points thumb toward body.

_____ Spins ball clockwise, using wrist and forearm.

_____ Makes ball rise into air 6 to 12 inches.

_____ Catches ball with both hands.

the stations. Encourage students to compete against their own scores—not against each other.

> Make your task cards do double duty by incorporating the option of a reciprocal lesson. To do this, list the critical elements for each skill on its card so students can check a partner's performance. When making your own task cards, be sure to include color and graphics, and laminate them so that they withstand the tests of time and of middle school students. You can also encourage your students to make task cards for you. Kids can create wonderful and effective task cards.

Worksheets

Worksheets give students directions and a set format for written responses. For example, students fill in their own data and follow the directions to calculate their own personal target heart rate range. Or for a weight training unit exercise, students could identify the muscle that they worked on a worksheet. Another type of worksheet is a data collection sheet on which students record quantity information (e.g., distance, time, accuracy, heart rate). Later have students transfer data to a computer spreadsheet or analyze their own data.

Like task cards, many teachers have found that worksheets help keep students on-task. But don't let your students become dependent on worksheets, use them as one option, along with open-ended questions and logs.

Textbooks

Textbooks are relatively new to physical education. Currently, three types are available: sport activity textbooks, fitness-specific textbooks, and conceptually based textbooks. The *Australian Physical Education* books by Blackall contain information (playing area, skills, rules) on a variety of traditional activities (e.g., basketball, volleyball) separated into one activity per chapter. Two fitness books, *Fitness for Life* (Corbin and Lindsey 1990) and *Personal Fitness and You* (Stokes, Moore, and Schultz 1993) provide students with comprehensive information on the topic of fitness. You can purchase *Fitness for Life* with a teacher resource book that gives you instructional ideas for the teaching of fitness. Finally, the three books by Spindt, Monti, and Hennessy (1992) provide the first comprehensive textbook series for middle school students. The sixth grade book is

Computing Your Target Heart Rate Range

Name _____ Date _____ Class _____

Purpose: To identify a target heart rate zone, which is the safe and comfortable level of overload that you should maintain to achieve a training effect.

Procedure:

	Example	Lower	Upper
1. Calculate your maximum heart rate according to your age. 220 − age = maximum heart rate (MHR). Do for both upper and lower columns.	220 − 14 ‾‾‾‾ 206 MHR	220 − ___ ‾‾‾	220 − ___ ‾‾‾
2. Determine your resting heart rate by counting your pulse for 15 seconds before you get out of bed in the morning, then multiply the number by 4. Subtract RHR from MHR.	− 70 RHR 136	− ___	− ___
3. Multiply this number by percent overload, 60% for the lower limit and 80% for the upper limit.	×.60 ‾‾‾ 81	×.60	×.80
4. Add the resting heart rate.	+ 70 RHR	+	+
5. A is your lower limit of target heart rate for training effect and B is your safe upper limit.	151	A=	B=

Recovery Heart Rate Data Worksheet

Minutes after exercise

1 minute	_____
2 minutes	_____
3 minutes	_____
4 minutes	_____
5 minutes	_____
6 minutes	_____

Chart results on the graph:

180

125

75

0   1   2   3   4   5   6

Muscular Strength and Endurance Worksheet

As you rotate through each exercise, match the exercise with the muscle or muscle group that it works.

Wings	Deltoid
Butterfly	Pectoralis major
Rowing machine	Biceps brachii
Knee lifts	Rectus abdominus
Leg press	Quadriceps femoris
Military press	Trapezius
Lateral pulls	Latissimus dorsi
Lunges	Gluteus maximus
Toe press	Gastrocnemius
Bar dips	Triceps
Leg curls (flexion)	Hamstrings

Textbooks for Student Use

Australian Physical Education: Book 1 by Blackall from the Macmillan Company of Australia.

Australian Physical Education: Book 2 by Blackall from the Macmillan Company of Australia.

Fitness for Life by Corbin and Lindsey from Scott, Foresman and Company.

Personal Fitness and You by Stokes, Moore, and Schultz from Hunter Textbooks.

Moving With Confidence by Spindt, Monti, and Hennessy from Kendall/Hunt.

Moving With Skill by Spindt, Monti, and Hennessy from Kendall/Hunt.

Moving as a Team by Spindt, Monti, and Hennessy from Kendall/Hunt.

entitled *Moving With Confidence*, the seventh grade book is *Moving With Skill*, and the eighth grade book is *Moving as a Team*. This series covers motor skills, fitness, social skills, self-esteem concepts, pursuing lifelong movement activities, and promoting individual excellence. You can purchase the series with a portfolio and teacher resource book containing instructional suggestions and ideas for each grade level.

Although textbooks are an excellent resource for students, be careful how you use them in physical education. Using limited instructional time to sit students down to read a chapter in their books is not consistent with physical education goals. You can, however, instruct students to read a section of a textbook as homework to prepare them for a physical activity they'll be doing during class time. Another approach to using textbooks is to create a reading station in a circuit of more traditional physical activities. Here, you can have students read a section of the book. If, like many physical educators, you have limited equipment for practice, a reading station can give those students who might otherwise be waiting to use a piece of equipment a valuable learning experience. Another advantage of using textbooks in the station approach, is that you may only need four to eight copies of the textbook, thereby saving your limited funds. Finally, you can make a variety of textbooks available to students who are working on projects to use as a resource.

Simulations

Simulations are lifelike events that allow students to experience situations that they typically can not experience otherwise due to risk of injury, lack of real-life equipment, or lack of access to the real situation. Figure 12.1 shows an example of a simulation that gives students the opportunity to travel through the cardiorespiratory system. Using different pieces of physical education apparatus and equipment, you create a route that approximates the path that blood takes through the heart and lungs. Students then follow the route, disposing of blue balls and collecting red balls to simulate the exchange of carbon monoxide for oxygen in the lungs. The second time they go though the course, they encounter stress factors that cause heart attacks, strokes, and blood clots. You can simulate the stress factors by raising the temperature in the gym and altering the course by clogging an aorta. This simulation is available from U.S. Games (see appendix D) or you can create your own.

You can also simulate—either in the gymnasium or on the playground—a self-defense scenario; swimming, gymnastics, or track and field meets; a Medieval festival; an orienteering event; and an Olympic festival. An easier vehicle for simulations, however, is the computer. I'll discuss several examples of computer simulations in the "Instructional Software" and "Virtual Reality" sections later in this chapter.

Videos, Laser Discs, and Instructional Television

Earlier in this chapter, we discussed single still images as a form of visual aids. Still images can show your students key positions for different phases of a motor skill, but only moving images can provide students with a complete demonstration of the skill or strategic play. So in this section, we'll discuss moving images in the form of videos (see appendix D for a list of videos I recommend and sources), laser discs, and instructional television.

As physical educators, many of us are not able to demonstrate a perfect model of every motor skill. To fill your skill gaps, use recorded model performances from video, laser disc, or television in physical education. In addition, use video images to illustrate strategic plays or at the beginning of a unit to create excitement about the upcoming sport or activity.

Suggested Videos

Golf With Al Geiberger from SyberVision

Juggling Star from Human Kinetics

The Jump Rope Primer Video from Human Kinetics

The Science and Myths of Tennis from Human Kinetics

Teaching Lifetime Fitness by David Laurie and Chuck Corbin from Audio Visual Designs of Manhattan

PE-TV from Whittle Communications

Most of us know about videotapes and their players, but what are laser discs? How can they help in physical education? Laser discs are round silver discs about the size of a vinyl record. Each laser disc holds over 54,000 frames of video or stills on each side. Each laser disc also has two audio channels (left and right), which you can use for stereo sound or two different audio tracks (e.g., English and Spanish or music and voice). In order to play the laser discs, you need a laser disc player.

The main difference between videos and laser discs is that you can access any image on the laser disc within a few seconds while accessing a particular clip on video requires a linear search and risks going past the desired image. Moreover, laser discs are more durable and produce much clearer images. For both video and laser discs, you will need a large monitor to display the images and cables to connect the monitor to the appropriate player.

Budget limited? You can record a television broadcast (be sure to check federal guidelines) and show it to your students without having to purchase a video—if what you want is being televised in your area. Sporting events, instructional television shows, and the Olympics are excellent shows to record. Television shows with messages about self-esteem or the demonstration of prosocial skills are also appropriate in physical education (e.g., *Wonder Years* or *After School Specials*). After viewing clips of such shows, have students describe their feelings about the incident you showed or stop the show before the issue is resolved and have students write their own endings to the stories.

But don't misuse this technology, giving into the temptation of showing an entire video, television show, or disc. Preview the show prior to showing it to your students, selecting only those clips that depict the concept or skill you are teaching. Then show the clips to the entire class or use them at a station.

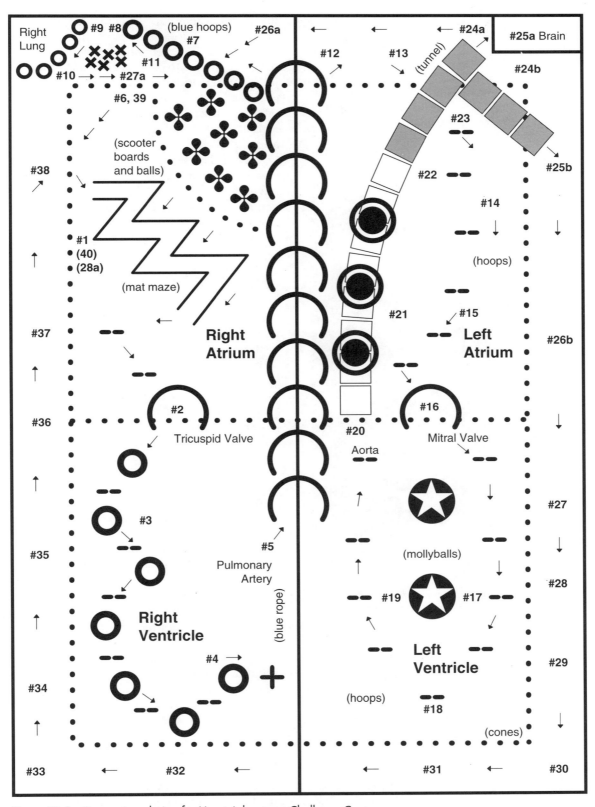

Figure 12.1   Gymnasium design for Heart Adventures Challenge Course.
Reprinted, with permission, from *Journal of Physical Education, Recreation & Dance,* February 1995, 19. *JOPERD* is a publication of the American Alliance for Health, Physical Education, Recreation and Dance, 1900 Association Drive, Reston, VA 22091.

Camcorders

Camcorders (see figure 12.2) are especially effective devices in helping students master skills and analyze strategy. You can train students to record each other performing motor skills or participating in a scrimmage so they can immediately view their performances. The new video cameras that have a three- or four-inch viewfinder are ideal for physical education because students can replay the video in the camera and still see the images clearly. For cameras with a one-inch viewfinder, students will need to either hook the camera up to a monitor, remove the videotape and play it through a video casette recorder or video casette player, or try to view the video through the eye piece.

Figure 12.2 Camcorders are ideal for physical education because students can get immediate feedback on their performances.

Give students a form that lists the critical features for the motor skill or the main concepts of the strategy they are observing, so that they analyze their own performances as they observe them. In order for this learning process to be most effective, allow students to stop and start the video at their own discretion. You should act as a facilitator, questioning the students regarding the significance of particular movements, actions, or behaviors at a station while keeping an eye on the rest of the stations.

Using the camcorder to collect video clips of students throughout the learning process demonstrates to students and others the actual learning and skill development that occurs in physical education. Refer to the discussion in chapter 8 of how you can digitize these images to place in electronic student portfolios. In addition, you can apply software programs to these images for biomechanical analysis. (See *BioMachanics* from Brown and Benchmark and *Measurement in Motion* from Learning in Motion in appendix D.)

You can also allow students to use a camcorder to create individual projects about fitness concepts, movement patterns, and new games they have invented. Refer to the discussion of the creation and assessment of student projects in chapter 8 for more information.

Software for Teaching Efficiency

Computer software can help you perform many of your daily tasks more efficiently and effectively, including creating instructional materials. Integrated software programs such as *Microsoft Works* and *Claris Works*, both of which include word processing, desktop publishing (graphics), a data base, and a spreadsheet, can help you create newsletters, worksheets, task cards, visual aids, locker systems, budgets, inventories, and grading systems. You can also use fitness software to create fitness reports for your students so you can more easily monitor student progress (see figure 12.3).

You may wonder if using a computer for fitness reports and grades is really a time-saver when you have to write down the information while on the field and then key the information into the computer once you're back in your office. One answer is to use a handheld computer for data collection on the field (see figure 12.4). Today, you can choose from several models and programs. The Apple Newton handheld computer with *GradePoint* software for traditional grading or *Learner Profile* for authentic assessment offers great promise for an efficient electronic assessment system for physical educators (see also chapter 8). For more information contact Sunburst Software (see appendix D).

Other Technological Devices

We've discussed how you may use technology to assist with your many tasks, but what about your students? Technology can assist students with the learning process, in addition to preparing students to live in the 21st century. Many commercial fitness

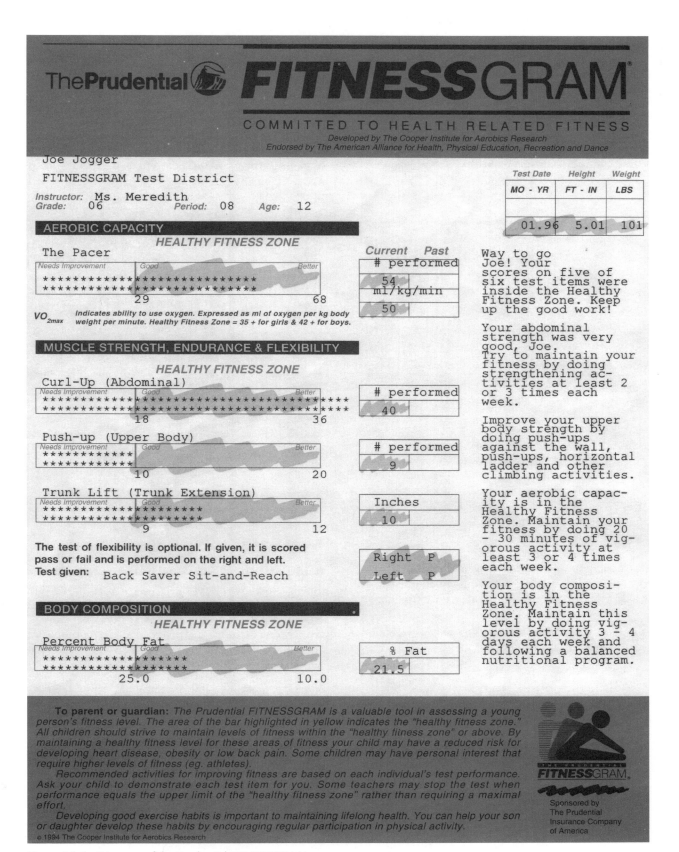

Figure 12.3 Diagram of the Prudential FITNESSGRAM computer output.
Reprinted with permission from The Cooper Institute for Aerobics Research, Dallas, TX.

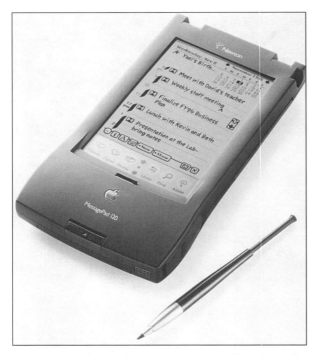

Figure 12.4 The Apple Newton is an excellent device for collecting data on the field.
©Apple Computer, Inc. Used with permission.

centers already use technology, so you will be preparing students for healthy lifestyles, including participation at fitness centers.

Specifically, devices such as electronic blood pressure machines, heart monitors, and body composition analyzers help students learn more about the scientific side of fitness (see appendix D for vendors). Granted, many times the school versions of these devices don't compare with the more sophisticated—and expensive—models available to professionals, but they do motivate students, increasing their understanding of exercise physiology concepts while introducing them to the use of technology in physical activity.

Electronic blood pressure devices (approximately $60 to $200) allow students to take each other's blood pressure. If a student's blood pressure reading is abnormal, you should refer the student to a nurse or physician. Some of these machines take readings on the index finger, but I recommend that you use a cuff model with either an automatic inflation or manual bulb inflator. A cuff model works by inflating until the screen display reads 180. The machine then deflates the cuff as it reads the systolic and diastolic blood pressure as well as the pulse rate, displaying all three on the screen for viewing.

When teaching students to reach and maintain the pulse in the target heart rate training zone, consider

using heart rate monitors to make tracking easier (see figure 12.5). Students can program their target heart rate zones into these devices, which, in turn, give a visual and sometimes an auditory signal when the heart rate goes above or below the target heart rate zone. Although heart rate monitors come in various forms such as ear clips and head bands, I recommend the heart rate monitors that have a wireless transmitter attached to a chest strap and a receiver on a wrist strap.

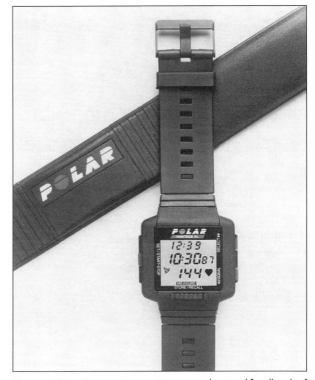

Figure 12.5 Heart rate monitors provide visual feedback of students' heart rates during exercise.
Courtesy of Polar Electro Inc.

When purchasing heart rate monitors for use in physical education, I recommend either the bottom or the top of the Polar line (see appendix D). The models in between don't seem to meet the needs of most physical educators. The heart rate monitor at the bottom of the line (approximately $70) simply displays the student's heart rate. The top of the line (approximately $300) can store 33 hours of heart rate, recorded in eight different files, and is available with an interface (approximately $450) that rapidly transfers data from the heart monitor to an IBM (or a compatible) or a Macintosh computer (see figure 12.6). The software, which comes with the interface, displays each student's heart rate as a data table, line graph, or bar graph you can print out.

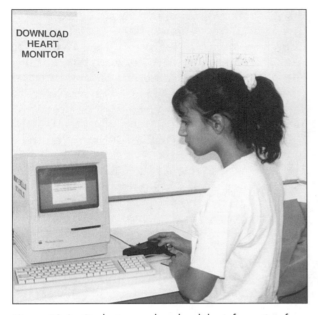

Figure 12.6 Students can download the information from their heart rate monitors into the computer for analysis.

Figure 12.7 Heart rate monitors motivate students and provide them with essential information during aerobic activity.

Although you may not be able to purchase a heart rate monitor for each student, you can have students share these devices so that they wear one every week or month (see figure 12.7). Use heart rate monitors to collect data during aerobic workouts, to compare heart rates for different activities (e.g., football and jump rope), and to determine fitness levels by analyzing the recovery heart rates (how long it takes to return the heart rate to normal after a workout).

Body composition analyzers cost between $800 and $3000 (see figure 12.8). Two different types are widely available: bioelectric impedance and infrared instruments. Although each model collects data

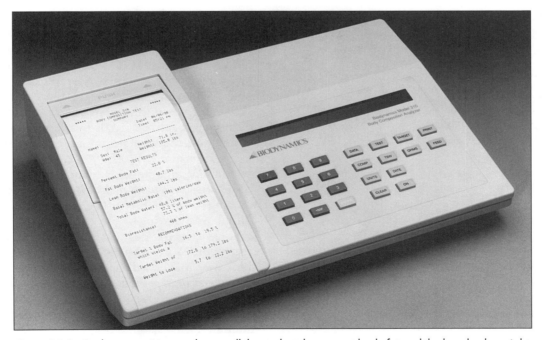

Figure 12.8 Body composition analyzers tell the student the percent body fat and the lean body weight.

somewhat differently, they all report the percent body fat. For example, the Futrex 5000 asks the student to answer a few questions and then asks for two infrared readings at the biceps. A printout tells the student the percent body fat and percent lean body weight. The printout also makes recommendations for increasing or decreasing body fat. Although there has been some controversy throughout the profession regarding the validity and accuracy of these devices, they are becoming more accurate. When purchasing one of these models, be sure that it works with children, since there are different models for adults and children. Consider putting the body composition analyzer on your wish list, asking for it if your funds permit or adding it to your next grant proposal.

Telecommunications

If you have access to telecommunications, you can share information about instructional techniques, lesson plans, and student worksheets with teachers at other schools. In order to participate in telecommunications, you will need a computer (see figure 12.9), modem, telephone line (or a direct line to the Internet), and telecommunications software. If you are purchasing a new modem, be sure to get one that has a speed of at least 28,800 baud.

Once you have all the necessary hardware and software, find a service provider. Talk to a technology expert in your area about local service provid-

Figure 12.9 One of the Macintosh computers.
© Apple Computer, Inc. Used with permission.

ers. At a minimum, the provider should assign you an e-mail address, connect you to the Internet, and allow you to browse the World Wide Web. If you cannot find a local service provider, then I recommend America Online for beginners and Earthlink for intermediate users. Most of these providers allow you to check out their services free for 10 hours.

Once you have an e-mail address you can send and receive mail just like you do with snail mail (Internet users' name for the United States Postal Delivery Service). If you would like to send a message, feel free to send me one at: **bonnie_mohsen @ocde.k12.ca.us**. The difference between e-mail and snail mail is that your message is immediately delivered and, if the receiver is available, immediately answered.

One extension of electronic mail is a listserv, which works much like a mailing list. You can send one message to the listserv distribution address, and a copy of the message goes to everyone on the list. If you would like to join a physical education listserv, send me an e-mail message stating that you would like to join pedlist. Be aware that many listservs, like USPE (**listserv@listserv.vt.edu**), require you to leave the subject line of your message blank and put subscribe *nameOfList* (e.g., subscribe USPE-L) in the body of the message when joining. Once you are subscribed to a list, you will be e-mailed the address where you can send messages for distribution.

Finally, World Wide Web (WWW) browsers (e.g., Netscape, Mosaic) provide an easy way to search the Internet for information. World Wide Web browsers have done for the Internet what Windows 95 did for the IBM and IBM compatible computer—provided it with a graphic user interface. You can now click on an "open" button, type in an address such as **http://www.humankinetics.com/** and press the return key to travel half-way across the country or the world to see what is on another computer. The address I listed will take you to a computer that contains information on Human Kinetics and physical education. You can also access information by clicking on the search button, typing in the name of a topic, and clicking on the go button to return a list of Internet addresses that contain information on your topic. Then, you can click on any one of the addresses and it will take you to information on your topic. Be sure when typing in e-mail and World Wide Web addresses that you type them in exactly as they are written—without extra spaces or punctuation. (Please keep in mind that addresses given here were correct at time of publication but may change due to unforeseen circumstances.)

Instructional Software

Instructional software can enhance the learning process as students interact with computers. Several different types of instructional software have been developed. Tutorial software, such as *MacBowling Tutorial* and *MacSoftball Basic Defense*, guide students through information and then has them answer questions on the material. The *MacBowling Tutorial* teaches students how to count the score in bowling, and the *MacSoftball Basic Defense* teaches students where to throw the ball, depending on the number of outs and runners on base. (See also appendix D for a list of recommended software, software publishers, and addresses.)

Simulation software, such as *Mac Heart Monitor Tutorial and Simulation, MacSoftball Rules Game, MacFootball Rules Game, Body & Mind*, and the *John Rae—Survival Series* provide students with situations that require them to use higher-order thinking skills. In the *MacFootball Rules Game*, students play a simulated touchdown game by answering rule questions. They get four questions, which can be 5-yard, 10-yard, or 15-yard questions, to move their team past the next quarter line. If they are successful, they get four more questions, otherwise, they go on the

Suggested Instructional Software

Body & Mind from Fitness Lifestyle Design, Inc.

DINE Healthy from DINE Systems

John Rae—Survival Series from CompTech Systems Design

MacBowling Tutorial from Bonnie's Fitware

MacFootball Rules Game from Bonnie's Fitware

MacHealth-Related Fitness from Bonnie's Fitware

Mac Heart Monitor Tutorial and Simulation from Bonnie's Fitware

MacPortfolio from Bonnie's Fitware

MacSoftball Basic Defense from Bonnie's Fitware

MacSoftball Rules Game from Bonnie's Fitware

MacVolleyball Complete from Bonnie's Fitware

The Total Heart from IVI Publishing

defensive. *MacSoftball Rules Game* (see figure 12.10) is similar except the students select from single, double, or triple questions and an incorrect answer

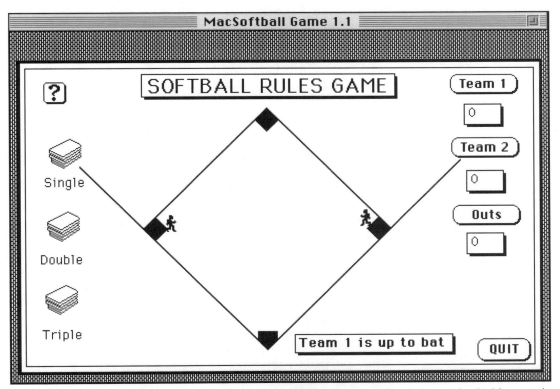

Figure 12.10 A screen from Bonnie's Fitware *MacSoftball Rules Game*. Students select single, double, or triple questions to answer. If their answers are correct, their players advance; if an answer is incorrect, it results in an out.

results in an out. In the *Mac Heart Monitor Tutorial and Simulation* (see figure 12.11) students learn how to set the Polar Vantage Heart Monitor and are then presented with a simulated heart monitor that they can program as if it were the real thing. In the *John Rae—Survival Series*, students must deal with unexpected events in the wilderness in order to survive. *Body & Mind* allows students to simulate alternative fitness plans. The program immediately displays the consequences of adding or deleting exercises or changing the overload variables.

Reference software, such as encyclopedias and *The Total Heart*, provide students with detailed reference information, including pictures, graphs, and short video clips (see figure 12.12). Students can search for the information they seek by typing the name of the topic in the "Find Box" or they can click on related information until they find the appropriate information. Most reference software comes on CD-ROM (small silver disc) which is a computer storage media that holds much more (600+ times) information than a computer floppy disk. We are also beginning to see more and more of these CD-ROMs on various sports, such as *Interactive Volleyball* and *Interactive Soccer* from SISU and *Mountain Biking* and *Rock Climbing* from Media Mosaic.

Some laser disc players can also be hooked up to a computer to create what is called a "level III" interactive video disc system. The computer software used in this system contains instructions for the laser disc player to show live action video clips at appropriate times throughout the software program. Although quite a few of these laser disc systems for health are available, none currently exist specifically for physical education. Fortunately, ABC News Interactive, which produced many of the health programs, has plans for a fitness program.

Software authoring programs, such as *HyperStudio* for the Apple and Macintosh, *HyperCard* for the Macintosh, and *LinkWay Live* for IBM and IBM compatibles, provide students with an open-ended program with which to create any project they want. These programs give students the tools to add text, pictures, video, sound, and animation to their electronic projects. There is no limit to what students can create! It is similar to giving students a Lego set with which to build whatever they want—only this set is computerized. In some physical education classes, students have even created their own computer programs for different sports, such as tennis, volleyball, and soccer.

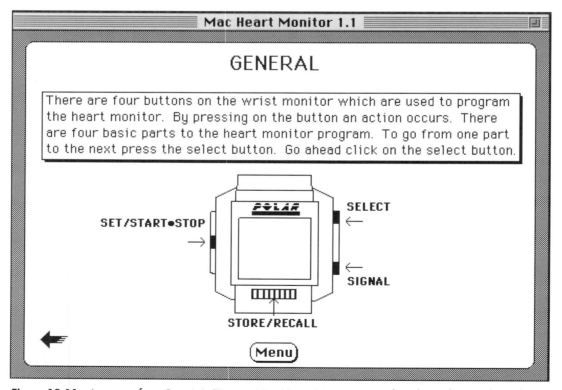

Figure 12.11 A screen from Bonnie's Fitware *Mac Heart Monitor Tutorial and Simulation.* This software teaches students and teachers how to set the Polar Vantage heart rate monitors.

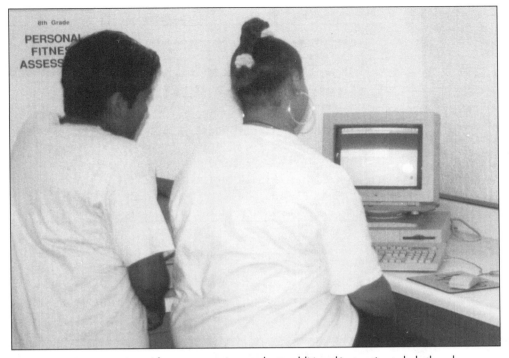

Figure 12.12   Interaction with computers gives students additional instruction to help them learn new information.

Using Technology

We offer a nine-week course "Personal Sport and Technology" in which eighth grade students select their own personal sport for an in-depth study and investigate through technology the benefits of fitness and the development of sport skills. Technology is used with heart rate analysis (heart monitors and spreadsheets), skill analysis (HyperStudio, video, and laser discs), and research efforts (on-line services). The course culminates with a multimedia presentation by every student that highlights their learning experiences from their studies.

—Physical Educator Carol Chestnut, Simmons Middle School, Birmingham, Alabama

Students can also use *HyperStudio*, *HyperCard*, and *LinkWay Live* to design their own electronic portfolios (see also chapter 8). Or they can use preset generic electronic portfolios, such as *Grady Profile* or *Scholastic's Electronic Portfolio* into which students simply add their own pictures, writings, and video clips. Finally, preset electronic portfolios tailored to physical education needs are available into which students can add video clips of their motor skills, rate their performances based on preset rubrics, and analyze their own fitness scores—among other things. These programs include *MacHealth-Related Fitness Tutorial and Portfolio* (see figure 12.13), *MacPortfolio* (see figure 12.14), and *MacVolleyball Complete* (see figure 12.15) for physical education.

At Montebello Intermediate School in California, students use videotapes, camcorders, computer software, and heart rate monitors in their physical education classes. Physical educators use a computer presentation system to demonstrate new software to the students. All seventh and eighth grade students maintain electronic portfolios using *MacHealth-Related Fitness Tutorial and Portfolio*. They keep track of their fitness levels, goals, and quarterly progress and create personalized fitness plans. They can also access information on health-related fitness because the electronic portfolio contains a database of fitness information.

For maximum learning to occur, it is important that instructional software requires students to be actively engaged in learning. Tutorial software simply asks students to answer questions, reference software provides students with an opportunity to look up information; simulations put students in lifelike situations; and authoring software and portfolio software require students to apply

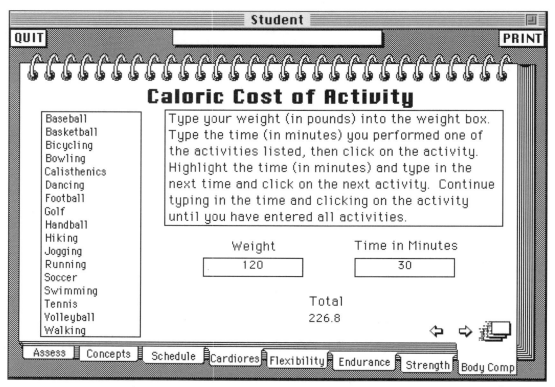

Figure 12.13   A screen from Bonnie's Fitware *MacHealth-Related Tutorial and Portfolio*. Students can access information on health-related fitness and maintain their own electronic fitness portfolios.

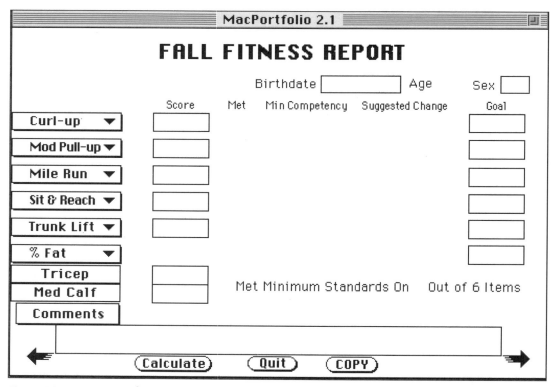

Figure 12.14   A screen from Bonnie's Fitware *MacPortfolio*. Students can store evidence of learning and physical development in the forms of journal entries, fitness scores, and video clips.

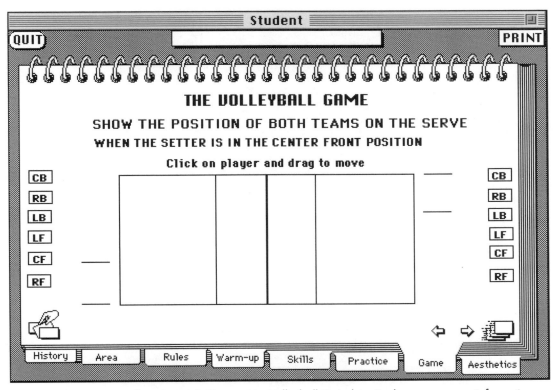

Figure 12.15   A screen from Bonnie's Fitware *MacVolleyball Complete*. Students can access information on volleyball and maintain their own electronic volleyball portfolios.

information and create a new product. Therefore, interactive types of software, such as simulations, project-based software, and electronic portfolios, are—in most cases—a better use of technology.

Virtual Reality

Virtual reality is the ultimate in computer hardware and software. A typical virtual reality system includes a computer, special user interfaces (gloves and a head-mounted display which contains two miniature monitors) connected to the computer, and software that controls the visual images on the television sets and the pressure exerted on the tactile stimulators in the gloves. This gives the user the sensory illusion of being in a different environment. The user can interact with this environment by gesturing with the gloves or moving the helmeted head, and the computer responds appropriately. Virtual reality is appealing to most learners because of its novelty; however, it is especially effective with students whose primary intelligence is bodily-kinesthetic. Although few schools are currently using virtual reality, it is an emerging technology that could have a significant impact on the future of

physical education. Currently, a number of virtual reality systems that place the user in sport situations are available.

Virtual Racquetball, currently used in universities and colleges, places the user in an artificial, computer-generated, three-dimensional racquetball court. Players use a real racquetball racquet that interfaces with the computer. As a player swings the racquet, the computer generates a representation of the racquet in virtual space that corresponds to the movement of the real racquet and displays the image on the two television sets in the user's head-mounted display. The virtual game begins with a serve that rebounds off a virtual wall. As the player swings the real racquet, the virtual racquet attempts to make contact with the virtual ball, and the game is under way.

A virtual bicycling experience developed by the researchers at the University of North Carolina provides users with a stationary 10-speed mountain bicycle accompanied by a head-mounted display and headphones. By watching the visual images in the head-mounted display, the user steers through the virtual environment simply by turning the bike's handlebars. A mechanical device measures the rotation of the handlebars and the pedals, passing the information back to the computer, which calculates the next scene to be displayed on the monitors. As the user pedals up a virtual hill, the computer increases the resistance on the rear bicycle wheel, which, in turn, requires the user to exert more force on the pedals.

PGA Tour Gold from Electronic Arts provides players with a virtual reality version of golf that is played using a 3DO machine (a super powered video game system). The game uses fully digitized images of golfers, three-dimensional courses with accurate elevations, and a special golf club interface. Players plot their strategies, adjust for obstacles on the course, and play 18 holes of golf from a stationary position.

Other Resources

Many sport organizations provide free or inexpensive instructional materials just for the asking. For example, the United States Tennis Association has developed an instructional manual that they provide free to teachers who attend one of their free training sessions. Other associations listed in appendix D can assist you with instructional manuals, orienteering maps, and other materials that may be of benefit to your students. Simply write and request a list of their complimentary or inexpensive resources.

Summary

Technological devices, camcorders, videos, the Internet, and virtual reality systems offer students exciting ways to learn physical education concepts. Keep in mind that as we move into the 21st century, these tools will become commonplace, and our students need to know how to use them. Use the information in this chapter to get you started. In the next chapter, we'll look at ways you can stay current in physical education theory and practice.

CHAPTER 13

Continuing to Grow as a Professional

Are you familiar with the game of Midnight (a.k.a. What Time Is It, Mr. Fox?)? When I was first out of college 30 years ago, I played it with the kids because I didn't know any better. They played that game for a few minutes each day, and I just watched them and refereed. They all loved the game, and they followed the rules, but I knew they weren't learning anything, and it drove me crazy. It didn't take me long to realize that I couldn't spend my life being a referee: I had to teach them something. So I started by changing the games they seemed to like.

—Vinnie Minotti

Reprinted from Petersen, Allen, and Minotti, 1994, "Teacher knowledge and reflection," *Journal of Physical Education, Recreation & Dance*, 32.

With knowledge doubling every year, change is coming so quickly that we can barely adjust to one change and another is on our doorstep. Thus, as we leave the 20th century and enter the 21st, we must learn to accept and adjust effectively to constant change. This affects the teaching of physical education because, as information increases, we gain a better understanding of the world around us, which, in turn, requires us to adjust our programs to reflect the most recent information and research. The three terms which most accurately describe education in the 21st century are learn, unlearn, and relearn.

If you are ready to apply the concepts addressed in this book, you have already accepted the challenge of change. This makes you one of the "paradigm pioneers." Remember, however, that the pioneers often take the arrows as they clear the way for the next group of settlers. As a pioneer, or teacher-leader, you must not only learn to deal effectively with change personally, you must also learn to help your colleagues see the benefits of and accept change. For if we have learned nothing else, we have learned that change must be systemic (system-wide) and not piecemeal (single-person) to be effective. In this chapter, I'll share methods and strategies to help you and your colleagues prepare for and implement the many changes that lie ahead.

Change

It helps to view change in the 21st century as a process and not an event. This process is highly personal because it gives each of us an opportunity to reinvent ourselves and the world around us. Indeed, change takes a different length of time for different individuals. Moreover, it is not unusual for life to seem chaotic during the process. It is important, however, that throughout what appears to be chaos and uncertainty you stay focused on your values and ultimate purpose so that the decisions you make during these times of confusion are aligned with your ultimate purpose.

Eight Basic Lessons of the New Paradigm of Change

You can't mandate what matters.

Change is a journey, not a blueprint.

Problems are our friends.

Vision and strategic planning come later.

Individualism and collectivism must have equal power.

Neither centralization nor decentralization works exclusively.

Connection with the wider environment is critical for success.

Every person is a change agent.

Summarized from *Change Forces: Probing the Depths of Educational Reform* by M. Fullan (1993).

Requisites for Change

Change requires vision, skills, resources, and an action plan. Vision is a clearly defined, yet flexible, view of what your program will look like after the change occurs. To get on-track, list the positive benefits that the change will create. Although the vision is often articulated by the leader, it must include everyone's view and everyone must buy into it.

Skills refer to both knowledge and processing skills. Knowledge provides the information necessary to create the vision. For example, you—whether

you're a teacher or an administrator—need to understand authentic assessment in order to put it into practice. In addition, process skills are necessary to help a department or committee go through the process of change. Teacher-leaders who possess process skills can form groups, help those groups make decisions, and facilitate effective communication between group members.

Resources are the equipment, supplies, and other financial requirements needed to facilitate the change. For example, to implement a swimming program, you either need a pool or access and transportation to a pool. In order to train teachers in a new instructional strategy, you need money for either stipends or substitutes.

Finally, an action plan requires a well-defined step-by-step blueprint that identifies the activities necessary to implement change and defines a clear pathway to the vision. Your action plan, however, must be open-ended, allowing for changes along the way. The open-ended structure has always been an important feature of any action plan, but as rapidly as change is occurring, it becomes essential to an effective plan.

Model for Change

Change is much more effective when a group, such as the physical education department, embraces the change collectively, deciding to try a new program together. Still, if you have successfully implemented the changes in your classes it will be easier to sell them to your colleagues. Taking time to share with your colleagues and provide them with resources is a great way to ensure that the new program is adopted by all members of the department.

It may appear to you at times that everyone has different concerns about implementing the new program. Remember, everyone will move toward the changes at their own pace. In fact, according to the CBAM Model (Hall, Wallace, Dossett 1973), everyone will progress through a seven-step process on their way to adopting any new program. By becoming aware of the seven steps, you can appropriately assist an individual who is having difficulty with the changes.

Practical Ideas for Change

You, as a teacher-leader, must also keep in mind strategies that have proven effective for other teacher-leaders. If you have several new ideas that you wish to implement in your program and you

CBAM Model and Suggestions for Assisting Persons at Each Stage

Awareness: Little Concern About or Involvement With the Innovation

Involve individuals in discussions and decisions about the innovation and its implementation.

Share enough information to arouse interest, but not so much that it overwhelms.

Take steps to minimize gossip and inaccurate sharing of information about the innovation.

Informational: A General Awareness of the Innovation and Interest in Learning More Detail

Use a variety of ways to share information: oral, written, and through any other available media.

Have individuals who have used the innovation in other settings talk with your teachers.

Help individuals see how the innovation relates to their current practices.

Personal: Individual Is Uncertain About the Demands of the Innovation

Legitimize the existence and expression of personal concerns.

Connect these individuals with others whose concerns have diminished.

Do not push innovation, rather, encourage and support it.

Management: Attention Focuses on the Processes and Tasks of Using the Innovation

Provide answers that address the small specific "how to" issues.

Demonstrate exact and practical solutions to the logistical problems.

Consequence: Attention Focuses on Impact of the Innovation on Students

Provide these individuals with opportunities to visit other settings where the innovation is in use.

Give them positive feedback and necessary support.

Find opportunities for these persons to share their skills with others.

Collaboration: Attention Focuses on Coordination and Cooperation With Others

Provide these individuals with opportunities to develop those skills necessary for working collaboratively.

Use these individuals to provide technical assistance to others who need assistance.

Encourage the collaborators, but don't attempt to force collaboration on those who are not interested.

Refocusing: Attention Focuses on Exploration of More Universal Benefits From the Innovation

Help these individuals access the resources they may need to refine their ideas and put them into practice.

Be aware of and willing to accept the fact that these persons may replace or significantly modify the existing innovations.

Adapted from G.E. Hall, R.C. Wallace, and W.A. Dossett, 1973, *A Developmental Conceptualization of the Adoption Process Within Educational Institutions.*

encounter resistance either from the administration or other teachers, pick one new idea at a time on which to focus your attention. Once you are successful with that idea, progress to the next.

Staff Development

Staff development is a process through which you'll learn about new ideas and begin the process of transferring these new ideas to your classes. Unfortunately, however, many physical educators feel that staff development is useless. This opinion is based on their many experiences with school-wide

in-services that did not relate directly to their jobs. The typical problem with these school-wide staff development seminars is not the content *per se* (cooperative learning, restructuring, technology), but the inability of the presenter to relate the content to physical education. Yet, physical educators can benefit from understanding cooperative learning strategies, instructional technology, and the issues related to restructuring. Still, when the presenter discusses cooperative learning only in the context of classroom situations with a small number of students, it is difficult for the physical educators to apply the suggestions. You can address this problem either by educating the presenter on how to

Practical Steps to Change

Secure as much information as possible about the change from in-services, videotapes, audiotapes, discussions, and observations.

Set written goals for implementing the change.

Experiment with one class.

Visit other teachers who are also attempting to implement the change.

Share information, successes, and failures with other teachers who are attempting to implement the change.

Modify the new approach if it seems necessary.

Implement the change in all your classes.

Adapt the change as necessary.

Document your success.

Invite administrators to visit your classes.

Staff Development Topics

Understanding middle school students

Setting up a positive environment

Developing an effective curriculum

Examining the content of physical education

Exploring student learning styles

Increasing effective teaching behaviors

Exploring teaching styles

Expanding your teaching strategies

Selecting instructional materials

Selecting assessment tools

Implementing assessment strategies

relate his topic to physical educators, by allowing time after the presentation for each department to debrief its members as to how they can apply the information, or by encouraging the administration to schedule separate presentations for each department on the same topic.

Characteristics of Effective, Ongoing Professional Development

Based on school's strategic long-term staff development plan

Built on a professional network of teachers

Presents theory

Focuses on students' needs and desired learning outcomes

Views teachers as learners

Supports collegiality and collaboration

Commits to a long-term financial investment

Focuses on teachers' questions, needs, and concerns

Encourages initial practice in the workshop

Provides for adequate follow-up, including prompt feedback from a coach in the classroom

Effective staff development programs require sustained, ongoing efforts through which teachers have time to learn and try new ideas in a safe, controlled situation. Moreover, they must address one or more of the skills necessary to teach physical education. Indeed, you should be able to see a direct relationship between the staff development program and what goes on in your classes. Staff development can take on many different forms. Let's examine a few.

In-Services

In-services are learning experiences that are planned and organized for current teachers within a fairly local geographic area (county, district, or school). These in-services can take the form of a single meeting on one topic to a series of meetings on one or more topics. They can be times for teachers to share with each other or times for teachers to learn new information from visiting experts. Some districts and schools set up a number of in-service days or times per year for specific subject area issues. In this way, the physical educators are not excluded from school-wide in-services as is too often the case; instead, all departments are able to benefit from some in-service time devoted to their specific content field.

A new direction for in-services is on-demand staff development. In this model, teachers can participate in learning situations anytime and anywhere. This occurs via the Internet using e-mail, listservs, chat sessions, virtual auditoriums, and video conferencing. If you are tired of traditional staff development, seek out an on-demand training program.

Physical Education Clinics

I have encouraged clinics that are conducted by the physical education teachers. Teachers who are experts in a particular activity would conduct a training session for the rest of the physical education staff. We would get together at 7:00 P.M. for two hours. This really helped our program. These evening clinics, for example, contributed to making our gymnastics units an outstanding feature in this district.

From Butler and Mergardt, 1994, "The many forms of administrative support," 45.

Conferences

Conferences provide opportunities for teachers from a wider geographic area to come together and share ideas and activities on a wider variety of topics than in-services. For example, the American Alliance for Health, Physical Education, Recreation and Dance (AAHPERD) holds a national convention each year as well as a number of specialty conferences. Most of the state AHPERD organizations (depending on the size of the state) offer yearly conferences as well in addition to a number of local conferences.

Reflections

Opportunities to attend conferences and in-services are only two pieces of the learning puzzle. But opportunities to reflect on those learning endeavors and your teaching experiences extends your thinking and learning. As Petersen, Allen, and Minotti (1994) state, "It was through experience that thoughtful teachers gained much of their professional knowledge, but it was through reflection that they effectively used that knowledge to build outstanding programs and maintain their motivation to continue to gain knowledge" (p. 31). Refer to the quote at the beginning of this chapter as one example of a teacher's reflection regarding his own teaching and what he learned from it.

Peer Coaching

Many new teachers feel isolated because they have no one with whom to share successes or concerns. At the other end of the spectrum is the teacher who suffers from burnout. Having done the same job day in and day out for 20 years with the daily stresses inherent to teaching, many experienced teachers experience the burnout syndrome. These teachers tend to plan less, become inflexible in their views, and expect less both from themselves and their students. Teachers on both ends of this continuum can benefit from peer coaching. Peer coaching gives teachers someone to share ideas and concerns with. The peer coach can also help the teacher implement new ideas. In order for peer coaching to work, however, it must take place in a safe environment in which the teacher being observed invites the peer into his or her class—not the other way around. Training on how to observe and give feedback to peers also facilitates the process.

Peer Coaching

There is evidence that peer coaching, a system of collegial support and feedback, can greatly facilitate transfer of learning. Peer coaching provides companionship, provides technical feedback, extends executive control, helps teachers adapt to students, and provides personal facilitation. The end result is that teachers achieve a higher level of mastery and are better able to adapt innovations to unique demands.

From Randall, 1992, *Systematic supervision for physical education*, 210.

Visitations

The common saying "A picture is worth a thousand words" certainly holds true for implementing a new teaching idea or strategy. Teachers who can see the actual technique in action with adolescents are more likely to believe the technique is valuable and therefore are more likely to try the technique. These visits can be to schools whose teachers have mastered the new technique or to schools whose teachers are in the beginning stages of implementing the new technique. Either way, beyond the actual observation, the visiting teachers can benefit from discussions with other practicing teachers.

Visitations, whenever possible, should be done in teams, or at least with a colleague. The dialogue that results between two or more participants can be much more valuable than the single thoughts of one individual. It is also important to determine ahead of time the specific questions to ask and points to observe, so that you are ready to benefit from the experience.

Even teachers who are not ready to try a specific new technique may benefit from visiting other programs. This is because such visits tend to give us a wealth of new ideas and confirm for us what we are already doing well. As with visits made by more enthusiastic teachers, a visit by reluctant teachers should be a two-way exchange of information, covering successes, concerns, and failures. Indeed, you may find that reluctant teachers have their fears allayed and join your reform efforts after all.

Your state's Association for Health, Physical Education, Recreation and Dance and your state's department of education are great places to start looking for schools to visit. Many states have program or exemplary status awards, which they grant to physical education programs that are implementing new and exciting ideas. Ask for a list of award winners. You can also ask colleagues from other schools in your district where they have visited.

Video Learning

Often you hear of schools you would like to visit but are unable to travel to them. In these instances, ask if the school has a video of their program to share. For example, one demonstration school, Montebello Intermediate in the Montebello (California) Unified School District, has developed a video that they send out for the cost of the video and shipping to any other school interested in their program. In addition, the Educational Telecommunications Network (ETN) has produced over a dozen videos on quality physical education designed to be used as part of in-service programs. Each ETN video includes a discussion on a specific topic and footage of actual classes implementing the concept. (See appendix D for addresses and phone numbers.)

Reading, Listening, or Discussing: Do It Your Way

In chapter 9, we discussed how students learn in different ways. Of course, this is also true for teachers. Some teachers like to belong to discussion groups, some like to listen to audiotapes, and others like to read. Whatever is your preferred learning style, find a way to keep abreast of current research (yes, I did say the "R" word) and its application to your instructional program. If you like to read, avail yourself of books, journals, the Internet and, if you like to listen, make use of the many excellent audiotapes on the market (e.g., *Presentation Success Skills, How to Use Accelerated Learning,*

Mind Mapping: Your Learning Tool). See appendix D for lists of resources.

Graduate School

A great way to stay on top of current information and move up the pay scale at the same time is to attend graduate school. Many colleges and universities offer degree programs in physical education pedagogy, making their programs relevant to your teaching situation. If you are interested in pursuing an administrative position, graduate programs can help you pursue a master's degree in educational administration, while fulfilling the credentialing requirements.

Contributing to the Profession

Contributing to the profession is one way to give something back to the profession as you extend the change process beyond your own school. Moreover, many professionals have found that contributing to the profession renews their own excitement about the role they play in the lives of their students. Finally, the contact with other professionals can make you feel that your own ideas and feelings are valid.

Committee Work

Become involved in your professional association, if not as an officer, then as a committee member, working on an area of interest to you. The time to pitch in has never been better as more professional associations are establishing committees through which most of their work is actually done. This is because they find that, in general, their members like the idea of working on one project that interests them, rather than taking on the role of an officer.

Of course, you can also become involved in committee work at your local school. All too often, physical educators have chosen to remain in their isolated offices never to interact with the rest of the staff. This often leads to feelings of isolation as well as the perception on the part of the other staff members that the physical education department is outside the educational realm. Don't let this happen to you and your department! By becoming involved in school committees, you can participate in an area that may be of interest to you as well as educate the other committee members as to the role and importance of physical education. Perhaps most importantly, however, your inclusion on the committee also ensures that physical education will be represented and included in the committee's project.

Supervise a Student Teacher

Another way that you as an experienced teacher can give something back to the profession is through supervising a student teacher. Although having a student teacher is often thought of as a one-way process through which the master teacher provides the student teacher with the wisdom he or she has gained over the years, many master teachers often learn as much from student teachers. Many times, student teachers have recently completed their physical education classes (exercise physiology, motor learning, biomechanics) and can share this information with you and the rest of the department. Be certain, however, if you are interested in taking on a student teacher, that you truly are an outstanding teacher who has kept up with the times and that you are willing to spend the extra time necessary to work directly with the student teacher. Then you must prove to the university in question that you're qualified to supervise.

Make Presentations

When you teach a middle school physical education class, you reach 20, 30, 40, or more students. But by making a presentation to other teachers, you can reach 100 to 300 students multiplied by the number of the teachers in the audience. Indeed, many experienced teachers have wonderful ideas that other teachers are interested in learning. State AHPERD conferences, district or county in-services, and school-based in-services are all excellent places to offer your services as a speaker. If you are new to making presentations, pick your best lesson or unit and build your presentation around that. Then as you shape your presentation, remember what we have discussed about student learning in terms of learning styles, multiple intelligences, and learning modalities because these concepts also apply to teachers. Finally, make sure as with adolescent students that the information you provide is relevant to your audience.

The physical educators at one middle school decided that they wanted their entire school staff to understand how they were working with students in the area of social skills. They asked for and were given one of the school-wide in-service days. The physical educators divided the staff into four groups and rotated them through four stations:

1. Low ropes course elements
2. Physical challenges
3. In-class social initiatives
4. Debriefing activities

The physical education staff assumed the leadership role at each station. At the conclusion of the day, the school staff decided that the school's focus the following year should be on social skill development. They decided that this would entail all subject areas addressing one social skill each month. The physical education department was asked to provide monthly in-service training on how to address each new social skill.

You can also employ and hone your speaking skills at the local parent and teacher association, community service organizations, and boards of education. Naturally, the topic of your speech should be different from what you presented to other teachers because these groups will not be as interested in how to teach physical education. Rather, they'll be interested in the benefits of physical education, how they can help their youngsters or the youngsters in their community perform well in physical education, and other important issues associated with physical education.

Summary

Well, we've come to the end of our journey. Or is it the beginning? At any rate, it's time for you to chart your own course and follow your own path. To help you further, I'll outline sixth, seventh, and eighth grade programs, complete with lesson plan outlines, appropriate tasks, and specific authentic assessment tools, in the next three chapters. But before you read chapters 14 through 16, take a look at the scenario I asked you to write in chapter 2. Now that you have read through the book, would you change that scenario? Go ahead: Make those changes and spell out the steps you will take next year, the year after that, and the third year. I trust that the path you have chosen to follow leads you toward quality physical education. Now let's take a look at our destination: a quality middle school physical education program.

PART IV

Discover Your Destination

Physical education textbooks that address curriculum, instruction, and assessment are common. These books are filled with dos and don'ts, and conclude with well wishes for you, the reader, to translate the information into a real day-to-day program. In contrast, it has been important to me to share real-life scenarios as well as concrete examples of the ideas we've discussed throughout this book. Now, it is especially important for me to provide concrete examples as we look at a sample middle school program. But please don't view my sample program as the only program! Instead, use my ideas as springboards for your own ideas. Adopt, adapt, and discard what you will because only you know how you want your program to look. So as you prepare to implement your quality physical education program for the 21st century, view the next three chapters, which outline a sixth grade program, a seventh grade program, and an eighth grade program, as the additional stimuli I intend them to be.

CHAPTER 14

A Sixth Grade Program: Learning Skills Through Cooperation

Traditionally, the middle school physical education curriculum has been activity centered. The activity was viewed as the end. However, a skill theme curriculum reverses the means-ends relationship. The curriculum is organized around specific skills or groups of skills. The focus is on student performance outcomes. The activities now become the means through which the student can practice, refine, and develop competence in the skills. The end is students who are able to use skills in a variety of contexts and situations.

—*Palm Beach County Middle School Physical Education Curriculum Focus, Florida*

In this chapter and the next two, we will take a closer look at how to teach skills and concepts to students at each grade level. I have organized these chapters based on the standards and instructional units I identified in chapters 6 and 7. Keep in mind, however, that you should not view the instructional units I suggest here as the definitive answer for your middle school physical education program. Instead,

look at these units as one example of how to organize a middle school program that ensures that you are teaching the grade level standards through a variety of activities, each provided for a sufficient duration for learning to occur. Then make your final curriculum decisions based on your school environment, culture, and expected outcomes.

For each unit of instruction in chapters 14, 15, and

16, I will briefly discuss the reason for using the particular unit; I'll list equipment, facilities, and instructional materials you'll need to implement the unit; I'll suggest interdisciplinary and community ideas for making the unit more like real life; and I'll alert you to class environment issues associated with the unit. After each introduction, I'll list the unit standards that are linked directly to the grade level standards. This will be followed by a unit plan, which contains a day-by-day outline for what you should teach, explaining how the information and activities connect to the unit standards. Look for the motivational, learning, assessment, teaching style, and strategy ideas I have embedded in these daily plans. But don't confuse these unit outlines with detailed lesson plans, which would elaborate on each of the daily agendas, providing detailed drills, activities, and learning experiences. Also, please keep in mind that, depending on the initial general ability level and progress of your students, you may need to teach preliminary concepts as well as review new concepts frequently throughout a unit. Ongoing monitoring of progress can be a big help to you in this regard.

As we discussed in chapter 8, some teachers provide an assessment tool for each unit standard while others only provide assessment tools for each grade level standard. You can choose to follow one of these two strategies or combine the two in the way that works best for you. To guide you, I will provide the numbers of the grade level standards through the unit standards, activities, and assessment ideas. Assessments that can be completed in one day will be noted as assessment opportunities, whereas those being assigned and collected later will be noted as assessment assignment opportunities. Many assessment assignment opportunities are noted as homework and are collected the next day, unless otherwise indicated. Unit 11 ties all of the assessments together. As you read through part IV, think about how you can apply the concepts we have discussed in the first 13 chapters to these model units as well as to your own program.

In this chapter, I have selected "Learning Skills Through Cooperation" as the theme for my sample sixth grade program. As I mentioned in chapter 7, my sixth graders are coming to me from a less than ideal elementary experience, so I want to ensure that they are competent in the basic motor skills before moving on to sport-specific skills. In addition, I want to set the tone for both the physical education and school environments by focusing on

Sixth Grade Standards

By the end of sixth grade, each student should be able to demonstrate the following:

1.0 Applies the correct techniques for locomotor, nonlocomotor, and manipulative skills in a variety of cooperative activities.

2.1 Gives appropriate feedback to a partner while developing or improving movement skills.

2.2 Analyzes movement performance using Newton's Third Law in order to learn or improve a movement skill.

2.3 Creates a cooperative game by combining a variety of locomotor, nonlocomotor, and manipulative skills.

3.0 Participates daily in some form of physical activity based on personal interests and capabilities.

4.0 Assesses personal fitness, compares scores to health-related standards, sets goals for improvement or maintenance, and develops a one-day personal fitness plan.

5.0 Works cooperatively and productively in a group to accomplish goals in physical activity settings.

6.1 Analyzes the variables of physical development within his peer group and their effect on movement performance as he works cooperatively with both more- and less-skilled peers.

6.2 Describes the development and role of movement-related activities and physical education in the ancient world and their influences on physical activities today.

7.0 Analyzes patterns in physical activities to determine the influence that the qualities of movement have on the aesthetic impact of these activities.

Modified from Region 9's *Physical Education Curriculum*, 1994 and NASPE's *National Physical Education Standards: A Guide to Content and Assessment*, 1995.

social skill development during the students' first year in middle school.

As we discussed in chapter 7, I have used the skills theme approach to guide my selection of most sixth grade units of instruction because my emphasis is on basic skill acquisition. I do, however, conclude the year with an opportunity for students to apply these skills in the fun setting of circus activities and in the creation of their own games. Specifically, the units for sixth grade include:

- introduction and fitness pretesting,
- cooperative activities,
- body management,
- locomotor skills,
- underhand and sidearm throwing and catching,
- overhand throwing and catching,
- striking with body parts,
- striking with objects,
- circus skills,
- creating new games, and
- closing and fitness posttesting.

Notice that I move from simple to complex units throughout the year: body management to locomotor skills, to underhand to sidearm to overhand throwing and catching, to striking with body parts to striking with objects. Such sequencing is important so that students can develop their skills progressively. In addition, within each of the skills themes in sixth grade, I move students from simple to complex learning tasks through informing, extending, refining, and finally applying each skill. In the informing stage, I present the new skill. In the extending stage, I increase the complexity or difficulty of the skill, for example, by decreasing the size of the target or increasing the distance to the target. In the refining stage, I focus more on the critical elements of the skill performance, improving the technique aspects of the skill performance. Finally, I encourage the most complex learning to occur by having students apply the skill in an activity. It is vital that your own unit plans incorporate each of these stages as well.

Unit 1: Introduction and Fitness Pretesting

As is appropriate, this unit serves as a basic introductory unit for sixth grade students. For my students, this is the first time they don't stay together as a class for every subject, including physical education. Therefore, I emphasize having them get to know each other so they can start feeling comfortable with new classmates in a new school under new circumstances—a very important issue to young adolescents. This introductory unit also gives me the opportunity to set my expectations as I teach the class rules to the students. Finally, in this unit, I assess the students' fitness levels and show them how to set yearly goals for fitness development.

You can conduct this particular unit in just about any facility. If you must have students perform exercises on the ground or grass, however, be sure to provide students with carpet squares or some other material so that they don't get dirty. The equipment necessary to implement the unit depends on the type of introductory games you choose and the fitness tests you plan to administer. I will be administering the Prudential FITNESSGRAM health-related fitness test battery, including the back-saver sit-and-reach, curl-ups, skinfold measurements, push-ups, trunk lift, and one-mile run. You can order the test administration procedures from The Cooper Institute for Aerobic Research (see appendix D). You will see in the sample daily agendas that my students will prepare for the fitness test through different aerobic activities, including the use of a videotape on step aerobics. In addition, the students will enter their fitness scores into their own electronic portfolios (*MacHealth-Related Fitness Tutorial and Portfolio*). Unless otherwise noted, refer to appendix C for exercise and activity descriptions.

This introductory unit is especially effective when the other sixth grade teachers also focus on students learning each other's names, getting to know one another, learning class and school rules, and connecting students to their new school. Certainly, the most important aspect of this introductory unit is that it creates a psychologically safe environment, setting the stage for learning throughout the year. It is especially important for you to model acceptance of all students regardless of skill or fitness level during this unit. If you focus on including everyone from the start, you will do much to set the stage for students to accept each other's strengths and weaknesses. Furthermore, if you protect the privacy of students during fitness assessments, this approach will go far in showing students that you have respect for them as individuals. In turn, students will be more likely to respect you as well as each other.

Unit Standards

1.0 – Applies the correct techniques for locomotor, nonlocomotor, and manipulative skills to physical fitness and getting acquainted activities.

2.1 – Explains the reasons for giving feedback to a partner.

2.2 – States Newton's Third Law.

2.3 – Creates a game that focuses on learning each other's names.

3.0 – Identifies physical activities of interest based on own strengths and weaknesses.

4.0 – Explains the role of pretesting and goal setting in terms of fitness improvement and actually assesses personal fitness, compares scores to health-related standards, and sets personal goals.

5.0 – States other students' names.

6.1 – Identifies areas of skill-related fitness, health-related fitness, and physical characteristics.

6.2 – Describes fitness training during ancient times.

7.0 – Describes qualities of movement.

Unit Outline

Day 1

Establish a roll call order.   **5.0**

Introduce class rules.

Discuss the use of feedback for learning rules, social skills, and motor skills.   **2.1**

Give students feedback as they play Toss-a-Name Game. (See appendix C.)   **1.0 / 2.1 / 5.0**

Day 2

Review class rules.

Discuss qualities of movement.   **7.0**

Give students feedback as they play Toss-a-Name Game, having them toss the ball using different qualities of movement.   **1.0 / 2.1 / 5.0 / 7.0**

Have students play Toss-and-Catch-a-Name Game. (See appendix C.)   **1.0 / 5.0**

Explain how to open lockers.

Ask students if anyone can say the names of half the students in the class. (Assessment opportunity: structured observation.)   **5.0**

Day 3

Review class rules.

Give students feedback as they play Toss-and-Catch-a-Name Game, using different qualities of movement.   **1.0 / 2.1 / 5.0 / 7.0**

Discuss the types of fitness training that occurred during ancient times.   **6.2**

Have students watch "Lifetime Fitness" on the *Slim Goodbody Presents All Fit* (vol. 1) video.   **4.0 / 6.1**

In small groups, ask students to review and discuss the types of fitness training that occurred during ancient times. Have resources (books and articles) available. Assign lockers to one group at a time.   **6.2**

Have students practice opening lockers.

Day 4

Have students dress for physical education.

Review class rules.

Discuss the five areas of health-related fitness.   **4.0 / 6.1**

Have students perform exercises for each area of health-related fitness. (See appendix C for sample exercises under each area of health-related fitness.)   **1.0 / 4.0**

Ask students to review the types of fitness training that occurred during ancient times. (Assessment opportunity: structured observation.)   **6.2**

Give students feedback as they play Toss-and-Catch-a-Name Game, having them use different qualities of movement.   **1.0 / 2.1 / 5.0 / 7.0**

Day 5

Review class rules.

Have students perform exercises for each area of health-related fitness, allocating more time to cardiorespiratory exercise in preparation for the one-mile run.   **1.0 / 4.0**

Give students feedback as they play Toss-and-Catch-a-Name Game, having them use different qualities of movement. (Assessment opportunity: structured observation.)   **1.0 / 2.1 / 5.0 / 7.0**

Have students watch "Fitness" on the *Slim Goodbody Presents All Fit* (vol. 2) video, then discuss what they learned.   **4.0 / 6.1**

Ask students to state in a journal entry the reasons for giving feedback when learning something new. (Assessment opportunity: journal entry.)   **2.1**

Day 6

Review class rules.

Have students perform exercises for each area of health-related fitness, allocating more time to cardiorespiratory exercises in preparation for the one-mile run.   **1.0 / 4.0**

Discuss Newton's Third Law, relating it to one of the warm-up exercises.   **2.2**

Have students play Introducer. (See appendix C.)   **5.0**

Discuss the six areas of skill-related fitness.   **6.1**

Have students watch "Speed and Power" on the *Slim Goodbody Presents All Fit* (vol. 2) video, then discuss what they learned.   **6.1**

Day 7

Have students perform exercises for each area of health-related fitness, allocating more time to cardiorespiratory exercise in preparation for the one-mile run.   **1.0 / 4.0**

Discuss Newton's Third Law, relating it to another exercise.   **2.2**

Have students play Interest Circle. (See appendix C.)   **5.0**

Have students watch "Coordination and Agility" on the *Slim Goodbody Presents All Fit* (vol. 2) video, then discuss what they learned.   **6.1**

Ask students to describe Newton's Third Law. (Assessment opportunity: structured observation.)   **2.2**

Day 8

Have students perform exercises for each area of health-related fitness.   **1.0 / 4.0**

Discuss Newton's Third Law, relating it to another exercise.   **2.2**

Have students participate along with the *Slim Goodbody Presents Step by Step for Kids* video.   **1.0 / 4.0**

Ask students to describe Newton's Third Law. (Assessment opportunity: essay.)   **2.2**

Day 9

Have students perform warm-up exercises for the back-saver sit-and-reach test.   **4.0**

Assign students randomly to groups of four.

Explain the back-saver sit-and-reach test, why you are giving it, and how physical characteristics affect test performance. (See figure 14.1.)   **4.0 / 6.1**

Figure 14.1   Back-saver sit-and-reach test for hamstring flexibility.

Have each group create a game to learn each other's names.   **1.0 / 2.3 / 5.0**

Administer the back-saver sit-and-reach test to one group at a time. (Assessment opportunity: fitness test.)   **4.0**

Ask students if anyone knows the names of all the students in the class. (Assessment opportunity: structured observation.)   **5.0**

Day 10

Have students perform warm-up exercises for the curl-up test.   **4.0**

Explain the curl-up test, why it is given, and how physical characteristics affect test performance. (See figure 14.2.)   **4.0 / 6.1**

Figure 14.2   Curl-up test for abdominal strength and endurance.

Have each group present its name game to other groups. (Assessment opportunity: structured observation.)   **1.0 / 2.3 / 5.0**

While the groups are sharing their name games, administer the curl-up test to two groups at a time. (Assessment opportunity: fitness test.)   **4.0**

Ask students if anyone knows the names of all the students in the class. (Assessment opportunity: structured observation.)   **5.0**

Day 11

Explain the skinfold test, why you are giving it, and how physical characteristics affect test performance. (See figures 14.3 and 14.4.)   **4.0 / 6.1**

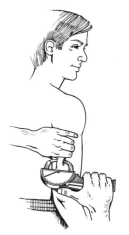 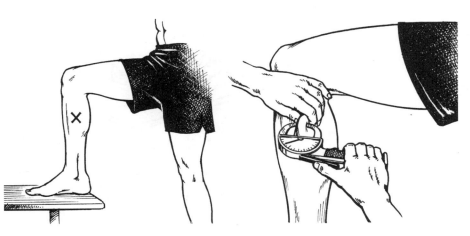

Figure 14.3 Triceps skinfold measurement.

Figure 14.4 Medial calf skinfold measurement.

Have students watch "Balance" from the *Slim Goodbody Presents All Fit* (vol. 3) video.   **6.1**

Administer the skinfold or body mass index test to students one at a time in private, while the others watch the video. (Assessment opportunity: fitness test.)   **4.0**

Ask students to describe the six areas of skill-related fitness. (Assessment opportunity: structured observation.)   **6.1**

Day 12

Have students perform warm-up exercises for the push-up test.   **4.0**

Explain the push-up test (see figure 14.5), why you are giving it, and how physical characteristics affect test performance.   **4.0 / 6.1**

Figure 14.5 Push-up test for upper body strength and endurance.

Have each group present its name game to other groups. (Assessment opportunity: structured observation.)   **1.0 / 2.3 / 5.0**

While the groups are sharing their games, administer the push-up test to one group at a time. (Assessment opportunity: fitness test.)   **4.0**

Day 13

Have students perform warm-up exercises for the trunk lift test.   **4.0**

Explain the trunk lift test, why you are giving it, and how physical characteristics affect test performance. (See figure 14.6.)   **4.0 / 6.1**

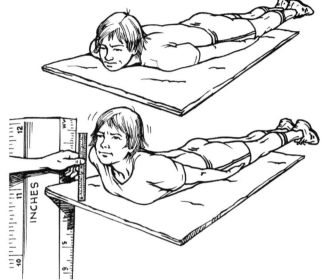

Figure 14.6   Trunk lift test for trunk extensor strength and flexibility.

Have students participate in a flexibility circuit.   **1.0 / 4.0**

Administer the trunk lift test at one station in the circuit. (Assessment opportunity: fitness test.)   **4.0**

Ask students to describe the types of physical characteristics. (Assessment opportunity: structured observation.)   **6.1**

Day 14

Have students perform warm-up exercises for the one-mile run.   **4.0**

Explain the one-mile run test, why you are giving it, and how physical characteristics affect test performance.   **4.0 / 6.1**

Administer the one-mile run test to half the class at a time, using the other half of the class as testing assistants, who keep track of the number of laps. (Assessment opportunity: fitness test.)   **4.0**

Ask students to describe the five areas of health-related fitness. (Assessment opportunity: structured observation.)   **6.1**

Day 15

Have students perform warm-up exercises, depending on the fitness test(s) they need to make up due to absences.   **4.0**

Administer makeup tests. (Assessment opportunity: fitness test.)   **4.0**

Have students enter their scores into their electronic portfolios on computers in order to compare their scores to the minimum competencies and set goals for the year. (Assessment opportunity: electronic log.)   **4.0**

Have students identify their strengths and weaknesses related to physical activity.   **3.0**

For homework, have students create a list of activities that interest them, using their strengths and weaknesses as a guide. (Assessment assignment opportunity: log.)   **3.0**

Unit 2: Cooperative Activities

This unit provides students with an opportunity to extend, refine, and apply their social skills, especially those we associate with cooperation, during many different types of physical challenges. Specifically, I'll employ the teaching strategies that help develop cooperation and social skills during this unit. I'll also show you how to give students opportunities to learn different ways of working together to accomplish a specific goal. In order to address standard four, I'll begin each lesson with a series of warm-up and flexibility exercises and will include cardiorespiratory, muscular strength, and muscular endurance exercises every other day. See the muscular strength and endurance exercises appropriate for middle schoolers that I have listed in appendix C. If you are fortunate enough to have access to a weight room, emphasize correct lifting techniques, not the amount of weight that a student can lift. I'll review warm-up and cooldown concepts related to health-related fitness development daily during the warm-up period. After participating in an activity that requires cooperation and trust, ask your students a number of debriefing questions, including "Did you cooperate to solve the challenge? Did you support one another? Did you feel you could trust your partner? What will you do differently next time?"

As with the first unit, you can conduct this instructional unit in a variety of locations and the equipment you need depends on the type of challenges or cooperative activities you choose. For the challenges that I have selected, you'll need hula hoops, scarves, long ropes, balloons, small balls, cones, and either carpet squares or polyspots (rubber discs). I will continue to use the *Slim Goodbody Presents All Fit* video series to convey the cognitive concepts related to health-related fitness.

This unit is also an extension of the last in terms of developing a supportive and psychologically safe environment through which students can feel comfortable with their physical abilities. It is an opportunity for students to continue to get to know one another and extend their relationships through cooperation and trust building. Students will also have the opportunity to extend their learning into the community as they research opportunities for physical activities in the community. Ideally, the other sixth grade teachers at your school will also use this time to continue to help students develop their social and cooperative skills so that by the end of this unit you and your colleagues will have set the stage for a supportive school environment in which the students can learn during their next three years of school.

Unit Standards

1.0 – Applies the correct techniques for locomotor, nonlocomotor, and manipulative skills to a variety of cooperative activities.

2.1 – Identifies when and how feedback should be given.

2.2 – Explains Newton's Third Law.

2.3 – Experiences a variety of cooperative games and activities.

3.0 – Identifies opportunities for physical activity in and out of school.

4.0 – Participates in a wide variety of exercises for all five areas of health-related fitness as well as ones for warm-up and cooldown and explains the purpose of warm-up and cooldown exercises and the five principles of fitness development.

5.0 – Describes cooperative skills and gives examples.

6.1 – Analyzes how physical development varies within the peer group.

6.2 – Describes the relationship between the role of physical activities and getting to know people from other cultures.

7.0 – Associates different qualities of movement with different expressions.

Unit Outline

Day 1

Have students watch "Warm-Up/Cool-Down" on the *Slim Goodbody Presents All Fit* (vol. 2) video, then discuss what they learned.   **4.0**

Introduce the unit.

Discuss the relationship between the role of games and sports and getting to know people from other cultures.   **5.0 / 6.2**

Have students play Interest Circle, having them focus only on physical activity interests. (See appendix C.)   **1.0 / 2.3 / 5.0**

Debrief the activity, including discussing the relationship between the roles of games and sports and getting to know people from other cultures. (Assessment opportunity: structured observation.)   **5.0 / 6.2**

Day 2

Brainstorm social skills related to cooperation.   **5.0**

Discuss Newton's Third Law and how it applies to cooperation.   **2.2**

Have students brainstorm a list of what encouragement looks and sounds like. (Make a T-chart.)   **5.0**

Give students feedback as they participate and encourage one another in Switch, Stand Up, and Everyone Up in Pairs. (See appendix C.)   **1.0 / 2.1 / 2.2 / 2.3 / 5.0**

Debrief each activity, including how Newton's Third Law and the use of encouragement are related to success in the partner activities. (Assessment opportunity: structured observation.)   **2.2 / 4.0**

Day 3

Review cooperation skills.   **5.0**

Discuss when and how students should give feedback.   **2.1**

Review Newton's Third Law.   **2.2**

Have students participate and encourage one another in Greeter, Bottoms Up, and Inchworm while you provide feedback. (See appendix C.)   **1.0 / 2.1 / 2.2 / 2.3**

Debrief each activity, including how Newton's Third Law and the use of encouragement are related to success in these partner activities. (Assessment opportunity: structured observation)   **2.2 / 4.0**

Day 4

Discuss the meaning of "trust."   **5.0**

Have students brainstorm a list of what trust looks like and sounds like. (Make a T-chart.)   **5.0**

Give students feedback as they participate in Trust Walk and Two-Person Trust Fall. (See appendix C.)   **1.0 / 2.1 / 2.3 / 5.0**

Debrief each activity.   **5.0**

Day 5

Review the meaning of "trust."   **5.0**

Give students feedback as they participate in Two-Person Trust Fall and Yeah, But. (See appendix C.)   **1.0 / 2.1 / 2.3 / 5.0**

Debrief each activity.   **5.0**

Day 6

Discuss trusting other people.   **5.0**

Have students participate in Switch, Touch Knees, Stand Up, Everyone Up in Pairs, Greeter, Two-Person Trust Fall, Bottoms Up, Inchworm, Trust Walk, and Yeah, But by rotating through stations. Have half the students rotate clockwise and the other half rotate counterclockwise so that each person has a new partner for each activity. (See appendix C.)   **1.0 / 2.1 / 2.3 / 5.0**

Debrief each activity before students rotate to the next station.   **5.0**

Day 7

Assign students randomly to groups of four.

Review warm-up and cooldown principles.   **4.0**

Have students watch "Training Principles" on the *Slim Goodbody Presents All Fit* (vol. 2) video.   **4.0**

Have students discuss how physical development varies within their groups and the affect this will have on their working together.   **6.1**

Ask students to discuss warm-up, cooldown, and training principles. (Assessment opportunity: structured observation.)   **4.0**

For homework, have students create a brochure depicting physical activity opportunities available to them in and out of school. (Assessment assignment opportunity: project.)   **3.0**

Day 8

Discuss working cooperatively in a group.   **5.0**

Discuss the relationship between qualities of movement and different expressions.   **7.0**

Give students feedback as they play Ice Breaker, Booop, and Blind Polygon. (See appendix C.)   **1.0 / 2.1 / 2.3 / 5.0**

Debrief each activity, including discussing the qualities of movement and different expressions. (Assessment opportunity: structured observation.)   **5.0 / 7.0**

Day 9

Review working cooperatively in small groups.   **5.0**

Have students brainstorm a list of what courtesy looks like and sounds like. (Make a T-chart.)   **5.0**

Give students feedback as they play Everyone Up, Courtesy Tag, and Shark Attack. (See appendix C.)   **1.0 / 2.1 / 2.3 / 5.0**

Debrief each activity, including discussing the qualities of movement and different expressions as well as the use of courtesy. (Assessment opportunity: structured observation.)   **5.0 / 7.0**

Day 10

Review working cooperatively in small groups using courtesy.   **5.0**

Give students feedback as they play Across the Great Divide and Moon Ball. (See appendix C.)   **1.0 / 2.1 / 2.3 / 5.0**

Debrief each activity, including discussing the qualities of movement and different expressions, as well as the use of courtesy. (Assessment opportunity: structured observation.)   **5.0 / 7.0**

Day 11

Review working cooperatively in small groups.   **5.0**

Have students brainstorm a list of what positive disagreement looks like and sounds like. (Make a T-chart.)   **5.0**

Give students feedback as they play Turnstile and Knots. (See appendix C.)   **1.0 / 2.1 / 2.3 / 5.0**

Debrief each activity, including discussing the qualities of movement and different expressions as well as what positive disagreement is, then have students note their own feelings in their journals. (Assessment opportunity: journal entry.)   **5.0 / 7.0**

Day 12

Review working cooperatively in small groups and what positive disagreement is.   **5.0**

Give students feedback as they play Group Juggle and Traffic Jam. (See appendix C.)   **1.0 / 2.1 / 2.3 / 5.0**

Debrief each activity, including discussing when and how students should use feedback and positive disagreement.   **2.1 / 5.0**

Day 13

Discuss trust development related to working in groups.   **5.0**

Have students brainstorm a list of what active listening looks like and sounds like. (Make a T-chart.)   **5.0**

Give students feedback as they play Yurt Circle and Minefield. (See appendix C.)   **1.0 / 2.1 / 2.3 / 5.0**

Debrief each activity, including discussing when and how students should use feedback as well as how to listen actively. (Assessment opportunity: structured observation.)   **2.1 / 5.0**

Day 14

Review trust development when working in groups.   **5.0**

Have students brainstorm a list of what acceptance of others looks like and sounds like. (Make a T-chart.)   **5.0 / 6.1**

Give students feedback as they play Trust Circle and Levitation. (See appendix C.)   **1.0 / 2.1 / 2.3 / 5.0**

Debrief each activity, including discussing how the variables of physical development within the group affected participation in Levitation.   **5.0 / 6.1**

Have students describe their feelings related to participation in Levitation in their journals. (Assessment opportunity: journal entry.)   **5.0 / 6.1**

Day 15

Review trust development, active listening, and acceptance of others related to working in small groups.   **5.0 / 6.1**

Give students feedback as they participate in Sherpa Walk. (See appendix C.)   **1.0 / 2.1 / 2.3 / 5.0**

Debrief the activity.   **5.0**

For homework, have students write an essay describing cooperative skills and giving specific examples of how they have demonstrated different cooperative skills. (Assessment assignment opportunity: essay.)   **5.0**

Unit 3: Body Management

This unit begins our focus on the skills theme units starting with how our bodies can assume different shapes either in stationary or moving situations. Specifically, this unit focuses on balance, weight transfer, flight, and rolling. Building on the trust developed between students throughout the last unit, you can begin to have students spot one another as they attempt to perform activities in this body management unit. In order to address standard four, I'll continue to cover physical fitness during the daily warm-up and flexibility exercises as well as include cardiorespiratory and muscular strength and endurance exercises every other day, performed through the station approach. I'll review the flexibility concepts related to health-related fitness development daily during the warm-up period. From days 4 through 11, I'll have the students rotate from station to station, performing activities in five or more categories. As students demonstrate competency in the first skill in each category, I will have them document their performances on their progress cards, then practice the next skill in that category. I have used this inclusion style of teaching throughout the unit. The following lists describe the categories and related activities included in this unit.

Note: If you are unfamiliar with these skills, refer to *Physical Education for Elementary School Children* by Kirchner and *A Manual for Tumbling and Apparatus Stunts* by Ryser and Brown (see Bibliography).

Static balance:

- Balancing on different body parts (alone and with a partner)
- Knee scale
- Crane stand
- Tripod
- Three-point tip-up
- Headstand (see figure 14.7)

Figure 14.8 Handstand.

Figure 14.7 Headstand.

- Wall walk-up
- Switcheroo
- Teeter-totter
- Handstand (see figure 14.8)

Dynamic balance:

- Thread-the-needle

- Jump-through
- Walking on a balance beam
- Walking on a balance beam with a dip
- Single-leg circle

Rolling:

- Log roll
- Shoulder roll
- Triple roll
- Back shoulder roll
- Squat forward roll (see figure 14.9)
- Double roll
- Squat backward roll (see figure 14.10)
- Pike forward roll
- Straddle roll

Weight transfer:

- Pivoting in place
- Pivoting on a balance beam

Figure 14.9   Squat forward roll.

Figure 14.10   Squat backward roll.

- Squat turning on the balance beam
- Tumbling sequences
- Balance beam sequences
- Cartwheel (see figure 14.11)
- Round-off
- Handstand roll-out
- Back extension

Flight:

- Heel click
- Heel slap
- Running and jumping for height
- Running and jumping for distance
- Running and leaping
- Running and leaping for distance
- Running, hopping, and jumping on a springboard
- Running, hopping, and jumping on a springboard for height
- Running, hopping, and jumping on a springboard for height and distance

Depending on the number of students in each class, you can double each of the stations and add a video station. In lieu of performing the exercises at the beginning of the instructional period, you can add abdominal strength, upper body strength, and cardiorespiratory stations.

It is best if you conduct this unit inside a gymnasium or closed area. You can, however, conduct this unit outside in an open area, but only if you can bring mats or some other protective material outside. Although I will make several references to a balance beam, you can have students use a line on the gym floor if a balance beam is unavailable. And students can perform the flight skills without the springboard, but it does give students an additional challenge. Instructional material for this unit includes recorded gymnastics performances from television broadcasts. The visual images of these performances provide students with model performances for the many movements they will attempt during the unit. Once again, I'll use the *Slim Goodbody Presents All Fit* video series to convey the cognitive concepts related to health-related fitness (see appendix D).

This unit aligns well with sixth grade history and social science studies, especially as students investi-

Figure 14.11 Cartwheel.

gate the type of activities and games played by the ancient Babylonians. If you're able to work on an interdisciplinary team, the history/social science teacher can assess students' knowledge of the different types of physical activities and physical education experienced by the ancient Babylonians. And because it requires students to express through movement different emotions or characters they are reading about in books, this unit aligns well with language arts as well. Finally, through this unit, your students will also begin to connect more with your community as they begin participating in areas of physical activity of interest to them outside of school.

Unit Standards

1.0 – Applies the correct techniques for locomotor and nonlocomotor skills to a variety of body management activities.

2.1 – Gives appropriate feedback to a partner when developing or improving body management skills.

2.2 – Describes how Newton's Third Law applies to body management.

2.3 – Experiences a variety of cooperative activities that involve body management.

3.0 – Chooses to participate in physical activities of interest outside of physical education.

4.0 – Participates in a wide variety of exercises for all five areas of health-related fitness and explains the intensity and time concepts for flexibility.

5.0 – Displays cooperative skills when working with a partner during a movement-related experience.

6.1 – Describes how skills are developed and what can be done to assist with skill development.

6.2 – Describes physical activities and physical education from ancient Babylon.

7.0 – Demonstrates body management skills, using various qualities of movement to convey different expressions in a student-created routine.

Unit Outline

Day 1

Introduce unit.

Assign students to groups of four.

Have students watch "Flexibility" on the *Slim Goodbody Presents All Fit* (vol. 1) video, then discuss what they learned. **4.0**

Review with students the intensity and time concepts related to flexibility. **4.0**

Discuss the physical activities and physical education experiences of ancient Babylonians. **6.2**

For homework, have students begin to monitor their participation in activities of interest outside of physical education. (Assessment assignment opportunity: log.) **3.0**

Day 2

Demonstrate, then have students perform the first skill in each category. **1.0**

- Static balance: balancing on different body parts
- Dynamic balance: thread-the-needle
- Rolling: log roll
- Weight transfer: pivoting in place
- Flight: heel click

Have students brainstorm about different ways they can use each of these skills. **1.0**

Day 3

Explain station approach and hand out a checklist on which students may record their progress in the skills in each category.

Discuss how students can improve body management skills; discuss the influence of physical development. **6.1**

Discuss giving feedback to a partner when working on body management skills. **2.1**

Have students practice giving feedback as you demonstrate skills. **2.1**

Have students brainstorm about what it means to work cooperatively with a partner at each station. **5.0**

Have pairs perform the first skill in each category, giving each other feedback. **1.0**

- Static balance: finding five positions of balance on four body parts, then finding five positions of balance on three body parts
- Dynamic balance: thread-the-needle
- Rolling: log roll
- Weight transfer: pivoting in place
- Flight: heel click

Days 4 and 5

Demonstrate one or two new skills in each category **1.0**

Have pairs practice the skills, giving feedback to each other as they rotate through the stations in groups of four. **1.0 / 2.1 / 2.3 / 5.0**

Have students brainstorm about how Newton's Third Law applies to the body management skills they performed.   **2.2**

Have students brainstorm about the different ways they can apply to other situations each skill they practiced.   **1.0**

Days 6 and 7

Demonstrate one or two new skills in each category.   **1.0**

Have pairs practice the skills, giving each other feedback as they rotate through the stations in groups of four.   **1.0 / 2.1 / 2.3 / 5.0**

Have students brainstorm about how Newton's Third Law applies to the body management skills they performed.   **2.2**

Have students brainstorm about the different ways they can apply each skill they practiced.   **1.0**

Days 8 and 9

Demonstrate one or two new skills in each category   **1.0**

Have pairs practice the skills, giving each other feedback as they rotate through the stations in groups of four.   **1.0 / 2.1 / 2.3 / 5.0**

Have students brainstorm about how Newton's Third Law applies to the body management skills they performed.   **2.2**

Have students brainstorm about the different ways they can apply each skill they practiced.   **1.0**

Days 10 and 11

Demonstrate one or two new skills in each category.   **1.0**

Have pairs practice the skills, giving each other feedback as they rotate through the stations in groups of four. (Assessment opportunity: structured observation.)   **1.0 / 2.1 / 2.3 / 5.0**

Have students brainstorm about how Newton's Third Law applies to the body management skills they performed.   **2.2**

Have students brainstorm about the different ways they can apply each skill they practiced.   **1.0**

For homework, have students write an essay describing how Newton's Third Law applies to one of the body management skills they performed. (Assessment assignment opportunity: essay.)   **2.2**

Day 12

Review the qualities of movement.   **7.0**

In groups of four, have students create their own body management routines, using various qualities of movement to convey a message.   **7.0**

Days 13 and 14

Have groups work on their routines.   **7.0**

Day 15

Have each group demonstrate their routine to one other group, explaining what they learned and how their physical development helped them succeed. (Assessment opportunity: structured observation.)   **1.0 / 6.1 / 7.0**

Collect student logs on participation in physical activity outside of physical education. (Assessment opportunity: log.)   **3.0**

Unit 4: Locomotor Skills

In this unit, the second of the skills theme approach, I'll expand on body management by reviewing basic locomotor skills (walking, running, hopping, skipping, jumping, leaping, galloping, sliding) with students. Then I'll apply these skills to rhythm activities such as tinikling, jumping rope, and dancing. For those unfamiliar with tinikling, it originated in the Republic of the Philippines and involves dance steps performed to music over two moving parallel poles. The dances selected for this unit align with the various countries being studied in sixth grade history and social science, but you can use different dances from other countries, depending on the history and social science units taught at your school. Be aware, however, that I have sequenced the dances in this sample unit so that the locomotor skills presented in the first dance are repeated in subsequent dances. To address standard four, I will continue to cover physical fitness during the daily warm-up and flexibility exercises as well as have students perform muscular strength and endurance exercises every other day. Tinikling, jumping rope, and dancing satisfy the need for cardiorespiratory training. I'll review the cardiorespiratory endurance and body composition concepts related to health-related fitness development daily during the warm-up period.

This particular unit works best in a closed area or gymnasium, but you can present it outside. If you must conduct the unit outside, it is best to choose a secluded area so that students do not feel self-conscious about performing to music in front of other classes. For equipment, you'll need short jump ropes, long jump ropes, and bamboo poles or plastic pipes (three-quarter-inch diameter PVC plumbing pipe), 10 to 12 feet long for the tinikling poles. You may prefer to use JumpBands (one-inch-wide elastic bands) available from Kathryn Short Productions as a safer alternative to bamboo poles or plastic pipes for tinikling. Naturally, because this is a rhythms and dance unit, you'll need a variety of music. We will also use *The Jump Rope Primer Video* to introduce many of the jump rope skills and the *Slim Goodbody Presents All Fit* video series to convey the cognitive concepts related to health-related fitness (see appendix D). Throughout the unit, I have students wear heart rate monitors to determine whether they are in their target heart rate zones long enough to improve their cardiorespiratory endurance. On different days, I have different students download the data from their heart rate monitors into the computer, then I have them place the computer-generated graphs into their electronic portfolios. (See appendix D for music, equipment, software, and video sources.)

This unit aligns well with sixth grade history and social science studies as the students study the countries of origin of rope jumping, tinikling, and the various dances they will perform. This unit also aligns well with sixth grade music studies because I ask students to create and perform a dance using locomotor skills, incorporating various qualities of movement in order to convey an expression. At the conclusion of this unit, you can take your students to shopping centers or malls to demonstrate to the community the various dances they have learned.

Unit Standards

1.0 – Applies the correct techniques for locomotor skills to activities performed to music.

2.1 – Gives appropriate feedback to a partner when developing or improving locomotor skills.

2.2 – Describes how Newton's Third Law applies to locomotor skills.

2.3 – Explains the elements of a cooperative game.

3.0 – Chooses to participate in physical activities of interest outside physical education.

4.0 – Participates in a wide variety of exercises for all five areas of health-related fitness and explains intensity and time concepts for cardiorespiratory endurance and body composition.

5.0 – Displays cooperative skills in small groups during a movement-related experience.

6.1 – Describes what happens when individuals are forced to learn before they are ready.

6.2 – Describes the origins of rhythmic activities and dances performed during class and their influence on dances performed today.

7.0 – Demonstrates locomotor skills, using various qualities of movement in repetitive patterns set to music in order to convey different expressions.

Unit Outline

Day 1

Introduce unit.

Randomly assign students to groups of four.

Demonstrate all eight locomotor skills (running, hopping, skipping, jumping, leaping, galloping, sliding, walking).   **1.0**

Have students perform all eight locomotor skills while you play music.   **1.0**

Give students new logs for charting their participation in physical activities outside physical education. (Assessment assignment opportunity: log.)   **3.0**

Day 2

Have students watch "Cardiorespiratory Fitness" on the *Slim Goodbody Presents All Fit* (vol. 1) video, then discuss what they learned.   **4.0**

Have students review intensity and time concepts related to cardiorespiratory endurance.   **4.0**

Review the qualities of movement.   **7.0**

Have students perform all eight locomotor skills while you play music, using various qualities of movement as you call them out.   **1.0**

Have students perform all eight locomotor skills while you play music at a speed fast enough to raise their heart rates into their target heart rate zones.   **1.0**

Have students brainstorm a list of various motor skills that use each of the locomotor skills.   **1.0**

Day 3

Discuss how students can improve locomotor skills and how physical development affects locomotor skills.   **6.1**

Discuss giving feedback to a partner when working on locomotor skills.   **2.1**

Review with students what it means to work cooperatively with a partner.   **5.0**

Demonstrate the basic jump forward and the basic jump backward using short ropes.   **1.0**

Have pairs practice the basic jump forward and the basic jump backward using short ropes, giving each other feedback.   **1.0 / 2.1 / 5.0**

Day 4

Review how students can improve locomotor skills and how physical development affects locomotor skills.   **6.1**

Discuss with students what happens when individuals are forced to learn a new skill before they are ready.   **6.1**

Review giving feedback and working cooperatively with a partner when working on locomotor skills.   **2.1 / 5.0**

Demonstrate the basic jump and the front and back entries for long ropes.   **1.0**

Have students, in their groups of four, practice the basic jump and the front and back entries for long ropes, giving each other feedback.   **1.0 / 2.1 / 5.0**

Have students describe why they are now ready to learn long rope skills. (Assessment assignment opportunity: journal entry.)   **6.1**

Day 5

Introduce tinikling and its origin.   **1.0 / 6.2**

Demonstrate striker skills for tinikling or ender skills for JumpBands.   **1.0**

Have students practice striker skills.   **1.0**

Demonstrate the basic jump for tinikling. (See figure 14.12.)   **1.0**

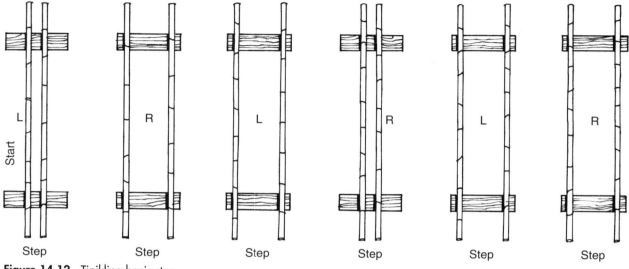

Figure 14.12   Tinikling basic step.

Have students practice striker skills and the basic jump for tinikling while partners give feedback.
1.0 / 2.1 / 5.0

Have students discuss how Newton's Third Law applies to tinikling.   **2.2**

Days 6 and 7

Note: New skills being introduced are in parentheses.

Introduce new skills by demonstrating them or by showing *The Jump Rope Primer Video*.   **1.0**

Have students rotate through the following stations: tinikling (rocker step, crossover step; see figure 14.13), short ropes (jogging step, straddle step, can can, switches), long ropes (toss and catch ball).
1.0 / 2.1 / 5.0

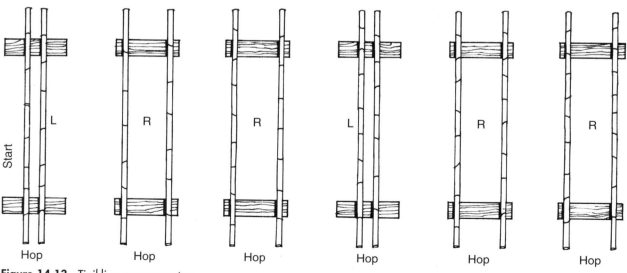

Figure 14.13   Tinikling crossover step.

Have students discuss how Newton's Third Law applies to the new skills.   **2.2**

Have students discuss how they encouraged a partner today.   **5.0**

Days 8 and 9

Introduce new skills by demonstrating them or by showing *The Jump Rope Primer Video*.   **1.0**

Have students rotate through stations: tinikling (circle poles, fast tinikling trot), short ropes (leg swing, continuous sideswing open, continuous forward crossover, continuous backward crossover), long ropes (dribble ball). (Assessment opportunity: rubric.)   **1.0 / 2.1 / 5.0**

Have students discuss how Newton's Third Law applies to the new skills.   **2.2**

Have students discuss how they encouraged a partner today.   **5.0**

Days 10 and 11

Introduce new skills by demonstrating them or by showing *The Jump Rope Primer Video*.   **1.0**

Stations: tinikling (side jump, crossover, straddle step), short ropes (partners), long ropes (eggbeater). (Assessment opportunity: rubric.)   **1.0 / 2.1 / 5.0**

Have students discuss how Newton's Third Law applies to the new skills.   **2.2**

Days 12 and 13

Introduce new skills by demonstrating them or by showing *The Jump Rope Primer Video*.   **1.0**

Stations: tinikling (review steps), combination long and short rope skills, long ropes (double Dutch). (Assessment opportunity: rubric.)   **1.0 / 2.1 / 5.0**

Have students discuss how Newton's Third Law applies to the new skills.   **2.2**

Day 14

Have students watch "Body Composition" on the *Slim Goodbody Presents All Fit* (vol. 1) video, then discuss what they learned.   **4.0**

Have students review intensity and time concepts related to body composition in textbooks or hand-outs.   **4.0**

Discuss the elements of a cooperative game.   **2.3**

For homework, have students outline the elements of a cooperative game. (Assessment assignment opportunity: written assignment for portfolio.)   **2.3**

Day 15

Note: Directions for most dances come with the music, or check out *International Playtime: Classroom Games and Dances From Around the World* by Nelson and Glass. (See Bibliography.)

Introduce clapping.   **1.0**

Teach the clapping dance (Ghana).   **1.0**

Describe the origin of the clapping dance.   **6.2**

Have students practice the clapping dance with feedback from their partners.   **1.0 / 2.1 / 5.0 / 7.0**

Day 16

Introduce shovel, step, and clapping movements   **1.0**

Teach the tanko bushi (Japan).   **1.0**

Describe the origin of the tanko bushi.   **6.2**

Have students practice the tanko bushi with feedback from their partners.   **1.0 / 2.1 / 5.0 / 7.0**

Have students review the clapping dance with feedback from their partners.   **1.0 / 2.1 / 5.0 / 7.0**

Day 17

Introduce walking and bending movements.   **1.0**

Teach the limbo (West Indies).   **1.0**

Describe the origin of the limbo.   **6.2**

Have students practice the limbo with feedback from their partners.   **1.0 / 2.1 / 5.0 / 7.0**

Have students review the tanko bushi with feedback from their partners.   **1.0 / 2.1 / 5.0 / 7.0**

Day 18

Introduce walking and swinging movements.   **1.0**

Teach the apat apat (Philippines).   **1.0**

Describe the origin of the apat apat.   **6.2**

Have students practice the apat apat with feedback from their partners.   **1.0 / 2.1 / 5.0 / 7.0**

Have students review the limbo with feedback from their partners.   **1.0 / 2.1 / 5.0 / 7.0**

Day 19

Introduce step, kick, and toes in and out movements.   **1.0**

Teach the pata pata (Africa).   **1.0**

Describe the origin of the pata pata.   **6.2**

Have students practice the pata pata with feedback from their partners.   **1.0 / 2.1 / 5.0 / 7.0**

Have students review the apat apat with feedback from their partners.   **1.0 / 2.1 / 5.0 / 7.0**

Day 20

Introduce the crossover, pivot, and two-step.   **1.0**

Teach the miserlou (Greece).   **1.0**

Describe the origin of the miserlou.   **6.2**

Have students practice the miserlou with feedback from their partners.   **1.0 / 2.1 / 5.0 / 7.0**

Have students review the pata pata with feedback from their partners.   **1.0 / 2.1 / 5.0 / 7.0**

Day 21

Discuss dance project: Research, learn, and present a dance and its history. (Assessment assignment opportunity: project.)   **1.0 / 6.2**

Introduce running and arch movements.   **1.0**

Teach the troika (Russian).   **1.0**

Describe the origin of the troika.   **6.2**

Have students practice the troika with feedback from their partners.   **1.0 / 2.1 / 5.0 / 7.0**

Have students practice the miserlou with feedback from their partners.   **1.0 / 2.1 / 5.0 / 7.0**

Day 22

Introduce schottische and break step.   **1.0**

Teach the korobushka (Russian).   **1.0**

Describe the origin of the korobushka.   **6.2**

Have students practice the korobushka with feedback from their partners.   **1.0 / 2.1 / 5.0 / 7.0**

Have students practice troika with feedback from their partners.   **1.0 / 2.1 / 5.0 / 7.0**

Day 23

Introduce the grapevine step.   **1.0**

Teach the hora (Israel).   **1.0**

Describe the origin of the hora.   **6.2**

Have students practice the hora with feedback from their partners.   **1.0 / 2.1 / 5.0 / 7.0**

Have students practice the korobushka with feedback from their partners.   **1.0 / 2.1 / 5.0 / 7.0**

Day 24

Introduce the stamp.   **1.0**

Teach the alunelul (Romanian).   **1.0**

Describe the origin of the alunelul.   **6.2**

Have students practice the alunelul with feedback from their partners.   **1.0 / 2.1 / 5.0 / 7.0**

Have students practice the hora with feedback from their partners.   **1.0 / 2.1 / 5.0 / 7.0**

Day 25

Review the grapevine and stomps.   **1.0**

Teach the ali pasa (Turkey).   **1.0**

Describe the origin of the ali pasa.   **6.2**

Have students practice the ali pasa with feedback from their partners.   **1.0 / 2.1 / 5.0 / 7.0**

Have students practice the alunelul with feedback from their partners. (Assessment opportunity: rubric.) **1.0 / 2.1 / 5.0 / 7.0**

Day 26

Introduce the twist and jump.   **1.0**

Teach the halay (Armenian).   **1.0**

Describe the origin of the halay.   **6.2**

Have students practice the halay with feedback from their partners.   **1.0 / 2.1 / 5.0 / 7.0**

Have students practice the ali pasa with feedback from their partners. (Assessment opportunity: rubric.)   **1.0 / 2.1 / 5.0 / 7.0**

Day 27

Introduce the hop, heel touch, skip, shuffle or blek, and two-step.   **1.0**

Teach the la raspa (Mexico).   **1.0**

Describe the origin of the la raspa.   **6.2**

Have students practice the la raspa with feedback from their partners.   **1.0 / 2.1 / 5.0 / 7.0**

Have students practice the halay with feedback from their partners. (Assessment opportunity: rubric.) **1.0 / 2.1 / 5.0 / 7.0**

Day 28

Introduce the polka step, swing, clap, and the grand right and left.   **1.0**

Teach the kalvelis (Lithuanian). **1.0**

Describe the origin of the kalvelis. **6.2**

Have students practice the kalvelis with feedback from their partners. **1.0 / 2.1 / 5.0 / 7.0**

Have students practice the la raspa with feedback from their partners. (Assessment opportunity: rubric.) **1.0 / 2.1 / 5.0 / 7.0**

Days 29 and 30

Have students hand in their logs showing participation in activities outside of physical education. (Assessment opportunity: log.) **3.0**

Have each group present their dance to another small group; have them explain the history of the dance and its influence on dancing today as well. (Assessment opportunity: project.) **1.0 / 5.0 / 6.2 / 7.0**

For homework, have students describe how Newton's Third Law applies to locomotor skills. (Assessment opportunity: essay.) **2.2**

Unit 5: Underhand and Sidearm Throwing and Catching

In our third skills theme unit, we move on to the manipulation of objects. The underhand and sidearm throw and catch are used in many of our traditional sports. I have assumed for this unit and the next three that, although students may not be proficient in these skills, they have been introduced to them during their elementary physical education experience. Specifically, the purpose of this unit is to ensure that the students learn the correct techniques for both the underhand and sidearm throws and then to extend those skills to throwing for distance and throwing for accuracy. Once the students have acquired some distance and accuracy, I have them explore throwing at moving objects and, finally, throwing while they are moving. Each step of the way brings the students closer to applying the skills to game-like settings, specifically in this unit to bowling and Frisbee activities. To address standard four, I will continue to cover physical fitness activities during the daily warm-up and flexibility exercises as well as have students perform muscular strength, muscular endurance, and cardiorespiratory exercises every other day. I'll also review muscular endurance concepts related to health-related fitness development daily during the warm-up period.

You can conduct the rolling skills activities on any blacktop area and the underhand and sidearm throws in any open area, indoors or outdoors. So that students can see that they can apply the underhand and sidearm throws and catches to a wide variety of activities, provide a variety of objects (e.g., fleece balls, softballs, bowling balls, Frisbees, and other balls) for students to practice throwing.

Provide a variety of targets, including bowling pins, so that students can practice their accuracy in several different situations. Use plastic liter bottles and student-made targets to create new challenges for students. Appropriate instructional materials include *Learn to Bowl* and *Learn to Bowl II*, both of which provide students with visual images of model bowlers, *MacBowling Tutorial*, a software program that teaches students bowling scoring, and *Disc Video*, which gives students visual images of model Frisbee players. In addition, I will continue to use the *Slim Goodbody Presents All Fit* video series to convey the cognitive concepts of health-related fitness. (See appendix D for instructional material sources.)

This unit and the next three lend themselves especially well to interdisciplinary links with the science curriculum and math curriculum. As students strive to improve both distance and accuracy, the scientific principles of how these occur come into play. Specifically, I'll have students focus on Newton's Third Law and how it applies to throwing and catching and to the striking of an object. Because this approach may surprise your students and their parents, it's important that you explain your use of the skills theme approach with manipulatives to both students and parents because often their perception is that students should be learning to play softball, basketball, and football. Spend time showing students the links between these fundamental skills and a wide variety of sport-specific skills to help both them and their parents understand your goals.

Unit Standards

1.0 – Applies the correct techniques for locomotor, nonlocomotor, and manipulative skills to underhand and sidearm throwing and catching skills in a variety of activities.

2.1 – Gives appropriate feedback to a partner when developing or improving underhand and sidearm throwing and catching skills.

2.2 – Describes how Newton's Third Law applies to underhand and sidearm throwing and catching.

2.3 – Creates a cooperative game using underhand and sidearm throwing and catching skills.

3.0 – Chooses to participate in physical activities of interest outside physical education.

4.0 – Participates in a wide variety of exercises to develop all five areas of health-related fitness and explains intensity and time concepts for muscular endurance.

5.0 – Describes cooperative goal setting.

6.1 – Analyzes the variables of physical development within her peer group and their affects on her own learning of the underhand and sidearm throwing and catching skills.

6.2 – Describes physical activities and physical education in ancient Greece and Egypt.

7.0 – Demonstrates underhand and sidearm throwing and catching skills, using various qualities of movement in repetitive patterns to convey different expressions.

Unit Outline

Day 1

Assign students to heterogeneous groups of four.

Give students new logs for charting their participation in physical activities outside physical education. (Assessment assignment opportunity: log.)   **3.0**

Have students watch "Muscular Strength and Endurance" on the *Slim Goodbody Presents All Fit* (vol. 1) video, then discuss what they learned.   **4.0**

Have students review intensity and time concepts related to muscular endurance. (Assessment opportunity: structured observation.)   **4.0**

Demonstrate rolling and catching a ball.   **1.0**

Have students roll and catch with their partners.   **1.0**

Have students roll and catch with partners, using various qualities of movement (e.g., rolling the ball fast, low, in a straight line, in a curved line). (Assessment opportunity: structured observation.)   **1.0 / 7.0**

Day 2

Review rolling skill.   **1.0**

Discuss giving appropriate feedback to a partner when working on throwing and catching skills.   **2.1**

Have students rotate through several stations, rolling different-sized balls at a variety of stationary targets from different distances with feedback from their partners.   **1.0 / 2.1**

Have students play Goalie Ball in pairs using the skill of rolling. (See appendix C.)   **1.0**

Day 3

Introduce bowling as an activity that applies rolling.   **1.0**

Figure 14.14   Four-step bowling approach.

Have students watch the *Learn to Bowl* video, then discuss what they learned.   **1.0**

Discuss the history of bowling and other activities played in ancient Egypt.   **6.2**

Demonstrate the proper bowling ball grip.   **1.0**

Have students practice gripping a ball with feedback from their partners.   **1.0 / 2.1**

Demonstrate the bowling four-step approach. (See figure 14.14.)   **1.0**

Have students practice the four-step approach with and without a ball with feedback from their partners.   **1.0 / 2.1**

Explain spot bowling to students.   **1.0**

Ask students what they think is the relationship between rolling a ball and physical development. (Assessment opportunity: journal entry.)   **6.1**

Days 4, 5, and 6

Discuss with students how they are going to practice and improve their bowling and rolling skills over the next three days.   **5.0**

	1	2	3	4	5	6	7	8	9	10
You	7 ◿	5 3	9 ◿	F 6	5 –	⊠	⊠	8 ◿	⊠	⊠⊠⊠
	15	23	33	39	44	72	92	112	142	172

	10 + 5	5 + 3	10 + 0	0 + 6	5 + 0	10+10+ 8	10+8+2	10 + 10	10+10+10	10+10+10
	15	+8	+10	+6	+5	+28	+20	+20	+30	+30

Figure 14.15   Sample bowling score sheet. ◿ stands for a spare, ⊠ stands for a strike, and F stands for a foul.

In groups, have students discuss how a group can determine a cooperative goal (e.g., skill improvement for all members of the group). (Assessment opportunity: structured observation.)   **5.0**

Review the bowling grip, the four-step approach, and spot bowling.   **1.0**

Have students rotate through three stations: the bowling four-step approach with feedback from their partners, scoring in bowling (using computer software, see figure 14.15), and bowling history and rules (reading from a book). (Assessment opportunity: structured observation.)   **1.0 / 2.1**

Ask students what they think the relationship between Newton's Third Law and the bowling ball striking the pins is. (Assessment opportunity: essay.)   **2.2**

Day 7

Demonstrate underhand throwing and catching.   **1.0**

Have students throw and catch a ball, using an underhand motion with their partners.   **1.0**

In partners, have students throw and catch a ball, using an underhand motion and various qualities of movement (e.g., throwing the ball high, low, softly, hard). (Assessment opportunity: structured observation.)   **1.0 / 7.0**

Have students rotate through several stations, using an underhand motion to throw a variety of different-sized objects (e.g., balls, Frisbees) at a variety of stationary targets from different distances with feedback from their partners.   **1.0 / 2.1**

Day 8

Review the underhand throw and catch.   **1.0**

Show the pancake catch for catching a Frisbee on the *Disc Video*.   **1.0**

Have students rotate through several stations, using an underhand motion to throw different-sized objects at a variety of stationary targets from different distances with feedback from their partners. (Assessment opportunity: rubric.)   **1.0 / 2.1**

Have students play Goalie Ball in pairs, using the underhand throwing skill.   **1.0**

Day 9

Demonstrate the sidearm throwing and catching skills.   **1.0**

Have students throw and catch a ball with their partners, using the sidearm motion.   **1.0**

Have students throw and catch a ball with their partners, using the sidearm motion and employing various qualities of movement (e.g., throwing the ball high, low, softly, hard). (Assessment opportunity: structured observation.)   **1.0 / 7.0**

Have students rotate through several stations, using the sidearm motion to throw a variety of different-sized objects (e.g., balls, Frisbees) at a variety of stationary targets from different distances while receiving feedback from their partners.   **1.0 / 2.1**

Ask students to brainstorm a list of the various sport skills and activities that utilize a sidearm throwing motion.   **1.0**

Days 10 and 11

Show the sidearm backhand Frisbee throw on the *Disc Video*.   **1.0**

Demonstrate thumb-up and thumb-down catches with a Frisbee.   **1.0**

In groups of four, have two students throw and catch a Frisbee, using a sidearm backhand throw while two students give feedback.   **1.0 / 2.1**

Have students rotate through several stations, using a sidearm backhand motion to throw a Frisbee at a variety of stationary and moving targets from different distances while receiving feedback from their partners. You can turn this into a Frisbee Golf activity if you wish. (Assessment opportunity: rubric.)   **1.0 / 2.1**

Day 12

Show the sidearm backhand Frisbee throw and catch while moving on the *Disc Video*. **1.0**

In groups of four, have students use the sidearm backhand Frisbee throw, running up and down the field while their partners give feedback. **1.0 / 2.1**

Describe how to play Ultimate Frisbee with four players on a team. **1.0**

Ask students how Newton's Third Law applies to throwing a Frisbee back and forth while running up and down the field. (Assessment opportunity: essay.) **2.2**

Day 13

Discuss physical activities and physical education in ancient Greece, identifying modern activities that had their origins in Greece. **6.2**

Have students play Ultimate Frisbee four-on-four. (Assessment opportunity: rubric.) **1.0**

Day 14

Review the elements of a cooperative game. **2.3**

Have students create a cooperative game, using either underhand and (or) sidearm throwing and catching skills. (Assessment assignment opportunity: project.) **1.0 / 2.3**

Ask students to brainstorm about the relationship between their cooperative games and games played in either ancient Greece or Egypt. (Assessment opportunity: open-ended question.) **6.2**

Day 15

Have each group teach their cooperative game to another group. (Assessment opportunity: project.) **1.0 / 2.3**

Have students hand in their logs, showing their participation in activities outside of physical education. (Assessment opportunity: log.) **3.0**

Unit 6: Overhand Throwing and Catching

This skills theme focuses on the skills of throwing overhand and catching an overhand throw. The overhand throw is one of the most common skills used in sports. So I teach this unit to ensure that the students have the correct overhand throw technique, then I extend that skill to both throwing for distance and throwing for accuracy. Once the students have acquired some distance and accuracy, then I'll have them explore throwing at moving objects and, finally, throwing while they are moving. As with the underhand and sidearm throwing and catching skills, each step of the way brings the student closer to applying the overhand throwing skill to game-like settings, specifically in this unit to settings similar to team handball and basketball. To address standard four, I will continue to cover physical fitness during the daily warm-up and flexibility exer-

cises as well as have students perform muscular strength, muscular endurance, and cardiorespiratory exercises every other day. In this unit, I'll review daily the concept of muscular strength related to health-related fitness development during the warm-up period.

You can conduct this unit on blacktop or in a gymnasium. As in the last unit, it's important to provide students with a wide variety of objects (e.g., team handballs, fleece balls, softballs, footballs, and basketballs) as well as a variety of targets to throw the objects at. It also helps to have goals for team handball and baskets for basketball available for applying the overhand throw during lead-up games. Students also enjoy watching the Harlem Globetrotters and then attempting to create their own ball-handling routines to the Harlem Globetrotters' music.

Unit Standards

1.0 – Applies the correct techniques for locomotor, nonlocomotor, and manipulative skills to overhand throwing and catching skills in a variety of activities.

2.1 – Gives appropriate feedback to a partner when developing or improving overhand throwing and catching skills.

2.2 – Describes how Newton's Third Law applies to overhand throwing and catching skills.

2.3 – Creates a cooperative game, using overhand throwing and catching skills.

3.0 – Chooses to participate in physical activities of interest outside physical education.

4.0 – Participates in a wide variety of exercises for all five areas of health-related fitness and explains intensity and time concepts for muscular strength.

5.0 – Displays cooperative goal setting when working with a partner.

6.1 – Analyzes how physical development varies within his peer group and how these variations affect his learning of the overhand throwing and catching skills.

6.2 – Describes the first Olympics.

7.0 – Demonstrates overhand throwing and catching, using various qualities of movement in repetitive patterns to convey different expressions.

Unit Outline

Day 1

Introduce unit.

Assign students to heterogeneous groups of four.

Discuss the frequency and intensity concepts related to muscular strength.   **4.0**

Give students new logs for charting their participation in physical activities outside physical education. (Assessment assignment opportunity: log.)   **3.0**

Demonstrate the overhand throw and catch. (See figure 14.16.)   **1.0**

Figure 14.16 The correct technique for the overhand throw.

Have students practice the overhand throw and catch with a partner.   **1.0**

Have students throw and catch with a partner, using various qualities of movement (e.g., throwing the ball fast, low, high). (Assessment opportunity: rubric.)   **1.0 / 7.0**

Day 2

Review the overhand throw and catch.   **1.0**

Have students experiment with different release angles, forces, and mechanics in order to determine the most effective way to throw an object for distance.   **1.0**

Ask students to summarize the variables that produce a long throw. (Assessment opportunity: log.)   **1.0**

For homework, ask students to describe the relationship between Newton's Third Law and throwing overhand for distance. (Assessment assignment opportunity: essay.)   **2.2**

Day 3

Discuss giving appropriate feedback to a partner when working on throwing and catching skills.   **2.1**

Have students rotate through several stations, throwing different-sized balls at a variety of stationary targets from different distances while receiving feedback from their partners.   **1.0 / 2.1**

Have students identify the various sport skills and activities that utilize the overhand throwing motion.   **1.0**

Ask students to identify which of the activities that utilize an overhand throwing motion are in the Olympics.   **6.2**

Discuss the first Olympics.   **6.2**

Day 4

Demonstrate throwing overhand at a moving target or player.   **1.0**

Have students practice throwing overhand at moving targets while their partners give feedback.   **1.0 / 2.1**

Review the jump-stop and pivot from the body management unit.   **1.0**

Have students practice throwing overhand at moving players who catch the ball, perform a jump-stop, then pivot while a partner gives feedback.   **1.0 / 2.1**

Ask students to research the first Olympics. (Assessment assignment opportunity: report, in conjunction with history/social science.)   **6.2**

Day 5

Review throwing overhand at a moving target.   **1.0**

Review the two-step stop and pivot.   **1.0**

Have students practice throwing overhand at moving players who catch the ball, then perform a two-step stop and pivot while a partner gives feedback.   **1.0 / 2.1**

Have students play Goalie Ball. (See appendix C.)   **1.0**

Ask students to brainstorm about the relationship between overhand throwing ability and physical development. (Assessment opportunity: open-ended question.)   **6.1**

Day 6

Demonstrate throwing overhand at a moving target while moving.   **1.0**

In groups of four, have students perform an overhand throw and catch while moving up and down the field while their partners give feedback.   **1.0 / 2.1**

Have students play Pickle, while the fourth person provides feedback. (See appendix C.)   **1.0**

Day 7

Review the overhand throw and catch.   **1.0**

Have students rotate through a variety of stations: throwing overhand at stationary targets; the sequence of throwing overhand, catching, stopping, and pivoting; throwing overhand at moving targets; throwing overhand while moving; and throwing overhand at a moving target while moving. (Assessment opportunity: rubric.)   **1.0 / 2.1**

Days 8 and 9

Introduce Modified Four-on-Four Team Handball.   **1.0**

Discuss and practice throwing to open areas.   **1.0**

Have students play Modified Four-on-Four Team Handball, scoring by throwing the ball into the goal area. (Assessment opportunity: rubric.)   **1.0**

Day 10

Demonstrate the basketball set shot.   **1.0**

Have students practice the basketball set shot while receiving feedback from their partners. (Assessment opportunity: rubric.)   **1.0 / 2.1**

Introduce Two-on-Two No-Dribble Basketball.   **1.0**

Day 11

Have students play Two-on-Two No-Dribble Basketball. (Assessment opportunity: rubric.)   **1.0**

Have students discuss the similarities and differences between basketball and team handball.

Day 12

Have students brainstorm what cooperative goal setting looks like and sounds like when working with a partner (make a T-chart).   **5.0**

Demonstrate several ball-handling activities (body circles, figure eight).   **1.0**

Have students practice ball-handling activities.   **1.0**

Have students in pairs create a ball-handling routine to go along with the Harlem Globetrotters' music. (Assessment assignment opportunity: project.)   **1.0 / 2.1 / 5.0 / 7.0**

Day 13

Have each pair teach their ball-handling routine to another pair. (Assessment opportunity: project.)   **1.0 / 2.1 / 5.0 / 7.0**

Have students brainstorm both the qualities of movement and repetitive patterns observed in the routines. (Assessment opportunity: structured observation.)   **7.0**

Day 14

Review the elements of a cooperative game.   **2.3**

Have students, in groups of four, create a cooperative game, using overhand throwing and catching skills. (Assessment assignment opportunity: project.)   **1.0 / 2.3**

Day 15

Have each group teach their cooperative game to another group. (Assessment opportunity: project.)   **1.0 / 2.3**

Have students hand in their logs, showing participation in activities outside of physical education. (Assessment opportunity: log.)   **3.0**

Have students turn in their reports on the first Olympics. (Assessment opportunity: report.)   **6.2**

Unit 7: Striking With Body Parts

This skills theme looks at the skill of striking with body parts (e.g., hands and feet). Teach this unit to ensure that your students have the correct technique for striking with various body parts. Then extend the skill by having students strike objects at moving targets and strike while students are moving and by applying the skills to game-like settings, specifically in this unit to settings similar to volleyball and soccer. To address standard four, I'll continue to cover physical fitness during the daily warm-up and flexibility exercises and will have students perform muscular strength, muscular endurance, and cardiorespiratory exercises every other day. I'll also continue to review the cognitive concepts related to health-related fitness development daily during the warm-up period, preparing students to write a one-day plan for improving or maintaining muscular strength and endurance.

You can conduct this unit in any open area; however, a grassy area is best for practicing the kicking skills. As in the previous two units, students need a wide variety of objects (e.g., volleyballs, soccer balls, rubber playground balls, beach balls, balloons) as well as a variety of targets to aim at. It also helps to have soccer goals and volleyball nets available for applying the skills in lead-up games.

The assignment to research physical activity and physical education during ancient Rome is interdisciplinary in nature. Your students' history or social science teacher should assess the assignment from an historical perspective, their language arts teacher should assess the assignment from a writing perspective, and you should assess the assignment from the perspective of physical activity and physical education. I have assumed that students will have research time during their history/social science and language arts classes.

Unit Standards

1.0 – Applies the correct techniques for locomotor, nonlocomotor, and manipulative skills to striking with body parts to a variety of activities.

2.1 – Gives appropriate feedback to a partner when developing or improving striking with body parts skills.

2.2 – Describes how Newton's Third Law applies to striking with body parts skills.

2.3 – Creates a cooperative game, using striking with body parts skills.

3.0 – Chooses to participate in physical activities of interest outside physical education.

4.0 – Participates in a wide variety of exercises for all five areas of health-related fitness and creates a one-day personal fitness plan for improving muscular strength and muscular endurance.

5.0 – Works cooperatively and productively in a small group to accomplish goals in a physical activity setting.

6.1 – Analyzes how physical development varies within his peer group and how these variations affect his learning of striking with body parts skills.

6.2 – Describes physical activity and physical education in ancient Rome.

7.0 – Demonstrates striking with body parts skills, using various qualities of movement in repetitive patterns to convey different expressions.

Unit Outline

Day 1

Introduce the striking with body parts unit.

Assign students to heterogeneous groups of four.

Give students new logs for charting their participation in physical activities outside physical education. (Assessment assignment opportunity: log.)   **3.0**

Figure 14.17 The correct technique for hand dribbling.

Review intensity and time concepts related to muscular strength and endurance. **4.0**

Assign a one-day fitness plan for improving muscular strength and endurance. (Assessment assignment opportunity: project.) **4.0**

Demonstrate hand dribbling while standing still. (See figure 14.17.) **1.0**

Have students practice hand dribbling alone while standing still. **1.0**

Have students practice hand dribbling alone, using various qualities of movement (e.g., dribble fast, high, following a curved line). (Assessment opportunity: structured observation.) **1.0 / 7.0**

Assign students a written report about physical activities and physical education in ancient Rome. (Assessment assignment opportunity: report.) **6.2**

Day 2

Review hand dribbling. **1.0**

Discuss giving appropriate feedback to a partner when working on striking with body parts. **2.1**

Demonstrate dribbling and have students practice giving you feedback. **2.1**

Have students practice dribbling while their partners give feedback. **1.0 / 2.1**

Have students practice dribbling around an obstacle course while their partners give feedback. **1.0**

Ask students to describe the relationship between Newton's Third Law and performing hand dribbling. (Assessment opportunity: structured observation.) **2.2**

Day 3

Review hand dribbling. **1.0**

Have students play Dribble Tag. (See appendix C.) (Assessment opportunity: rubric.) **1.0**

Ask students to identify the various sport skills and activities that utilize hand dribbling. **1.0**

Ask students to discuss in small groups whether boys or girls have better dribbling ability and, if one group does, to explain why that may be so (guide answer toward more practice). **6.1**

Day 4

Demonstrate one-handed underhand striking of a ball.   **1.0**

Have students practice one-handed underhand striking of a ball.   **1.0**

Have students strike the ball over a volleyball net, allowing them to choose how far from the net they wish to stand.   **1.0**

Have students strike the ball over a volleyball net, aiming for a spot on the other side. Allow students to choose how far from the net they wish to stand. (Assessment opportunity: rubric.)   **1.0**

Ask students to identify the various sport skills and activities that utilize underhand striking of a ball.   **1.0**

Day 5

Demonstrate two-handed underhand striking of a ball.   **1.0**

In groups of four, have two students practice two-handed underhand striking of a ball to each other while the other students give feedback.   **1.0 / 2.1**

In groups of four, have two students practice two-handed underhand striking of a ball while aiming at a target while the other students give feedback   **1.0 / 2.1**

Day 6

Demonstrate one-handed overhand striking of a ball.   **1.0**

Have students practice one-handed overhand striking of a ball.   **1.0**

Have students strike the ball over a volleyball net, allowing them to choose how far from the net they wish to stand.   **1.0**

Have students strike the ball over a volleyball net, aiming for a spot on the other side. Allow students to choose how far from the net they wish to stand.   **1.0**

Ask students to identify the various sport skills and activities that utilize overhand striking of a ball. **1.0**

For homework, ask students to analyze how the variables of physical development affect striking ability. (Assessment assignment opportunity: essay.)   **6.1**

Day 7

Demonstrate two-handed overhand striking of a ball.   **1.0**

In groups of four, have two students practice two-handed overhand striking of a ball to each other while the other students give feedback.   **1.0 / 2.1**

In groups of four, have students practice two-handed overhand striking of a ball while aiming at a target while the other students give feedback.   **1.0 / 2.1**

For homework, ask students to describe the relationship between Newton's Third Law and performing the overhand strike. (Assessment assignment opportunity: essay.)   **2.2**

Day 8

Review striking with hand skills (dribbling, overhand, underhand).   **1.0**

Teach students to play Keep-It-Up. (See appendix C.)   **1.0**

Have students rotate through stations, practicing the skills and receiving feedback: dribbling, underhand strike, overhand strike, Keep-It-Up. (Assessment opportunity: rubric.)   **1.0 / 2.1**

Day 9

Have students rotate through stations, practicing the skills and receiving feedback: dribbling, underhand strike, overhand strike, Keep-It-Up. (Assessment opportunity: rubric.)   **1.0 / 2.1**

Figure 14.18 The correct technique for the kick.

Day 10

Demonstrate kicking a stationary object (see figure 14.18) and the sole-of-foot trap.   **1.0**

Have students practice kicking a stationary object to a partner who traps it using the sole-of-foot trap. **1.0**

Demonstrate kicking to a partner who is moving.   **1.0**

Have students practice kicking to a partner who is moving; have the partner use the sole-of-foot trap. **1.0**

Demonstrate kicking on the run to a partner who is moving.   **1.0**

Have students practice kicking back and forth to a partner while both are moving.   **1.0**

Day 11

Demonstrate foot dribbling.   **1.0**

Have students practice foot dribbling alone.   **1.0**

Have students practice foot dribbling alone, using various qualities of movement (e.g., dribble fast, slow, in a straight line, in a curved line). (Assessment opportunity: structured observation.)   **1.0 / 7.0**

For homework, ask students to describe the relationship between Newton's Third Law and foot dribbling or kicking. (Assessment assignment opportunity: essay.)   **2.2**

Day 12

Review foot dribbling.   **1.0**

Have students practice foot dribbling around an obstacle course while their partners give feedback. (Assessment opportunity: rubric.)   **1.0 / 2.1**

Have students play Dribble Tag. (See appendix C.) (Assessment opportunity: rubric.)   **1.0**

For homework, ask students to analyze the variables of physical development and foot dribbling or kicking. (Assessment assignment opportunity: essay.)   **6.1**

Day 13

Teach students Two-on-Two Soccer.   **1.0**

Have students play Two-on-Two Soccer. (Assessment opportunity: rubric.)   **1.0**

Day 14

Review the elements of a cooperative game.   **2.3**

Discuss working cooperatively and productively in a small group to accomplish a goal.   **5.0**

In their groups of four, have students create a cooperative game, using striking with body parts skills. (Assessment assignment opportunity: project.)   **1.0 / 2.3 / 5.0**

Day 15

Have each group teach their cooperative game to another group. (Assessment opportunity: project.) **1.0 / 2.3 / 5.0**

Have students hand in their logs, showing participation in activities outside of physical education. (Assessment opportunity: log.)   **3.0**

Have students turn in their one-day fitness plans for muscular strength and endurance. (Assessment opportunity: project.)   **4.0**

Have students turn in their physical activity and physical education in ancient Rome report. (Assessment opportunity: report.)   **6.2**

Unit 8: Striking With Objects

This skills theme unit looks at the skill of striking with objects. Teach this unit to ensure that your students have the correct technique for striking with a variety of objects, then extend that skill for both distance and accuracy. Once your students have acquired some distance and accuracy, then have them explore aiming at moving objects and aiming while moving. Finally, apply the skill of striking to game-like settings, specifically in this unit to settings similar to tennis and hockey. To address standard four, I will continue to cover physical fitness during the daily warm-up and flexibility exercises and will have students perform muscular strength, muscular endurance, and cardiorespiratory exercises every other day. I'll also continue to review the cognitive concepts related to health-related fitness development daily during the warm-up; specifically, students will prepare to write a one-day plan for improving cardiorespiratory endurance.

Conduct this unit in any open area; however, a blacktop area is best for racket and hockey skills (street hockey) and grass is best for batting skills. If you choose to teach field hockey instead of street hockey, then conduct the hockey skill lessons on the grass as well. As in the previous three units, students need a wide variety of objects (e.g., rubber balls, softballs, tennis balls, hockey pucks) as well as striking objects (e.g., bats, rackets, golf clubs, hockey sticks). In addition, a variety of targets will keep interest level high as they work on accuracy. It also helps to have tennis nets and hockey goals available for applying the skills in lead-up games.

Unit Standards

1.0 – Applies the correct techniques for locomotor, nonlocomotor, and manipulative skills to striking with an object in a variety of activities.

2.1 – Gives appropriate feedback to a partner when developing or improving striking with object skills.

2.2 – Describes how Newton's Third Law applies to striking with an object.

2.3 – Creates a cooperative game, using striking with an object skills.

3.0 – Chooses to participate in activities of interest outside physical education.

4.0 – Participates in a wide variety of exercises for all five areas of health-related fitness and creates a one-day fitness plan for improving cardiorespiratory endurance.

5.0 – Works cooperatively and productively in a small group to accomplish goals in physical activity settings.

6.1 – Analyzes how physical development varies within his peer group and how these variations affect his learning of striking with object skills.

6.2 – Describes physical activities and physical education in ancient China.

7.0 – Demonstrates striking with an object, using various qualities of movement in repetitive patterns to convey different expressions.

Unit Outline

Figure 14.19 The correct technique for performing a sidearm strike with an object such as a bat.

Day 1

Introduce striking with an object unit.

Assign students to heterogeneous groups of four.

Review intensity and time concepts related to cardiorespiratory endurance.   **4.0**

Ask students to write a one-day fitness plan for improving cardiorespiratory endurance. (Assessment assignment opportunity: project.)   **4.0**

Give students new logs for charting their participation in physical activities outside physical education. (Assessment assignment opportunity: log.)   **3.0**

Demonstrate striking a stationary object, using a variety of implements.   **1.0**

Have students practice striking a stationary object, using a variety of implements (e.g., bat, paddle, racket).   **1.0**

For homework, students research the physical activities and physical education in ancient China. (Assessment assignment opportunity: report.)

Day 2

Review striking a stationary object.   **1.0**

Discuss giving appropriate feedback to a partner when working on striking with implements.   **2.1**

Have students practice striking at a stationary object, using a variety of implements (e.g., bat, racket), while their partners give feedback. (See figure 14.19.)   **1.0 / 2.1**

Demonstrate striking an object tossed by the striker.   **1.0**

Have students practice striking at an object they toss for themselves, using a variety of implements (e.g., bat, paddle, racket), while their partners give feedback.   **1.0 / 2.1**

For homework, ask students to describe the relationship between Newton's Third Law and performing the sidearm strike. (Assessment assignment opportunity: essay.)   **2.2**

Day 3

Review striking a self-tossed object.   **1.0**

Have students practice striking a self-tossed object, using a variety of implements (e.g., bat, paddle, racket).   **1.0 / 2.1**

Demonstrate striking an object tossed by a partner.   **1.0**

Have students practice striking an object tossed by their partners, using a variety of implements, while their partners give feedback.   **1.0 / 2.1**

For homework, ask students to analyze the variables of physical development and performing the sidearm strike. (Assessment assignment opportunity: essay.)   **6.1**

Day 4

Demonstrate striking an object that has rebounded off a wall.   **1.0**

Have students pick either striking a self-tossed object, striking an object tossed by a partner, or striking an object that has rebounded off a wall, using a variety of implements (e.g., bat, paddle, racket), while a partner gives feedback. Insist that students make all strikes forehanded, aiming for a target. (Assessment opportunity: rubric.)   **1.0 / 2.1**

Day 5

Demonstrate No-Serve Tennis.   **1.0**

Have students pick from tennis rackets and paddles to play No-Serve Tennis, using only forehand strokes.   **1.0**

Have students review the most important points to remember about forehand strokes.   **1.0**

Day 6

Demonstrate employing a backhand stroke to strike at an object, using a variety of implements (e.g., paddle, racket).   **1.0**

Have students practice the backhand stroke striking a self-tossed object, using a variety of implements (e.g., paddle, racket).   **1.0 / 2.1**

Demonstrate using a backhand stroke to strike an object tossed by a partner.   **1.0**

Have students practice using the backhand stroke to strike an object tossed by a partner, using a variety of implements, while their partners give feedback.   **1.0 / 2.1**

Have students record in their journals how it feels to receive feedback. (Assessment opportunity: journal entry.)   **2.1**

Day 7

Demonstrate using a backhand stroke to strike an object that has rebounded off a wall.   **1.0**

Have students pick either striking a self-tossed object, striking an object tossed by a partner, or striking an object that has rebounded off a wall, using a variety of implements (e.g., paddle, racket), while their partners give feedback on their backhand strokes. (Assessment opportunity: rubric.)   **1.0 / 2.1**

Day 8

Have students choose to use either tennis rackets or paddles to play No-Serve Tennis, using both the forehand and backhand strokes.   **1.0**

Figure 14.20   The correct technique for performing an underhand strike with an object such as a hockey stick.

Have students brainstorm a list of various sports and sport skills that use the sidearm striking motion. **1.0**

Day 9

Demonstrate the underhand striking motion, using a variety of implements (e.g., golf club, hockey stick).   **1.0**

Have students practice the underhand striking motion, using a variety of implements at a stationary object, while their partners give feedback. (See figure 14.20.)   **1.0 / 2.1**

Have students practice the underhand striking motion, using a variety of implements at a stationary object and aiming at a target, while their partners give feedback.   **1.0 / 2.1**

Have students brainstorm a list of various sports and sport skills that use the underhand striking motion.   **1.0**

Day 10

Review underhand striking of a stationary object, using a variety of implements.   **1.0**

Have students practice underhand striking of a stationary object, using a variety of implements, while aiming at a variety of targets.   **1.0**

Demonstrate underhand striking back and forth with a partner while moving, using a hockey stick.   **1.0**

Have pairs practice underhand striking back and forth while moving, using a hockey stick.   **1.0**

Day 11

Demonstrate dribbling, using a hockey stick or variety of hockey sticks.   **1.0**

Have students practice dribbling while their partners give feedback.   **1.0 / 2.1**

Have students practice dribbling, using various movement qualities (e.g., dribbling fast, slow, in a straight line, in a curved line), while their partners give feedback. (Assessment opportunity: rubric.) **1.0 / 2.1 / 7.0**

Have students dribble around obstacles while their partners give feedback. (Assessment opportunity: rubric.)   **1.0 / 2.1**

Q198 Teaching Middle School Physical Education

Day 12

Discuss physical activities and physical education in ancient China.   **7.0**

Review hockey dribbling.   **1.0**

Have students play One-on-One Hockey. (Assessment opportunity: rubric.)   **1.0**

Day 13

Teach Two-on-Two Hockey.   **1.0**

Have students play Two-on-Two Hockey. (Assessment opportunity: rubric.)   **1.0**

Ask students what they remember about physical activities and physical education in ancient China. (Assessment opportunity: written test.)   **7.0**

Day 14

Review the elements of a cooperative game.   **2.3**

Review working with a group to accomplish a goal.   **5.0**

Have groups create a cooperative game, using striking with object skills. (Assessment assignment opportunity: project.)   **1.0 / 2.3 / 5.0**

Day 15

Have each group teach their cooperative game to another group. (Assessment opportunity: project.)   **1.0 / 2.3 / 5.0**

Have students hand in their logs, showing participation in activities outside of physical education. (Assessment opportunity: log.)   **3.0**

Have students turn in their one-day fitness plans for cardiorespiratory endurance. (Assessment opportunity: report.)   **4.0**

Unit 9: Circus Skills

Now that we have provided students with instruction in the major skills theme areas (body management, locomotor, underhand and sidearm throw and catch, striking with body parts, and striking with objects), let's give them an opportunity to review these fundamental skills and apply them to a circus skills unit. But because not all students will have mastered the techniques for all the fundamental skills or be ready to apply the skills to some of the more challenging circus skills, I'll return to the inclusion style of teaching after the first two days. To this end, I'll use a station approach for instruction so that students may select the skill they wish to work on while their partners give feedback. To address standard four, I will continue to cover physical fitness during our daily warm-up and flexibility exercises and will have students perform muscular strength, muscular endurance, and cardiorespiratory exercises every other day. I'll also continue to review daily the cognitive concepts related to health-related fitness development during the warm-up period as students prepare to write their one-day plans for warm-up, cooldown, and flexibility.

This unit can take place in any open area; however, it is best to unicycle on a blacktop area and do slack rope walking and use stilts over a protective ground covering. Please note that this unit requires some unique equipment, but you can substitute as noted. Juggling scarves (baggies), juggling balls (beanbags or paper balls with masking tape around them), hackey sacks (beanbags or paper balls with masking tape around them), unicycles and helmets, spinning balls (volleyballs), slack rope (prestretched yachting rope with a drop of about 1.5 meters, hung so the bottom of the rope is around 10 centimeters off the ground), and stilts. There are other circus events you may want to include in your unit. I'll use the station approach throughout this unit so you only have to purchase a few of each type of equipment because only a few students will be using one type of equipment at a time.

Many of the specific skills introduced in this unit are unique to you and your students, so the use of video is very appropriate. You can choose from several juggling videos, such as, *Juggle Time, Juggle Jam*, and *Juggling Star*; I'll be using *Juggling Star*. And you can choose from several unicycling videos, such as, *Rough Terrain Unicycling, International Unicycling Federation Achievement Skill Levels*, and *Unicycle*; I'll be using *Unicycle*. In addition, I've incorporated video clips showing the Harlem Globetrotters to help students progress to using ball-spinning skills in the their ball-handling routines as well as the *Footbag Video*, which will give visual images of hackey sack, or footbag, skills. (See appendix D for video sources.)

If you wish, have students use the skills they gain in this unit, performing at an open house, during Na-tional Physical Education Week events, or in shopping center demonstrations. One way to approach this unit is to let students select one circus skill event (e.g., juggling, footbag, stilts) in which to specialize and create a routine. The other option, which I'll present in detail, is to give students instruction in each area, *then* let them specialize and create a group routine. Either way, the demonstration of the skills or routines in front of a live audience is definitely an authentic assessment. If you're able to take an interdisciplinary approach, the assessment of standard 6.2 can be made by your students' history/social science teacher as they assess students' understanding of ancient Spartan history, including the type of physical activities and physical education of the time.

Unit Standards

1.0 – Applies the correct techniques for locomotor, nonlocomotor, and manipulative skills to circus activities.

2.1 – Gives appropriate feedback to a partner when developing or improving circus activity skills.

2.2 – Analyzes movement performance, using Newton's Third Law in order to learn or improve circus activity skills.

2.3 – Creates a cooperative game, using one or more circus activity skills.

3.0 – Chooses to participate in physical activities of interest outside of physical education.

4.0 – Participates in a wide variety of exercises for all five areas of health-related fitness and creates a one-day fitness plan for warm-up, cooldown, and flexibility.

5.0 – Works cooperatively and productively in a group to accomplish goals in physical activity settings.

6.1 – Analyzes how physical development varies within her peer group and how these variations affect her learning of circus-type skills.

6.2 – Describes physical activities and physical education of the ancient Spartans.

7.0 – Demonstrates circus skills, using different qualities of movement in repetitive patterns to convey different expressions.

Unit Outline

Day 1

Introduce circus skills unit.

Assign students to heterogeneous groups of four.

Give students new logs for charting their participation in physical activities outside physical education. (Assessment assignment opportunity: log.)   **3.0**

Discuss and assign the creation of a one-day warm-up, cooldown, and flexibility plan. (Assessment assignment opportunity: project.)   **4.0**

Demonstrate a one-scarf cascade.   **1.0**

Have students practice the one-scarf cascade.   **1.0**

Demonstrate the two-scarf cascade.   **1.0**

Have students practice the two-scarf cascade.   **1.0**

Demonstrate the three-scarf cascade.   **1.0**

Have students practice the three-scarf cascade.   **1.0**

Review Newton's Third Law with the students, discussing how it applies to juggling scarves.   **2.2**

Day 2

Review the three-scarf cascade.   **1.0**

Discuss the variables of physical development and their influences on learning circus skills.   **6.1**

Show one-ball juggling on the *Juggling Star* video.   **1.0**

Have students practice one-ball juggling.   **1.0**

Show two-ball juggling on the *Juggling Star* video.   **1.0**

Have students practice two-ball juggling.   **1.0**

Show three-ball juggling on the *Juggling Star* video.   **1.0**

Discuss giving appropriate feedback to a partner when working on throwing and catching skills.   **2.1**

Have students practice three-ball juggling while receiving feedback from partners.   **1.0 / 2.1**

For homework, ask students how Newton's Third Law applies to ball juggling. (Assessment opportunity: essay.)   **2.2**

Day 3

Discuss physical activities and physical education the ancient Spartans participated in.   **6.2**

Describe the use of stations and the importance of feedback and cooperation when working in small groups.   **2.1 / 5.0**

Show the instep footbag kick on the *Footbag Video*.   **1.0**

Have students rotate through the following stations: instep footbag kick; one-scarf, two-scarf, or three-scarf cascade; instep footbag kick; one-ball or basic ball-juggling cascade; instep footbag kick; and upper body strength and endurance.   **1.0 / 2.1 / 5.0**

For homework, ask students how physical development relates to the instep footbag kick. (Assessment opportunity: essay.)   **6.1**

Day 4

Discuss physical activities and physical education during the time of the ancient Spartans.   **6.2**

Show inside and outside spins from video clips of the Harlem Globetrotters.   **1.0**

Demonstrate the reverse cascade for scarf juggling.   **1.0**

Have students rotate through stations: instep kick; one-scarf, two-scarf, three-scarf, or reverse cascade; ball spinning; one-ball or basic ball-juggling cascade; ball spinning; and cardiorespiratory endurance.   **1.0 / 2.1 / 5.0**

For homework, ask students how physical development variables relate to ball spinning. (Assessment opportunity: essay.)   **6.1**

Day 5

Explain to students that, as they go from station to station over the next seven days, they will be recording how Newton's Third Law and physical development variables relate to the circus skill practiced at each station. (Assessment opportunity: log.)   **2.2 / 6.1**

Demonstrate stilt walking.   **1.0**

Show the overhand throw for ball juggling on *Juggling Star*.   **1.0**

Have students rotate through stations: instep kick; one-scarf, two-scarf, three-scarf, or reverse cascade; ball spinning; one-ball juggling, basic ball-juggling cascade, or overhand throw juggle; stilt walking; and upper body strength and endurance. **1.0 / 2.1 / 5.0**

Day 6

Demonstrate slack rope walking. **1.0**

Show the knee kick for footbag skills on the *Footbag Video*. **1.0**

Have students rotate through stations: instep kick or knee kick; one-scarf, two-scarf, three-scarf, or reverse cascade; ball spinning; one-ball juggling, basic ball-juggling cascade, or overhand throw juggle; stilt walking and slack rope walking; and cardiorespiratory endurance. **1.0 / 2.1 / 5.0**

Day 7

Show unicycling on the *Unicycle* video. **1.0**

Demonstrate the pivot in place on the slack rope. **1.0**

Show outside kick for footbag skills on the *Footbag Video*. **1.0**

Show columns juggling with scarves. **1.0**

Have students rotate through stations: instep kick or knee kick; one-scarf, two-scarf, three-scarf, or reverse cascade; ball spinning; basic ball-juggling cascade, or overhand throw juggle; slack rope walking with pivot in place; stilt walking; unicycle riding; outside kick; columns juggling with scarves; and upper body strength and endurance. **1.0 / 2.1 / 5.0**

Day 8

Show the standard mount on the *Unicycle* video. **1.0**

Show the back kick on the *Footbag Video*. **1.0**

Show catch-ball-on-finger skill for ball spinning from a video clip of the Harlem Globetrotters' video. **1.0**

Have students rotate through stations: instep kick, knee, or outside kick; cascade, reverse cascade, or columns skill for scarf juggling; ball spinning; basic ball-juggling cascade or overhand throw juggle; slack rope walking with pivot in place; stilt walking; unicycle riding and standard mount; back kick; catch-ball-on-finger skill for ball spinning; one-handed ball juggling; and cardiorespiratory endurance. **1.0 / 2.1 / 5.0**

Day 9

Demonstrate the reverse pivot on slack rope. **1.0**

Demonstrate the reverse pivot when stilt walking. **1.0**

Show the side mount on the *Unicycle* video. **1.0**

Demonstrate shower skill for scarves juggling. **1.0**

Demonstrate clawing for ball juggling. **1.0**

Have students rotate through stations: instep kick, knee, back, or outside kick; cascade, reverse cascade, or columns skill for scarves juggling; ball spinning; basic ball-juggling cascade, overhand throw juggle, or one-handed juggling; slack rope walking with reverse pivot; stilt walking with reverse pivot; unicycle riding and side mount; shower skill for scarves juggling; catch-ball-on-finger skill for ball spinning; clawing for ball juggling; and upper body strength and endurance. (Assessment opportunity: rubric.) **1.0 / 2.1 / 5.0**

Day 10

Demonstrate forward pivot while slack rope walking. **1.0**

Demonstrate the reverse mount for unicycle riding. **1.0**

Have students rotate through stations: instep kick, knee, back, or outside kick; cascade, reverse cascade, or columns skill for scarves juggling; ball spinning with catch on finger; basic ball-juggling cascade, overhand throw for juggling, or one-handed juggling; slack rope walking with forward pivot; stilt walking; unicycle riding and reverse mount; shower skill for scarves juggling; ball spinning; clawing for ball juggling; and cardiorespiratory endurance. (Assessment opportunity: rubric.)   **1.0 / 2.1 / 5.0**

Day 11

Show column juggling for balls on *Juggling Star*.   **1.0**

Demonstrate ball-on-ball spinning or show it from video clips of the Harlem Globetrotters' video.   **1.0**

Have students rotate through stations: instep kick, knee, back, or outside kick; cascade, reverse cascade, or columns skill for scarves juggling; ball spinning with catch on finger; basic ball-juggling cascade, overhand throw juggling, one-handed juggling, or column juggling; slack rope walking with forward pivot; stilt walking; unicycle riding and reverse mount; shower skill for scarves juggling; ball-on-ball spinning; clawing for ball juggling; and upper body strength and endurance. (Assessment opportunity: rubric.)   **1.0 / 2.1 / 5.0**

Tell students that tomorrow they will be creating a cooperative game or activity, using one or more circus skills.   **2.3**

Day 12

Review the elements of a cooperative game.   **2.3**

In groups of four, have students create a cooperative game or activity, using one or more circus skills. (Assessment assignment opportunity: project.)   **2.3**

Day 13

Have each group teach their cooperative game or activity to another group. (Assessment opportunity: project.)   **1.0 / 2.3 / 5.0**

Discuss the influences of qualities of movement related to the creation of a circus routine.   **7.0**

Discuss working cooperatively and productively in a group to accomplish a common goal.   **5.0**

Have groups create a circus skills routine. (Assessment assignment opportunity: project)   **1.0 / 5.0 / 7.0**

Day 14

Have groups work on their circus skills routines.   **1.0 / 5.0 / 7.0**

Day 15

Have students hand in their logs, showing participation in activities outside of physical education. (Assessment opportunity: log.)   **3.0**

Have students turn in their one-day fitness plans for warm-up, cooldown, and flexibility. (Assessment opportunity: project)   **4.0**

Have each group demonstrate their circus skills routine to another group. (Assessment opportunity: project.)   **1.0 / 5.0 / 7.0**

Have students describe the qualities of movement and patterns observed in the routines. (Assessment opportunity: structured observation.)   **7.0**

Have students describe in journals how their group worked together to create their routine. (Assessment opportunity: journal entry.)   **5.0**

Unit 10: Creating New Games

Several times throughout my sample curriculum, I have had the sixth graders create games, using the specific skills addressed in each unit. In this unit, however, we will take a more comprehensive look at games and how they are played around the world and will elaborate on the various elements of a game. The primary resource for the games listed in this unit plan is *International Playtime: Classroom Games and Dances From Around the World* by Nelson and Glass (1992). This is an excellent resource, covering the rules and history of various games and dances, helping students understand how games are played fairly. As we move toward the 21st century, this knowledge of fair play is far more important than remembering the official rules for every sport. Moreover, students need to see how they can adapt games, depending on the situation. For example, individuals may enjoy playing football but they are not often in situations in which they have 11 players on a team so they must know how to modify football or any other game.

You can teach this unit in any open area, keeping in mind the specific requirements of each game. The specific pieces of equipment will also depend on the game; however, make a wide variety available as your students start to create their final new games for the year. If you like, use the video *New Games From Around the World* from Sportime to illustrate different elements of a game (see appendix D). Finally, encyclopedias, either on CD-ROM or hard copy, along with the students' history books and access to either the Internet or library, will provide resources for the research study in this unit.

I've saved this unit until the end of the school year for two reasons: First, it applies the various skills the students have learned and practiced throughout the year, and second, it includes games from various countries around the world as the sixth graders conclude their ancient civilizations course in history class and begin to compare and contrast the cultures they have studied throughout the year. Because of this physical education unit, students can include the area of games and recreation in their comparisons.

Elements of a Game

Purpose of a Game

Developing motor skills

Improving fitness

Enjoyment

Practicing problem solving

Developing social skills

Players

Individuals	Teams of various sizes
Partners	

Movements

Locomotor	Manipulative
Nonlocomotor	

Objects (Type and Quantity)

Balls	Mats
Bats	Ropes
Racquets	Hoops
Gloves	

Organization

Line	Diamond
Circle	Random
Zone	

Limits (Rules)

Time limits	Legal play
Scoring	Penalties for illegal play
Boundaries	

Unit Standards

1.0 – Applies the correct techniques for locomotor, nonlocomotor, and manipulative skills in ancient games and in student-created games.

2.1 – Gives appropriate feedback to a partner when developing or improving skills while engaged in ancient games and student-created games.

2.2 – Analyzes movement performance using Newton's Third Law in order to learn or improve a movement skill used in an ancient game or student-created game.

2.3 – Creates a cooperative game by combining a variety of locomotor, nonlocomotor, and manipulative skills.

3.0 – Chooses to participate in physical activities of interest outside of physical education.

4.0 – Participates in a wide variety of exercises for all five areas of health-related fitness, computes the difference between caloric input and output for one day, and creates a one-day fitness plan that addresses body composition.

5.0 – Works cooperatively and productively in a group to accomplish goals in physical activity settings.

6.1 – Adapts games so that they are appropriate for everyone on the team.

6.2 – Describes the origin of ancient games played in class and their influences on games today.

7.0 – Analyzes patterns in games to determine the influences that qualities of movement have on aesthetic impact.

Unit Outline

Day 1

Introduce games unit.

Assign students to heterogeneous groups of four.

Give students new logs for charting their participation in physical activities outside physical education. (Assessment assignment opportunity: log.)   **3.0**

Discuss caloric input and output.   **4.0**

Provide students with sample diets and activities and the related caloric information and have them practice computing the caloric differences.   **4.0**

Day 2

Discuss games and their components.   **2.3**

Discuss the origin of games with students.   **2.3**

Have students discuss how games can be modified so that they are appropriate for everyone.   **6.1**

Provide students in their work groups with a number of games and have them modify a game for someone who is visually impaired, hearing impaired, and physically impaired. (Assessment opportunity: open-ended question.)   **6.1**

Day 3

Discuss giving feedback to a partner about game skills.   **2.1**

Discuss working cooperatively with group members to achieve a goal in a game.   **5.0**

Teach the rules and history of Catch the Dragon's Tail (China). (See Nelson and Glass 1992 for game descriptions throughout this unit.)   **1.0 / 6.2**

Have students play Catch the Dragon's Tail.   **1.0 / 2.1 / 5.0**

Teach the rules and history of Hop-Sing Game (Liberia).   **1.0 / 6.2**

Have students play Hop-Sing Game.   **1.0 / 2.1 / 5.0**

Have students analyze these two games, looking for common traits.   **2.3**

Have students brainstorm about how Newton's Third Law applies to these two games.   **2.2**

Have students discuss common patterns that occurred during the two games, determining the influences that qualities of movement have on aesthetics.   **7.0**

Day 4

Teach the rules and history of Hunter and Gazelle (Africa).   **1.0 / 6.2**

Have students play Hunter and Gazelle.   **1.0 / 2.1 / 5.0**

Teach the rules and history of Don-Don Ba Ji (Sudan).   **1.0 / 6.2**

Have students play Don-Don Ba Ji.   **1.0 / 2.1 / 5.0**

Have students analyze these two games, looking for common traits.   **2.3**

Have students brainstorm about how Newton's Third Law applies to these two games.   **2.2**

Have students discuss common patterns that occurred during the two games, determining the influences that qualities of movement have on aesthetics.   **7.0**

Day 5

Teach the rules and history of Ichi-Ni-San (Japan).   **1.0 / 6.2**

Have students play Ichi-Ni-San.   **1.0 / 2.1 / 5.0**

Teach the rules and history of Tug-of-Rope (Egypt).   **1.0 / 6.2**

Have students play Tug-of-Rope.   **1.0 / 2.1 / 5.0**

Have students analyze these two games, looking for common traits.   **2.3**

Have students brainstorm about how Newton's Third Law applies to these two games.   **2.2**

Have students discuss common patterns that occurred during the two games, determining the influences that qualities of movement have on aesthetics.   **7.0**

Day 6

Teach the rules and history of Bli Yadayim (Israel).   **1.0 / 6.2**

Have students play Bli Yadayim.   **1.0 / 2.1 / 5.0**

Teach the rules and history of Ver Ver Aras Lama (New Guinea).   **1.0 / 6.2**

Have students play Ver Ver Aras Lama.   **1.0 / 2.1 / 5.0**

Have students analyze these two games, looking for common traits.   **2.3**

Have students brainstorm about how Newton's Third Law applies to these two games.   **2.2**

Have students discuss common patterns that occurred during the two games, determining the influences that qualities of movement have on aesthetics.   **7.0**

Day 7

Teach the rules and history of Gutera Uriziga (Rwanda).   **1.0 / 6.2**

Have students play Gutera Uriziga.   **1.0 / 2.1 / 5.0**

Teach the rules and history of Kukla (Turkey).   **1.0 / 6.2**

Have students play Kukla.   **1.0 / 2.1 / 5.0**

For homework, have students analyze these two games, looking for common traits. (Assessment assignment opportunity: open-ended question.) **2.3**

Day 8

Teach the rules and history of Kick-Swing (Vietnam). **1.0 / 6.2**

Have students play Kick-Swing. (Assessment opportunity: structured observation.) **1.0 / 2.1 / 5.0**

Teach the rules and history of Sheep Dog (Australia). **1.0 / 6.2**

Have students play Sheep Dog. (Assessment opportunity: structured observation.) **1.0 / 2.1 / 5.0**

Have students analyze these two games, looking for common traits. **2.3**

For homework, have students brainstorm about how Newton's Third Law applies to these two games. (Assessment opportunity: essay.) **2.2**

Day 9

In small groups, research another ancient game: rules, skills, history, and adaptations for the physically, visually, and hearing impaired. (Assessment assignment opportunity: project.) **1.0 / 5.0 / 6.2**

Day 10

Have each group continue to research an ancient game: rules, skills, history, adaptations. **5.0 / 6.2**

Have each group teach the game they researched, including its rules, skills, and history, to another group, suggesting adaptations for the physically, visually, and hearing impaired. (Assessment opportunity: project.) **1.0 / 5.0 / 6.1 / 6.2**

Day 11

Hand out the Create a Cooperative Game Worksheet. **2.3**

In small groups, have students create a cooperative game, using a variety of locomotor, nonlocomotor, and manipulative skills and including adaptations for the physically, visually, and hearing impaired. (Assessment assignment opportunity: project.) **1.0 / 2.3 / 5.0 / 6.1**

Day 12

Assign a one-day computation between caloric input and output, based on students' own eating and activities. (Assessment assignment opportunity: project.) **4.0**

Have groups continue working on creating cooperative games. **1.0 / 2.3 / 5.0 / 6.1**

Day 13

Have groups continue working on creating cooperative games. **1.0 / 2.3 / 5.0 / 6.1**

Have groups try out the games they designed. **1.0 / 2.3 / 5.0 / 6.1**

Day 14

Have each group teach their new game to another group and then play their two groups' games. (Assessment opportunity: project.) **1.0 / 2.3 / 5.0 / 6.1**

For homework, have students describe which game they enjoyed playing the most and why. (Assessment assignment opportunity: open-ended question.) **7.0**

Day 15

Have each group teach their new game to another group and then play their two groups' games. (Assessment opportunity: project.) **1.0 / 2.3 / 5.0 / 6.1**

Create a Cooperative Game Worksheet

Purpose of the game:

Players:

Movements:

Equipment:

Organization:

Rules with penalties:

Have students hand in their logs, showing participation in activities outside of physical education. (Assessment opportunity: log.) **3.0**

Have students turn in their one-day computations between caloric input and output. (Assessment opportunity: project.) **4.0**

Unit 11: Closing and Fitness Posttesting

This unit creates appropriate closure for your school year, including the chance to ensure that the students are able to demonstrate the grade level standards. Although students have been working on projects throughout the year, this unit provides an opportunity for them to focus on depth over breadth. Moreover, while your students focus on completing their demonstrations of their learning and creating and collecting work for their portfolios, you are free to administer the fitness posttests and to act as a resource for student projects.

For this unit, I present students with the 10 standards for the sixth grade and ask them to present evidence of their learning related to each standard. For some of the standards, students will be able to demonstrate their learning by looking through their working portfolios and pulling from work that they have already accomplished during the year. For other standards, students will be able to pull from interdisciplinary projects that they have accomplished throughout the year. For still other standards, students will need to create new projects during this closure unit to demonstrate their learning. Once the students have collected their evidence, it goes into their performance portfolios. Then I ask students to write a reflection paper (a one-page essay) on their cumulative learning throughout sixth grade physical education. Ideally, the students then present their portfolios not only to their peers but also to their parents. In this case during a parent, teacher, and student conference, the student is in charge of the conference as she presents the evidence that she has accumulated during the year and explains how the evidence demonstrates her learning of the various standards. This conference can focus exclusively on physical education or be a comprehensive conference in which the student explains her learning in all subject areas.

Like the introduction and fitness pretesting unit, you can conduct this unit in just about any facility. I recommend, however, that if you are having your students perform exercises on the ground or grass that you provide them with carpet squares or some other material so they won't get dirty. An indoor facility is also helpful for the project development phase of this unit. In addition, many teachers reserve the library or at least make arrangements for some of their students to do research in the library. Of course, the equipment necessary to implement the unit depends on the type of fitness tests you plan to administer. I will be administering the same Prudential FITNESSGRAM tests that I gave at the beginning of the school year. After the posttests, the students will be able to enter their fitness posttest scores into their own electronic portfolios so that you and they can compare these scores to pretests, standards, and goals. Students will also need access to reference books, CD-ROMs, computers, videotape players, monitors, camcorders, and other materials to assist project development.

Sample Evidence for Each Sixth Grade Standard

1.0 Applies the Correct Techniques for Locomotor, Nonlocomotor, and Manipulative Skills in a Variety of Cooperative Activities

Student and teacher assessment during each instructional unit based on a rubric determines whether or not a student has reached this standard. The following is a sample rubric for underhand throwing:

6: Performs a mature underhand throwing pattern in a game or activity situation.

5: Performs a mature throwing pattern when underhand throwing for accuracy and distance.

4: Performs a mature underhand throwing pattern.

_____ Faces the direction of the throw.

_____ Keeps shoulders perpendicular to the line of throw.

_____ Swings arm in pendulum action on preferred side of body.

_____ Steps forward on opposite foot.

_____ Transfers weight to forward foot.

_____ Follows through in direction of throw.

3: Moving toward a mature underhand throwing pattern.

2: Performs an immature underhand throwing pattern.

1: Randomly attempts an immature underhand throwing pattern.

2.1 Gives Appropriate Feedback to a Partner While Developing or Improving Movement Skills

Student and teacher chart the amount and type of feedback during skill development of various skills.

2.2 Analyzes Movement Performance Using Newton's Third Law in Order to Learn or Improve a Movement Skill

Have student take one skill that he has not perfected and write an essay, explaining how Newton's Third Law can assist him in becoming more proficient at the skill.

2.3 Creates a Cooperative Game By Combining a Variety of Locomotor, Nonlocomotor, and Manipulative Skills

Have groups of four create and teach a cooperative game to another group.

3.0 Participates Daily in Some Form of Physical Activity Based on Personal Interests and Capabilities

Throughout the year, have student maintain a log of participation in fitness activities outside of the school day.

4.0 Assesses Personal Fitness, Compares Scores to Health-Related Standards, Sets Goals for Improvement or Maintenance, and Develops a One-Day Personal Fitness Plan

Have student create a chart, essay, video, or computer program that shows his one-day fitness plan, explaining how it relates to his current fitness level and goals for the year.

5.0 Works Cooperatively and Productively in a Group to Accomplish Goals in Physical Activity Settings

Student and teacher evaluate the extent and quality of cooperative skills used during various activities. The following is a sample rubric for judging this standard:

6: Consistently exhibits cooperative skills with all during physical activity, during class time, nutrition, and lunch.

5: Consistently exhibits cooperative skills with all during physical activity during class time.

4: Consistently works cooperatively with team members during physical activity in the school setting.

3: Inconsistently works cooperatively with team members during physical activity in the school setting.

2: Rarely works cooperatively with team members during physical activity in the school setting.

1: Does not cooperate with others.

6.1 Analyzes Physical Development Within His Peer Group and the Variables of Their Effect on Movement Performance as He Works Cooperatively With Both More- and Less-Skilled Peers

Have student take one activity and describe the skill levels of the different members of his group, relating skill levels to how their physical characteristics and abilities play a role in their performances of the skill or activity.

6.2 Describes the Development and Role of Movement-Related Activities and Physical Education in the Ancient World and Their Influences on Physical Activities Today

Have groups of four explain the history of one activity that originated in the ancient world to another group.

7.0 Analyzes Patterns in Physical Activities to Determine the Influence That the Qualities of Movement Have on the Aesthetic Impact of These Activities

Have student write an essay or draw a picture depicting how different people in his group perform a variety of activities. Student comments on what he likes or doesn't like about different expressions of movement.

Unit Standards

1.0 – Applies the correct techniques for locomotor, nonlocomotor, and manipulative skills in a variety of cooperative activities.

2.1 – Gives appropriate feedback to a partner while developing or improving movement skills.

2.2 – Analyzes movement performance using Newton's Third Law in order to learn or improve a movement skill.

2.3 – Creates a cooperative game by combining a variety of locomotor, nonlocomotor, and manipulative skills.

3.0 – Participates daily in some form of physical activity, based on personal interests and capabilities.

4.0 – Reassesses personal fitness and compares scores to pretest scores, health standards, and personal goals, then finalizes a one-day personal fitness plan.

5.0 – Works cooperatively and productively in a group to accomplish goals in physical activity settings.

6.1 – Analyzes how physical development varies within her peer group and how these variations affect motor performance as she works cooperatively with both more- and less-skilled peers.

6.2 – Describes the development and role of movement-related activities and physical education in the ancient world and its influence on activities today.

7.0 – Analyzes patterns in physical activity to determine the influence that qualities of movement have on the aesthetic impact of these activities.

Unit Outline

Day 1

Assign students to work in groups of four.   **4.0**

Remind students why you administer fitness tests twice a year.   **4.0**

Remind students why you administer the one-mile run test.   **4.0**

Administer the one-mile run test to half the class at a time, while the other half helps to count laps for the runners.   **4.0**

Day 2

Describe the projects and portfolios you expect students to complete in this unit.   **1.0-7.0**

Describe the project and portfolio design steps.   **1.0-7.0**

Have students begin to work on their projects and portfolios.   **1.0-7.0**

Remind students why you administer the curl-up test.   **4.0**

Administer the curl-up test to one group at a time.   **4.0**

Day 3

Remind students why you administer the skinfold or body mass index test.   **4.0**

Have students work on their projects and portfolios.   **1.0-7.0**

Administer the skinfold or body mass index test privately to one student at a time.   **4.0**

Day 4

Remind students why you administer the back-saver sit-and-reach or shoulder stretch and trunk lift tests.   **4.0**

Have students work on their projects and portfolios.   **1.0-7.0**

Administer the back-saver sit-and-reach or shoulder stretch and trunk lift tests to one group at a time.   **4.0**

Day 5

Remind students why you administer the push-up, flexed arm hang, modified pull-up, or pull-up test.   **4.0**

Have students work on their projects and portfolios.   **1.0-7.0**

Administer the push-up, flexed arm hang, modified pull-up, or pull-up test to one group at a time.   **4.0**

Day 6

Administer makeup fitness tests to one group at a time.   **4.0**

Have students work on their projects and portfolios, including entering their fitness scores into their electronic portfolios.   **1.0-7.0**

Days 7 Through 12

Have students work on their projects and portfolios.   **1.0-7.0**

Day 13

Have each group share their projects and portfolios with another group.   **1.0-7.0**

Day 14

Have other groups share their projects and portfolios.   **1.0-7.0**

Day 15

Debrief projects, portfolios, and the entire year.   **1.0-7.0**

Summary

Use the ideas and model outline in this sample year-long curriculum for the sixth grade as a guide for your own planning, keeping in mind that this is one sample and not the definitive sixth grade program. Your particular environment, standards, student needs, and faculty will shape your sixth grade program. Indeed, be flexible, creative, and innovative when developing the program that is best for *your* situation.

CHAPTER 15

A Seventh Grade Program: Taking Acceptable Risks Through Problem Solving

An innovative teaching idea is not so much reinventing the wheel but a spark of potential energy mounting in your head that your kids inspired. It is the students that stretch our thinking and constantly call upon us to get them thinking and creating new ideas. In their processing and coming up with unique ways to respond, they continually take us to new levels, helping us to go beyond what we know and expect. These moments make teaching personal, real, and exciting.

—*Physical Educator Anne Fontaine, Florida*

In this chapter, I'll describe a sample seventh grade program, having selected "Taking Acceptable Risks Through Problem Solving" as the theme. As we discussed in chapter 7, seventh graders are passing through a critical stage in their development in which they find personal identify and establish self-worth and confidence. Students in this age group like to experiment with new challenges, and unless the school provides opportunities for appropriate risk-taking, students are likely to experiment with inappropriate risk-taking activities, such as experimenting with illegal drugs. Specifically in physical education, we can encourage appropriate risk-taking by providing students with exciting new activities that require creative thinking and problem solving in a controlled, safe environment.

I have based my program on my sample standards. Review your grade level standards for seventh grade before planning your own program. As I discussed in chapter 7, I have used the activity approach for selecting the seventh grade units of instruction. The units for the seventh grade include

- introduction and fitness pretesting,
- tumbling and gymnastics,
- outdoor education,

Seventh Grade Standards

By the end of seventh grade, each student should be able to demonstrate the following:

1.0 Applies the correct techniques for locomotor, nonlocomotor, and manipulative skills to appropriate risk-taking activities.

2.1 Sets goals and monitors changes in the development of movement skills in order to improve performance.

2.2 Analyzes movement performances using rotation principles in order to learn or improve a movement skill.

2.3 Creates an individual or dual game with scoring options and a penalty system.

3.0 Participates daily in some form of physical activity, including new and appropriate risk-taking activities.

4.0 Assesses personal fitness, compares scores to health-related standards, sets goals for improvement or maintenance, and designs a one-week personal fitness plan.

5.0 Applies collaborative problem solving techniques in physical activity settings.

6.1 Explains the growth rates of body segments and how they relate to movement experiences.

6.2 Describes the development and role of movement-related activities and physical education during Medieval times and their influences on physical activities today.

7.0 Appreciates the aesthetic features or stylistic differences of own approach to movement activities.

Modified from Region 9's *Physical Education Curriculum*, 1994 and NASPE's *National Physical Education Standards: A Guide to Content and Assessment*, 1995.

- racket sports,
- aquatics,
- golf,
- self-defense,
- Medieval times activities, and
- closing and fitness posttesting.

Each of these units challenges my students in one way or another. In activities such as tumbling and gymnastics, outdoor education, aquatics, and self-defense they face the challenge of what I call "physi-cal fear" as they strive to overcome ingrained fear for their own safety by taking acceptable risks. In addition, because golf and racket sports are new to my students, they experience the physical challenges of mastering new sports. The Medieval times activities unit extends the history and social science content my seventh graders are studying. Moreover, many of the activities participated in during Medieval times, such as chariot races, wrestling, track and field events, and jousting, both challenge students and help them understand history better.

In this chapter, I will present the units in the same format as I did in chapter 14. Please keep in mind that I do not intend for the lesson outlines to take the place of detailed lesson plans. Instead, elaborate on my brief day-by-day instructions by including innovative activities for discussions and skill practice in your own plans, tailoring them to meet the needs of your students, teaching preliminary concepts and reviewing new concepts as necessary throughout each unit.

Unit 1: Introduction and Fitness Pretesting

This unit serves as a basic introductory unit for seventh grade students. It gives students time to get reacquainted and to meet new members of the class. I also use this introductory unit to set my expectations, to teach the class rules, to assess the students' fitness levels, and to guide them as they set their year-long goals for fitness development.

You can conduct this particular unit in just about any facility. It does help, however, if you are performing exercises on the ground or grass to provide students with carpet squares or some other material so they don't get dirty. The equipment necessary to implement the unit depends on the type of introductory games you choose and the fitness tests you administer. I will be administering the Prudential FITNESSGRAM health-related fitness test battery, including the back-saver sit-and-reach, curl-ups, skinfold measurements, push-ups, trunk lift, and one-mile run. You can order the test administration procedures for Prudential FITNESSGRAM from The Cooper Institute for Aerobic Research (see appendix D). You will see in the daily agendas that my students will be preparing for the fitness test and the students will again be entering their fitness scores into their own electronic portfolios (*MacHealth-Related Fitness Tutorial and Portfolio*; see appendix D).

Unit Standards

1.0 – Applies the correct techniques for locomotor, nonlocomotor, and manipulative skills to fitness and getting acquainted activities.

2.1 – Sets fitness goals based on teacher recommendations.

2.2 – Explains the scientific principles associated with rotation.

2.3 – Creates a game to learn more about each other.

3.0 – Identifies activities that are new or involve appropriate risk-taking.

4.0 – Assesses personal fitness, compares scores to health-related standards, and sets personal goals.

5.0 – Knows other students' names.

6.1 – Explains the relationships between growth rates and fitness performance.

6.2 – Describes fitness training during Medieval times and the Renaissance period.

7.0 – Identifies the variables that affect the beauty of a performance.

Unit Outline

Day 1

Establish a roll call order.   **5.0**

Introduce the class rules.

Students participate in Toss-a-Name Game. (See appendix C for description of game.)   **1.0 / 5.0**

Day 2

Review class rules.

Review how to open lockers.

Have students participate in Toss-a-Name Game.   **1.0 / 5.0**

Have students participate in Toss-and-Catch-a-Name Game. (See appendix C for description of game.)   **1.0 / 5.0**

Ask students if anyone can name half the students in the class. (Assessment opportunity: structured observation.)   **5.0**

Day 3

Review class rules.

Have students watch "Lesson 2: Cardiorespiratory Endurance" on the *PE-TV* video, then discuss material covered on video.   **4.0**

Assign lockers while students watch the video.

Have students practice opening lockers.

Day 4

Have students dress for physical education.

Review class rules.

Assign students randomly to groups of four.

Have students perform exercises for each area of health-related fitness. (See appendix C for sample exercises for each area of health-related fitness.)   **1.0 / 4.0**

Day 5

Review class rules.

Have students perform exercises for each area of health-related fitness.   **1.0 / 4.0**

Review the qualities of movement.   **7.0**

Have students perform various locomotor movements using qualities of movement as called out by the teacher (e.g., run at a fast pace, walk at a low level, jump at a slow pace).   **4.0 / 7.0**

Day 6

Review class rules.

Have students perform exercises for each area of health-related fitness, allocating more time to cardiorespiratory exercise in preparation for the one-mile run.   **1.0 / 4.0**

Have students play Booop, while referring to each other by name. (See appendix C.)

Using a balloon and a beach ball, introduce the scientific principles associated with rotation.   **2.2**

Day 7

Have students perform exercises for each area of health-related fitness, allocating more time to cardiorespiratory exercise in preparation for the one-mile run.   **1.0 / 4.0**

Have students participate in Circle the Circle, while referring to each other by name. (See appendix C.)   **1.0 / 5.0**

Have students read and discuss fitness training during Medieval times.   **6.2**

For homework, ask students to describe the fitness training that occurred during Medieval times. (Assessment assignment opportunity: essay.)   **6.2**

Day 8

Have students perform exercises for each area of health-related fitness, allocating more time to cardiorespiratory exercise in preparation for the one-mile run.   **1.0 / 4.0**

Have students participate in Across the Great Divide, while referring to each other by name. (See appendix C; assessment opportunity: structured observation.)   **1.0 / 5.0**

Have students participate in Knots, while referring to each other by name. (See appendix C; assessment opportunity: rubric.)   **1.0 / 5.0**

Have students brainstorm the variables that affect the beauty of a performance (e.g., what was beautiful about what they did today?). (Assessment opportunity: journal entry.)   **7.0**

Day 9

Have students perform warm-up exercises for the back-saver sit-and-reach test.   **1.0 / 4.0**

Explain the back-saver sit-and-reach test, why you give it, and the influences of growth rates on test performance.   **4.0 / 6.1**

Have each group create a game to learn more about each other. (Assessment assignment opportunity: project.)   **1.0 / 2.3 / 5.0**

Administer the back-saver sit-and-reach test to one group at a time. (Assessment opportunity: fitness test.)   **1.0 / 4.0**

Ask students if anyone knows the names of all the students in the class. (Assessment opportunity: structured observation.)   **5.0**

Day 10

Have students perform warm-up exercises for the curl-up test.   **4.0**

Explain the curl-up test, why you give it, and the influences of growth rates on test performance. **4.0 / 6.1**

Have each group present its game to another group. (Assessment opportunity: project.)   **1.0 / 2.3 / 5.0**

Administer the curl-up test to two groups at a time. (Assessment opportunity: fitness test.)   **1.0 / 4.0**

Ask students if anyone knows the names of all the students in the class. (Assessment opportunity: structured observation.)   **5.0**

Day 11

Explain the skinfold test, why you give it, and the influences of growth rates on test performance. **4.0 / 6.1**

Have students watch "Lesson 4: Nutrition" on the *PE-TV* video.   **4.0**

Administer the skinfold or body mass index test to students one at a time in private. (Assessment opportunity: fitness test.)   **4.0**

Discuss material covered on video.   **4.0**

Day 12

Have students perform warm-up exercises for the push-up test.   **1.0 / 4.0**

Explain the push-up test, why you give it, and the influences of growth rates on test performance. **4.0 / 6.1**

Have students participate in a flexibility circuit.   **1.0 / 4.0**

Administer the push-up test at one station in the circuit. (Assessment opportunity: fitness test.) **1.0 / 4.0**

Day 13

Have students perform warm-up exercises for the trunk lift test.   **1.0 / 4.0**

Explain the trunk lift test, why you give it, and the influences of growth rates on test performance. **4.0 / 6.1**

Have students participate in a flexibility circuit.   **1.0 / 4.0**

Administer the trunk lift test at one station in the circuit. (Assessment opportunity: fitness test.) **1.0 / 4.0**

Day 14

Have students perform warm-up exercises for the one-mile run.   **1.0 / 4.0**

Explain the one-mile run test, why you give it, and the influences of growth rates on test performance.   **4.0 / 6.1**

Administer the one-mile run test to half the class at a time, using the other half of the class as testing assistants to count laps. (Assessment opportunity: fitness test.)   **1.0 / 4.0**

Day 15

Have students perform warm-up exercises, depending on the fitness test(s) they need to make up.   **1.0 / 4.0**

Administer makeup tests. (Assessment opportunity: fitness test.)   **1.0 / 4.0**

Have students enter their scores into their electronic portfolios so they can compare them to the minimum competencies and set goals for the year. (Assessment opportunity: electronic log.)   **2.1 / 4.0**

For homework, have students create a list of new and risk-taking physical activities that interest them. (Assessment assignment opportunity: log.)   **3.0**

Unit 2: Tumbling and Gymnastics

In this unit, we'll begin to focus on taking appropriate risks by having the students challenge themselves to participate in body management activities relating to tumbling and gymnastics. Because many tumbling and gymnastics moves involve rotation, this unit is ideal for teaching students how the scientific principles associated with rotation relate to movement. To address standard four, I'll continue to cover physical fitness during the daily warm-up and flexibility exercises as well as have students perform cardiorespiratory, muscular strength, and endurance exercises every other day. I'll also review flexibility concepts related to health-related fitness development daily during the warm-up period. From days 5 through 22, I'll have students rotate through 10 stations. Initially, I repeat some of the stations; however, as the unit progresses, I'll make the activities more specific and unique. As students demonstrate competency in the first skill in each category, I'll have them document their performances on their progress cards, then practice the next skill in the category. I have found that this inclusion style of teaching works well throughout the entire unit. The following list outlines the categories and related activities for this unit.

Floor exercise, transitions:
   V-sit
   Front seat support

Floor exercise, forward sequence:
   Log roll
   Front shoulder roll
   Forward roll
   Forward roll walk-out
   Pike forward roll
   Forward roll combinations

Floor exercise, backward sequence:
   Log roll
   Back shoulder roll
   Backward roll
   Back roll to standing
   Backward roll combinations
   Back extension

Floor exercise, headstand sequence:
   Trust fall

   Tripod
   Three-point tip-up
   Headstand
   Headstand roll-out

Floor exercise, handstand sequence:
   Wall walk-up
   Switcheroo
   Teeter-totter
   Handstand
   Front walkover

Floor exercise, lateral sequence:
   Cartwheel
   Round-off

Balance beam:
   Walk
   Walk with dip
   Arabesque
   Straddle support mount
   Squat turn
   Jump dismount
   Backward roll

Horizontal bar:
   Wide-arm chinning
   Skin-the-cat
   Knee hang
   Front pullover
   Swing turn
   Penny drop
   Forward hip circle
   Forward hip circle dismount

Parallel bars:
   Forward hand walk
   Half-turn
   Back hand walk
   Forward hand jump
   Swing in a straight-arm support
   Series of straddle seats
   Shoulder stand
   Shoulder roll
   Front dismount from straight-arm support

Pommels:

   Jump front support

   Hand walk

   Flank mount to rear support

   Rear mount to rear support

   Single-leg cut

   Front dismount from straight-arm support

   Single-leg circle

Vaulting:

   Squat mount

   Jump dismount

   Knee spring dismount

   Squat vault

   Flank vault

   Straddle vault

Long horse vaulting:

   Straddle dismount from croup

   Straddle vault

   Squat dismount from croup

Video:

   New stunts for the lesson

You can also include stations for cardiorespiratory endurance, muscular strength, and muscular endurance in the rotation so that the class can move into the station approach immediately after warm-up and flexibility exercises. Depending on the number of students in each class, you can double each of the stations. If you have a camcorder available, you can use it to take video clips of the students as they perform various stunts, giving them immediate feedback.

If at all possible, teach this unit in a gymnasium or other indoor facility. Tumbling mats or other floor padding are a must. Additional gymnastics equipment, such as a beam, low beam, pommel horse, side horse, long horse, horizontal bar, and parallel bars add to the effectiveness of this unit. In lieu of balance beams, however, draw a line on the floor for your students to use. In addition, if you only have one horse, then you can either focus on one use of the horse or use the horse as a pommel horse one day, a side horse the next day, and a long horse on the third day. For instructional materials, use recorded television gymnastics meets and *PE-TV* for the cognitive aspects of health-related fitness.

Tumbling and gymnastics provide an excellent opportunity to integrate physical science with physical education. Students can learn a variety of physics principles, including those associated with rotation, during their science classes and then apply the concepts as they participate in the tumbling and gymnastics stunts. As a final project for science, you can have your students take one gymnastics stunt and apply the various physics concepts to performing the stunt correctly.

Unit Standards

1.0 – Applies the correct techniques for locomotor and nonlocomotor skills to tumbling and gymnastic stunts.

2.1 – Monitors changes in fitness development.

2.2 – Describes how the scientific principles associated with rotation apply to tumbling and gymnastic activities.

2.3 – Describes the elements of an individual or dual game.

3.0 – Demonstrates appropriate risk-taking through participation in tumbling and gymnastic activities outside of physical education.

4.0 – Participates in a variety of exercises for all five areas of health-related fitness and describes the frequency, intensity, time, and type concepts related to flexibility development.

5.0 – Describes problem solving techniques.

6.1 – Explains the growth rates of body segments from birth through adolescence.

6.2 – Describes the role of recreation and physical education during Medieval times.

7.0 – Creates a tumbling or gymnastics routine based on own sense of aesthetics.

Unit Outline

Day 1

Introduce tumbling and gymnastics and discuss safety.

Assign students to work in groups of four.

For homework, have students begin to monitor participation in tumbling and gymnastics activities outside of physical education. (Assessment assignment opportunity: log.)   **3.0**

Discuss the origin and history of tumbling and gymnastics.   **6.2**

Discuss the role of recreation and physical education during Medieval times.   **6.2**

Discuss the elements of individual and dual games and activities.   **2.3**

Introduce exercises for all five areas of health-related fitness specific to tumbling and gymnastics.   **1.0 / 4.0**

For homework, ask students to list the elements of individual and dual games and activities. (Assessment opportunity: written assignment.)   **2.3**

Day 2

Have students watch "Lesson 6: Flexibility" on the *PE-TV* video, then discuss the information presented on the video.   **4.0**

Have students review the frequency, intensity, time, and type concepts related to flexibility. (Assessment opportunity: structured observation.)   **4.0**

Give students a form on which to record their fitness scores once every other week during the year at home. (Assessment assignment opportunity: log.)   **2.1 / 4.0**

For homework, ask students to review the role of recreation and physical education during Medieval times. (Assessment opportunity: essay.)   **6.2**

Day 3

Demonstrate the log roll.   **1.0**

Have students perform log rolls.   **1.0**

Demonstrate the V-sit.   **1.0**

Have students perform V-sits.   **1.0**

Demonstrate the front seat support.   **1.0**

Have students perform front seat supports.   **1.0**

Demonstrate the trust fall.   **1.0**

Have students perform trust falls.   **1.0**

Discuss how body segments grow from birth through adolescence and the effects on physical performance.   **6.1**

Ask students to brainstorm about the relationships among the log roll, V-sit, front seat support, trust falls, and growth in body segments. (Assessment opportunity: structured observation.)   **6.1**

Day 4

Review the log roll, V-sit, front seat support, and trust fall.   **1.0**

Have students perform log rolls, V-sits, front seat supports, and trust falls.   **1.0**

Demonstrate the front shoulder roll.   **1.0**

Have students perform front shoulder rolls.   **1.0**

Discuss and experiment with the scientific principles associated with rotation.   **2.2**

Ask students to brainstorm when they might use a front shoulder roll. (Assessment opportunity: structured observation.)   **1.0**

Days 5 and 6

Explain to students the station approach to tumbling and gymnastics, and provide students with forms on which to keep track of their progress. (Assessment assignment opportunity: log.)   **1.0**

Demonstrate the new stunts.   **1.0**

Have students rotate through these stations: floor exercise, transitions (V-sit); floor exercise, transitions (front seat support); floor exercise, forward sequence (log roll); floor exercise, forward sequence (front shoulder roll); floor exercise, backward sequence (back shoulder roll); floor exercise, headstand sequence (trust fall); floor exercise, headstand sequence (tripod); floor exercise, handstand sequence (wall walk-up); beam (walking); and video of tumbling clips.   **1.0**

For homework, ask students to describe the relationships between the scientific principles associated with rotation and the stunts they performed today. (Assessment opportunity: essay.)   **2.2**

For homework, ask students to describe the relationships between stunts they performed today and growth in body segments. (Assessment opportunity: essay.)   **6.1**

Days 7 and 8

Demonstrate the new stunts.   **1.0**

Have students rotate through stations (I have listed the skills that are the new or newest; students can work on the new skill or any previous skill in that category): floor exercise, transitions (V-sit); floor exercise, transitions (front seat support); floor exercise, forward sequence (forward roll); floor exercise, backward sequence (backward roll); floor exercise, headstand sequence (tripod); floor exercise, handstand sequence (switcheroo); beam (walk with dip); horizontal bar (wide-arm chinning); parallel bars (forward hand walk); and video of tumbling clips.   **1.0**

For homework, ask students to describe the relationships between the scientific principles associated with rotation and the stunts they performed today. (Assessment opportunity: essay.)   **2.2**

For homework, ask students to describe the relationships between stunts they performed today and growth in body segments. (Assessment opportunity: essay.)   **6.1**

Days 9 and 10

Demonstrate the new stunts.   **1.0**

Have students rotate through stations: floor exercise, forward sequence (forward roll); floor exercise, backward sequence (backward roll); floor exercise, headstand sequence (three-point tip-up); floor exercise, handstand sequence (teeter-totter); beam (arabesque); horizontal bar (skin-the-cat); parallel bars (half-turn, back hand walk); pommels (jump front support, hand walk); vaulting (squat mount, jump dismount); and video of tumbling and gymnastics clips.   **1.0**

For homework, ask students to describe the relationships between the scientific principles associated with rotation and the stunts they performed today. (Assessment opportunity: essay.)   **2.2**

For homework, ask students to describe the relationships between stunts they performed today and growth in body segments. (Assessment opportunity: essay.)   **6.1**

Days 11 and 12

Demonstrate the new stunts. (See figure 15.1.)   **1.0**

Have students rotate through stations: floor exercise, forward sequence (forward roll walk-out); floor exercise, backward sequence (back roll to standing); floor exercise, headstand sequence (three-point tip-up); floor exercise, handstand sequence (handstand); beam (straddle support mount); horizontal bar (knee hang); parallel bars (forward hand jump); pommels (flank mount to rear support); vaulting (knee spring dismount); and video of gymnastics clips.   **1.0**

Figure 15.1   The correct technique for the straddle support mount on the balance beam.

Days 13 and 14

Demonstrate the new stunts. (See figures 15.2 and 15.3.)   **1.0**

Have students rotate through stations: floor exercise, forward sequence (forward roll walk-out); floor exercise, backward sequence (back roll to standing); floor exercise, headstand sequence (headstand); floor exercise, handstand sequence (handstand); beam (straddle support mount); horizontal bar (front pullover); parallel bars (swing in a straight-arm support); pommels (rear mount to rear support); side horse (squat vault); long horse (straddle dismount from croup).   **1.0**

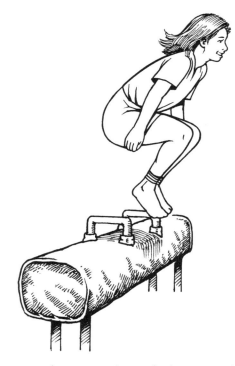

Figure 15.2   The correct technique for the squat vault for the side horse.

Figure 15.3   The correct technique for the front pullover on a horizontal bar.

Days 15 and 16

Demonstrate the new stunts.   **1.0**

Have students rotate through stations: floor exercise, forward sequence (pike forward roll); floor exercise, backward sequence (backward roll combinations); floor exercise, headstand sequence (headstand); floor exercise, lateral sequence (cartwheel); beam (squat turn); horizontal bar (front pullover); parallel bars (series of straddle seats); pommels (single-leg cut); vaulting (squat vault); long horse (straddle dismount from croup).   **1.0**

Days 17 and 18

Demonstrate the new stunts. (See figures 15.4 and 15.5.)   **1.0**

Have students rotate through stations: floor exercise, forward sequence (pike forward roll); floor exercise, backward sequence (backward roll combinations); floor exercise, headstand sequence (headstand); floor exercise, lateral sequence (cartwheel); beam (jump dismount); horizontal bar (swing turn); parallel bars (shoulder stand); pommels (single-leg cut); vaulting (flank vault); and long horse (straddle vault).   **1.0**

Figure 15.4 The correct technique for the shoulder stand on the parallel bars.

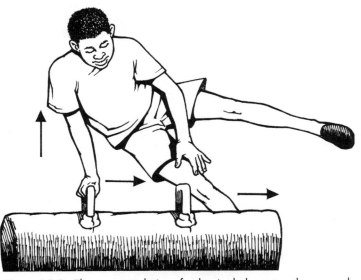

Figure 15.5 The correct technique for the single-leg cut on the pommel horse.

Days 19 and 20

Review and experience the qualities of movement.   **7.0**

Describe to students the routine you will require them to create. (Assessment assignment opportunity: project.)   **1.0 / 7.0**

Discuss problem solving techniques.   **5.0**

Ask groups to use problem solving techniques to determine which individual will create a routine for which event (only one student per group may perform in a particular event).   **1.0 / 5.0 / 7.0**

Demonstrate the new stunts. (See figure 15.6.)   **1.0**

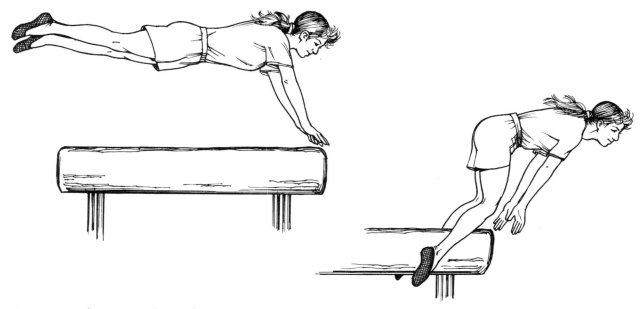

Figure 15.6 The correct technique for the straddle vault on the long horse.

Have students rotate through stations: floor exercise, forward sequence (forward roll combinations); floor exercise, backward sequence (back extension); floor exercise, headstand sequence (headstand roll-out); floor exercise, lateral sequence (round-off); beam (jump dismount); horizontal bar (penny drop); parallel bars (shoulder roll); pommels (front dismount from straight-arm support); vaulting horse (flank vault); long horse (straddle vault).   **1.0**

For homework, ask students to begin to create their routines. (Assessment assignment opportunity: project.)   **1.0 / 7.0**

Days 21 and 22

Demonstrate the new stunts.   **1.0**

Have students rotate through stations: floor exercise, backward sequence (back extension); floor exercise, headstand sequence (headstand roll-out); floor exercise, handstand sequence (front walkover); floor exercise, lateral sequence (round-off); beam (backward roll); horizontal bar (forward hip circle, forward hip circle dismount); parallel bars (front dismount from straight-arm support); pommels (single-leg circle); vaulting horse (straddle vault); and long horse (squat dismount from croup).   **1.0**

For homework, ask students to brainstorm about the relationships between the scientific principles associated with rotation and the stunts they performed today. (Assessment opportunity: essay.)   **2.2**

For homework, ask students to brainstorm about the relationships between stunts they performed today and growth in body segments. (Assessment opportunity: essay.)   **6.1**

Days 23 and 24

Have students work on their routines.   **1.0 / 7.0**

Collect stunt progress logs. (Assessment opportunity: log.)   **1.0**

Day 25

Have students perform their routines for their groups. (Assessment opportunity: project.)   **1.0 / 7.0**

Collect student logs of participation in tumbling and gymnastics outside of physical education. (Assessment opportunity: log.)   **3.0**

Collect fitness monitoring forms. (Assessment opportunity: log.)   **2.1 / 4.0**

Have students describe in their journals how their routine was an expression of their own sense of aesthetics. (Assessment opportunity: journal entry.)   **7.0**

Unit 3: Outdoor Education

This unit continues our focus on taking appropriate risks by having the students challenge themselves to participate in body management activities relating to outdoor education. You may elect to have students hike, bicycle, wall climb, camp, or orienteer for outdoor education, depending on your situation. Because of the physical nature of life in the inner city where my school is located, I have opted to focus on orienteering. To address standard four, I will continue to cover physical fitness during our daily warm-up and flexibility exercises as well as have students perform cardiorespiratory, muscular strength, and muscular endurance exercises every other day. I'll also review the warm-up and cooldown concepts related to health-related fitness development daily during the warm-up period.

Ideally, you should conduct this unit on open terrain so students can actually perform real-life orienteering events; however, any open outdoor area will do. Even in an inner city setting, students can experience orienteering through simulated events held on the school campus. To culminate simulated events, you may opt to take students on a field trip for their final orienteering challenge. In this unit, students must learn to use a compass and a topographic map; you can order the maps from the National Cartographic Information Center (see appendix D). In addition, I'll use the video *Finding Your Way in the Wild* to introduce some of the orienteering concepts (see appendix D).

Orienteering is an excellent activity to integrate physical education with history/social science. Reading maps, understanding map symbols, and following route directions help students in physical education, in the regular classroom, and—most importantly—in real life. Ideally, you should have your students' history/social science teacher cover the types of maps, reading of maps, and meaning of map symbols just prior to the start of your orienteering unit.

Unit Standards

1.0 – Applies the correct techniques for locomotor and nonlocomotor skills in outdoor education activities.

2.1 – Sets goals and monitors changes in outdoor education skills.

2.2 – Describes how the scientific principles associated with rotation apply to outdoor education.

2.3 – Creates an outdoor education game.

3.0 – Chooses to participate in physical activities outside of physical education.

4.0 – Participates in a variety of exercises for all five areas of health-related fitness and describes concepts related to warm-up and cooldown.

5.0 – Uses problem solving techniques with a partner when solving outdoor education challenges.

6.1 – Explains how growth rates of body segments relate to movement performances in general.

6.2 – Describes the type of tournaments held during Medieval times.

7.0 – Describes the variables that affect the beauty of a performance.

Unit Outline

Day 1

Introduce outdoor education and orienteering.

Show "Introduction" section on the *Finding Your Way in the Wild* video, then discuss the information presented in the video.   **1.0**

Assign students to work in groups of four.

Discuss concepts related to warm-up and cooldown.   **4.0**

Have students set goals for outdoor education activities.   **2.1**

Give students a form on which to record their progress toward outdoor education goals. (Assessment assignment opportunity: log.)   **2.1**

Have students record concepts related to warm-up and cooldown. (Assessment opportunity: log.)   **4.0**

For homework, have students begin to monitor their participation in physical activities outside of physical education. (Assessment assignment opportunity: log.)   **3.0**

Days 2 and 3

Review warm-up and cooldown principles.   **4.0**

Discuss the history of orienteering.   **1.0 / 6.2**

Have students read about the types of tournaments held during Medieval times.   **6.2**

For homework, have students write an essay on the types of tournaments held during Medieval times. (Assessment opportunity: essay.)   **6.2**

Days 4 and 5

Show "Topographic Maps" section on the *Finding Your Way in the Wild* video, then discuss the information presented in the video.   **1.0**

Discuss topographic maps. (See figure 15.7.)   **1.0**

Review key points related to topographic maps: opening, folding, and protecting the map; the four cardinal directions; symbols; contour lines; scale; and orienting a map.   **1.0**

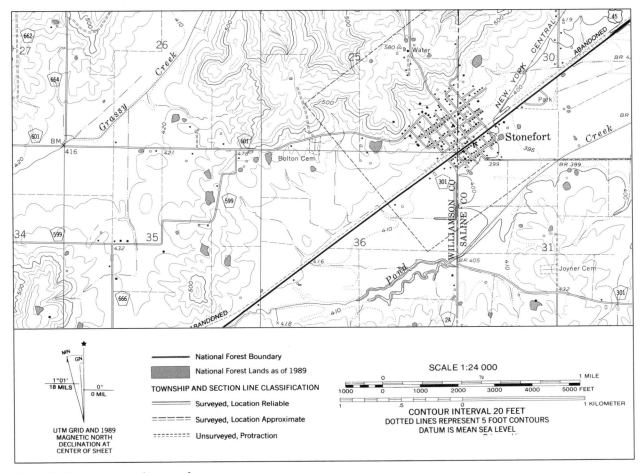

Figure 15.7 A topographic map for orienteering.

Discuss the scientific principles associated with rotation and how they might apply to topographic maps. **2.2**

Discuss how growth rates of body segments (length of step) relate to the use of topographic maps. **6.1**

Have students identify different types of mountains and hills on a topographic map. **1.0**

Have students identify the meanings of the symbols on a topographic map. **1.0**

Have students find the distance between several points marked on a map. **1.0**

For homework, have students create a topographic map of the school. (Assessment assignment opportunity: project.) **1.0**

Days 6, 7, and 8

Show "Compass" section on the *Finding Your Way in the Wild* video, then discuss the information presented in the video. **1.0**

Review parts of a compass, orienting a compass, and taking and following a bearing. (See figure 15.8.) **1.0**

Have students take a bearing on a physical feature (e.g., a point in the gym). **1.0**

Have students participate in an activity in which they walk 20 steps and turn 90 degrees, repeating it four times to end up in the original location. **1.0**

Have students participate in an activity in which they walk 20 steps and turn 120 degrees, repeating it three times to end up in the original location. **1.0**

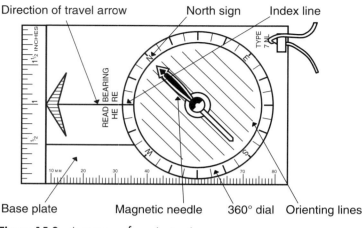

Figure 15.8   A compass for orienteering.

Have students walk 10 steps at a 30-degree bearing, 15 steps at a 40-degree bearing, and 20 steps at a 60-degree bearing.   **1.0**

Review how to use problem solving techniques with a partner.   **5.0**

Create a bearing route with a partner (lie at paper plates and note the bearing between the plates). (Assessment opportunity: project.)   **1.0 / 5.0**

With a partner, have students participate in the bearing route activity created by the other two members of their group. (Assessment opportunity: rubric.)   **1.0 / 5.0**

Discuss the scientific principles associated with rotation and how they might apply to compass reading.   **2.2**

Days 9, 10, and 11

Show "Declination" on the *Finding Your Way in the Wild* video, then discuss the information presented in the video.   **1.0**

Discuss declination (the difference between true north and magnetic north).   **1.0**

Have students take a map bearing (bearing between two points on a map) and then convert it to a real bearing based on the declination. (Assessment opportunity: structured observation.)   **1.0**

Show students how to read an isogenic chart.   **1.0**

Have students take a map bearing on an isogenic chart, determining the real bearing. (Assessment opportunity: structured observation.)   **1.0**

Day 12

Discuss pace and route choice.   **1.0**

Have students determine the most effective route between two points on a map.   **1.0**

Discuss how growth rates of body segments relate to pacing.   **6.1**

Have students determine the number of steps they must take to go between the two points on the map. (Assessment opportunity: structured observation.)   **1.0 / 6.1**

Day 13

Discuss with students the variables that affect the beauty of a performance.   **7.0**

Explain control marker, control code, control description, and control feature.   **1.0**

Describe an orienteering activity.   **1.0**

Have students describe what might make an orienteering experience beautiful. (Assessment opportunity: journal.)   **7.0**

For the first orienteering activity, give students the map to study overnight.   **1.0**

Days 14 and 15

Review problem solving techniques.   **5.0**

Have students working in pairs participate in the first orienteering activity. (Assessment opportunity: structured observation.)   **1.0 / 5.0 / 6.1**

Days 16 and 17

Have pairs participate in the second orienteering activity. (Assessment opportunity: structured observation.)   **1.0 / 5.0 / 6.1**

Days 18 and 19

Have each group create their own outdoor education or orienteering-like game.   **2.3**

Have each group teach their game to another group. (Assessment opportunity: project.)   **2.3**

Day 20

Collect student logs of participation in physical activity outside of physical education. (Assessment opportunity: log.)   **3.0**

Collect fitness monitoring forms. (Assessment opportunity: log)   **2.1 / 4.0**

Unit 4: Racket Sports

Because racket sports are new to my students, this unit continues the focus on taking appropriate risks. I'll cover tennis skills and introduce students to other racket sports, including badminton, table tennis, paddle tennis, pickleball, and racquetball. To address standard four, I will continue to cover physical fitness during the daily warm-up and flexibility exercises as well as have students perform cardio-respiratory, muscular strength, and muscular endurance exercises every other day. I'll also review body composition concepts related to health-related fitness development daily during the warm-up period.

Naturally, it's helpful if you have access to any or all of the following facilities, but you can conduct this unit in any open outdoor area: a tennis court, a paddle tennis court, a racquetball court, and a badminton court. Check with your local racket club or park district to see if you can gain free or low-cost access to appropriate facilities—at least to culminate the unit. While you can do without proper courts, rackets (any or all: tennis, paddle tennis, racquetball, table tennis, pickleball, or badminton) are essential to this unit. If you are unfamiliar with teaching tennis or lack equipment or facilities, the United States Tennis Association provides free training, curriculum materials, rackets, and balls. Perhaps most importantly, their curriculum guide is based on teaching tennis in an open area without regular tennis courts. Simply call the United States Tennis Association and ask for the office near you (see appendix D). In addition, I'll use the video *Tennis by Vic Braden* to illustrate different strokes, *The Science and Myths of Tennis* to illustrate how the scientific principles associated with rotation relate to playing tennis, and *PE-TV* to teach and reinforce other tennis and racket sport concepts. (See appendix D for video sources.)

Unit Standards

1.0 – Applies the correct techniques for locomotor, nonlocomotor, and manipulative skills to racket activities.

2.1 – Sets goals and monitors changes in racket skill development.

2.2 – Describes how the scientific principles associated with rotation apply to racket skills.

2.3 – Creates a dual game with scoring options, using a racket and an object.

3.0 – Chooses to participate in physical activities outside of physical education.

4.0 – Calculates caloric input and output for an entire week and performs exercises for all five areas of health-related fitness.

5.0 – Works with a partner to apply problem solving techniques in situations that arise during racket activities.

6.1 – Explains the growth rates of body segments and their relationships to racket activities.

6.2 – Describes the types of ball games popular during Medieval times.

7.0 – Appreciates the stylistic differences of own approach to racket activities.

Unit Outline

Day 1

Introduce tennis and other racket sports, including discussing safety, equipment, and unit overview. **1.0**

Have students watch "Lesson 11: Racket Sports" on the *PE-TV* video, then discuss the information presented in the video.   **1.0**

Describe the history of tennis as well as other ball games popular during Medieval times.   **6.2**

Assign students to work in groups of four.

Have students set goals for racket sports activities.   **2.1**

Give students a form on which to record their progress toward racket sport goals. (Assessment assignment opportunity: log.)   **2.1**

For homework, have students begin to monitor participation in physical activities outside of physical education. (Assessment assignment opportunity: log.)   **3.0**

Day 2

Review the meaning of stylistic differences in movement.   **7.0**

Have students watch "Forehand Drive" segment on the *Tennis by Vic Braden* video, then discuss the information presented in the video.   **1.0**

Review the ready position, grip (see figure 15.9), and forehand drive (see figure 15.10).   **1.0**

Figure 15.9 The correct technique for the forehand grip in tennis.

Figure 15.10 The correct technique for the forehand drive in tennis.

Have students demonstrate the ready position and the grip to you so you can provide feedback   **1.0**

Have pairs of students practice dropping the ball and executing the forehand drive, using any or all of the following: tennis racket, paddle tennis racket, pickleball racquet, and racquetball racket.   **1.0**

Have students brainstorm about the stylistic differences that can occur among tennis participants.   **7.0**

Day 3

Have pairs of students practice dropping the ball and executing the forehand drive, using any or all of the following: tennis racket, paddle tennis racket, pickleball racquet, and racquetball racket.   **1.0**

Have pairs who are ready practice tossing the ball to each other and executing the forehand drive, using any or all of the following: tennis racket, paddle tennis racket, pickleball racquet, and racquetball racket.   **1.0**

Have students brainstorm about the relationships between the scientific principles associated with rotation and a forehand drive.   **2.2**

Have students brainstorm about the relationships between growth rates of body segments and the execution of a forehand drive.   **6.1**

Day 4

Demonstrate the footwork necessary to move to the ball to execute a forehand drive.   **1.0**

Have students demonstrate the necessary footwork as you model it.   **1.0**

Have pairs of students practice dropping the ball and executing the forehand drive, using any or all of the following: tennis racket, paddle tennis racket, pickleball racquet, and racquetball racket.   **1.0**

Have pairs who are ready practice tossing the ball to each other and executing the forehand drive, using any or all of the following: tennis racket, paddle tennis racket, pickleball racquet, and racquetball racket.   **1.0**

Have pairs who are ready begin hitting back and forth to each other with forehand drives, using any or all of the following: tennis racket, paddle tennis racket, pickleball racquet, and racquetball racket.   **1.0**

Have pairs who are ready hit the ball back and forth with forehand drives, counting the number of hits they can make without missing, using any or all of the following: tennis racket, paddle tennis racket, pickleball racquet, and racquetball racket.   **1.0**

Have students brainstorm about the differences and similarities between using a tennis racket, paddle tennis racket, pickleball racquet, and racquetball racket.   **1.0**

Day 5

Have students watch "Backhand Drive" segment on the *Tennis by Vic Braden* video, then discuss the information presented in the video.   **1.0**

Review the ready position, backhand grip (see figure 15.11), and backhand drive (see figure 15.12).   **1.0**

Have pairs of students practice dropping the ball and executing the backhand drive, using any or all of the following: tennis racket, paddle tennis racket, pickleball racquet, and racquetball racket.   **1.0**

Have students brainstorm about the stylistic differences among tennis players.   **7.0**

Figure 15.11   The correct technique for the backhand grip in tennis.

Figure 15.12   The correct technique for the backhand drive in tennis.

Day 6

Have pairs practice dropping the ball and executing the backhand drive, using any or all of the following: tennis racket, paddle tennis racket, pickleball racquet, and racquetball racket.   **1.0**

Have pairs who are ready practice tossing the ball to each other and executing the backhand drive, using any or all of the following: tennis racket, paddle tennis racket, pickleball racquet, and racquetball racket.   **1.0**

For homework, have students analyze the relationships between the scientific principles associated with rotation and the backhand drive. (Assessment opportunity: essay.)   **2.2**

For homework, have students analyze the relationships between growth rates of body segments and the execution of the backhand drive. (Assessment opportunity: essay.)   **6.1**

Day 7

Demonstrate the footwork necessary to move to the ball to execute a backhand drive.   **1.0**

Have students demonstrate the necessary footwork as you model it.   **1.0**

Have pairs of students practice dropping the ball and executing the backhand drive, using any or all of the following: a tennis racket, paddle tennis racket, pickleball racquet, and racquetball racket.   **1.0**

Have pairs who are ready practice tossing the ball to each other and executing the backhand drive, using any or all of the following: tennis racket, paddle tennis racket, pickleball racquet, and racquetball racket.   **1.0**

Have pairs who are ready begin hitting back and forth to each other with backhand drives, using any or all of the following: tennis racket, paddle tennis racket, pickleball racquet, and racquetball racket.   **1.0**

Have pairs who are ready hit the ball back and forth with backhand drives, counting the number of hits they can make without missing, using any or all of the following: tennis racket, paddle tennis racket, pickleball racquet, and racquetball racket.   **1.0**

Day 8

Have students watch the "Serve" segment on the *Tennis by Vic Braden* video, then discuss the information presented in the video.   **1.0**

Review the serves for different types of racket sports. (See figure 15.13.)   **1.0**

Have pairs of students practice tossing the ball.   **1.0**

Have pairs of students practice tossing the ball and serving, using any or all of the following: tennis racket, paddle tennis racket, pickleball racquet, and racquetball racket.   **1.0**

Have students brainstorm about the stylistic differences among players' serves. (Assessment opportunity: journal.)   **7.0**

Day 9

Have students watch "Why Take the Ball on the Rise," "Why Hitting a Cross Court Shot Down the Line Is Dangerous" and other segments related to the scientific principles associated with rotation on *The Science and Myths of Tennis* video, then discuss the information presented in the video.   **1.0 / 2.2**

Have pairs of students practice tossing the ball and serving, using any or all of the following: tennis racket, paddle tennis racket, pickleball racquet, and racquetball racket.   **1.0**

For homework, have students analyze the relationships between the scientific principles associated with rotation and a serve. (Assessment opportunity: essay.)   **2.2**

For homework, have students analyze the relationships between growth rates of body segments and the execution of a serve. (Assessment opportunity: essay.)   **6.1**

Figure 15.13 The correct technique for the tennis serve.

Day 10

Have pairs of students discuss problem solving techniques with a partner over situations that occur during games. **5.0**

In their groups of four, have students begin to create a rubric for the striking skill (e.g., serve, forehand). (Assessment assignment opportunity: project.) **1.0 / 2.0**

Teach modified racket sport rules. **1.0**

Have pairs of students play modified racket sports, using the same type of racket. (Assessment opportunity: structured observation.) **1.0 / 5.0**

Day 11

Have students watch the "Volley" segment on the *Tennis by Vic Braden* video, then discuss the information presented in the video. **1.0**

Review the volley. **1.0**

Have pairs practice tossing the ball and executing a volley, using any or all of the following: tennis racket, paddle tennis racket, pickleball racquet, and racquetball racket. **1.0**

Have students brainstorm about the stylistic differences among players' volleys. (Assessment opportunity: journal.) **7.0**

Day 12

Have pairs practice tossing the ball and executing the volley, using any or all of the following: tennis racket, paddle tennis racket, pickleball racquet, and racquetball racket. **1.0**

Have pairs who are ready practice tossing the ball to each other and executing the volley, using any or all of the following: tennis racket, paddle tennis racket, pickleball racquet, and racquetball racket. **1.0**

For homework, have students analyze the relationships between the scientific principles associated with rotation and a volley. (Assessment opportunity: essay.) **2.2**

For homework, have students analyze the relationships between growth rates of body segments and the execution of a volley. (Assessment opportunity: essay.)   **6.1**

Day 13

Have students complete their rubrics for one striking skill. (Assessment opportunity: project.)   **1.0 / 5.0**

Have pairs of students play modified racket sports, using same racket of choice. (Assessment opportunity: rubric.)   **1.0 / 5.0**

Day 14

Discuss caloric input and output.   **4.0**

Give students a form on which to keep track of their caloric input and output for one week. (Assessment assignment opportunity: log.)   **4.0**

Days 15 Through 18

Introduce students to the concept of using stations to practice racket sport skills.   **1.0**

Have students participate in the following racket sport stations—volley practice, modified pickleball game, serving practice station, modified tennis game, backhand drive practice station, modified racquetball game, forehand drive practice station, modified paddle tennis game—while using their rubrics to assess one another. (Assessment opportunity: rubric.)   **1.0 / 5.0**

Day 19

Have each group create a new game, using a racket and a ball. (Assessment assignment opportunity: projects.)   **1.0 / 2.3 / 5.0**

Day 20

Have each group share their new game with another group. (Assessment opportunity: project.)   **1.0 / 2.3 / 5.0**

Collect student logs of participation in physical activity outside of physical education. (Assessment opportunity: log.)   **3.0**

Collect fitness monitoring forms. (Assessment opportunity: log.)   **2.1 / 4.0**

Collect racket sport and tennis goals and monitoring forms. (Assessment opportunity: log.)   **2.1**

Collect one-week caloric input and output calculations. (Assessment opportunity: log.)   **4.0**

Unit 5: Aquatics

This unit continues our focus on taking appropriate risks by having students challenge themselves in a water setting. Because this unit is directly related to student safety, it is one of the most important units that physical education can offer. Most of my students are beginning swimmers, although a few have more advanced skills. Before I allow my students in the water, they must pass a water safety test in their native language to demonstrate that they understand the safety principles associated with swimming. I will use the *American Red Cross Swimming Program* to teach my students swimming skills.

This program identifies skills in six categories: water adjustment, buoyancy and breath control, water entry and exit, locomotion, turns, and personal safety and rescue. The program also outlines seven courses (water exploration, primary skills, stroke readiness, stroke development, stroke refinement, skill proficiency, and advanced skills) that provide a sequence of development and refinement for water skills. I encourage you to become certified by the American Red Cross in Water Safety Instruction (WSI). To meet standard four, I'll continue to address physical fitness during the daily warm-up and flexibility exercises, and, every other day, I'll have students perform cardiorespiratory and muscular strength and endurance exercises. I'll review the cognitive concepts related to cardiorespiratory endurance development daily during the warm-up period.

Naturally, this unit does require a swimming pool or other aquatic facility. If a pool is unavailable, you can still teach water safety concepts to your students; however, this approach makes for a much shorter unit. *Longfellow's Whales Tales* available from the American Red Cross provides you with the instructional materials you need to put together a no-water aquatics unit. Life jackets, kickboards, objects that sink, snorkels, masks, and fins still help with this unit, but you can conduct it without these items. In addition, I'll use the videos *Water, The Deceptive Power* and *Home Pool Safety* to teach water safety principles and *PE-TV* to teach and reinforce health-related fitness concepts (see appendix D).

Unit Standards

1.0 – Applies the correct techniques for locomotor and nonlocomotor skills to aquatics.

2.1 – Sets goals and monitors changes in aquatic skills.

2.2 – Describes how the scientific principles associated with rotation apply to aquatics.

2.3 – Creates an aquatic individual or dual game with scoring options.

3.0 – Chooses to participate in physical activities outside physical education.

4.0 – Participates in a variety of exercises for all five areas of health-related fitness and describes the frequency, intensity, time, and type concepts related to cardiorespiratory development.

5.0 – Uses problem solving techniques in a small group when solving aquatic challenges.

6.1 – Explains the growth rates of body segments and their relationships to aquatics.

6.2 – Describes the role of aquatic activities during the Renaissance period.

7.0 – Appreciates the stylistic features of own approach to aquatics.

Unit Outline

Day 1

Introduce aquatics unit.

Explain the safety rules.   **1.0**

Have students watch *Water, The Deceptive Power*, then discuss the information presented in the video.   **1.0**

Administer a written water safety test. (Assessment opportunity: written test.)   **1.0**

Day 2

Have students watch "Lesson 3: Cardiorespiratory Endurance" on the *PE-TV* video, then discuss the information presented in the video.   **4.0**

Review frequency, intensity, time, and type concepts related to cardiorespiratory endurance.   **4.0**

Have students practice taking their pulses and calculating their target heart rates.   **4.0**

Have students take a partner's blood pressure, using an electronic blood pressure device.   **4.0**

Have students record frequency, intensity, time, and type concepts related to cardiorespiratory endurance. (Assessment opportunity: log.)   **4.0**

Discuss the role of aquatic activities during the Renaissance period.   **6.2**

Figure 15.14 The correct technique for the elementary backstroke.

For homework, have students begin to monitor participation in physical activities outside of physical education. (Assessment assignment opportunity: log.) **3.0**

Day 3

Assess students' current skill levels in swimming (see figures 15.14-15.18), then assign each to one of the American Red Cross swimming courses. **1.0**

Have students set goals for aquatics activities. **2.1**

Give students a form on which to record their progress toward aquatics goals. (Assessment assignment opportunity: log.) **2.1**

Have students brainstorm about how the scientific principles associated with rotation apply to aquatics. **2.2**

Have students brainstorm about how growth rates of body segments relate to aquatics. **6.1**

Days 4 Through 13

Have students progress through the skills (holding breath through swimming underwater) based on their current ability levels. (Assessment opportunity: checklist.) **1.0**

Work with one group at a time, assigning practice tasks for the other groups. **1.0**

Have students brainstorm about how the scientific principles associated with rotation apply to aquatics. **2.2**

Have students brainstorm about how the growth rates of body segments relate to aquatics. **6.1**

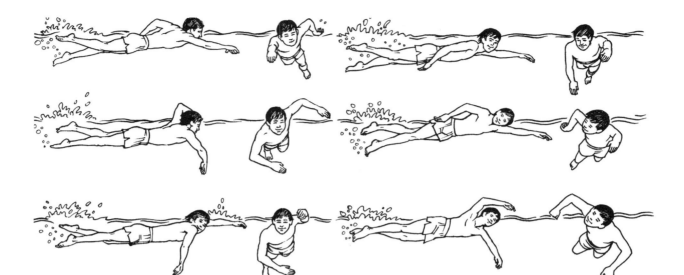

Figure 15.15 The correct technique for the front crawl.

Figure 15.16 The correct technique for the back crawl.

Days 14 Through 18

Have students continue to progress through the skills (holding breath through swimming underwater), based on their current ability levels. (Assessment opportunity: checklist)   **1.0**

Work with one group at a time, assigning practice tasks to the other groups.   **1.0**

Introduce skin diving skills to one group at a time, starting with the most advanced group while other groups practice tasks. (The group working on skin diving interrupts their progression to work on skin diving skills.)   **1.0**

For homework, have students describe how the scientific principles associated with rotation apply to aquatics. (Assessment opportunity: essay.)   **2.2**

Figure 15.17 The correct technique for the breaststroke.

For homework, have students describe how growth rates of body segments relate to aquatics. (Assessment opportunity: essay.)   **6.1**

Day 19

Discuss how to use problem solving techniques in a small group.   **5.0**

Have each group create an aquatic game with scoring options. (Assessment assignment opportunity: project.)   **1.0 / 2.3 / 5.0**

Have students write an essay, describing how their own sense of aesthetics has affected their development of an aquatics game. (Assessment opportunity: essay.)   **7.0**

Figure 15.18 The correct technique for the sidestroke.

Day 20

Have groups teach their aquatic game to another group and then allow them to play each other's games. (Assessment opportunity: project.)   **1.0 / 2.3 / 5.0**

Collect student logs of participation in physical activity outside of physical education. (Assessment opportunity: log.)   **3.0**

Collect fitness monitoring forms. (Assessment opportunity: log.)   **2.1 / 4.0**

Collect aquatics goals and monitoring forms. (Assessment opportunity: log.)   **2.1**

Unit 6: Golf

This unit continues our focus on taking appropriate risks by having students challenge themselves in an activity that very few of them have ever tried: golf. I teach golf and tennis (and other racket sports) to students not only to challenge them but also to introduce them to two lifetime sports. Most students at my school are not introduced to these activities in a community or park setting; however, golf and tennis are the type of sports adults are more likely to play as they get older. To address standard four, we will continue to work on physical fitness during the daily warm-up and flexibility exercises and will have students perform cardiorespiratory and muscular strength and endurance exercises every other day. I'll also review the health-related fitness cognitive concepts related to muscular endurance daily during the warm-up period.

As you might expect, this unit requires a grass facility. In addition, you'll need golf clubs (woods, irons, and putters), golf balls, and cones. If you do not have access to golf equipment, then contact your local driving range or golf association. They often have surplus equipment to donate to schools. The type of ball you use will depend on the amount of space you have available for the golf unit. You can use regular golf balls, Wiffle golf balls, or special golf balls for limited spaces developed by Cayman and available from Wittek Golf Company. In addition, I'll use the video *Golf With Al Geiberger* to reinforce golfing techniques and *PE-TV* to teach and reinforce concepts related to health-related fitness (see appendix D for sources).

Unit Standards

1.0 – Applies the correct techniques for locomotor, nonlocomotor, and manipulative skills to golf.

2.1 – Sets goals and monitors changes in golf skill development.

2.2 – Describes how the scientific principles associated with rotation apply to golf skills.

2.3 – Creates an individual game with scoring options, using a golf club and an object.

3.0 – Chooses to participate in physical activities outside of physical education.

4.0 – Participates in a variety of exercises for all five areas of health-related fitness and describes the frequency, intensity, time, and type concepts related to muscular endurance development.

5.0 – Applies problem solving techniques to working in a small group on situations that arise during golf.

6.1 – Explains the growth rates of body segments and their relationships to golf.

6.2 – Describes the role of physical activity and physical education during the Renaissance period.

7.0 – Appreciates the stylistic differences of own approach to golf.

Unit Outline

Day 1

Introduce golf unit.

Review golf safety and equipment.   **1.0**

Assign students to work in groups of four.

Have students watch "Lesson 5: Muscular Strength and Endurance" on the *PE-TV* video, then discuss the information presented in the video.   **4.0**

Review frequency, intensity, time, and type related to muscular endurance.   **4.0**

Have students record frequency, intensity, time, and type related to muscular endurance. (Assessment opportunity: log.)   **4.0**

For homework, have students monitor participation in physical activities outside of physical education. (Assessment assignment opportunity: log.)   **3.0**

Day 2

Discuss the history of golf as well as the role of physical activity and physical education during the Renaissance period.   **6.2**

Have students pick an activity played during the Renaissance period and write a report about it, including modern sports that have grown out of the activity. (Assessment assignment opportunity: report.)   **6.2**

Have students watch Al Geiberger practice his iron swing on the *Golf With Al Geiberger* video, then discuss the information presented in the video.   **1.0**

Have students set goals for golf activities.   **2.1**

Give students a form on which to record their progress toward their golf goals. (Assessment assignment opportunity: log.)   **2.1**

Days 3 and 4

Review the grip (see figure 15.19), stance, address, and swing (see figure 15.20).   **1.0**

Check each student's grip.   **1.0**

Check each student's stance.   **1.0**

Check each student's address.   **1.0**

Check each student's swing.   **1.0**

Have students brainstorm about the relationships between the scientific principles associated with rotation and the golf swing.   **2.2**

Have students brainstorm about the relationships between the growth of body segments and the golf swing.   **6.1**

Days 5 and 6

Demonstrate incorrect grip, stance, address, and swing, asking the students for feedback.   **1.0**

Have pairs practice the iron swing, giving each other feedback.   **1.0**

Figure 15.19 The correct technique for the golf grip.

Figure 15.20 The correct technique for the golf swing.

Day 7

Have students watch Al Geiberger demonstrate the pitching swing on the *Golf With Al Geiberger* video, then discuss the information presented in the video. **1.0**

Have students discuss Al Geiberger's stylistic approach to golf. **7.0**

Give students feedback as they practice the pitching swing. **1.0**

Give students feedback as they practice the pitching swing over an obstacle (e.g., football goal crossbar). **1.0**

Day 8

Demonstrate an incorrect pitching swing, asking for feedback from the students. **1.0**

Have pairs practice the pitching swing, giving each other feedback. **1.0**

Have students brainstorm about the relationships between the scientific principles associated with rotation and the pitching swing. **2.2**

Have students brainstorm about the relationships between the growth of body segments and the pitching swing. **6.1**

Day 9

Have students watch Al Geiberger demonstrate the chipping swing on the *Golf With Al Geiberger* video, then discuss the information presented in the video.   **1.0**

Have students discuss Al Geiberger's stylistic approach to golf. (Assessment opportunity: journal.)   **7.0**

Give students feedback as they practice the chipping swing.   **1.0**

Day 10

Demonstrate an incorrect chipping swing, asking for feedback from the students.   **1.0**

Have pairs of students practice the chipping swing, giving each other feedback.   **1.0**

Have students brainstorm about the relationships between the scientific principles associated with rotation and the chipping swing.   **2.2**

Have students brainstorm about the relationships between the growth of body segments and the chipping swing.   **6.1**

Day 11

Have students watch Al Geiberger demonstrate the wood swing on the *Golf With Al Geiberger* video, then discuss the information presented in the video.   **1.0**

Have students discuss Al Geiberger's stylistic approach to golf. (Assessment opportunity: journal.)   **7.0**

Give feedback to students as they practice the wood swing.   **1.0**

Day 12

Demonstrate an incorrect wood swing, asking for feedback from the students.   **1.0**

Have pairs of students practice the wood swing, giving each other feedback.   **1.0**

For homework, have students explain the relationships between the scientific principles associated with rotation and the golf swing. (Assessment opportunity: essay.)   **2.2**

For homework, have students explain the relationships between the growth of body segments and the golf swing. (Assessment opportunity: essay.)   **6.1**

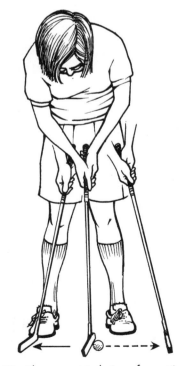

Day 13

Have students watch Al Geiberger demonstrate putting on the *Golf With Al Geiberger* video, then discuss the information presented in the video.   **1.0**

Have students discuss Al Geiberger's stylistic approach to golf. (Assessment opportunity: journal.)   **7.0**

Review putting technique. (See figure 15.21.)   **1.0**

Give students feedback as they practice putting.   **1.0**

Figure 15.21 The correct technique for putting.

Set up a miniature golf course for students to practice on.   **1.0**

Day 14

Discuss how to use problem solving techniques in small groups to identify golfing errors.   **5.0**

Provide students, in their groups, with a list of common golf problems (e.g., hook, slice), asking them to determine the causes of the problems in their groups. (Assessment opportunity: written test.) **1.0 / 5.0**

Have students watch *Golf With Al Geiberger* again for a review of golf skills, then discuss the information presented in the video.   **1.0 / 7.0**

For homework, have students write an essay comparing their own stylistic approach to golf with Al Geiberger's approach to golf (Assessment opportunity: essay.)   **7.0**

Days 15 and 16

Explain the golf stations to students.

Have students rotate through the stations, aiming at targets to practice their strokes: iron swing, putting, chipping, pitching, and wood swing. (Assessment opportunity: rubric.)   **1.0**

Days 17 and 18

Teach students the rules of golf as well as how to be courteous when playing golf.   **1.0**

Have students play on a simulated golf course. (Assessment opportunity: rubric.)   **1.0**

Day 19

Review how to use problem solving techniques in small groups.   **5.0**

Have each group create a new game with scoring options, using a golf club and a ball. (Assessment assignment opportunity: project.)   **1.0 / 2.3 / 5.0**

Day 20

Have each group teach another group how to play their game, then allow them to play each other's games. (Assessment opportunity: project.)   **1.0 / 2.3 / 5.0**

Collect student logs of participation in physical activity outside of physical education. (Assessment opportunity: log.)   **3.0**

Collect fitness monitoring forms. (Assessment opportunity: log.)   **2.1**

Collect golf goals and monitoring forms. (Assessment opportunity: log.)   **2.1**

Have students turn in their history essays. (Assessment opportunity: essay.)   **6.2**

Unit 7: Self-Defense

This unit continues our focus on taking appropriate risks by challenging students in the area of self-defense. Like outdoor education, this is another area especially important for physical educators to teach as it is directly related to student safety in our increasingly violent society. Be careful, however, to emphasize how to *defend*—not how to fight. I'll start the unit by teaching students to be more aware of potentially unsafe situations and how to avoid them. Discussing survival skills, such as staying alert, walking assertively with purse or bag under an arm and keys in hand, staying in lighted areas, staying away from suspicious-looking strangers, installing dead bolts, and not hitchhiking, set the tone for the unit. Then, and only then, will I instruct students as to how to protect themselves if they are attacked. To address standard four and to prepare students for the physical requirements necessary for self-defense, I'll continue to cover physical fitness during the daily warm-up and flexibility exercises as well as have students perform cardio-respiratory, muscular strength, and muscular endurance exercises every other day. I'll also review the muscular strength concepts related to health-related fitness development daily during the warm-up period.

You can teach this unit in any open area; however, I have found it preferable to teach it inside. In addition, air bags (Self-Defense Publications; see appendix D), Styrofoam "heads" on PVC pipe, football equipment, soccer shin guards, and bleach bottles with faces painted on them are necessary both to ensure safety and to create an effective unit of instruction. Finally, I often bring in a guest speaker for this unit, usually someone connected with a law enforcement agency. I either have the guest assist with the demonstrations or teach additional information on self-defense.

Unit Standards

1.0 – Applies the correct techniques for locomotor and nonlocomotor skills in self-defense.

2.1 – Sets goals and monitors changes in self-defense skills.

2.2 – Describes how the scientific principle of rotation applies to self-defense skills in order to learn skills or improve performance.

2.3 – Creates a combative-type game.

3.0 – Participates in appropriate self-defense activities outside of physical education.

4.0 – Participates in a variety of exercises in all five areas of health-related fitness and describes the frequency, intensity, time, and type concepts related to muscular strength.

5.0 – Applies problem solving techniques to real-life self-defense scenarios.

6.1 – Explains the growth rates of body segments and their relationship to activities in self-defense.

6.2 – Describes combat activities from Medieval times and the Renaissance period.

7.0 – Appreciates the stylistic differences of own approach to self-defense.

Unit Outline

Day 1

Assign students to work in groups of four.

Introduce self-defense and its safety rules.

Discuss the history of self-defense, martial arts, and combatives during Medieval times and the Renaissance period.   **6.2**

Have students select one martial art to research and write a report on, including a discussion of the stylistic differences related to the martial art they are studying. (Assessment assignment opportunity: report.)   **6.2 / 7.0**

Have students set goals for self-defense activities.   **2.1**

Give students a form on which to record their progress toward self-defense goals. (Assessment assignment opportunity: log.)   **2.1**

For homework, have students begin to monitor participation in self-defense activities outside of physical education. (Assessment assignment opportunity: log.)   **3.0**

Days 2 and 3

Review frequency, intensity, time, and type concepts related to muscular strength.   **4.0**

Have students record frequency, intensity, time, and type concepts related to muscular strength. (Assessment opportunity: log.)   **4.0**

Discuss ways to eliminate danger.   **1.0**

Discuss problem solving techniques related to self-defense.   **5.0**

Give students several scenarios in which they must determine ways to eliminate danger. (Assessment opportunity: simulation.)   **1.0 / 5.0**

Personal Weapons		**Vulnerable Areas**	
Voice	Elbows and hands	Knees and shins	Nose
Legs and feet	Fingers and thumbs	Groin	Eyes
Knees		Throat or neck	Ears

Day 4

Demonstrate the self-defense stance and correct breathing.   **1.0**

Give students feedback as they assume the self-defense stance and practice correct breathing.   **1.0**

Introduce personal weapons.   **1.0**

Introduce vulnerable areas.   **1.0**

Have students discuss personal weapons and vulnerable areas with their partners.   **1.0**

Day 5

Have a guest speaker.   **1.0**

Day 6

Discuss general attacking principles.   **1.0**

Review providing feedback to a partner on skill performance.

Demonstrate stomps.   **1.0**

Demonstrate knee kicks.   **1.0**

Have groups of four perform stomps and knee kicks, giving feedback to each other.   **1.0**

Have students brainstorm about how the principles associated with rotation apply to stomps and knee kicks.   **2.2**

Have students brainstorm about how growth rates of body segments relate to stomps and knee kicks.   **6.1**

Days 7 and 8

Demonstrate the correct technique for the front snap kick. (See figure 15.22.)   **1.0**

Demonstrate the correct technique for the side kick.   **1.0**

Have groups of four perform front snap kick and side kick, giving feedback to each other.   **1.0**

Review previously introduced skills.   **1.0**

Have students brainstorm about how the principles associated with rotation apply to the front snap kick and side kick.   **2.2**

Have students brainstorm about how growth rates of body segments relate to the front snap kick and side kick.   **6.1**

Figure 15.22   The correct technique for the front snap kick.

Days 9 and 10

Demonstrate the correct technique for the rear kick.   **1.0**

Demonstrate the correct technique for the round kick.   **1.0**

Have groups of four perform the rear kick and round kick, giving each other feedback.   **1.0**

Review previously introduced skills.   **1.0**

Have students brainstorm about how the scientific principles associated with rotation apply to the rear kick and round kick.   **2.2**

Have students brainstorm about how growth rates of body segments relate to the rear kick and round kick.   **6.1**

Day 11

Review how to participate in a circuit.

Have groups of four rotate through kicking stations (stomps, knee kicks, front snap kick, side kick, rear kick, and ground kick), giving each other feedback and identifying the scientific principles associated with rotation and relationships between growth of body segments and success with the skills. (Assessment opportunity: rubric.)   **1.0**

Day 12

Demonstrate the correct technique for the elbow strike.   **1.0**

Demonstrate the correct technique for the palm heel strike. (See figure 15.23.)   **1.0**

Have groups of four perform the elbow and palm heel strikes, giving each other feedback.   **1.0**

Review previously introduced skills.   **1.0**

Have students brainstorm about how the scientific principles associated with rotation apply to the elbow and palm heel strikes.   **2.2**

Have students brainstorm about how growth rates of body segments relate to the elbow and palm heel strikes.   **6.1**

Figure 15.23   The correct technique for the palm heel strike.

Day 13

Demonstrate the correct technique for the ear slap.   **1.0**

Have groups of four perform the ear slap, giving each other feedback.   **1.0**

Review previously introduced skills.   **1.0**

Have students brainstorm about how the scientific principles associated with rotation apply to the ear slap.   **2.2**

Have students brainstorm about how growth rates of body segments relate to the ear slap.   **6.1**

Day 14

Have groups rotate through striking stations (elbow strike, palm heel strike, and ear slap), giving each other feedback and identifying the scientific principles associated with rotation and relationships between growth of body segments and success with the skills. (Assessment opportunity: rubric.)   **1.0**

Day 15

Demonstrate the correct technique for side falls.   **1.0**

Have groups of four perform side falls, giving each other feedback.   **1.0**

Review previously introduced skills.   **1.0**

Have students brainstorm about how the scientific principles associated with rotation apply to side falls.   **2.2**

Have students brainstorm about how growth rates of body segments relate to side falls.   **6.1**

Day 16

Demonstrate the correct technique for the wrist release. (See figure 15.24.)   **1.0**

Have groups of four perform the wrist release, giving feedback to each other.   **1.0**

Review previously introduced skills.   **1.0**

Have students brainstorm about how the scientific principles associated with rotation apply to the wrist release.   **2.2**

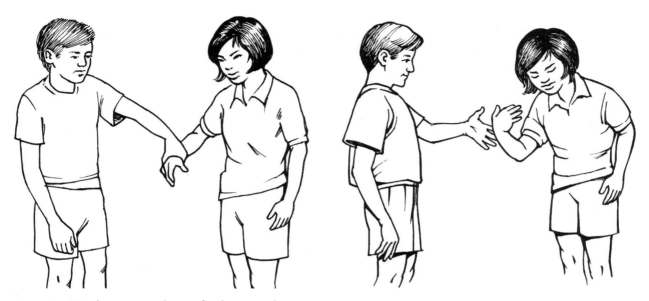

Figure 15.24   The correct technique for the wrist release.

Have students brainstorm about how growth rates of body segments relate to the wrist release.   **6.1**

Day 17

Demonstrate the correct technique for the front choke release.   **1.0**

Have groups of four perform the front choke release, giving each other feedback.   **1.0**

Review previously introduced skills.   **1.0**

Have students brainstorm about how the scientific principles associated with rotation apply to the front choke release.   **2.2**

Have students brainstorm about how growth rates of body segments relate to the front choke release.   **6.1**

Day 18

Demonstrate the correct technique for the rear choke release.   **1.0**

Have groups of four perform the rear choke release, giving each other feedback.   **1.0**

Review previously introduced skills.   **1.0**

Have students brainstorm about how the scientific principles associated with rotation apply to the rear choke release.   **2.2**

Have students brainstorm about how growth rates of body segments relate to the rear choke release.   **6.1**

Day 19

Demonstrate the correct technique for the ground release.   **1.0**

Demonstrate the correct technique for hair release.   **1.0**

Have groups of four perform the ground release and hair release, giving each other feedback.   **1.0**

Review previously introduced skills.   **1.0**

Have students brainstorm about how the scientific principles associated with rotation apply to the ground release and hair release.   **2.2**

Have students brainstorm about how growth rates of body segments relate to the ground release and hair release. **6.1**

Days 20 and 21

Have groups rotate through kicking, striking, and release stations, giving each other feedback and identifying the scientific principles associated with rotation and the relationships between growth of body segments and success with the skills. (Assessment opportunity: rubric and log.) **1.0 / 2.2 / 6.1**

Day 22

Have each group create a combative-type game. (Assessment assignment opportunity: project.) **1.0 / 2.3 / 5.0**

Day 23

Have each group teach another group their new combative-type game, then allow them to play their games. (Assessment opportunity: project.) **1.0 / 2.3 / 5.0**

Self-Defense Simulations

You are walking along a deserted street as an assailant approaches.

An assailant grabs both of your wrists.

An assailant grasps one of your wrists and attempts to pull you into his car.

An assailant grabs you in a rear bear hug.

An assailant grabs you in a front bear hug.

An assailant grabs your hair and attempts to pull you into the bushes.

An assailant pushes you to the ground.

An assailant grabs your throat in a front choke.

An assailant grabs your throat in a rear choke.

An assailant leaps into your car at a stoplight.

Day 24

Have students discuss and act out simulation scenarios. (Assessment opportunity: simulation.) **1.0 / 5.0**

Day 25

Continue simulations. (Assessment opportunity: simulation.) **1.0 / 5.0**

Collect student logs of practice of self-defense skills outside of physical education. (Assessment opportunity: log.) **3.0**

Collect fitness monitoring forms. (Assessment opportunity: log.) **2.1**

Collect self-defense goals and monitoring forms. (Assessment opportunity: log.) **2.1**

Collect martial arts reports. (Assessment opportunity: report.) **6.2 / 7.0**

Unit 8: Medieval Times Activities

This unit continues our focus on taking appropriate risks by having students challenge themselves in activities that were played during Medieval times and the modern day counterparts of these activities. And, like the orienteering unit, this unit dovetails nicely with what my students are studying in history/social science. I like to conduct this unit at the end of the school year because it lends itself to an interdisciplinary culminating activity in which the school holds a Medieval times festival, including sporting events. To address standard four, I will continue to cover physical fitness during our daily warm-up and flexibility exercises and will have students perform cardiorespiratory, muscular strength, and muscular endurance exercises every other day. I'll review all of the cognitive concepts related to health-related fitness development daily during the warm-up period.

You can conduct this unit in any open area, but several of the activities (e.g., chariot races, javelin, discus) require a grassy surface for safety reasons. It also helps to have a track, long jump pit, high jump pit, shot put area, and discus area. The equipment required for this unit includes football gear for running in armor, shot puts, hammers, discuses, hurdles, PVC pipe insulation for javelin and jousting, burlap bags for chariot races, measuring tape, and stopwatches.

Unit Standards

1.0 – Applies the correct techniques for locomotor, nonlocomotor, and manipulative skills to a variety of Medieval times activities.

2.1 – Sets goals and monitors changes in Medieval times activities.

2.2 – Analyzes movement performance using the scientific principles associated with rotation in order to learn or improve a movement skill related to Medieval times.

2.3 – Creates an individual or dual game with scoring options, using equipment from Medieval times.

3.0 – Participates in appropriate risk-taking in Medieval times activities outside of physical education.

4.0 – Performs exercises for all five areas of health-related fitness and designs a one-week fitness plan.

5.0 – Discusses use of problem solving techniques during Medieval times.

6.1 – Explains the growth rates of body segments and their relationships to Medieval times activities.

6.2 – Demonstrates games and activities from Medieval times.

7.0 – Appreciates the stylistic features of own approach to Medieval times activities.

Unit Outline

Day 1

Introduce Medieval times unit.   **6.2**

Assign students to work in groups of four.

Review games and activities from Medieval times that you have addressed already this year in physical education.   **6.2**

Discuss the problem solving strategies common in Medieval times.   **5.0**

Explain and assign a one-week fitness plan. (Assessment assignment opportunity: project.)   **4.0**

Have students set goals for Medieval times activities.   **2.1**

Give students a form on which to record their progress toward Medieval times goals. (Assessment assignment opportunity: log.)   **2.1**

For homework, have students begin to monitor participation in Medieval times activities outside of physical education. (Assessment assignment opportunity: log.)   **3.0**

Day 2

Demonstrate the correct technique for a sprint start.   **1.0**

Give students feedback as they practice the sprint start.   **1.0**

Have students brainstorm about how the scientific principles associated with rotation apply to sprint starts.   **2.2**

Have students brainstorm about how growth rates of body segments relate to the sprint start.   **6.1**

Day 3

Have pairs practice sprint starts, giving each other feedback.   **1.0**

Demonstrate the correct technique for sprinting.   **1.0**

Give students feedback as they practice sprinting.   **1.0**

Have students brainstorm about how the scientific principles associated with rotation apply to sprinting.   **2.2**

Have students brainstorm about how growth rates of body segments relate to sprinting.   **6.1**

Day 4

Have students review sprint starts and sprinting, receiving feedback from their partners.   **1.0**

Explain the history of and demonstrate the correct technique for running the hurdles. (See figure 15.25.)   **1.0 / 6.2**

Figure 15.25   The correct technique for running the hurdles.

Give students feedback as they practice running the hurdles.   **1.0**

Have students brainstorm about how the scientific principles associated with rotation apply to running the hurdles.   **2.2**

Have students brainstorm about how growth rates of body segments relate to running the hurdles.   **6.1**

Day 5

Have pairs practice hurdles, giving each other feedback.   **1.0**

Demonstrate running in armor.   **1.0**

Have students practice running in armor.   **1.0**

Day 6

Review the station approach to practice.

Have groups rotate through stations (sprint start, sprinting, hurdles, running in armor), giving each other feedback. (Assessment opportunity: rubric.)   **1.0**

Day 7

Demonstrate and explain the history of chariot races.   **1.0 / 6.2**

Have students participate in chariot races, rotating driver and rider positions.   **1.0**

Day 8

Explain the history of and demonstrate the correct technique for the long jump.   **1.0 / 6.2**

Give students feedback as they practice the long jump.   **1.0**

Have students brainstorm about how the scientific principles associated with rotation apply to the long jump.   **2.2**

Have students brainstorm about how growth rates of body segments relate to the long jump.   **6.1**

Day 9

Have students practice long jumping, receiving feedback from their partners.   **1.0**

Explain the history of and demonstrate the correct technique for the triple jump. (See figure 15.26.)   **1.0 / 6.2**

Give students feedback as they practice the triple jump.   **1.0**

Have students brainstorm about how the scientific principles associated with rotation apply to the triple jump.   **2.2**

Figure 15.26 The correct technique for the triple jump.

Have students brainstorm about how growth rates of body segments relate to the triple jump.   **6.1**

Day 10

Have pairs practice the triple jump, giving each other feedback.   **1.0**

Explain the history and demonstrate the correct technique for the high jump.   **1.0 / 6.2**

Give students feedback as they practice the high jump.   **1.0**

Have students brainstorm about how the scientific principles associated with rotation apply to the high jump.   **2.2**

Have students brainstorm about how growth rates of body segments relate to the high jump.   **6.1**

Day 11

Explain the history of and demonstrate the correct technique for the shot put release. (See figure 15.27.)   **1.0 / 6.2**

Figure 15.27 The correct technique for the shot put release.

Give students feedback as they practice the shot put release.   **1.0**

Have groups rotate through stations (long jump, high jump, shot put), giving each other feedback. (Assessment opportunity: rubric.)   **1.0**

Have students brainstorm about how the scientific principles associated with rotation apply to the shot put.   **2.2**

Have students brainstorm about how growth rates of body segments relate to the shot put.   **6.1**

Day 12

Explain the history of and demonstrate the correct technique for the hammer release.   **1.0 / 6.2**

Give students feedback as they practice the hammer release.   **1.0**

Have groups rotate through stations (long jump, high jump, shot put, hammer), giving each other feedback. (Assessment opportunity: rubric.)   **1.0**

Have students brainstorm about how the scientific principles associated with rotation apply to the hammer throw.   **2.2**

Have students brainstorm about how growth rates of body segments relate to the hammer throw.   **6.1**

Day 13

Explain the history of and demonstrate the correct technique for the discus release. **1.0 / 6.2**

Give students feedback as they practice the discus release. **1.0**

Have groups rotate through stations (long jump, high jump, shot put, hammer, and discus), giving each other feedback. (Assessment opportunity: rubric.) **1.0**

Have students brainstorm about how the scientific principles associated with rotation apply to the discus throw. **2.2**

Have students brainstorm about how growth rates of body segments relate to the discus throw. **6.1**

Day 14

Explain the history of and demonstrate the correct technique for the javelin release. **1.0 / 6.2**

Give students feedback as they practice the javelin release. **1.0**

Have groups rotate through stations (long jump, high jump, shot put, javelin, hammer, and discus), giving each other feedback. (Assessment opportunity: rubric.) **1.0**

For homework, have students describe how the scientific principles associated with rotation apply to one skill in this unit. (Assessment opportunity: essay.) **2.2**

For homework, have students describe how growth rates of body segments relate to one skill in this unit. (Assessment opportunity: essay.) **6.1**

Day 15

Explain the history of and demonstrate the correct technique for wrestling (standing up and trying to maneuver partner out of a circle). **1.0 / 6.2**

Give students feedback as they practice wrestling. **1.0**

Have groups rotate through stations (long jump, high jump, shot put, discus, javelin, hammer, and wrestling), giving each other feedback. (Assessment opportunity: rubric.) **1.0**

Day 16

Explain the history of and demonstrate the correct technique for jousting. **1.0 / 6.2**

Give students feedback as they practice jousting. **1.0**

Have groups rotate through stations (long jump, high jump, hammer, shot put, discus, javelin, wrestling, jousting), giving each other feedback. (Assessment opportunity: rubric.) **1.0**

Day 17

Have each group create a game, using equipment from Medieval times. (Assessment assignment opportunity: project.) **1.0 / 2.3 / 5.0**

Day 18

Have each group teach another group their game. (Assessment opportunity: project.) **1.0 / 2.3 / 5.0**

Days 19 and 20

Hold a school-wide "Medieval Times Festival." (Assessment opportunity: structured observation.) **1.0 / 5.0 / 6.2**

Collect student logs of participation in Medieval times activities outside of physical education. (Assessment opportunity: log.) **3.0**

Collect fitness monitoring forms. (Assessment opportunity: log.) **2.1**

Collect Medieval times goals and monitoring forms. (Assessment opportunity: log.) **2.1**

Collect one-week fitness plans. (Assessment opportunity: project.) **4.0**

For homework, have students write a one-page essay on own stylistic approach to activities from Medieval times. (Assessment opportunity: essay.) **7.0**

Unit 9: Closing and Fitness Posttesting

This unit, like the sixth grade closing and fitness posttesting unit, provides an opportunity for closure, including the chance to ensure that the students are able to demonstrate the standards. As with the sixth graders, the seventh graders have been working on projects throughout the year; here in this final unit, however, I will have them focus on depth over breadth. Direct students to focus on completing their demonstration of learning by collecting and creating work for their portfolios, freeing you to administer the fitness posttesting and to act as a resource for the student projects.

Sample Evidence for Each Seventh Grade Standard

1.0 Applies the Correct Techniques for Locomotor, Nonlocomotor, and Manipulative Skills to Appropriate Risk-Taking Activities

Student and teacher assessment during each instructional unit based on a rubric determines whether or not the student has reached this standard. The following is a sample rubric for striking with an object:

6: Performs a mature striking pattern when striking in a game or activity situation.

5: Performs a mature striking pattern when striking for distance and accuracy.

4: Performs a mature striking pattern.

_____ Turns trunk to side in anticipation of tossed ball.

_____ Keeps eyes on ball.

_____ Keeps dominant hand above nondominant hand.

_____ Before swing, twists body back.

_____ Holds elbows up and away from body.

_____ Shifts weight back and forward during swing.

_____ Segments body rotation from foot to pelvis to spine to shoulders.

_____ Swings object level, contacting ball at point of complete extension.

_____ On contact, ensures forward leg is straight.

_____ Follows through beyond point of contact.

3: Moving toward a mature striking pattern.

2: Attempts an immature striking pattern when a ball is tossed to him or her.

1: Randomly attempts an immature striking pattern.

2.1 Sets Goals and Monitors Changes in the Development of Movement Skills in Order to Improve Performance

Student sets goals in the fall and monitors improvement on a chart. Student then writes an essay describing own skill improvements throughout the year.

2.2 Analyzes Movement Performances Using Rotation Principles in Order to Learn or Improve a Movement Skill

Have student videotape herself performing a skill that utilizes the scientific principles associated with rotation. Then have student write an essay, analyzing her performance, based on the scientific principles associated with rotation.

2.3 Creates an Individual or Dual Game With Scoring Options and a Penalty System

Have groups of four create a game and teach it to another group.

3.0 Participates Daily in Some Form of Physical Activity, Including New and Appropriate Risk-Taking Activities

Throughout the year, have student maintain a log of participation in fitness activities outside of class.

4.0 Assesses Personal Fitness, Compares Scores to Health-Related Standards, Sets Goals for Improvement or Maintenance, and Designs a One-Week Personal Fitness Plan

Have student devise a chart that shows personal fitness scores, health standards for age and gender, and goals for the year. Then have student write an essay, describing the role of pretesting and goal setting and how personal physical development limits performance on fitness tests. Then have student design a one-week personal fitness plan and write it on a week-long calendar.

5.0 Applies Collaborative Problem Solving Techniques in Physical Activity Settings

Students and teacher evaluate the extent and quality of collaborative problem solving skills used during various activities. The following is a sample rubric:

6: Demonstrates collaborative problem solving skills in a real conflict in a physical activity setting.

5: Demonstrates collaborative problem solving skills in a simulation based on a real conflict.

4: Demonstrates collaborative problem solving skills in a simulation with friends.

3: Demonstrates some collaborative problem solving skills in a simulation with friends.

2: Demonstrates a few collaborative problem solving skills in a simulation with friends.

1: No evidence of collaborative problem solving.

6.1 Explains the Growth Rates of Body Segments and How They Relate to Movement Experiences

Have student take one activity and describe the relationship between own performance and length of own body segments.

6.2 Describes the Development and Role of Movement-Related Activities and Physical Education During Medieval Times and Their Influences on Physical Activities Today

Groups of four write a history of one activity that has its roots in Medieval times, describing its influence on activities today.

7.0 Appreciates the Aesthetic Features or Stylistic Differences of Own Approach to Movement Activities

Student creates and demonstrates a tumbling or gymnastics routine while describing the aesthetic features in their routine.

For this unit, I present students with the 10 standards for the seventh grade and ask them to present evidence of their learning related to each standard. For some of the standards, students will be able to demonstrate their learning by looking through their working portfolios and pulling from work that they have already accomplished during the year. For other standards, students will be able to pull from interdisciplinary projects that they have accomplished throughout the year. For still other standards, students will need to create new projects during this closing unit to demonstrate their learning. Once the students have collected their evidence, it goes into their performance portfolios. Then I ask them to write a reflection paper (a one-page essay) on their cumulative learning throughout seventh grade physical education. Ideally, the students then present their portfolios not only to their peers but also to their parents. In this case during a parent, teacher, and student conference, the student is in charge of the conference as he presents the evidence that he has accumulated during the year and explains how the evidence demonstrates his learning of the various standards. This conference can focus exclusively on physical education or be a comprehensive conference in which the student explains his learning in all subject areas.

Like the introduction unit, you can conduct this unit in just about any facility. I recommend, however, that if you are having your students perform exercises on the ground or grass that you provide them with carpet squares or some other material so they won't get dirty. An indoor facility is also helpful for the project development phase of this unit. In addition,

many teachers reserve the library or at least make arrangements for some of their students to do research in the library. Of course, the equipment necessary to implement the unit depends on the type of fitness tests you plan to administer. I will be administering the same Prudential FITNESSGRAM tests that I gave at the beginning of the school year. After the posttests, the students will be able to enter their fitness posttest scores into their own electronic portfolios so that you and they can compare these scores to pretests, standards, and goals. Students will also need access to reference books, CD-ROMs, computers, videotape players, monitors, camcorders, and other materials to assist project development.

Unit Standards

1.0 – Applies the correct techniques for locomotor, nonlocomotor, and manipulative skills to appropriate risk-taking activities.

2.1 – Sets goals and monitors changes in the development of movement skills in order to improve performance.

2.2 – Analyzes movement performances using the scientific principles associated with rotation in order to learn or improve a movement skill.

2.3 – Creates an individual or dual game with scoring options.

3.0 – Participates daily in some form of physical activity, including new and appropriate risk-taking activities.

4.0 – Reassesses personal fitness and compares scores to pretest scores, health standards and personal goals, and finalizes one-week fitness plan.

5.0 – Applies problem solving techniques to physical activity settings.

6.1 – Explains how the growth rates of body segments relate to movement experiences.

6.2 – Describes the origin of movement-related activities and physical education during Medieval times and this time period's influence on physical activities today.

7.0 – Appreciates the aesthetic features or stylistic differences of own approach to movement activities.

Unit Outline

Day 1

Assign students to work groups.

Remind students why you administer fitness tests twice a year.   **4.0**

Remind students why you administer the one-mile run test.   **4.0**

Administer the one-mile run test to half the class at a time, while the other half assists with counting the runner's laps.   **4.0**

Day 2

Describe the projects and portfolios to be completed in this unit.   **1.0-7.0**

Describe the project and portfolio design steps.   **1.0-7.0**

Have students begin to work on their projects and portfolios.   **1.0-7.0**

Remind students why you administer the curl-up test.   **4.0**

Administer the curl-up test to one group at a time.   **4.0**

Day 3

Remind students why you administer the skinfold or body mass index test.   **4.0**

Have students work on their projects and portfolios.   **1.0-7.0**

Administer the skinfold or body mass index test to one student at a time in private.   **4.0**

Day 4

Remind students why you administer the back-saver sit-and-reach or shoulder stretch and trunk lift tests.   **4.0**

Have students work on their projects and portfolios.   **1.0-7.0**

Administer the back-saver sit-and-reach or shoulder stretch and trunk lift tests to one group at a time.   **4.0**

Day 5

Remind students why you administer the push-up, flexed arm hang, modified pull-up, or pull-up test.

Have students work on their projects and portfolios.   **1.0-7.0**

Administer the push-up, flexed arm hang, modified pull-up, or pull-up test to one group at a time.

Day 6

Administer makeup fitness tests to one group at a time.   **4.0**

Have students work on their projects and portfolios.   **1.0-7.0**

Days 7 Through 12

Have students work on their projects and portfolios.   **1.0-7.0**

Day 13

Have groups share their projects and portfolios with one other group.   **1.0-7.0**

Day 14

Have groups share their projects and portfolios with one other group.   **1.0-7.0**

Day 15

Debrief projects, portfolios, and the entire year. (Assessment opportunity: portfolios and projects.)   **1.0-7.0**

Summary

Use the ideas and model outline in this sample year-long curriculum for the seventh grade as a guide for your own planning, keeping in mind that this is one sample and not the definitive seventh grade program. Your particular environment, standards, student needs, and faculty will shape your seventh grade program. As always, be flexible, creative, and innovative when developing the program that is best for *your* situation.

CHAPTER 16

An Eighth Grade Program: Working as a Team to Develop Strategies for Success

I expect my students to solve various tactical problems within a game. My focus is on using skill to accomplish the tactics. This has resulted in students being highly engaged in skills and tactics that are game-related, rather than working on skills in an isolated situation.

—*Rebecca J. Berkowitz, Blendon Middle School, Westerville, Ohio*

In this chapter, I will describe a sample eighth grade program. I have selected "Working as a Team to Develop Strategies for Success" as the theme. As we discussed in Chapter 7, students at this grade level are ready for the complex team sports that are played in our society. But you should still set up the practice activities in modified settings. For example, you can teach soccer through practice scrimmages with four players on each team. This gives students a chance to understand the game of soccer while still getting many chances to participate and practice.

I have selected the activity approach for the eighth grade units of instruction. The units for the eighth grade include the following:

- introduction and fitness pretesting,
- Project Adventure,
- invasion team sports,
- team net sports,

Eighth Grade Standards

By the end of eighth grade, each student should be able to demonstrate the following:

1.0 Applies the correct techniques for locomotor, nonlocomotor, and manipulative skills to sport-specific skills in a variety of team-related activities.

2.1 Applies the principle of transfer of learning in order to facilitate the learning of a new skill.

2.2 Analyzes movement performance using spin and rebound principles in order to learn or improve a movement skill.

2.3 Creates a team game with scoring options and a penalty system.

3.0 Sets personal goals for participating in physical activities in and out of school, then participates and monitors progress.

4.0 Assesses personal fitness, compares scores to health-related standards, sets goals for improvement or maintenance, refines one-week personal fitness plan, and implements the plan.

5.0 Collaboratively solves problems by analyzing causes and potential solutions in physical activity settings.

6.1 Analyzes how growth in height and weight alters the mechanical nature of performance and how it affects the selection of developmentally appropriate activities.

6.2 Describes the development and role of movement-related activities and physical education in the United States during the 19th and 20th centuries, and their influences on physical activities today.

7.0 Appreciates the aesthetic features or stylistic differences of someone else's approach to movement activities.

Modified from Region 9's *Physical Education Curriculum*, 1994 and NASPE's *National Physical Education Standards: A Guide to Content and Assessment*, 1995.

- team field sports,
- square dancing, and
- closing and fitness posttesting.

Of course, invasion team sports, team net sports, and team field sports fit in well with the grade level theme. But so does square dancing because it's a team activity, requiring four couples or eight indi-

viduals to work together to achieve the final outcome—successfully dancing to the calls. Project Adventure is also a team building activity, ensuring early in the year that students know how to get along with one another before working together in team sports.

In this chapter, I will again briefly discuss the reason for using each particular unit; I'll list equipment, facilities, and instructional materials you'll need to implement each unit; I'll suggest interdisciplinary and community ideas for making each unit more like real life; and I'll alert you to class environment issues associated with each unit. After each introduction, I'll list the unit standards that are linked directly to the grade level standards. A unit plan will follow, containing a day-by-day outline of what you should teach, explaining how the information and activities connect to the unit standards. Again, remember that these are not lesson plans— they still need activities, drills, and learning experiences. However, do look for the motivational, learning, assessment, teaching style, and strategy ideas I have embedded in these daily agendas.

Unit 1: Introduction and Fitness Pretesting

This unit serves as a basic introductory unit for eighth grade students. It gives students a chance to get reacquainted and to meet new members of the class. I also use this introductory unit to set my expectations, to teach the class rules, to assess the students' fitness levels, and to guide them as they set their yearly goals for fitness development.

You can conduct this unit in just about any facility. It does help, however, if you are having students perform exercises on the ground or grass to provide them with carpet squares or some other material so they don't get dirty. The equipment necessary to implement the unit depends on the type of introductory games you choose and the fitness tests you administer. Once again, I will be administering the Prudential FITNESSGRAM health-related fitness test battery, including the back-saver sit-and-reach, curl-up, skinfold, push-up, trunk lift, and one-mile run tests. You can order the test administration procedures from the Cooper Institute for Aerobic Research (see appendix D). You will see in the daily agendas that I'll have my students prepare for the fitness tests, the results of which they will again enter into their own electronic portfolios.

Unit Standards

1.0 – Applies the correct techniques for locomotor, nonlocomotor, and manipulative skills to fitness and getting acquainted activities.

2.1 – Explains the benefits related to positive transfer of learning.

2.2 – Explains the scientific principles associated with rebound.

2.3 – Describes the elements of a team game.

3.0 – Sets goals for participating in physical activity outside physical education.

4.0 – Assesses personal fitness, compares scores to health standards, and sets personal goals.

5.0 – Knows other students' names.

6.1 – Analyzes how growth in height and weight alters the mechanical nature of performance and how it affects the selection of developmentally appropriate fitness activities.

6.2 – Describes fitness activities of 19th- and 20th-century America.

7.0 – Describes the stylistic differences in approaches to exercising.

Unit Outline

Day 1

Establish a roll call order.

Introduce the class rules.

Have students participate in Toss-a-Name Game. (See appendix C.)   **1.0 / 5.0**

Day 2

Review the class rules.

Have students participate in Toss-and-Catch-a-Name Game. (See appendix C.)   **1.0 / 5.0**

Review how to open lockers.

Ask students if anyone can name half the students in the class. (Assessment opportunity: structured observation.)   **5.0**

Day 3

Review the class rules.

Have students participate in Toss-and-Catch-a-Name Game.   **1.0 / 5.0**

Have students watch "Lesson 7: Speed, Reaction Time, and Agility" on the *PE-TV* video (appendix D), then discuss the information presented in the video.   **4.0 / 6.1**

Assign lockers.

Day 4

Have students dress for physical education.

Review the class rules.

Assign students randomly to groups of four.

Have students review exercises for each area of health-related fitness. (See appendix C for sample exercises under each area of health-related fitness.) **1.0 / 4.0**

Have students participate in Moon Ball, calling out the person's name who is contacting the beach ball. (See appendix C.) **1.0 / 5.0**

Demonstrating with a beach ball, discuss the concepts of spin and rebound. **2.2**

Day 5

Review the class rules.

Have students perform exercises for each area of health-related fitness, allocating more time to cardio-respiratory exercise in preparation for the one-mile run. **1.0 / 4.0**

Have students participate in Knots, referring to each other by name. (See appendix C.) **1.0 / 5.0**

Discuss the concept of positive transfer of learning. **2.1**

Have students brainstorm activities they performed in sixth and seventh grades that are similar to Knots. **2.1**

Day 6

Review the class rules.

Have students perform exercises for each area of health-related fitness, allocating more time to cardio-respiratory exercise in preparation for the one-mile run. **1.0 / 4.0**

Have students participate in Everyone Up, referring to each other by name. (See appendix C.) **1.0 / 5.0**

Describe the influences of growth in height and weight on exercise performance and the game Everyone Up. **6.1**

Day 7

Have students perform exercises for each area of health-related fitness, allocating more time to cardio-respiratory exercise in preparation for the one-mile run. **1.0 / 4.0**

Have students participate in Yurt Circle. (See appendix C.) **1.0 / 5.0**

Have students brainstorm about the elements of a team game. **2.3**

Day 8

Have students perform exercises for each area of health-related fitness, allocating more time to cardio-respiratory exercise in preparation for the one-mile run. **1.0 / 4.0**

Review the five areas of health-related fitness and the purpose of pretesting. **4.0**

Have students brainstorm about the different stylistic approaches to exercising. (Assessment opportunity: journal entry.) **7.0**

Day 9

Have students perform warm-up exercises for the back-saver sit-and-reach test. **1.0 / 4.0**

Explain the back-saver sit-and-reach test, why you give it, and how growth in height and weight influence test performance. **4.0 / 6.1**

Have students watch "Lesson 8: Rhythm and Coordination" on the *PE-TV* video, then discuss the information presented in the video. **4.0**

Administer the back-saver sit-and-reach test to one group at a time. (Assessment opportunity: fitness test.) **1.0 / 4.0**

Ask students if anyone knows the names of all the students in the class. (Assessment opportunity: structured observation.)   **5.0**

Day 10

Have students perform warm-up exercises for the curl-up test.   **1.0 / 4.0**

Explain the curl-up test, why you give it, and how growth in height and weight influence test performance.   **4.0 / 6.1**

Have students participate in a flexibility circuit.   **1.0 / 4.0**

Administer the curl-up test to two groups at a time. (Assessment opportunity: fitness test.)   **1.0 / 4.0**

Ask students if anyone knows the names of all the students in the class. (Assessment opportunity: structured observation.)   **5.0**

Day 11

Explain the skinfold test, why you give it, and how growth in height and weight influence test performance.   **4.0 / 6.1**

Have students watch "Lesson 9: Balance" on the *PE-TV* video, then discuss the information.   **4.0**

Administer the skinfold or body mass index test to students one at a time in private. (Assessment opportunity: fitness test.)   **4.0**

Day 12

Have students perform warm-up exercises for the push-up test.   **1.0 / 4.0**

Explain the push-up test, why you give it, and how growth in height and weight influence test performance.   **4.0 / 6.1**

Have students read about fitness during 19th- and 20th-century America.   **6.2**

Administer the push-up test to one group at a time. (Assessment opportunity: fitness test.)   **1.0 / 4.0**

For homework, ask students to describe the fitness training that occurred during 19th- and 20th-century America. (Assessment opportunity: essay.)   **6.2**

Day 13

Have students perform warm-up exercises for the trunk lift.   **1.0 / 4.0**

Explain the trunk lift test, why you give it, and how growth in height and weight influence test performance.   **4.0 / 6.1**

Have students participate in a flexibility circuit.   **1.0 / 4.0**

Administer the trunk lift test at one station in the circuit. (Assessment opportunity: fitness test.)   **1.0 / 4.0**

Day 14

Have students perform warm-up exercises for the one-mile run.   **1.0 / 4.0**

Explain the one-mile run test, why you give it, and the influences of growth in height and weight on test performance.   **4.0 / 6.1**

Administer the one-mile run test to half the class at a time, using the other half of the class as testing assistants to count laps. (Assessment opportunity: fitness test.)   **1.0 / 4.0**

For homework, ask students to describe how growth in height and weight influence performance in fitness activities. (Assessment opportunity: essay.)   **6.1**

Day 15

Have students perform warm-up exercises, depending on the fitness test(s) they need to make up. **1.0 / 4.0**

Administer makeup tests. (Assessment opportunity: fitness test.)   **1.0 / 4.0**

Have students enter their scores into their electronic portfolios so that they can compare their scores to the minimum competencies and set goals for the year. (Assessment opportunity: electronic log.)   **4.0**

For homework as part of their fitness plans, have students set goals for participating in physical activity outside of physical education. (Assessment opportunity: log.)   **3.0 / 4.0**

Unit 2: Project Adventure

In this unit, I'll begin to focus on working as a team to develop strategies for success. These activities are the same activities that business people go through in order to improve teamwork. To address standard four, I'll continue to cover physical fitness during the daily warm-up and flexibility exercises as well as have students perform cardiorespiratory, muscular strength, and muscular endurance exercises every other day. I'll also have students refine the warm-up and cooldown sections of their seventh grade one-week fitness plans, so I'll spend time during warm-ups reviewing warm-up and cooldown concepts.

You can teach this unit in any open area; however, it is preferable to have access to either a built-in or portable ropes course. The specific elements I'll use include the swinging rope, suspended log, and spider web. Additional equipment you'll need is as follows: trolleys, rope, planks (2 by 6 inches), poles (1.5 inches in diameter), broomstick, bucket, platform (12 by 12 inches), scarves, foam box, and foam cylinders. If you do not have access to a ropes course, you might want to consider forming a partnership with a local business and sharing the ropes course with that business. The school can use the course during the school day and the business can use and rent out the course during the evenings and on weekends.

This unit links well with the communications unit in health education. To make the connection clear to students, I have them perform the activities in physical education and then debrief their feelings related to the activities during health education. You can also involve the language arts teacher, who can have students write about their feelings after they have discussed them in health education.

Unit Standards

1.0 – Applies the correct techniques for locomotor and nonlocomotor skills to Project Adventure activities.

2.1 – Identifies the elements necessary for positive transfer of learning to occur.

2.2 – Explains the scientific principles associated with spin.

2.3 – Creates a problem solving challenge for a small group of students.

3.0 – Participates and monitors physical activity and fitness activity outside physical education, based on personal goals.

4.0 – Performs exercises for all five areas of health-related fitness and redesigns warm-up and cooldown sections of seventh grade one-week fitness plan.

5.0 – Demonstrates problem solving techniques in physical activity settings.

6.1 – Explains how growth in height and weight alters mechanical nature of physical performance.

6.2 – Describes the growth of physical education, playgrounds, recreation, and modern Olympics during 19th- and 20th-century America.

7.0 – Describes the stylistic differences in approaches to movement.

Unit Outline

Day 1

Introduce Project Adventure unit and review safety considerations.

Assign students to work in groups of four.

Review concepts related to warm-up and cooldown and assign refining seventh grade warm-up and cooldown section of one-week fitness plan as a project for this unit. (Assessment assignment opportunity: project.)   **4.0**

Discuss collaborative problem solving and conflict resolution strategies.   **5.0**

Have students work on Wordles in their new groups. (See appendix C.) (Assessment opportunity: structured observation.)   **5.0**

For homework, have students begin to monitor participation in physical activities outside of physical education, based on their own goals. (Assessment assignment opportunity: log.)   **3.0**

Day 2

Have groups work on "Lost in the Desert" written activity described in *Cooperative Learning: Resources for Teachers* by Spencer Kagan (1989).   **5.0**

Debrief activity, discussing aspects of team building.   **5.0**

Discuss positive transfer of learning and how students can apply the team building skills used in this written activity to the physical challenges coming in the next several weeks.   **2.1**

Have students describe team building and what it means to them. (Assessment opportunity: journal.)   **5.0**

Days 3, 4, and 5

Discuss the growth of physical education, playgrounds, and recreation during the 19th and 20th centuries and the history of Project Adventure.   **6.2**

Introduce Trolley, Amazon, and TP Shuffle. (See appendix C.)   **1.0**

Have students rotate through these stations: Trolley, Amazon, and TP Shuffle.   **1.0 / 5.0**

Debrief activities.   **5.0**

Have students brainstorm about how growth in height and weight influences their performances in these physical challenges.   **6.1**

Days 6, 7, and 8

Discuss the history of the modern Olympics.   **6.2**

Introduce All Aboard, Human Ladder, and Acid Pit. (See appendix C.)   **1.0**

Have students rotate through stations: All Aboard, Human Ladder, and Acid Pit. (Assessment opportunity: structured observation.)   **1.0 / 5.0**

Debrief activities.   **5.0**

Have students brainstorm about how growth in height and weight influences their performances in these physical challenges.   **6.1**

Have students brainstorm about the stylistic differences of the people in their groups as they approach these physical challenges.   **7.0**

Day 9

Introduce Levitation. (See appendix C.)   **1.0**

Have students practice Levitation in their groups.   **1.0**

Debrief activity.   **5.0**

Have students brainstorm about how growth in height and weight influences their performances in Levitation.   **6.1**

Have students brainstorm about the stylistic differences of the people in their groups as they approach Levitation.   **7.0**

Describe Spider's Web. (See appendix C.)   **1.0**

Days 10, 11, and 12

Introduce Spider's Web, Prouty's Landing, and Trust Circle. (See appendix C.)   **1.0**

Have students rotate through these stations: Spider Web, Prouty's Landing, and Trust Circle. (Assessment opportunity: rubric.)   **1.0 / 5.0**

Debrief activities.   **5.0**

Have students brainstorm about how growth in height and weight influences their performances in these physical challenges.   **6.1**

Have students brainstorm about the stylistic differences of the people in their groups as they approach these physical challenges.   **7.0**

Days 13 and 14

Introduce Sherpa Walk and Pharaoh's Stone. (See appendix C.)   **1.0**

Have students rotate through stations: Sherpa Walk and Pharaoh's Stone. (Assessment opportunity: rubric.)   **1.0 / 5.0**

Debrief activities. (Assessment opportunity: rubric.)   **5.0**

Have students brainstorm about how growth in height and weight influences their performances in these physical challenges.   **6.1**

Have students brainstorm about the stylistic differences of the people in their groups as they approach these physical challenges.   **7.0**

Days 15 and 16

Have students participate in Trust Circle.   **1.0**

Introduce Trust Walk. (See appendix C.)   **1.0**

Have students participate in Trust Walk.   **1.0**

Introduce the Two-Person Trust Fall. (See appendix C.)   **1.0**

Have students participate in the Two-Person Trust Fall.   **1.0**

Introduce the Trust Fall. (See appendix C.)   **1.0**

Have students participate in the Trust Fall.   **1.0**

Debrief activities.   **5.0**

For homework, have students brainstorm about how growth in height and weight influences their performance in physical challenges. (Assessment opportunity: essay.)   **6.1**

For homework, have students brainstorm about the stylistic differences of the people in their groups as they approach physical challenges. (Assessment opportunity: essay.)   **7.0**

Day 17

Give students a variety of balls and have them problem solve the effects of spin on each type of ball. (Assessment opportunity: log.) **2.2 / 5.0**

Debrief ball-spinning activity. (Assessment opportunity: structured observation.) **2.2 / 5.0**

Day 18

Have groups design several problem solving challenges. (Assessment assignment opportunity: project.) **1.0 / 2.3 / 5.0**

Day 19

Have groups work on their problem solving challenges. **1.0 / 2.3 / 5.0**

Day 20

Have each group present their problem solving challenges to another group, asking them to solve them. (Assessment opportunity: project.) **1.0 / 2.3 / 5.0**

Collect student logs of participation in physical activity outside of physical education. (Assessment opportunity: log.) **3.0**

Collect one-week fitness plans with updated warm-up and cooldown sections. (Assessment opportunity: project.) **4.0**

Unit 3: Invasion Team Sports

This unit ties together several invasion games (team handball, soccer, basketball, speed-a-way, and football), continuing our focus on working as a team to develop strategies for success. Although this unit takes 11 weeks, by presenting these games collectively, we can concentrate on similarities and differences as well as focus on standard 2.1, which stresses the positive transfer of learning to facilitate acquiring new skills. To address standard four, I'll continue to cover physical fitness during our daily warm-up and flexibility exercises as well as have students perform cardiorespiratory, muscular strength, and muscular endurance exercises every other day. I'll also have students refine the muscular strength and endurance sections of their seventh grade one-week fitness plans, so I'll spend time reviewing the health-related fitness concepts related to muscular strength and endurance during the daily warm-up.

You can teach this unit in any open area, but blacktop is preferable for basketball and team handball skills and grass is preferable for soccer, speed-a-way, and football. Of course, you'll need baskets for basketball and goals for the other sports. The supplies needed for this unit include: Frisbees, basketballs, team handballs, soccer balls, footballs, cones, and flags. In addition, I'll use videos to provide students with visual models for the ideal skill reproduction and illustrations of strategies. Specifically, I'll use *PE-TV*, *ESPN Teaching Kids Football*, *ESPN Teaching Kids Basketball*, and *New Soccer*. (See appendix D for video sources.)

Looking for a way to include math in your interdisciplinary plans? In this unit, students learn about open space and shortest points between distances in physical education, tying in well with their geometry lessons in math class. You can work with the math teacher to help students see the real-life applications of geometry. In addition, you can have students graph their improvements in both distance and accuracy as they continue to refine their motor skills.

Unit Standards

1.0 – Applies the correct techniques for locomotor, nonlocomotor, and manipulative skills to invasion sports.

2.1 – Applies the transfer of learning principle to learning new skills and strategies for invasion sports.

2.2 – Describes how the scientific principles associated with spin and rebound apply to invasion sports.

2.3 – Creates an invasion team game with scoring options.

3.0 – Participates in and monitors physical activity and fitness activity outside physical education, based on own goals.

4.0 – Performs exercises for all five areas of health-related fitness and redesigns the muscular strength and endurance section of the seventh grade one-week fitness plan.

5.0 – Defines steps in negotiating a resolution to a conflict of interests and demonstrates conflict resolution skills when working with a partner.

6.1 – Analyzes how growth in height and weight alters the mechanical nature of performance and how it influences the selection of player positions for invasion sports.

6.2 – Describes the development and role of basketball, team handball, soccer, speed-a-way, and football in the United States.

7.0 – Appreciates the stylistic differences of someone else's approach to invasion sports.

Unit Outline

Day 1

Assign students to work in groups of four.

Introduce team handball, soccer, basketball, speed-a-way, and football.   **1.0**

Briefly explain the histories of team handball, soccer, basketball, speed-a-way, and football.   **6.2**

Ask students to brainstorm the application of the principle of transfer of learning to invasion sports.   **2.1**

Discuss steps for negotiating a resolution when a conflict occurs.   **5.0**

Have students play Ultimate Frisbee (which they learned in sixth grade) as an introduction to invasion sports.   **1.0**

Have students debrief how they handled conflicts during the game.   **5.0**

Have students write in their journals how they handled conflict during the game. (Assessment opportunity: journal entry.)   **5.0**

Assign an essay due at the end of the unit that compares team handball, soccer, basketball, speed-a-way, and football in terms of skills, strategies, rules, and the reasons for their creation. (Assessment assignment opportunity: essay.)   **1.0 / 2.1 / 6.2**

For homework, have students begin to monitor their participation in physical activities outside of physical education, based on their own goals. (Assessment assignment opportunity: log.)   **3.0**

Days 2 and 3

Review concepts related to muscular strength and endurance and assign refining muscular strength and endurance section of the seventh grade one-week fitness plan as a project for this unit. (Assessment assignment opportunity: project.)   **4.0**

Have students participate in a muscular strength and endurance circuit, having them identify which stations are for developing muscular strength and which are for developing muscular endurance. (Assessment opportunity: log.) **4.0**

Review team handball. (See figure 16.1.) **1.0**

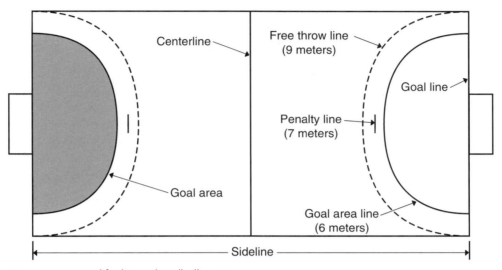

Figure 16.1 Modified team handball court.

Have students play Modified Four-on-Four Team Handball. **1.0 / 5.0**

Demonstrate chest pass, one- and two-handed overhead pass, and bounce pass. **1.0**

Give feedback as pairs practice the chest pass, overhead pass, and bounce pass, using a variety of balls. **1.0**

Demonstrate passing at stationary and moving targets. **1.0**

Have pairs rotate through stations, passing at stationary and moving targets, giving each other feedback. **1.0**

Days 4 and 5

Demonstrate the two-step stop and the jump-stop. **1.0**

Give feedback as pairs of students practice the two-step stop and the jump-stop. **1.0**

Demonstrate the pivot. **1.0**

Give feedback as students practice the pivot. **1.0**

Demonstrate game-like drills for passing and catching, using stops and pivots. **1.0**

Give feedback as students participate in passing, catching, stopping, and pivoting drills. **1.0**

Have students play Modified Four-on-Four Team Handball with no dribbling. **1.0 / 5.0**

Days 6 and 7

Demonstrate dribbling. **1.0**

Give students feedback as they practice dribbling with a variety of balls. **1.0**

Review giving feedback to a partner.

Discuss conflict resolution strategies as they apply to working with a partner. **5.0**

Have pairs rotate through a variety of dribbling stations (stationary, while moving, while defended), giving each other feedback.   **1.0**

Have students play Dribble Tag. (See appendix C.)   **1.0**

Have students brainstorm about how the scientific principles associated with spin and rebound apply to dribbling activities.   **2.2**

Have students brainstorm about how growth in height and weight influence dribbling activities.   **6.1**

Have students brainstorm about the stylistic differences among individuals participating in dribbling activities.   **7.0**

Days 8 and 9

Review passing, catching, stopping, pivoting, and dribbling.   **1.0**

Have pairs rotate through stations, practicing these skills with and without a team handball, giving each other feedback.   **1.0**

Have students play Modified Four-on-Four Team Handball.   **1.0**

Day 10

Demonstrate the set shot for team handball.   **1.0**

Give students feedback as they practice the team handball set shot, aiming at stationary targets.   **1.0**

Give students feedback as they practice the team handball set shot while moving, aiming at stationary targets.   **1.0**

Have students brainstorm about how the scientific principles associated with spin and rebound apply to set shot activities.   **2.2**

Have students brainstorm about how growth in height and weight influence set shot activities.   **6.1**

Have students brainstorm about the stylistic differences among individuals participating in set shot activities.   **7.0**

Day 11

Review the set shot.   **1.0**

Introduce the jump shot for team handball to students who are ready.   **1.0**

Demonstrate effective goalkeeping.   **1.0**

Have students participate in a game-like drill, involving the set shot (the jump shot for those who are ready) against a goalie, giving each other feedback.   **1.0**

Day 12

Demonstrate the basic offensive stance.   **1.0**

Give students feedback as they assume the basic offensive stance.   **1.0**

Demonstrate the basic defensive stance.   **1.0**

Give students feedback as they assume the basic defensive stance.   **1.0**

Have students play Modified Four-on-Four Team Handball.   **1.0**

Days 13 and 14

Explain the concepts of open and closed space as offensive and defensive strategies.   **1.0**

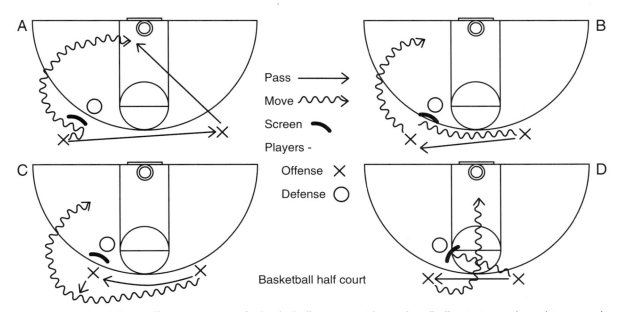

Figure 16.2   Two-player offensive strategies for basketball, soccer, and team handball: (a) give-and-go, (b) give-and-screen outside, (c) give-and-screen outside by receiver, and (d) give-and-screen inside.

Demonstrate two-player offensive strategies: give-and-go, give-and-screen outside, give-and-screen outside by receiver, give-and-screen inside. (See figure 16.2.)   **1.0**

Have students practice two-player offensive strategies (give-and-go, give-and-screen outside, give-and-screen outside by receiver, give-and-screen inside) with their groups.   **1.0**

Have students practice two-player offensive strategies (give-and-go, give-and-screen outside, give-and-screen outside by receiver, give-and-screen inside) against two-player defense teams.   **1.0**

Days 15 and 16

Have students play Modified Four-on-Four Team Handball. (Assessment opportunity: structured observation.)   **1.0 / 5.0**

Have students brainstorm a list of invasion sports.   **1.0**

Day 17

Introduce the history and sport of soccer.   **1.0**

Have students watch "Lesson 16: Soccer" on the *PE-TV* video, and then discuss.   **1.0**

Have students play Two-on-Two Soccer.   **1.0**

Day 18

Review the placekick and the sole-of-foot trap learned in sixth grade.   **1.0**

Have pairs practice the placekick and the sole-of-foot trap, giving each other feedback.   **1.0**

Demonstrate the instep kick and the inside-of-foot trap.   **1.0**

Have students watch a clip on the instep kick and the inside-of-foot trap from *New Soccer*.   **1.0**

Have pairs practice the instep kick and the inside-of-foot trap, giving each other feedback.   **1.0**

Have students participate in Soccer Golf (kicking at targets and keeping personal score).   **1.0**

Have students brainstorm about how the scientific principles associated with spin and rebound apply to placekick activities.   **2.2**

Have students brainstorm about how growth in height and weight influence placekick activities.   **6.1**

Have students brainstorm about the stylistic differences among individuals participating in placekick activities.   **7.0**

Day 19

Demonstrate goalkeeping and discuss the similarities and differences between goalkeeping in team handball and goalkeeping in soccer.   **1.0 / 2.1**

Have students watch a clip on goalkeeping from *New Soccer*.   **1.0**

In groups of four, have students practice the instep shot against a goalie while partners give feedback.   **1.0**

Assign students to groups of four: two students practice the instep kick and shot against a goalie (two-on-one) while the fourth student gives feedback.   **1.0**

Have students brainstorm about how the scientific principles associated with spin and rebound apply to instep kick activities.   **2.2**

Have students brainstorm about how growth in height and weight influence instep kick activities.   **6.1**

Have students brainstorm about the stylistic differences among individuals participating in instep kick activities.   **7.0**

Day 20

Demonstrate the soccer dribble and discuss the similarities and differences between dribbling in team handball and dribbling in soccer. (See figure 16.3.)   **1.0 / 2.1**

Figure 16.3 The correct technique for foot dribbling.

Have students watch a clip on dribbling from *New Soccer*.   **1.0**

Give students feedback as they practice the soccer dribble.   **1.0**

Have pairs rotate through a variety of dribbling stations, giving each other feedback.   **1.0**

Have students play Dribble Tag. (See appendix C.)   **1.0**

Have students brainstorm about how the scientific principles associated with spin and rebound apply to dribbling activities.   **2.2**

Have students brainstorm about how growth in height and weight influence dribbling activities.   **6.1**

Have students brainstorm about the stylistic differences among individuals participating in dribbling activities.   **7.0**

Day 21

Have students participate in game-like drills that combine dribbling, passing, shooting, and goalkeeping while group members give feedback. (Assessment opportunity: rubric.)   **1.0**

Day 22

Demonstrate dodging, feinting, and tackling.   **1.0**

Have students practice one-on-one feinting and dodging against tackles.   **1.0**

Have students play Keep-Away (two-on-one).   **1.0**

Day 23

Have students practice two-on-one dribbling, passing, dodging, and feinting against tackles.   **1.0**

Days 24 and 25

Explain Modified Four-on-Four Soccer rules.   **1.0**

Emphasize that students must stay in relative location and not bunch up.   **1.0**

Have students play Modified Four-on-Four Soccer. (Assessment opportunity: structured observation.)   **1.0 / 5.0**

Have students discuss the similarities and differences between team handball and soccer.   **1.0 / 2.1**

Day 26

Review basketball.   **1.0**

Have students watch "Lesson 10: Basketball" on the *PE-TV* video, and then discuss.   **1.0**

Have students play Two-on-Two Basketball to review passing, catching, stopping, pivoting, and dribbling.   **1.0**

Have students compare basketball to team handball.   **1.0 / 2.1**

Days 27 and 28

Have students use basketballs in game-like combination drills, passing, catching, stopping, pivoting, and dribbling (including the three-person weave).   **1.0**

Demonstrate the one-handed set shot for basketball and compare it to team handball. (See figure 16.4.)   **1.0 / 2.1**

Have students watch a clip on set shots from *ESPN Teaching Kids Basketball*.   **1.0**

Give students feedback as they practice one-handed set shot for basketball.   **1.0**

Figure 16.4 The correct technique for the basketball set shot.

Have students practice one-handed set shot for basketball while partners give feedback. **1.0**

Have pairs practice one-handed set shot from various locations, giving each other feedback. **1.0**

Have students brainstorm about how the scientific principles associated with spin and rebound apply to one-handed set shot activities. **2.2**

Have students brainstorm about how growth in height and weight influence one-handed set shot activities. **6.1**

Have students brainstorm about the stylistic differences among individuals participating in one-handed set shot activities. **7.0**

Days 29 and 30

Review the one-handed set shot. **1.0**

Demonstrate the layup. (See figure 16.5.) **1.0**

Have students watch a clip on layups from *ESPN Teaching Kids Basketball*. **1.0**

Give students feedback as they practice the layup for basketball. **1.0**

Have pairs practice the layup for basketball, giving each other feedback. **1.0**

Have students brainstorm about how the scientific principles associated with spin and rebound apply to layup activities. **2.2**

Have students brainstorm about how growth in height and weight influence layup activities. **6.1**

Have students brainstorm about the stylistic differences among individuals participating in layup activities. **7.0**

Day 31

Review the layup. **1.0**

Demonstrate the rebound.   **1.0**

Have students watch a clip on rebounding from *ESPN Teaching Kids Basketball*.   **1.0**

Give students feedback as they practice the layup and rebound for basketball.   **1.0**

Have pairs practice the layup and rebound for basketball, giving each other feedback.   **1.0**

Have students brainstorm about how the scientific principles associated with spin and rebound apply to rebound activities.   **2.2**

Have students brainstorm about how growth in height and weight influence rebound activities.   **6.1**

Have students brainstorm about the stylistic differences among individuals participating in rebound activities.   **7.0**

Day 32

Review the offensive and defensive basic stances for basketball and compare to soccer and team handball.   **1.0 / 2.1**

Give students feedback as they practice the defensive basic stance (slide forward, back, right, and left).   **1.0**

Review the concepts of open and closed spaces.   **1.0**

Review offensive strategies (give-and-go, give-and-screen outside, give-and-screen outside by receiver, and give-and-screen inside), using a basketball, and compare to team handball.   **1.0**

Figure 16.5 The correct technique for the basketball layup.

Have students practice offensive strategies, using a basketball.   **1.0**

Have students practice offensive strategies against a defense.   **1.0**

Days 33, 34, and 35

Teach basketball the way it was originally played.   **1.0**

Have students play the original game of basketball.   **1.0 / 5.0**

Teach basketball the way it was played in the early 1900s.   **1.0**

Have students play basketball the way it was played in the early 1900s.   **1.0 / 5.0**

Teach basketball the way women played it in the 1960s.   **1.0**

Have students play basketball the way women played it in the 1960s.   **1.0 / 5.0**

Teach Modified Two-on-Two Basketball.   **1.0**

Have students play Modified Two-on-Two Basketball. (Assessment opportunity: rubric.)   **1.0 / 5.0**

Teach modern basketball.   **1.0**

Have students play modern basketball. (Assessment opportunity: rubric.)   **1.0 / 5.0**

Have students brainstorm about the similarities and differences among soccer, team handball, original basketball, and basketball today. (Assessment opportunity: structured observation.)   **1.0 / 2.1**

Day 36

Review speed-a-way.   **1.0**

Have students watch "Lesson 14: Disc Activities" on the *PE-TV* video.   **1.0**

Have students play Modified Two-on-Two Speed-a-Way, using hand skills only.   **1.0**

Day 37

Review passing and trapping using feet; compare to soccer.   **1.0 / 2.1**

Have students practice passing and trapping using feet as teammates give feedback.   **1.0**

Review dribbling and compare to soccer.   **1.0 / 2.1**

Have students rotate through a variety of dribbling, passing, and trapping stations as their group members give feedback.   **1.0**

Days 38 and 39

Demonstrate one-foot lift to self (see figure 16.6), two-foot stationary lift to self, moving ball lift, and lift to teammate.   **1.0**

Figure 16.6   The correct technique for the one-foot lift to self used in speed-a-way.

Have pairs rotate through lifting stations, practicing each type of lift, giving each other feedback.   **1.0**

Have students play Modified Two-on-Two Speed-a-Way. (Assessment opportunity: rubric.)   **1.0**

For homework, have students explain how the scientific principles associated with spin and rebound apply to one of the skills taught in this unit. (Assessment opportunity: essay.)   **2.2**

For homework, have students explain how growth in height and weight influence their ability to perform one of the skills in this unit. (Assessment opportunity: essay.)   **6.1**

For homework, have students describe the stylistic differences among individuals participating in one of the skills in this unit. (Assessment opportunity: essay.)   **7.0**

Day 40

Students give feedback to each other as they participate in a variety of dribbling, foot passing, overhead passing, and lifting combinations. (Assessment opportunity: rubric.)   **1.0**

Day 41

Review dodging, feinting, and tackling; compare to soccer. **1.0 / 2.1**

Review the concepts of open and closed spaces. **1.0**

Demonstrate flag pulling. **1.0**

Have students work on offense and defense in one-on-one combinations. **1.0**

Have students work on offense and defense in two-on-two combinations. **1.0**

Days 42 and 43

Teach Modified Four-on-Four Speed-a-Way. **1.0**

Have students play Modified Four-on-Four Speed-a-Way. (Assessment opportunity: structured observation.) **1.0 / 5.0**

Have students debrief the similarities and differences among team handball, soccer, basketball, and speed-a-way. (Assessment opportunity: structured observation.) **1.0 / 2.1**

Day 44

Review football. **1.0**

Have students play Modified Four-on-Four Flag Football. **1.0**

Day 45

Demonstrate centering, forward passing, and catching of a football. **1.0**

Have students watch clips on centering, passing, and catching from *ESPN Teaching Kids Football*. **1.0**

Have students practice the forward pass and catching the football (stationary target, passing for distance). **1.0**

Demonstrate centering. **1.0**

Have students participate in game-like drills, involving centering, the forward pass, and catching the football activities (including passing for accuracy and moving while passing for accuracy). **1.0**

Day 46

Demonstrate ball carrying. **1.0**

Explain pass patterns. **1.0**

Give students feedback as they run through different pass patterns. (See figure 16.7.) **1.0**

Have students participate in game-like drills, involving centering, forward pass, pass patterns, and catching activities (including passing to a moving target and moving while passing to a moving target). **1.0**

Day 47

Demonstrate the basic defensive stance and blocking. **1.0**

Give students feedback as they demonstrate the basic defensive stance and blocking. **1.0**

Demonstrate laterals. **1.0**

Have students watch a clip on laterals from *ESPN Teaching Kids Football*. **1.0**

Have students participate in centering, lateral, and catching activities. **1.0**

Demonstrate rushing. **1.0**

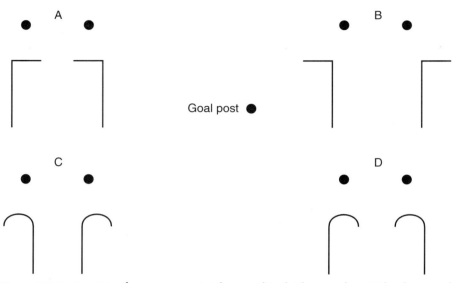

Figure 16.7   A variety of pass patterns: (a) down and in, (b) down and out, (c) hook out, and (d) hook in.

In groups of four, have students participate in centering, lateral, and catching activities against a defensive rusher.   **1.0**

For homework, have students describe the stylistic differences among individuals participating in lateral activities. (Assessment opportunity: essay.)   **7.0**

Day 48

Review laterals.   **1.0**

Demonstrate handoffs. (See figure 16.8.)   **1.0**

Have students watch a clip from *ESPN Teaching Kids Football*.   **1.0**

Have students participate in centering and handoff activities.   **1.0**

In groups of four, have students participate in centering and handoff activities against a defensive rusher.   **1.0**

Days 49 and 50

Review the concepts of open and closed spaces.   **1.0**

Demonstrate the basic offensive formation for four players.   **1.0**

Demonstrate the basic defensive formation for four players.   **1.0**

Introduce the concept of offensive plays.   **1.0**

Have each group create three offensive plays.   **1.0**

Videotape each group performing their three offensive plays. (Assessment opportunity: rubric.)   **1.0**

Days 51 and 52

Teach Modified Four-on-Four Flag Football.   **1.0**

Have students watch the video of each team's three offensive plays.   **1.0**

Have students play Modified Four-on-Four Flag Football. (Assessment opportunity: rubric.)   **1.0 / 5.0**

Have students describe similarities and differences among team handball, basketball, soccer, speed-a-way, and football.   **1.0 / 2.1**

Figure 16.8 The correct technique for the football handoff.

Day 53

Have students rotate through stations, playing modified versions of team handball, basketball, soccer, speed-a-way, and football. (Assessment opportunity: rubric.)   **1.0 / 2.1**

Have students describe similarities and differences among team handball, basketball, soccer, speed-a-way, and football. (Assessment opportunity: structured observation.)   **1.0 / 2.1**

Day 54

Have each group create a new team invasion game. (Assessment assignment opportunity: project.)   **1.0 / 2.3**

Day 55

Have each group teach another group how to play their game and then allow them to play it with the other group. (Assessment opportunity: project.)   **1.0 / 2.3**

Collect student logs of participation in physical activity outside of physical education. (Assessment opportunity: log.)   **3.0**

Collect student essays on comparing team handball, soccer, basketball, speed-a-way and football. (Assessment opportunity: essay.)   **1.0 / 2.1 / 6.2**

Collect one-week fitness plans with updated sections on muscular strength and endurance. (Assessment opportunity: log.)   **4.0**

Unit 4: Team Net Sports

This unit continues our focus on working as a team to develop strategies for success by teaching an-other type of team game: team net sports. For our purposes, we will only examine volleyball, since the other net sports fall into the individual and dual sport category (e.g., tennis, badminton, table tennis). To address standard four, I will continue to cover physical fitness during our daily warm-up and flexibility exercises as well as have students perform cardiorespiratory, muscular strength, and muscular endurance exercises every other day. I'll also have students refine the flexibility sections of their seventh grade one-week fitness plans, so I'll spend some warm-up time reviewing the health-related fitness concepts related to flexibility.

You can teach this unit in any open area; however, blacktop volleyball courts with nets are preferable. The only equipment required for this unit is volleyballs. But which of the many volleyballs available is best? I recommend the Volleyball Trainer from Sportime because it's lightweight and easy to use. In addition, I'll use volleyball clips from *The World of Volleyball* video and the volleyball segment on the *PE-TV* as well as *MacVolleyball Complete* software (see appendix D for sources). I have also found it effective to videotape students throughout the unit, so that they can add the tapes to their electronic portfolios as evidence of their growth in motor skills.

Science principles fit in with physical education more often then you might think. Because my students are studying spin and rebound in their science classes, I'll point out how they can apply these science concepts to real-life situations—developing their volleyball skills. To assess student understanding, I'll assign a cooperative project in which students must select one volleyball skill to analyze in depth, explaining how spin and rebound are involved with the skill.

Unit Standards

1.0 – Applies the correct techniques for locomotor, nonlocomotor, and manipulative skills in team net sports.

2.1 – Applies the transfer of learning principle to learning new skills in team net sports.

2.2 – Describes how the scientific principles associated with spin and rebound apply to team net sports.

2.3 – Creates a team net game with scoring options.

3.0 – Participates in and monitors physical activity and fitness activity outside physical education, based on own goals.

4.0 – Performs exercises for all five areas of health-related fitness and redesigns flexibility section of the seventh grade one-week fitness plan.

5.0 – Demonstrates conflict resolution skills when working in a group.

6.1 – Analyzes how growth in height and weight alters the mechanical nature of performance and how it affects the selection of player positions in net sports.

6.2 – Describes the development and role of volleyball in the United States.

7.0 – Appreciates the stylistic differences of someone else's approach to net sports.

Unit Outline

Day 1

Introduce the history and sport of volleyball. **6.2**

Assign students to work in groups of four.

Review concepts related to flexibility and assign refining the flexibility section of seventh grade one-week fitness plan as a project for this unit. (Assessment assignment opportunity: project.) **4.0**

Have students watch "Lesson 13: Volleyball" on the *PE-TV* video, and then discuss. **1.0**

Have students play Modified Four-on-Four Volleyball. **1.0**

Have students brainstorm a list of other net sports, and discuss their similarities and differences. **2.1**

For homework, have students write an essay on the relationship between what was going on in society and the invention of volleyball. (Assessment opportunity: essay.)   **6.2**

Days 2 and 3

Discuss conflict resolution skills as they apply to working in a group.   **5.0**

Demonstrate the ready position.   **1.0**

Give students feedback as they assume the ready position.   **1.0**

Demonstrate the forearm pass. (See figure 16.9.)   **1.0**

Figure 16.9 The correct technique for the forearm pass.

Have students watch a clip on the forearm pass from *The World of Volleyball*.   **1.0**

Give pairs feedback as they practice the forearm pass (from a toss and from a partner's forearm pass).   **1.0**

For homework, have students begin to monitor participation in physical activities outside of physical education. (Assessment assignment opportunity: log.)   **3.0**

Days 4 and 5

Review the forearm pass.   **1.0**

In groups of four, have students practice the forearm pass (from a toss, from a partner's forearm pass, and for accuracy) while the other students give feedback.   **1.0**

Have students participate in a forearm pass game (four-on-four).   **1.0**

Days 6 and 7

Demonstrate the underhand serve. (See figure 16.10.)   **1.0**

Give students feedback as they practice the underhand serve from as close to the net as they like.   **1.0**

Have pairs practice the underhand serve from as close to the net as they like, giving each other feedback.   **1.0**

Have pairs play a serving accuracy game.   **1.0 / 5.0**

Figure 16.10 The correct technique for the underhand serve.

Have students brainstorm about how the scientific principles associated with spin and rebound apply to the serve. **2.2**

Have students brainstorm about how growth in height and weight influence the serve. **6.1**

Have students brainstorm about the stylistic differences among individuals participating in the serve. **7.0**

Days 8 and 9

Review the forearm pass and underhand serve. **1.0**

Demonstrate the overhand pass. (See figure 16.11.) **1.0**

Figure 16.11 The correct technique for the overhand pass.

Have students watch a clip on the overhand pass from *The World of Volleyball*.   **1.0**

Give pairs feedback as they practice the overhand pass (from a toss and from a partner's forearm pass).   **1.0**

Have students brainstorm about how the scientific principles associated with spin and rebound apply to the overhand pass.   **2.2**

Have students brainstorm about how growth in height and weight influence the overhand pass.   **6.1**

Have students brainstorm about the stylistic differences among individuals participating in the over-hand pass.   **7.0**

Have students add information to their volleyball electronic portfolios. (Assessment opportunity: essay.)   **1.0**

Day 10

Review the overhand and forearm passes.   **1.0**

Have groups create rubrics for the forearm pass.   **1.0**

Have students participate in a variety of forearm pass to overhand pass activities while teammates give feedback. (Assessment opportunity: rubric.)   **1.0**

Days 11 and 12

Demonstrate the overhand serve. (See figure 16.12.)   **1.0**

Give students feedback as they practice the overhand serve from as close to the net as they like.   **1.0**

Have pairs practice the overhand serve from as close to the net as they like, giving each other feed-back.   **1.0**

Have pairs play a serving accuracy game.   **1.0 / 5.0**

Have students brainstorm about how the scientific principles associated with spin and rebound apply to the serve.   **2.2**

Have students brainstorm about how growth in height and weight influence the serve.   **6.1**

Figure 16.12 The correct technique for the overhand serve.

Have students brainstorm about the stylistic differences among individuals participating in the serve. **7.0**

Have students add information to their volleyball electronic portfolios. (Assessment opportunity: essay.) **1.0**

Days 13 and 14

Demonstrate the standing spike. **1.0**

Give students feedback as they practice the standing spike (from a hold, from a self toss, from a partner toss, and from an overhand pass). **1.0**

Have pairs practice the standing spike (from a hold, from a self toss, from a partner toss, from an overhand pass), giving each other feedback. **1.0**

Have students brainstorm about how the scientific principles associated with spin and rebound apply to the spike. (Assessment opportunity: structured observation.) **2.2**

Have students brainstorm about how growth in height and weight influence the spike. (Assessment opportunity: structured observation.) **6.1**

Have students brainstorm about the stylistic differences among individuals participating in the spike. (Assessment opportunity: structured observation.) **7.0**

Days 15 and 16

Demonstrate the jumping spike. **1.0**

Have students watch a clip on spiking from *The World of Volleyball*. **1.0**

Give students feedback as they practice the jumping spike (from a hold, from a self toss, from a partner toss, and from an overhand pass). **1.0**

Have pairs practice the jumping spike (from a hold, from a self toss, from a partner toss, and from an overhand pass), giving each other feedback. **1.0**

Have students add video clips to their volleyball electronic portfolios. (Assessment opportunity: structured observation.) **1.0**

Day 17

Demonstrate the block. **1.0**

Have students watch a clip on blocking from *The World of Volleyball*. **1.0**

Give students feedback as they practice the block. **1.0**

Have pairs practice the jump spike and block, giving each other feedback. **1.0**

For homework, have students explain how the scientific principles associated with spin and rebound apply to one of the volleyball skills. (Assessment opportunity: essay.) **2.2**

For homework, have students describe how growth in height and weight influence someone's ability in one of the volleyball skills. (Assessment opportunity: essay.) **6.1**

For homework, have students write about the stylistic differences among individuals participating in volleyball. (Assessment opportunity: essay.) **7.0**

Day 18

Review all volleyball skills. **1.0**

Have students rotate through a variety of practice stations: serving, forearm pass, forearm pass to overhand pass, overhand pass, spiking and blocking, and computer. (Assessment opportunity: rubric.) **1.0**

Have students add video clips to their electronic portfolios. (Assessment opportunity: rubric.)   **1.0**

Day 19

Review the concept of open and closed spaces.   **1.0**

Discuss the relationship between open and closed spaces for invasion team sports and net sports.   **2.1**

Demonstrate the basic defensive position.   **1.0**

Give students feedback as they assume the basic defensive position.   **1.0**

Demonstrate the basic rotation. (See figure 16.13.)   **1.0**

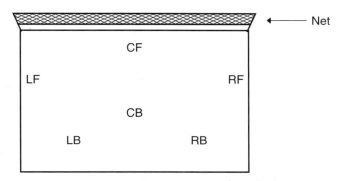

Figure 16.13   Basic rotation (W-position) for volleyball.

Give students feedback as they assume positions on the court and walk through the basic rotation.   **1.0**

Divide students into teams of six. Have one team toss the ball while the other team attempts to execute a pass and set and spike sequence, awarding one point to the team if they are successful, switching tossing team if unsuccessful.   **1.0**

Days 20 and 21

Demonstrate the 4–2 formation and rotation. (See figure 16.14.)   **1.0**

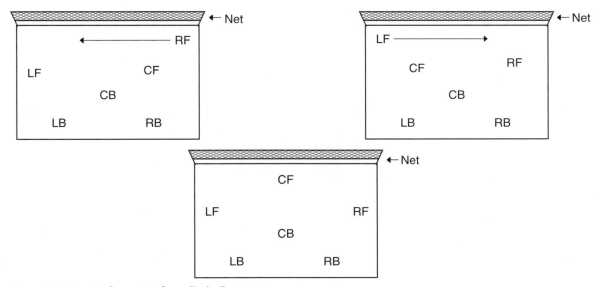

Figure 16.14   4–2 formation for volleyball.

Have each team determine who will be the setters and who will be the spikers. (Assessment opportunity: structured observation.) **5.0 / 6.1**

Give students feedback as they assume positions on the court and walk through the 4–2 rotation. **1.0**

Have one team toss the ball while the other team attempts to execute a pass and set and spike sequence, awarding one point to the team if they are successful, switching tossing team if unsuccessful. (Assessment opportunity: rubric.) **1.0**

Have students describe in their journals how they feel about being either a setter or a spiker. (Assessment opportunity: journal entry.) **5.0**

Days 22 and 23

Teach the game and rules of volleyball. **1.0**

Have students play volleyball. (Assessment opportunity: rubric.) **1.0**

Have students add information and video clips to their volleyball electronic portfolios. (Assessment opportunity: structured observation and essay.) **1.0**

Day 24

Have each group create a team net game. (Assessment assignment opportunity: project.) **1.0 / 2.3 / 5.0**

Day 25

Have each group teach another how to play their game and then allow them to play each other's games. (Assessment opportunity: project.) **1.0 / 2.3 / 5.0**

Collect student logs of participation in physical activity outside of physical education. (Assessment opportunity: log.) **3.0**

Collect one-week fitness plans with updated muscular flexibility sections. (Assessment opportunity: project.) **4.0**

For homework, have students write an essay, describing how their new team net game is similar to and different from volleyball. (Assessment opportunity: essay.) **2.1**

Unit 5: Team Field Sports

This unit continues our focus on working as a team to develop strategies for success by focusing on another type of team game: team field sports. For our purposes, we will only examine softball, since the other field sports are more elementary level recess games (e.g., kickball and sockball). As always, I'll continue to address standard four by covering physical fitness during the daily warm-up and flexibility exercises and by having students perform cardiorespiratory, muscular strength, and muscular endurance exercises every other day. I'll also have students refine the body composition sections of their seventh grade one-week fitness plans, so I'll spend some warm-up time reviewing the health-related fitness concepts related to body composition.

You can teach this unit in any open area; however, grass is preferable. Softball diamonds and backstops help, too. As for equipment, you'll need softballs, softball bats, softball gloves, bases, and—for safety reasons—catcher masks and chest protectors. In addition, I recommend showing students softball clips from the *VIP Softball Series* by the Amateur Softball Association and the softball segment on the *PE-TV* video and using *MacSoftball Basic Defense* and *MacSoftball Rules Game* software. (See appendix D for sources.)

Because my students are studying the 1800s in their history class, I have them study the history of softball and other team sports that developed during the 1800s to create an especially interesting interdisciplinary link. Have you heard about the controversies about who created baseball? I like to cooperate with my students' history teachers and create an interdisciplinary project by having students research the history of baseball, having them determine who, in fact, invented it and the reasons for the controversy.

Unit Standards

1.0 – Applies the correct techniques for locomotor, nonlocomotor, and manipulative skills to team field sports.

2.1 – Applies the transfer of learning principle to learning new skills in team field sports.

2.2 – Describes how the scientific principles associated with spin and rebound apply to team field sports.

2.3 – Creates a team field game with scoring options.

3.0 – Participates in and monitors physical activity and fitness activity outside physical education, based on personal goals.

4.0 – Performs exercises for all five areas of health-related fitness and refines the body composition section of the seventh grade one-week fitness plan.

5.0 – Develops offensive and defensive strategies, based on strengths and weaknesses of both teams.

6.1 – Analyzes how growth in height and weight alters the mechanical nature of performance and how it influences the selection of player positions in team field sports.

6.2 – Describes the development and roles of baseball and softball in the United States.

7.0 – Appreciates the stylistic differences of someone else's approach to softball.

Unit Outline

Day 1

Introduce softball, including discussing equipment and safety. **1.0**

Explain the history of softball and assign baseball research project. (Assessment assignment opportunity: project.) **6.2**

Review concepts related to body composition and assign refining body composition section of the seventh grade one-week fitness plan as a project for this unit. (Assessment assignment opportunity: project.) **4.0**

Have students watch "Lesson 17: Softball" on the *PE-TV* video, and then discuss. **1.0**

Have students play nine-on-nine softball. **1.0**

Have students brainstorm a list of other field sports, and discuss similarities and differences. **1.0**

Days 2 and 3

Assign students to work in groups of four.

Demonstrate the overhand throw and catch. **1.0**

Have students watch a clip on throwing and catching from *VIP Softball Series*. **1.0**

Give students feedback as they practice the overhand throw and catch (throwing at stationary object, throwing at moving object, throwing for distance, throwing for accuracy, throwing while moving, and throwing while moving at a moving target). **1.0**

Have pairs practice the overhand throw and catch (throwing at stationary object, throwing at moving object, throwing for distance, throwing for accuracy, throwing while moving, throwing while moving at a moving target), giving each other feedback. **1.0**

For homework, have students begin to monitor participation in physical activities outside of physical education. (Assessment assignment opportunity: log.) **3.0**

Day 4

Review the overhand throw and catch. **1.0**

Demonstrate the sidearm whip throw and catch. **1.0**

Give students feedback as they practice the sidearm whip throw and catch (throwing at stationary object, throwing at moving object, throwing for distance, throwing for accuracy, throwing while moving, and throwing while moving at a moving target). **1.0**

Have pairs practice the sidearm whip throw and catch (throwing at stationary object, throwing at moving object, throwing for distance, throwing for accuracy, throwing while moving, throwing while moving at a moving target), giving each other feedback. **1.0**

Have students brainstorm about how the scientific principles associated with spin and rebound apply to the sidearm whip throw. **2.2**

Have students brainstorm about how growth in height and weight influence the sidearm whip throw. **6.1**

Have students brainstorm about the stylistic differences among individuals performing the sidearm whip throw. **7.0**

Day 5

Review overhand throw and sidearm whip throw and catch. **1.0**

Demonstrate the underhand throw and catch. **1.0**

Give students feedback as they practice the underhand throw and catch (throwing at stationary object, throwing at moving object, throwing for accuracy, throwing while moving, and throwing while moving at a moving target). **1.0**

Have pairs practice the underhand throw and catch (throwing at stationary object, throwing at moving object, throwing for accuracy, throwing while moving, throwing while moving at a moving target), giving each other feedback. **1.0**

Have students brainstorm about how the scientific principles associated with spin and rebound apply to the underhand throw and catch. **2.2**

Have students brainstorm about how growth in height and weight influence the underhand throw and catch. **6.1**

Have students brainstorm about the stylistic differences among individuals performing the underhand throw and catch. **7.0**

Days 6 and 7

Review the overhand throw, sidearm whip throw, and underhand throw. **1.0**

Have students play Pickle. (See appendix C.) **1.0**

Demonstrate fielding ground balls. (See figure 16.15.) **1.0**

Have students watch a clip on fielding ground balls from *VIP Softball Series*. **1.0**

Give students feedback as they practice fielding ground balls (from a toss and from a toss to the side). **1.0**

Have pairs practice fielding ground balls (from a toss, from a toss to the side), giving each other feedback. **1.0**

Figure 16.15 The correct technique for fielding ground balls.

Have students brainstorm about how the scientific principles associated with spin and rebound apply to fielding ground balls.   **2.2**

Have students brainstorm about how growth in height and weight influence the fielding of ground balls.   **6.1**

Have students brainstorm about the stylistic differences among individuals fielding ground balls.   **7.0**

Days 8 and 9

Review fielding ground balls and throwing.   **1.0**

Demonstrate fielding fly balls. (See figure 16.16.)   **1.0**

Have students watch a clip on fielding fly balls from *VIP Softball Series*.   **1.0**

Give students feedback as they practice fielding fly balls (from a toss and from a toss to the side).   **1.0**

Have pairs practice fielding fly balls (from a toss and from a toss to the side), giving each other feedback.   **1.0**

Have students brainstorm about how the scientific principles associated with spin and rebound apply to fielding fly balls.   **2.2**

Have students brainstorm about how growth in height and weight influence the fielding of fly balls.   **6.1**

Have students brainstorm about the stylistic differences among individuals fielding fly balls.   **7.0**

Days 10 and 11

Review fielding ground balls and throwing.   **1.0**

Give students feedback as they practice throwing the ball from the shortstop position to catcher to first to second to third and back to catcher (also other sequences).   **1.0**

Demonstrate pitching. (See figure 16.17.)   **1.0**

Have students watch a clip on pitching from *VIP Softball Series*.   **1.0**

Give students feedback as they practice pitching (first technique, then accuracy).   **1.0**

Have pairs practice pitching (technique then accuracy), giving each other feedback.   **1.0**

Have students brainstorm about how the scientific principles associated with spin and rebound apply to pitching. (Assessment opportunity: structured observation.)   **2.2**

Have students brainstorm about how growth in height and weight influence pitching. (Assessment opportunity: structured observation.)   **6.1**

Have students brainstorm about the stylistic differences among individuals pitching. (Assessment opportunity: structured observation.)   **7.0**

Days 12 and 13

Demonstrate batting. (See figure 16.18.)   **1.0**

Figure 16.16 The correct technique for fielding fly balls.

Figure 16.17   The correct technique for pitching.

Have students watch a clip on batting from *VIP Softball Series*.   **1.0**

Give students feedback as they practice batting (off tee, from a toss, from a pitch, for distance, and for accuracy).   **1.0**

Have pairs practice batting (off tee, from a toss, from a pitch, for distance, and for accuracy), giving each other feedback.   **1.0**

Have students describe how the scientific principles associated with spin and rebound apply to batting.   **2.2**

Have students describe how growth in height and weight influence batting.   **6.1**

Have students describe the stylistic differences among individuals batting.   **7.0**

Days 14 and 15

Demonstrate bunting.   **1.0**

Have students watch a clip on bunting from *VIP Softball Series*.   **1.0**

Figure 16.18   The correct technique for batting.

Give students feedback as they practice bunting (off a tee, from a toss, from a pitch, for technique and accuracy).   **1.0**

Have pairs practice bunting (off a tee, from a toss, from a pitch, for technique and accuracy), giving each other feedback.   **1.0**

For homework, have students describe how the scientific principles associated with spin and rebound apply to softball skills. (Assessment opportunity: essay.)   **2.2**

For homework, have students describe how growth in height and weight influences softball-playing ability. (Assessment opportunity: essay.)   **6.1**

For homework, have students describe the stylistic differences among individuals playing softball. (Assessment opportunity: essay.)   **7.0**

Day 16

Demonstrate baserunning.   **1.0**

Give students feedback as they practice baserunning.   **1.0**

Have students practice baserunning for time, emphasizing self-improvement.   **1.0**

Have students brainstorm how growth in height and weight influence baserunning.   **6.1**

Have students brainstorm the stylistic differences among individual's baserunning.   **7.0**

Days 17 and 18

Review how to practice in stations.

Have pairs review skills by participating in a variety of softball stations (throwing and catching, fielding fly balls, fielding grounders, pitching, batting, bunting, and baserunning), giving each other feedback. (Assessment opportunity: rubric.)   **1.0**

Days 19 and 20

Discuss the development of offensive and defensive strategies in softball.   **5.0**

Review the concepts of open and closed spaces, along with the similarities and differences in net and invasion sports.   **1.0 / 2.1 / 5.0**

Give groups a variety of scenarios for which they must collectively determine the best offensive or defensive strategy. (Assessment opportunity: rubric.)   **5.0**

Have students play *MacSoftball Basic Defense* on the computer to reinforce softball basic defense skills.   **1.0 / 5.0**

Day 21

Assign students to groups of nine.

Teach Three-Pitch Softball and regulation softball.   **1.0**

Have students play *MacSoftball Rules Game* on the computer to reinforce softball rules.   **1.0**

Have students meet with their softball teams to determine who will play which position.   **1.0 / 5.0 / 6.1**

Days 22 and 23

Have students play Three-Pitch Softball. (Assessment opportunity: rubric.)   **1.0 / 5.0**

Have students play regulation softball. (Assessment opportunity: rubric.)   **1.0 / 5.0**

Have students discuss which softball game they like the best, and why.   **1.0**

Day 24

In their groups of four, have students create a team field game for teams of four. (Assessment assignment opportunity: project.)   **1.0 / 2.3 / 5.0**

Day 25

Have each group teach another how to play their game and then allow them to play each other's game. (Assessment opportunity: project.)   **1.0 / 2.3 / 5.0**

Collect student logs of participation in physical activity outside of physical education. (Assessment opportunity: log.) **3.0**

Collect one-week fitness plans with updated sections on body composition. (Assessment assignment opportunity: project.) **4.0**

Collect baseball research projects. (Assessment opportunity: project.) **6.2**

For homework, have students write an essay describing how their new team field game is similar to and different from softball. (Assessment opportunity: essay.) **2.1**

Unit 6: Square Dancing

By looking at how individuals need to work together to square dance successfully, this unit continues our focus on working as a team to develop strategies for success. And because square dance developed in America during the 1800s, it dovetails nicely with what my students are studying in history. This unit also reinforces the concept of the transfer of learning because dance skills used in one dance positively transfer to other dances. To address standard four, I'll continue to cover physical fitness during the daily warm-up and flexibility exercises as well as have students perform cardiorespiratory, muscular strength, and muscular endurance exercises every other day. I'll also have students refine the cardiorespiratory sections of their seventh grade one-week fitness plans, so I'll spend some warm-up time reviewing health-related fitness concepts related to cardiorespiratory endurance. To reinforce these concepts, I'll have students wear heart rate monitors as they dance to prove that dancing is an aerobic activity.

You can teach this unit in any open area; however, an indoor facility is preferable. Of course, you'll need compact discs, audiotapes, or records for each dance you teach as well as the appropriate player. A microphone will ensure that students can hear your voice over the music. Heart rate monitors, a heart rate monitor interface to a computer, and electronic blood pressure devices will help you teach about cardiorespiratory endurance.

Naturally, this unit ties in well with music education. My students learn more about the history of American square dance and the type and development of music that goes with the dancing in their music classes. Then in physical education, the students actually participate in the dances and learn the history from a physical education perspective.

Unit Standards

1.0 – Applies the correct techniques for locomotor and nonlocomotor skills to square dance activities.

2.1 – Applies the transfer of learning principle to learning new steps in square dancing.

2.2 – Describes how the scientific principles associated with spin apply to square dance skills.

2.3 – Creates a team game that involves square dancing.

3.0 – Participates in and monitors physical activity and fitness activity outside physical education, based on personal goals.

4.0 – Performs exercises for all five areas of health-related fitness and refines the cardiorespiratory section of the seventh grade one-week personal fitness plan.

5.0 – Solves problems by analyzing causes and potential solutions in physical activity settings.

6.1 – Describes relationship between height and weight and selection of developmentally appropriate activities.

6.2 – Describes the growth of square dancing throughout the 19th and 20th centuries.

7.0 – Appreciates the stylistic differences of someone else's approach to square dancing.

Unit Outline

Day 1

Introduce square dancing.   **1.0**

Assign students to work in groups of eight.

Explain the history of square dancing throughout the 19th and 20th centuries.   **6.2**

Review concepts related to cardiorespiratory endurance and assign refining cardiorespiratory endurance section of the seventh grade one-week fitness plan as a project for this unit. (Assessment assignment opportunity: project.)   **4.0**

Review wearing the heart rate monitor and downloading information.   **4.0**

Have students take each other's blood pressure.   **4.0**

For homework, have students begin to monitor their participation in physical activities outside of physical education. (Assessment assignment opportunity: log.)   **3.0**

Have students describe the history of square dancing throughout the 19th and 20th centuries. (Assessment assignment opportunity: report.)   **6.2**

Day 2

Discuss solving problems by analyzing causes and potential solutions.   **5.0**

Set up a square set (see figure 16.19) and describe the different positions.   **1.0**

Have students set up in a square and identify the different positions.   **1.0**

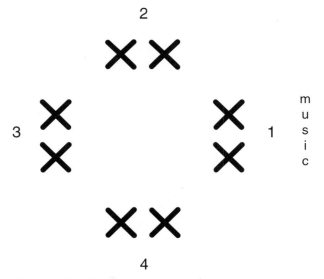

Figure 16.19 Square set in square dancing.

Using a jigsaw strategy, have students teach one another the following moves: courtesy turn, circle left and right, do-si-do, and forward and back.   **1.0 / 5.0**

Review courtesy turn, circle left and right, do-si-do, and forward and back.   **1.0**

Days 3 and 4

Have students review the courtesy turn, circle left and right, do-si-do, and forward and back.   **1.0**

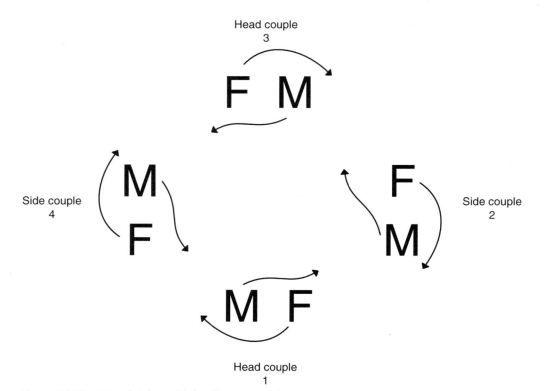

Figure 16.20 Grand right and left call in square dancing.

Demonstrate the grand right and left. (See figure 16.20.)   **1.0**

Have students practice the grand right and left.   **1.0**

Demonstrate the promenade.   **1.0**

Have students practice the promenade.   **1.0**

Demonstrate the swing.   **1.0**

Have students practice the swing.   **1.0**

Walk students through the song "Hinky Dinky."   **1.0**

Have students dance to "Hinky Dinky."   **1.0 / 5.0**

Have students brainstorm about the stylistic differences among individual approaches to "Hinky Dinky."   **7.0**

Day 5

Have students review "Hinky Dinky."   **1.0 / 5.0**

Demonstrate the alemande left.   **1.0**

Have students practice the alemande left.   **1.0**

Walk students through the song "Spoonful of Sugar."   **1.0**

Have students dance to "Spoonful of Sugar."   **1.0 / 5.0**

Have students brainstorm about the stylistic differences among individual approaches to "Spoonful of Sugar."   **7.0**

Day 6

Have students review "Spoonful of Sugar."   **1.0**

Demonstrate the star.   **1.0**

Have students practice the star.   **1.0**

Demonstrate the promenade outside.   **1.0**

Have students practice the promenade outside.   **1.0**

Walk students through the song "Gentle on My Mind."   **1.0**

Have students dance to "Gentle on My Mind."   **1.0 / 5.0**

Have students brainstorm about the stylistic differences among individual approaches to "Gentle on My Mind."   **7.0**

Day 7

Have students review "Gentle on My Mind."   **1.0**

Demonstrate the single file.   **1.0**

Have students practice the single file.   **1.0**

Demonstrate the couple star.   **1.0**

Have students practice the couple star.   **1.0**

Walk students through "Bad Bad Leroy Brown."   **1.0**

Have students dance to "Bad Bad Leroy Brown."   **1.0 / 5.0**

Have students brainstorm about the stylistic differences among individual approaches to "Bad Bad Leroy Brown."   **7.0**

Day 8

Have students review "Hinky Dinky," "Spoonful of Sugar," "Gentle on My Mind," and "Bad Bad Leroy Brown." (Assessment opportunity: rubric.)   **1.0**

Day 9

Demonstrate the divide ring.   **1.0**

Have students practice the divide ring.   **1.0**

Walk students through the song "Engine 9."   **1.0**

Have students dance to "Engine 9."   **1.0 / 5.0**

Have students brainstorm about the stylistic differences among individual approaches to "Engine 9."   **7.0**

Day 10

Have students review "Engine 9."   **1.0**

Demonstrate changing partners.   **1.0**

Have students practice changing partners.   **1.0**

Walk students through "Hey Lei Lee Li Lee."   **1.0**

Have students dance to "Hey Lei Lee Li Lee."   **1.0 / 5.0**

Have students brainstorm about the stylistic differences among individual approaches to "Hey Lei Lee Li Lee."   **7.0**

Day 11

Have students review "Hey Lei Lee Li Lee."   **1.0**

Demonstrate the ladies' chain.   **1.0**

Have students practice the ladies' chain.   **1.0**

Walk students through the song "King of the Road."   **1.0**

Have students dance to "King of the Road."   **1.0 / 5.0**

Have students brainstorm about the stylistic differences among individual approaches to "King of the Road."   **7.0**

Day 12

Have students review "King of the Road."   **1.0**

Demonstrate the four ladies' chain.   **1.0**

Have students practice the four ladies' chain.   **1.0**

Demonstrate the twirl.   **1.0**

Have students practice the twirl.   **1.0**

Walk students through the song "Kingston Town."   **1.0**

Have students dance to "Kingston Town."   **1.0 / 5.0**

Have students brainstorm about the stylistic differences among individual approaches to "Kingston Town."   **7.0**

Day 13

Have students review "Engine 9," "Hey Lei Lee Li Lee," "King of the Road," and "Kingston Town." (Assessment opportunity: rubric.)   **1.0**

Day 14

Demonstrate changing partners.   **1.0**

Walk students through the song "Just Because."   **1.0**

Have students dance to "Just Because."   **1.0 / 5.0**

Day 15

Have students review "Just Because."   **1.0**

Demonstrate the seesaw.   **1.0**

Have students practice the seesaw.   **1.0**

Demonstrate the right and left through.   **1.0**

Have students practice the right and left through.   **1.0**

Walk students through the song "Crawdad."   **1.0**

Have students dance to "Crawdad."   **1.0 / 5.0**

Day 16

Have students review "Crawdad."   **1.0**

Demonstrate the back to the center.   **1.0**

Have students practice the back to the center.   **1.0**

Walk students through the song "If They Could See Me Now."   **1.0**

Have students dance to "If They Could See Me Now."   **1.0 / 5.0**

Day 17

Have students review "Just Because," "Crawdad," and "If They Could See Me Now."   **1.0**

Have students brainstorm about the stylistic differences among individual approaches to "Just Because," "Crawdad," and "If They Could See Me Now." (Assessment opportunity: rubric.)   **7.0**

Day 18

Demonstrate the grand square. (See figure 16.21.)   **1.0**

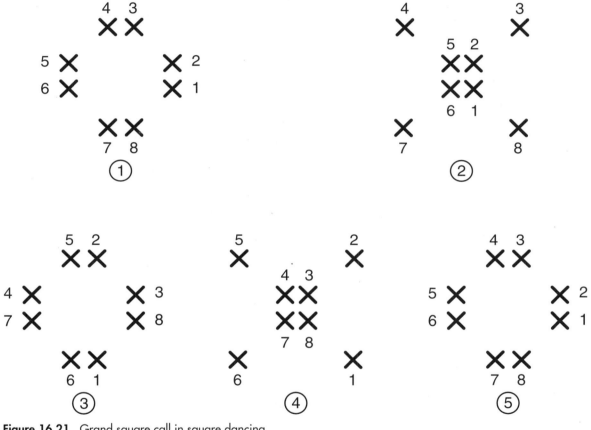

Figure 16.21   Grand square call in square dancing.

Have students demonstrate the grand square.   **1.0**

Walk students through the song "Wheels."   **1.0**

Have students dance to "Wheels."   **1.0 / 5.0**

Day 19

Have students learn how to dance to "Hey Look Me Over" by reading and following written directions for the dance. (Assessment opportunity: structured observation.)   **1.0 / 5.0**

Day 20

Have students review "Hey Look Me Over." **1.0**

Demonstrate the alemande right. **1.0**

Have students practice the alemande right. **1.0**

Have students learn how to dance to "Tie a Yellow Ribbon" by reading and following written directions for the dance. (Assessment opportunity: structured observation.) **1.0 / 5.0**

Day 21

Have students review "Wheels," "Hey Look Me Over," and "Tie a Yellow Ribbon." (Assessment opportunity: rubric.) **1.0**

Have students brainstorm about the stylistic differences among individual approaches to "Wheels," "Hey Look Me Over," and "Tie a Yellow Ribbon." (Assessment opportunity: structured observation.) **7.0**

Days 22 and 23

Review all dances learned in this unit. (Assessment opportunity: rubric.) **1.0**

For homework, have students describe how growth in height and weight relate to the selection of developmentally appropriate dances and activities. (Assessment opportunity: essay.) **6.1**

Day 24

Have each group create a square dance. (Assessment assignment opportunity: project.) **1.0 / 2.3 / 5.0 / 7.0**

For homework, have students explain whether or not the principles associated with spin and rebound have any application to square dancing. (Assessment opportunity: essay.) **2.2**

Day 25

Have each group teach their dance to another group. (Assessment opportunity: project.) **1.0 / 2.3 / 5.0 / 7.0**

Collect student logs of participation in physical activity outside of physical education. (Assessment opportunity: log.) **3.0**

Collect the one-week fitness plans with updated sections on cardiorespiratory endurance. (Assessment opportunity: project.) **4.0**

Collect the history of square dance essays. (Assessment opportunity: report.) **6.2**

For homework, have students write an essay, describing how their new dance is similar to and different from other square dances learned in this unit. (Assessment opportunity: essay.) **2.1**

Unit 7: Closing and Fitness Posttesting

This unit, similar to the sixth and seventh grade closing and fitness posttesting units gives students the opportunity to demonstrate whether or not they have reached the eighth grade standards. Although students have been working on projects throughout the year, I'll give them the chance to focus on depth over breadth in this unit. Direct students to focus on completing their demonstrations of learning by collecting and creating work for their portfolios, freeing you to administer the fitness posttesting and to act as a resource for the student projects.

Sample Evidence for Each Eighth Grade Standard

1.0 Applies the Correct Techniques for Locomotor, Nonlocomotor, and Manipulative Skills to Sport-Specific Skills in a Variety of Team-Related Activities

Student and teacher assessment during each instructional unit based on a rubric determines whether or not the student has reached this standard. The following is a sample rubric for kicking in soccer:

6: Performs a mature kick when kicking in a game or activity situation.

5: Performs a mature kick when kicking for distance and accuracy.

4: Performs a mature kick.

____ Stands behind ball slightly to nonkicking side of the ball.

____ Runs to ball and takes a small leap to get kicking foot in position.

____ Keeps eyes on ball.

____ Swings kicking leg back and then forcefully forward from hip.

____ Leans trunk backward.

____ Extends knee.

____ Contacts center of ball with instep.

____ Swings arm opposite kicking leg forward.

____ Follows through in an upward motion.

____ Takes small step forward on support foot after contact.

3: Moving toward mature kick.

2: Attempts an immature kick when a ball is rolled to him or her.

1: Randomly attempts an immature kick.

2.1 Applies the Principle of Transfer of Learning in Order to Learn a New Skill

Have student write an essay describing how the learning of one skill assisted in the learning of a new skill during the year.

2.2 Analyzes Movement Performance Using Spin and Rebound Principles in Order to Learn or Improve a Movement Skill

Have student videotape himself performing a skill that utilizes the principles associated with spin and rebound. Then have student write an essay analyzing his performance in terms of the scientific principles associated with spin and rebound.

2.3 Creates a Team Game With Scoring Options and a Penalty System

Have groups of four create and teach a game to another group.

3.0 Sets Personal Goals for Participating in Physical Activities in and out of School, Then Participates and Monitors Progress

Throughout the school year, have student maintain a chart of participation in fitness activities outside of class.

4.0 Assesses Personal Fitness, Compares Scores to Health-Related Standards, Sets Goals for Improvement or Maintenance, Refines One-Week Personal Fitness Plan, and Implements the Plan

Have student refine a chart, essay, video, or computer program that shows his one-week fitness plan, explaining how it relates to own current fitness level and goals for the year.

5.0   Collaboratively Solves Problems by Analyzing Causes and Potential Solutions in Physical Activity Settings

Have student write an essay describing the extent and quality of own problem solving skills, including analyzing causes of and potential solutions to problems arising during physical activity.

6.1   Analyzes How Growth in Height and Weight Alters the Mechanical Nature of Performance and How It Affects the Selection of Developmentally Appropriate Activities

Have student take one activity and analyze how height and weight relate to performance in the activity, including a discussion of at what point the activity would be developmentally appropriate for children (include how the activity could be modified for children of different ages).

6.2   Describes the Development and Role of Movement-Related Activities and Physical Education in the United States During the 19th and 20th Centuries, and Their Influendes on Physical Activities Today

Have student write an essay on the development of activities and physical education in the late 1800s and the relationship with what was going on in society at that time.

7.0   Appreciates the Aesthetic Features or Stylistic Differences of Someone Else's Approach to Movement Activities

Have student write an essay describing how participation in dance allows for self-expression and feelings of satisfaction.

For this unit, I present students with the 10 standards for the eighth grade and ask them to present evidence of their learning related to each standard. For some of the standards, students will be able to demonstrate their learning by looking through their working portfolios and pulling from work that they have already accomplished during the year. For other standards, students will be able to pull from interdisciplinary projects that they have accomplished throughout the year. For still other standards, students will need to create new projects during this closure unit to demonstrate their learning. Once the students have collected their evidence, it goes into their performance portfolios. Then I ask students to write a reflection paper (a one-page essay) on their cumulative learning throughout eighth grade physical education.

Ideally with eighth grade students, you and your students' other teachers should assign a final eighth grade project that incorporates all subject areas, affording students the opportunity to demonstrate their learning in all subject areas. Teachers in all subject areas should give students time to work on the eighth grade project as well as offer appropriate guidance. Thus, this closure unit is not only an opportunity for students to complete their physical education or comprehensive portfolios but also an opportunity to complete their eighth grade projects. In order to link the eighth grade project to real life, you and your colleagues should allow students to select the content they wish to investigate and create an opportunity to exhibit the projects. Often, schools invite community members into the school to the presentations of the eighth graders' final projects. These presentations can take the form of speeches, multimedia presentations, video reports, and demonstrations.

Like the introductory and pretesting unit, you can conduct this unit in just about any facility. But if you have students perform exercises on the ground or grass, provide them with carpet squares or some other material so they don't get dirty. An indoor facility is also helpful for the project development phase of this unit. Many times, teachers also reserve the library or at least make arrangements for some of their students to do research in the library. Of course, the equipment necessary to implement the unit depends on the fitness tests you plan to administer. I will be administering the same Prudential FITNESSGRAM tests that I gave at the beginning of the school year and during sixth and seventh grade. Once again, I'll have the students enter their fitness posttest scores into their own electronic portfolios so that they and I can compare the latest scores to pretests, standards, and goals and calculate their progress over the last three years. You'll also need to make sure students have access to reference books, CD-ROMs, computers, videotape players, monitors, camcorders, and other materials to assist with project development.

Unit Standards

1.0 – Applies the correct techniques for locomotor, nonlocomotor, and manipulative skills to sport-specific skills in a variety of team-related activities.

2.1 – Applies the principle of transfer of learning in order to facilitate the learning of a new skill.

2.2 – Analyzes movement performances in terms of scientific principles associated with spin and rebound in order to learn or improve a movement skill.

2.3 – Creates a team game with scoring options.

3.0 – Sets personal goals for participation in physical activity, then participates and monitors own progress.

4.0 – Reassesses personal fitness, comparing scores to pretest scores, health standards, and personal goals, then finalizes one-week fitness plan.

5.0 – Solves problems by analyzing causes and potential solutions in physical activity settings.

6.1 – Analyzes how growth in height and weight alters the mechanical nature of performance and how it influences the selection of developmentally appropriate activities.

6.2 – Describes the development and role of movement-related activities and physical education in the United States during the 19th and 20th centuries and their influence on physical activities today.

7.0 – Appreciates the aesthetic features or stylistic differences of someone else's approach to movement activities.

Unit Outline

Day 1

Assign students to work in groups of four.

Remind students why you administer fitness tests twice a year.   **4.0**

Remind students why you administer the one-mile run test.   **4.0**

Administer the one-mile run test to half the class at a time, while the other half assists with administering the test by counting laps. (Assessment opportunity: fitness test.)   **4.0**

Day 2

Describe projects and portfolios students must complete in this unit.   **1.0-7.0**

Describe the project and portfolio design steps.   **1.0-7.0**

Have students begin to work on their projects and portfolios.   **1.0-7.0**

Remind students why you administer the curl-up test.   **4.0**

Administer the curl-up test to one group at a time. (Assessment opportunity: fitness test.)   **4.0**

Day 3

Remind students why you administer the skinfold or body mass index test.   **4.0**

Have students work on their projects and portfolios.   **1.0-7.0**

Administer the skinfold or body mass index test to one student at a time in private. (Assessment opportunity: fitness test.)   **4.0**

Day 4

Remind students why you administer the back-saver sit-and-reach or shoulder stretch and trunk lift tests. **4.0**

Have students work on their projects and portfolios. **1.0-7.0**

Administer the back-saver sit-and-reach or shoulder stretch test and trunk lift tests to one group at a time. (Assessment opportunity: fitness test.) **4.0**

Day 5

Remind students why you administer the push-up, flexed arm hang, modified pull-up, or pull-up test. **4.0**

Have students work on their projects and portfolios. **1.0-7.0**

Administer the push-up, flexed arm hang, modified pull-up or pull-up test to one group at a time. (Assessment opportunity: fitness test.) **4.0**

Day 6

Administer makeup fitness tests to one group at a time. (Assessment opportunity: fitness test.) **4.0**

Have students work on their projects and portfolios. **1.0-7.0**

Days 7 Through 12

Have students work on their projects and portfolios. **1.0-7.0**

Day 13

Have groups share their projects and portfolios with one other team. **1.0-7.0**

Day 14

Have groups share their projects and portfolios with one other team. **1.0-7.0**

Day 15

Debrief projects, portfolios, and the entire year. (Assessment opportunity: portfolios and projects.) **1.0-7.0**

Summary

Use the ideas and model outline in this sample year-long curriculum for the eighth grade as a guide for your own planning, keeping in mind that this is one sample and not the definitive eighth grade program. Your particular environment, standards, student needs, and faculty will shape your eighth grade program. Indeed, throughout your entire middle school program, be flexible, creative, and innovative when developing the program that is best for *your* situation.

Characteristics of Middle School Students

Intellectual Development

1. Display a wide range of individual intellectual development as their minds experience transition from the concrete-manipulatory stage to the capacity for abstract thought. This transition ultimately makes possible:

   - Propositional thought
   - Consideration of ideas contrary to fact
   - Reasoning with hypotheses involving two or more variables
   - Appreciation for the elegance of mathematical logic expressed in symbols
   - Insight into the nuances of poetic metaphor and musical notation
   - Analysis of the power of a political ideology
   - Ability to project thought into the future, to anticipate, and to formulate goals
   - Insight into the sources of previously unquestioned attitudes, behaviors, and values
   - Interpretation of larger concepts and generalizations of traditional wisdom expressed through sayings, axioms, and aphorisms

2. Are intensely curious;

3. Prefer active over passive learning experiences; favor interaction with peers during learning activities;

4. Exhibit a strong willingness to learn things they consider to be useful; enjoy using skills to solve real life problems;

5. Are egocentric; argue to convince others; exhibit independent, critical thought;

6. Consider academic goals as a secondary level of priority; personal-social concerns dominate thoughts and activities;

7. Experience the phenomenon of metacognition—the ability to know what one knows and does not know;

8. Are intellectually at-risk; face decisions that have the potential to affect major academic values with lifelong consequences.

Physical Development

1. Experience accelerated physical development marked by increases in weight, height, heart size, lung capacity, and muscular strength;

2. Mature at varying rates of speed. Girls tend to be taller than boys for the first two years of early adolescence and are ordinarily more physically developed than boys;

3. Experience bone growth faster than muscle development; uneven muscle/bone development results in lack of coordination and awkwardness; bones may lack protection of covering muscles and supporting tendons;

4. Reflect a wide range of individual differences which begin to appear in prepubertal and pubertal stages of development. Boys tend to lag behind girls. There are marked individual differences in physical development for boys and girls. The greatest variability in physiological development and size occurs at about age thirteen;

5. Experience biological development five years sooner than adolescents of the last century; the average age of menarche has dropped from seventeen to twelve years of age;

6. Face responsibility for sexual behavior before full emotional and social maturity has occurred;

7. Show changes in body contour including temporarily large noses, protruding ears, long arms; have posture problems;

8. Are often disturbed by body changes:

   Girls are anxious about physical changes that accompany sexual maturation

   Boys are anxious about receding chins, cowlicks, dimples, and changes in their voices;

9. Experience fluctuations in basal metabolism which can cause extreme restlessness at times and equally extreme listlessness at other moments;

10. Have ravenous appetites and peculiar tastes; may overtax digestive system with large quantities of improper foods;

11. Lack physical health; have poor levels of endurance, strength, and flexibility; as a group are fatter and unhealthier;

12. Are physically at-risk; major causes of death are homicide, suicide, accident, and leukemia.

Psychological Development

1. Are often erratic and inconsistent in their behavior; anxiety and fear are contrasted with periods of bravado; feelings shift between superiority and inferiority;

2. Have chemical and hormonal imbalances which often trigger emotions that are frightening and poorly understood; may regress to more childish behavior patterns at this point;

3. Are easily offended and are sensitive to criticism of personal shortcomings;

4. Tend to exaggerate simple occurrences and believe that personal problems, experiences, and feelings are unique to themselves;

5. Are moody, restless; often self-conscious and alienated; lack self-esteem; are introspective;

6. Are searching for adult identity and acceptance even in the midst of intense peer group relationships;

7. Are vulnerable to naive opinions, one-sided arguments;

8. Are searching to form a conscious sense of individual uniqueness—"Who am I?";

9. Have emerging sense of humor based on increased intellectual ability to see abstract relationships; appreciate the "double entendre";

10. Are basically optimistic, hopeful;

11. Are psychologically at-risk; at no other point in human development is an individual likely to encounter so much diversity in relation to oneself and others.

Social Development

1. Experience often traumatic conflicts due to conflicting loyalties to peer groups and family;

2. Refer to peers as sources for standards and models of behavior; media heroes and heroines are also singularly important in shaping both behavior and fashion;

3. May be rebellious towards parents but still strongly dependent on parental values; want to make own choices, but the authority of the family is a critical factor in ultimate decisions;

4. Are impacted by high level of mobility in society; may become anxious and disoriented when

peer group ties are broken because of family relocation to other communities;

5. Are often confused and frightened by new school settings which are large and impersonal;

6. Act out unusual or drastic behavior at times; may be aggressive, daring, boisterous, argumentative;

7. Are fiercely loyal to peer group values; sometimes cruel or insensitive to those outside the peer group;

8. Want to know and feel that significant adults, including parents and teachers, love and accept them; need frequent affirmation;

9. Sense negative impact of adolescent behaviors on parents and teachers; realize thin edge between tolerance and rejection; feelings of adult rejection drive the adolescent into the relatively secure social environment of the peer group;

10. Strive to define sex role characteristics; search to establish positive social relationships with members of the same and opposite sex;

11. Experience low risk-trust relationships with adults who show lack of sensitivity to adolescent characteristics and needs;

12. Challenge authority figures; test limits of acceptable behavior;

13. Are socially at-risk; adult values are largely shaped conceptually during adolescence; nega-

tive interactions with peers, parents, and teachers may compromise ideals and commitments.

Moral and Ethical Development

1. Are essentially idealistic; have a strong sense of fairness in human relationships;

2. Experience thoughts and feelings of awe and wonder related to their expanding intellectual and emotional awareness;

3. Ask large, unanswerable questions about the meaning of life; do not expect absolute answers but are turned off by trivial adult responses;

4. Are reflective, analytical, and introspective about their thoughts and feelings;

5. Confront hard moral and ethical questions for which they are unprepared to cope;

6. Are at-risk in the development of moral and ethical choices and behaviors; primary dependency on the influences of home and church for moral and ethical development seriously compromises adolescents for whom these resources are absent; adolescents want to explore the moral and ethical issues which are confronted in the curriculum, in the media, and in the daily interactions they experience in their families and peer groups.

Reprinted, by permission, from *Caught in the middle: Educational reform for young adolescents in California public schools*, copyright 1987, California Department of Education, 515 L Street #250, Sacramento, CA 95814.

Middle School Grade Level Standards

Sample Sixth Grade Standards With Critical Information

1.0 – Applies the correct techniques for locomotor, nonlocomotor, and manipulative skills in a variety of cooperative activities.

- Locomotor skills consist of walking, running, jumping, hopping, skipping, leaping, galloping, and sliding.

- Nonlocomotor skills consist of curling, stretching, twisting, bending, turning, swinging, and swaying.

- Manipulative skills consist of throwing, catching, striking with body parts (including kicking and dribbling), striking with objects, and trapping.

- Cooperative activities consist of problem solving initiatives, stunts, tumbling, circus skills, tinikling, jump rope, dance, lead-up games, games from ancient civilizations, and games created by students.

2.1 – Gives appropriate feedback to a partner while developing or improving movement skills.

- Feedback improves the learning of motor skills by providing error detection and motivation for the learner.

- Feedback is based on the critical elements for each skill.

- Only one or two corrections should be identified for feedback after each performance.

- Feedback is delayed for a few seconds after the performance to give the performer an opportunity to reflect on his or her own performance.

- Feedback is given when the performer cannot see the result of the performance (e.g., technique).

- Feedback is not given when the performer can see the result of the performance (e.g., accuracy, speed, or distance).

- Feedback is most helpful when it is specific and meaningful.

- Feedback should be given frequently in the early stages of learning and then tapered off.

2.2 – Analyzes movement performance using Newton's Third Law in order to learn or improve a movement skill.

- For every action there is an equal and opposite reaction.
- When an object is contacted, it will rebound in the opposite direction with the same amount of force with which it was contacted.

2.3 – Creates a cooperative game by combining a variety of locomotor, nonlocomotor, and manipulative skills.

- A cooperative game requires players to work together for a common goal.
- The game's equipment consists of one or more objects.
- The organization pattern, player movement, limitations (rules), and penalties are determined by the creator.
- There is at least one means of scoring.

3.0 – Participates daily in some form of physical activity based on personal interests and capabilities.

- Trying a number of different activities increases the probability of finding a few activities of interest.
- Recording strengths and weaknesses in an activity helps to determine the activities of interest.
- Identifying physical activities, available in and out of school, helps to determine the activities of interest.

4.0 – Assesses personal fitness, compares scores to health-related standards, sets goals for improvement or maintenance, and develops a one-day personal fitness plan.

- All five areas (cardiorespiratory endurance, muscular strength, muscular endurance, flexibility, and body composition) of health-related fitness are assessed.
- Setting goals based on pretest scores, self-testing, and monitoring scores leads to improvement in health-related fitness.
- Warm-up exercises prepare the body for activity by raising body temperature for better oxygen delivery to muscles, improved muscle relaxation, improved coordination, and better utilization of fat for fuel.
- Cooldown, slow static stretching, is needed to prevent lactic acid buildup in muscles (soreness) following vigorous exercise.
- Flexibility exercises are held to the point of strain, but not pain, for 20-60 seconds.

- Cardiorespiratory exercises (e.g., swimming, dancing, jogging) are performed for fifteen to sixty minutes within the individual's target heart rate zone.
- Target heart rate range is calculated by: [(maximum heart rate (220) – age) × 70-85%].
- Muscular strength (the ability to lift something very heavy one time) exercises involve lifting a heavy object between 5 and 8 times for three sets.
- Muscular endurance (the ability to lift something light many times) exercises involve lifting a light object between 8 and 20 times for three sets.
- Body composition is a result of food intake and exercising. To lose one pound of fat, you must decrease your caloric intake by 3500 calories or increase your calorie expenditure by 3500 calories, or a combination of decreasing caloric intake and increasing caloric expenditure that equals 3500 calories (e.g., decrease your caloric intake by 1500 and increase your caloric expenditure by 2000).
- Application of the principle of specificity (there are specific exercises for each area of health-related fitness), principle of regularity (each exercise must be performed on a regular basis), principle of individuality (each person's exercise program is different), principle of progression (start off slow and increase gradually), and principle of overload (increase intensity gradually over time) lead to the improvement of the five health-related fitness areas.
- Participation in a wide variety of exercises during the school day and at home leads to improvement in health-related fitness.

5.0 – Works cooperatively and productively in a group to accomplish goals in physical activity settings.

- Cooperative skills are the social skills that help a group complete its task and build positive feelings among the group.
- Examples of cooperative skills include active listening, encouragement, courtesy, positive disagreement, and acceptance of personal differences.
- The setting of goals is based on the group's current level of ability.

6.1 – Analyzes the variables of physical development within his peer group and their effect on movement performance as he works cooperatively with both more- and less-skilled peers.

- The variables of physical development that affect motor performance include: skill-related fitness (coordination, balance, agility, reaction time, power, and speed), physical characteristics (body built, height, weight, vision, hearing, touch) and health-related fitness (muscular strength, flexibility, muscular endurance, cardiorespiratory endurance, and body composition).

- Girls are typically taller than boys from ten to thirteen and boys are typically taller after thirteen years of age.

- Adolescent boys have wider shoulders and adolescent girls have wider hips.

- Boys continue to improve their motor performance after puberty, but girls tend not to improve; this fact seems to be strongly influenced by culture.

- Individuals proceed through similar stages on their way to learning skills, but each progresses at a different rate.

- The opportunity to receive instruction and to practice gives students an advantage with motor performance.

- Equipment needs to be appropriate for the developmental stage.

- Exercise and diet promote bone and muscle growth which has a positive affect on motor performance.

- Attempting to teach students skills before they are physically ready is often frustrating and can sometimes be harmful if they have not yet developed the skeletal and muscular strength necessary for the skills.

6.2 – Describes the development and role of movement-related activities and physical education in the ancient world and their influences on physical activities today.

- The role of games, sports, and dance helps in getting to know and understand people of diverse cultures.

- In Babylon about 5000 years ago, boys and girls played with spinning tops.

- A game very much like field hockey was played thousands of years ago in ancient Egypt and Persia according to paintings in tombs in the Nile River Valley.

- Archaeologists have found a set of nine stone pins (bowling) in a child's tomb dated 5200 B.C. in Egypt.

- Early Olympic Games had only one event, the Stade, a footrace of about 200 meters; additional events were added each year (wrestling, Pentathlon, chariot races, boxing, race in armor).

- Athenian men spent much of their day at the gymnasium where they took part in sports such as boxing, discus and javelin throwing, and wrestling.

- Children in ancient Greece swung in swings.

- It is believed that the ancient Greeks began the sport of gymnastics.

- Romans enjoyed ball games based on throwing and catching and a form of handball.

- The skill of kicking was introduced by the Romans.

- Roman bath houses, where men participated in strenuous types of exercises like swinging lead weights, were popular between 4 B.C. and 65 A.D.

- Romans enjoyed chariot racing and gladiator contests.

- In ancient Athens, gymnastics and music (academics) were the two components of the curriculum.

- Physical education activities in Athens commenced at about age seven and began with general physical conditioning.

- Physical education in Athens included boxing, wrestling, jumping, ball games, games with hoops, military skills, running, wrestling, dancing, javelin and discus throwing, and the pancratium (a combination of boxing and wrestling).

- Wealthy Athenian families hired a paidotribe (physical education teacher) who owned his own palaestra (wrestling center) and charged a fee similar to today's private health clubs.

- Athenian women did not receive instruction in physical education.

- In Rome, the training or physical education of youth had one purpose: to make them obedient, disciplined, and ready to be a warrior. Children were taught running, jumping, swimming, wrestling, horsemanship, boxing, fencing, and archery.

- The ancient Chinese flew kites.
- Spartan approach of physical training was strictly for military purposes.
- Spartan youths were instructed in swimming, running, fighting, wrestling, boxing, ball games, horsemanship, archery, discus and javelin throwing, field marches, and pancratium.
- Spartan women participated in gymnastic exercises (military and physical training).

7.0 – Analyzes patterns in physical activities to determine the influence that the qualities of movement have on the aesthetic impact of these activities.

- Combinations of qualities of movement including time, space, energy, and flow form the basis for aesthetics.
- Aesthetic impact reflects the differences we see in the performance of the same skill.
- The aesthetic impact is influenced by taste (what people like) and is only a part of the entire impact of the experience.
- The aesthetic impact has some relatively stable intrinsic components and some extrinsic components which can be improved and changed.

Modified from Region 9's *Physical Education Curriculum*, 1994 and NASPE's *National Physical Education Standards: A Guide to Content and Assessment*, 1995.

Sample Seventh Grade Standards With Critical Information

1.0 – Applies the correct techniques for locomotor, nonlocomotor, and manipulative skills to appropriate risk-taking activities.

- Locomotor skills consist of walking, running, jumping, hopping, skipping, leaping, galloping, and sliding.
- Nonlocomotor skills consist of curling, stretching, twisting, bending, turning, swinging, and swaying.
- Manipulative skills consist of throwing, catching, striking with body parts (including kicking and dribbling), striking with objects, and trapping.
- Appropriate risk-taking activities consist of tumbling and gymnastics, outdoor education activities, self-defense, aquatics, racket games, golf, track and field, and Medieval games.

2.1 – Sets goals and monitors changes in the development of movement skills in order to improve performance.

- Setting goals, based on current ability, improves the learning of motor skills.
- Monitoring change in motor skill development based on the type of improvement desired (e.g., accuracy, distance, technique) improves the learning of motor skills.

2.2 – Analyzes movement performance using rotation principles in order to learn or improve a movement skill.

- Force should be applied away from the center of gravity if the object is to rotate.
- Direction of rotation is determined by the specific location where force is applied to the object.
- The shorter the radius of rotation, the greater the angular velocity or speed of rotation.
- The longer the radius of rotation the greater the force.
- Angular motion can increase linear speed if the point of release or transfer is at a right angle to the center of rotation.
- If linear movement is desired, force should be applied in line with an object's center of gravity.

2.3 – Creates an individual or dual game with scoring options and a penalty system.

- An individual or dual game consists of one or two players per team.
- The game's equipment consists of one or more objects.
- The organization pattern, player movement, limitations (rules), and penalties are determined by the creator.
- In order for the game to be played fairly, points for various scoring methods are based on the degree of difficulty of the task or challenge.

3.0 – Participates daily in some form of physical activity, including new and appropriate risk-taking activities.

- Selecting new or appropriate risk-taking activities for oneself increases the probability of future participation in the activity.
- Keeping track of accomplishments serves as an incentive for trying new activities.

4.0 – Assesses personal fitness, compares scores to health-related standards, sets goals for improvement or maintenance, and designs a one-week personal fitness plan.

- In addition to criteria for sixth grade standard 4.0, the following are included:
  — Flexibility exercises are performed four to six days per week.
  — Cardiorespiratory exercises (e.g., swimming, dancing, jogging) are performed four to six days per week.
  — Muscular strength and muscular endurance exercises are performed three to four days per week.
  — Basal metabolic rate and caloric output are compared to caloric intake to determine whether weight loss or gain will occur.

5.0 – Applies collaborative problem solving techniques in physical activity settings.

- The problem solving process includes the following steps:
  — Definition of the problem
  — Generation of the possible solutions
  — Selection and implementation of a solution
  — Testing for the success of the solution

6.1 – Explains the growth rates of body segments and how they relate to movement experiences.

- At birth the head is 1/2 adult size (25% of body length), but the legs are 1/5 adult length (30% of body length); making it impossible for the legs to support the body weight.
- At six the head makes up only 15% of total height, while the legs are nearly 40% of an individual's height; making it much easier to run, jump, and throw.
- Arms and legs grow faster than the rest of the body between age one and puberty.
- After birth, bone growth in length occurs at each end of the bone shaft called the growth plate.
- The potential exists for severe injury to the epiphyseal plate, since an accident can cut off the blood supply resulting in early cessation of growth at the site.
- The trunk grows most rapidly between puberty and mature stature.
- Longer limbs provide better leverage if accompanied by an increase in strength.

6.2 – Describes the development and role of movement-related activities and physical education during Medieval times and their influences on physical activities today.

- Ball games continued to be popular during the Middle Ages.
- Soule, which resembles the modern game of soccer with an indeterminate number of men on each side, was especially popular.
- Popular tournaments included joust (two mounted horsemen charging one another with long, wooden lances with the object to knock each other off the horse) and melee (groups of opposing knights engaging in hand-to-hand combat with dull swords).
- Other popular pastimes included hawking, hunting, le jeu de paume (form of handball), royal tennis, shuffleboard, billiards, and board games.
- Music, games, and dancing became acceptable pastimes during the Renaissance. Popular opinion of the time did not consider the activities evil, but rather that they contributed to good health.
- Abbasid rulers enjoyed recreation like falconry and backgammon.
- During the Middle Ages, the "ordinary" people enjoyed blood sports such as cock fighting, foot fighting, and wrestling.
- Leading educators of the Renaissance incorporated physical education into their educational curricula.
- The role of physical education during the Renaissance began to be looked upon for both military and health benefits. Students participated in games, riding, running, leaping, fencing, ball games, and during the summer would go hiking and camping.
- During the age of science, sport and physical education were more easily justified as philosophers came to accept the material world and the place bodies occupy in it.
- During the Renaissance period, new concern for hygiene brought an emphasis on swimming and water safety.
- Orienteering began as a Swedish military exercise.
- French played a game similar to tennis in 1300 when they batted the ball with an open hand.

- Romans, during the reign of Caesar, played a game resembling golf by striking a feather-stuffed ball with club-shaped branches.

- Dutch played a similar game on their frozen canals around the 15th century.

- In 1457 golf was banned in Scotland because it interfered with archery practice which was important to national defense.

- Martial arts originated in India among Buddhist monks around the 5th century B.C.

- From India martial arts moved to China then Japan.

7.0 – Appreciates the aesthetic features or stylistic differences of own approach to movement activities.

- Stylistic differences are reflected by altering the qualities of movement.

- Past achievements provide the source of present feelings of competence and confidence.

- Self-expression can be heightened by focusing on aesthetic features of motor skill, including improved form, greater ease, more clarity, and better precision.

- Personal identity can be developed by enhancing strengths and improving on weaknesses.

Modified from Region 9's *Physical Education Curriculum*, 1994 and NASPE's *National Physical Education Standards: A Guide to Content and Assessment*, 1995.

Sample Eighth Grade Standards With Critical Information

1.0 – Applies the correct techniques for locomotor, nonlocomotor, and manipulative skills to sport-specific skills in a variety of team-related activities.

- Locomotor skills consist of walking, running, jumping, hopping, skipping, leaping, galloping, and sliding.

- Nonlocomotor skills consist of curling, stretching, twisting, bending, turning, swinging, and swaying.

- Manipulative skills consist of throwing, catching, striking with body parts (including kicking and dribbling), striking with objects, and trapping.

- Team-related activities consist of softball, volleyball, basketball, team handball, soccer, speed-a-way, football, square dance, and Project Adventure.

2.1 – Applies the principle of transfer of learning in order to facilitate the learning of a new skill.

- Positive transfer occurs when previous learning has a favorable effect on new learning.

- Negative transfer occurs when prior learning interferes with learning new information or skills, or new skills interfere with previously learned tasks.

- Positive transfer occurs when there are a number of identical critical elements.

- Greater positive transfer occurs when the first task is well learned.

- Greater positive transfer occurs when similarities are pointed out to the learner.

2.2 – Analyzes movement performance using spin and rebound principles in order to learn or improve a movement skill.

- Spin results when force is applied away from an object's center of gravity.

- The object will spin in the direction the force is applied.

- Force below the center of gravity causes backward rotation (back spin) which results in the ball staying in the air longer, bouncing higher but shorter width and rolling a shorter distance.

- Force applied above the center of gravity causes forward rotating (top spin) which results in a quick drop with a longer but lower bounce and lengthened roll.

- Top spin increases velocity after impact.

- Back spin decreases velocity after impact.

- Spin is altered by the rebound angle and the elasticity of the object.

- A ball will rebound at an angle equal to that at which it strikes a surface unless the rebound is altered by the elasticity of the ball, the firmness of the surface, or the spin.

2.3 – Creates a team game with scoring options and a penalty system.

- A team consists of three or more players.

- The game's equipment consists of one or more objects.

- The organization pattern, player movement, limitations (rules), and penalties are determined by the creator.

- In order for the game to be played fairly, points for various scoring methods are based on the degree of difficulty of the task or challenge.

3.0 – Sets personal goals for participating in physical activities in and out of school, then participates and monitors progress.

- Writing down goals leads to a greater probability of the goals being met.

- Basing the goals on personal preferences and abilities increases the probability of the goals being met.

- Monitoring participation increases the probability of participation.

4.0 – Assesses personal fitness, compares scores to health-related standards, sets goals for improvement or maintenance, refines one-week personal fitness plan, and implements the plan.

- In addition to the criteria for sixth and seventh grade standard 4.0, the following are also included:

  — A more sophisticated target heart rate range calculation is: ((maximum heart rate (220) – age) – resting heart rate) × 60%-80% + resting heart rate.

  — Based on implementation progress and current fitness levels, the fitness plan is revised.

5.0 – Collaboratively solves problems by analyzing causes and potential solutions in physical activity settings.

- In addition to the criteria for seventh grade standard 5.0, the following are included:

  — Five basic steps in negotiating a resolution for a conflict of interests

  — Jointly defining the conflict

  — Exchanging reasons and rationale for their positions

  — Revising perspectives

  — Inventing options for mutual benefit

  — Reaching a wise agreement

6.1 – Analyzes how growth in height and weight alters the mechanical nature of performance and how it affects the selection of developmentally appropriate activities.

- Tall people tend to perform better in skills like the high jump.

- Shorter people tend to perform better at skills like gymnastics.

- Differences in weight distribution cause a higher or lower center of gravity. An individual with a lower center of gravity is more stable than an individual with a higher center of gravity.

- Longer limbs provide better leverage if accompanied by an increase in strength.

6.2 – Describes the development and role of movement-related activities and physical education in the United States during the 19th and 20th centuries, and their influences on physical activities today.

- The playground and recreation movements developed as an outgrowth of the Industrial Revolution with a concern about the poor health of children and the lack of space in which they could play.

- The first organized playground in the United States began in Boston in 1885.

- Sports and games became more popular as leisure time increased for the general population.

- The year 1896 marked the revival of the Olympic Games in Athens, Greece.

- Public schools showed little interest in physical education until the 1850s when some cities allowed a few minutes of calisthenics in the daily curriculum. In 1853, Boston became the first city to require daily exercise for school children.

- The Morrill Act of 1862 required military instruction in all state colleges, and affected physical education in the schools and colleges due to the inclusion of military drill as a form of physical activity. After the Civil War attention shifted to a strong emphasis toward physical exercise for the purpose of improving and maintaining a healthy body.

- During the late 1800s, training institutions specifically trained individuals for roles in physical education.

- By 1921 there was compulsory public school physical education in twenty-eight states.

- Team handball originated in Europe in late 1920s.

- The Greeks, Egyptians, Chinese, Japanese, Romans, and Native Americans all played games very similar to soccer.

- In 1863 soccer became an official school game, complete with rules and regulations.

- Dr. James A. Naismith introduced basketball to a class at the YMCA in Springfield, Massachusetts in 1891 as an indoor activity during bad weather and he used peach baskets on a gym rail as the first baskets.

- Speed-a-way was created in the 1940s at Edison High School in Stockton, California as a game that would serve as a lead-up game for field hockey.

- Present game of football began at Harvard University in spring of 1871 using a soccer ball and many of the soccer rules except players could pick up the ball and run with it. After being exposed to rugby, the Harvard football players adopted the oval-shaped rugby ball along with many of the rules.

- Volleyball originated in the United States in 1895 by William C. Morgan of Springfield College. The game was first played with the bladder of a basketball over a tennis net. Early version of game allowed for any number of players on the court, each server had three outs, and the game was played for nine innings. The new game was liked by businessmen at YMCA as a less strenuous alternative to basketball.

- Rounders, an older form of baseball, was around in the 1500s. Indoor baseball with larger balls, smaller bats, and modified rules originated in 1887 because baseball players wanted some sort of winter activity. When indoor baseball moved out doors it was first named playground ball and later softball.

- John Playford's epochal book, *English Dancing Master* published March 19, 1651, is credited with producing the movement from which American square dancing emerged. In the early 1800s dancing masters worked out sequences of moves that were memorized by the dancers.

- During the War of 1812 an American invented "calling" by a fiddler in the orchestra which made it unnecessary to memorize the dance steps. By 1890, a decline in square dancing began due to conservative masters of dance attacking swinging and dancers having to listen for the next step.

- In 1925 Henry Ford started a movement to bring back square dancing in order to counteract what he considered the evils of jazz.

7.0 – Appreciates the aesthetic features or stylistic differences of someone else's approach to movement activities.

- Stylistic differences are reflected by altering the qualities of movement.

- Assessment of another's performance is influenced by personal preference.

- Emphasis on the aesthetic features or stylistic differences allows for individual differences in the performance of the skill.

Modified from Region 9's *Physical Education Curriculum*, 1994 and NASPE's *National Physical Education Standards: A Guide to Content and Assessment*, 1995.

Exercises and Activities

Warm-Up Exercises

Jog in Place

Stay in stationary position.

Jog in place raising knees so thighs are parallel to the ground.

Jog One Lap

Slowly jog a designated distance.

Hop, Jump, or Jog in Place

On signal (one, two, or three whistles or taps on the tambourine), hop, jump, or jog.

Four Corners

Set up four cones in a rectangle, each with a sign listing one of the eight locomotor skills (walking, leaping, hopping, running, skipping, galloping, sliding, and jumping).

Staying on the outside of the rectangle, perform the locomotor skill listed on the sign until reaching the next cone, then change the locomotor skill accordingly.

Walk One Lap

Walk a designated distance starting slowly and gradually increasing speed.

Flexibility Exercises

Neck Roller

Stand.

Tuck chin to chest.

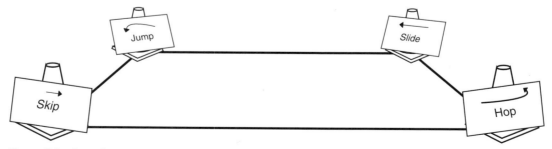

Figure C.1 Four Corners.

Rotate neck so left ear is over left shoulder.

Rotate neck so right ear is over right shoulder.

Shoulder Shrugs

Stand.

Raise both shoulders toward ear lobes.

Lower both shoulders.

Arm Lift

Grasp hands behind lower back.

Raise arms as high as possible.

Triceps Stretch (Elbow Pull)

Reach right hand over right shoulder and down the back.

Place left hand on right elbow.

Gently push on right elbow.

Switch arms and repeat.

Shoulder Stretch

Reach right arm across the chest, parallel to the ground.

Place left hand on right elbow.

Gently push right elbow.

Switch arms and repeat.

Low Back Flattener

Lie on back with knees bent at a 90-degree angle.

Press lower back into ground.

Low Back Stretch

Lie on back with knees bent at a 90-degree angle.

Grab the back of one thigh with both hands.

Pull thigh toward chest, keeping the knee at a 90-degree angle.

Switch legs and repeat.

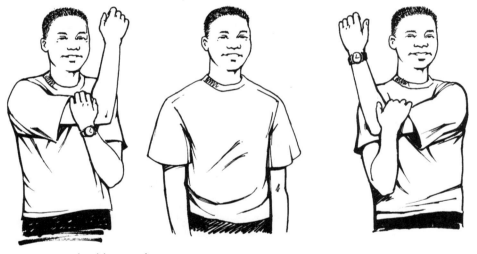

Figure C.2   Shoulder stretch.

Figure C.3   Low back stretch.

Figure C.4 Reverse hurdle stretch.

Reverse Hurdle Stretch

Sit with one leg extended and the other leg bent so that the sole of the foot is alongside the extended knee.

Bend the extended knee slightly.

Reach both hands toward toes of extended leg.

Switch legs and repeat.

Forward Lunge

Stand and extend one leg forward with knee bent at a 90-degree angle.

Lean forward so weight is over bent leg.

Keep rear leg extended.

Switch legs and repeat.

Calf Stretch

Stand three feet from a wall.

Lean toward the wall and place both hands on the wall in a push-up position.

Bend both elbows.

Muscular Endurance and Strength Exercises

Measuring Worm

Assume a push-up position.

Keep knees straight.

Walk feet toward hands.

Walk hands forward into push-up position.

Leg Change (Treadmill)

Assume a push-up position with one leg straight and the other bent.

Switch legs and repeat.

Figure C.5 Forward lunge.

Figure C.6 Calf stretch.

Figure C.7 Measuring worm.

Seal Walk

Assume a push-up position with tops of feet on the ground.

Walk hands forward dragging feet.

Keep body straight and head up.

Wall Push-Up

Stand three feet from wall and lean forward with both hands flat on the wall.

Lower body toward the wall by bending the elbows.

Keep body straight.

Raise body away from wall by extending the elbows.

Table Push-Up

Assume push-up position with hands on table.

Lower body toward table by bending the elbows.

Keep body straight.

Figure C.8 Leg change.

Figure C.9 Seal walk.

Raise body away from table by extending the elbows.

Chair Push-Up

Assume push-up position with hands on seat of chair.

Lower body toward chair by bending the elbows.

Keep body straight.

Raise body away from chair by extending the elbows.

Bench Push-Up

Assume push-up position with hands on bench.

Lower body toward bench by bending the elbows.

Keep body straight.

Raise body away from bench by extending the elbows.

Modified Push-Up

Assume push-up position with hands and knees on the floor.

Lower body toward floor by bending the elbows.

Keep body straight.

Raise body away from floor by extending the elbows.

Push-Up

Place both hands flat on the floor shoulder-width apart with body extended and weight on toes.

Lower body toward floor by bending the elbows.

Keep body straight.

Raise body away from floor by extending the elbows.

Elevated Push-Up

Assume push-up position with toes elevated on a bench, chair, or other object.

Lower body toward floor by bending the elbows.

Keep body straight.

Raise body away from floor by extending the elbows.

Negative Pull-Up

Set bar higher than the individual's reach.

Grasp bar with palms facing away from body.

Keep hands shoulder-width apart.

Raise chin above bar, using a chair or partner to get into elevated position.

Lower body until the arms are fully extended.

Modified Pull-Up

Set bar at chest height.

Grasp bar with palms facing away from body.

Keep hands shoulder-width apart.

Align chest directly below bar.

Raise body toward an elastic band strung seven to eight inches below and parallel to the bar by bending the elbows.

Keep body straight.

Lower body away from elastic band by extending the elbows.

Assisted Pull-Up

Set bar higher than the individual's reach.

Grasp bar with palms facing away from body.

Keep hands shoulder-width apart with body hanging.

Bend knees and cross lower legs.

Raise body toward the bar by bending elbows while letting a partner assist by pushing on lower legs where they cross.

Lower body away from bar by extending elbows.

Pull-Up

Set bar higher than the individual's reach.

Grasp bar with palms facing away from body.

Keep hands shoulder-width apart with body hanging.

Raise body toward the bar by bending elbows.

Lower body away from bar by extending elbows.

Rope Climb

Extend arms over head and grab rope with both hands.

Wrap one leg around the rope.

Climb rope using arms and legs.

Sit-Back

Sit with knees bent at 140-degree angle, keeping feet flat on the floor.

Cross arms over chest so hands rest on shoulders and arms touch chest.

Lean back to lying position.

Figure C.10 Modified pull-up

Assisted Sit-Up

Lie on back with knees bent at 140-degree angle.

Hold onto each thigh with one hand.

Pull on thighs to raise upper body so shoulder blades are off the ground.

Return to original position.

Curl-Up

Lie down on back.

Bend knees at 140-degree angle, keeping feet flat on floor and legs slightly apart.

Keep arms straight and parallel to trunk.

Rest palms of hands and head on the mat.

Keep feet in contact with the mat and curl up slowly until shoulder blades are off the ground.

Curl back down until head touches the mat.

Elevated Sit-Up

Lie on back on an elevated board.

Bend knees at 140-degree angle, keeping feet flat on floor and legs slightly apart.

Keep arms straight and parallel to trunk.

Rest palms of hands and head on the mat.

Keep feet in contact with the board and curl up slowly until shoulder blades are off the ground.

Curl back down until head touches the mat.

Cardiorespiratory and Body Composition Exercises

Power Walk

Walk at a pace that maintains the pulse in the target heart rate range.

Jogging

Jog at a pace that maintains the pulse in the target heart rate range.

Jumping Rope

Jump rope at a pace that maintains the pulse in the target heart rate range.

Four Corners

See directions in warm-up section.

Perform the locomotor skills at a pace that maintains the pulse in the target heart rate range.

Walk, Jog, Sprint

Alternate between walking, jogging, and sprinting either on teacher command or own initiative.

Perform walk, jog, and sprint at a pace that maintains the pulse in the target heart rate range.

Jog With Equipment

Jog while dribbling a basketball, dribbling a soccer ball, throwing and catching with a partner, or any other manipulative activity conducive to jogging. Pace must keep pulse in target heart rate range.

File Run

A group of four runs in a single file line with the last runner sprinting to the front and raising her hand to signal the next anchor runner to sprint. Pace must keep pulse in target heart rate range.

Line Dancing

Perform a variety of line dances. Pace must keep pulse in target heart rate range.

Step Aerobics

Using steps, perform aerobic movements to music. Pace must keep pulse in target heart rate range.

Aerobic Dance

Perform aerobic dance movements to music. Pace must keep pulse in target heart rate range.

Activity Descriptions

Acid Pit

Form groups of six.

Use a swinging rope over an imaginary acid pit, which is marked by jump ropes or hula hoops.

Objective is for the group to retrieve the swinging rope and all members of the group to cross the acid pit one at a time without touching the ground.

Across the Great Divide

Form groups of four.

Group members stand side by side with elbows locked and sides of feet touching.

The group must move from point A to point B (approximately 15 feet) keeping their elbows locked and sides of feet touching.

All Aboard

Form groups of eight.

The objective is to get the entire group balanced at once on a 12- by 12-inch platform for at least five seconds.

Both feet of each person must be off the ground.

Amazon

Form groups of four.

Give each group a plank (2 by 6 inches), a sturdy pole (1.5 inches diameter), a piece of rope (20 to 50 feet long), and a broomstick.

The objective is to retrieve a bucket of imaginary water placed some distance (15 to 30 feet) away using only the props provided without touching the ground.

Blind Polygon

Each group consists of four blindfolded people forming a circle holding on to a rope.

Ask groups to form a square, triangle, or some other polygon using the rope.

When a group decides that they have accomplished the task, they remove their blindfolds.

Booop

Form groups of four.

Form a circle and join hands except for person with balloon or beach ball.

To start the game, the person with balloon tosses it in the air and then joins hands with rest of group.

The objective is to keep the balloon in the air while hands remained joined.

Bottoms Up

Pairs sit facing each other with knees bent, feet held high, and soles touching.

The objective is to push against partner's feet until both bottoms are off the ground.

Circle the Circle

Form groups of four.

Join hands and form a circle with a hula hoop around one pair of joined hands.

Pass the hula hoop around the circle without letting go of joined hands.

Courtesy Tag

Keep whole class as one group.

Give each person a scarf.

Tell everyone they are "it."

When someone is tagged, he must go down on one knee and give his scarf to the tagger.

Players may have no more than two scarves in their hands at one time.

Players with two scarves may give one of their scarves to a player who is down.

The player receiving the scarf must say, "Thank you."

Dribble Tag

Keep whole class as one group or form pairs.

Each student has a flag or scarf tucked into waistband.

Each student dribbles a ball with hand or foot.

The objective is to take other players' flags while protecting your own.

Play continues until all flags have been taken.

Everyone Up

Form groups of four.

Sit on the ground in a small circle facing each other so that soles of feet are touching the adjoining person.

Grasp hands tightly with the adjoining person.

The objective is to stand up without letting go of hands.

Everyone Up in Pairs

Sit facing a partner with knees bent and bottoms of toes touching.

Join hands.

The objective is to pull one another up.

Goalie Ball

Form pairs.

One player is the goalie and stands between two markers.

The other player is the thrower or roller and stands behind a parallel line, 10 to 20 feet from the goal.

The thrower or roller gets five tries to throw or roll the ball past the goalie.

Switch positions.

Greeter

Pairs shake hands.

Bend low.

One partner steps over joined hands.

Second partner steps over joined hands.

Partners are now standing bottom-to-bottom.

First partner steps over joined hands with other leg.

Second partner steps over joined hands with other leg.

Partners are now standing face-to-face.

Group Juggle

Six to eight people form a circle with one person holding a ball.

The group determines the order in which they will toss the ball so that everyone in the group catches and throws.

Teacher continues to add more balls that the group must throw in the same order.

Group Juggle With Thank Yous

Four people form a circle with one person holding a ball.

The group determines the order in which they will toss the ball so that everyone in the group catches and throws.

Person throwing the ball calls out the intended receiver's name.

Person catching the ball must say, "Thank you," and the thrower's name.

Teacher continues to add one, two, and then three more balls that must be thrown in the same order.

Put two groups together to form a group of eight.

Repeat the activity.

Human Ladder

Form groups of eight.

Three pairs stand face-to-face, each pair holding a short pole (a rung) between them.

The three pairs line up side-by-side, the six of them forming the sides of the ladder.

The seventh person is the climber and eighth person is the spotter.

The climber starts at one end of the ladder and climbs from rung to rung.

The spotter walks alongside the climber in case the climber falls.

As the climber leaves one rung, that pair moves to the front of the line until the climber completes six rungs.

Ice Breaker

Form groups of four.

Loop a rope around each group three or four times and tie it loosely.

The group moves from point A to point B while each person shares something about themselves.

Once the group reaches point B, each member must repeat what the other members shared.

Inchworm

Pairs face each other, sitting on each other's feet.

Grasp each others elbows or upper arms.

The objective is to move forward or backward with bottoms in the air or on each other's feet.

Interest Circle

Keep whole class as one group.

Form a circle with you as the first leader.

You walk across the circle stating something you have done (e.g., climbed a mountain, swam in the ocean).

Everyone else who has done the same thing also walks across the circle to the other side.

The person currently to the teacher's right is the next person to walk out and state something he or she has done.

Continue so that the person on the right side of the previous leader is the new leader, until everyone has had a turn to be leader or time is up.

Introducer

Keep whole class as one group.

Students walk up to another person to shake hands, introduce themselves, and state something they like to do.

On a signal from the teacher, students change partners.

This time students first describe the last person they shook hands with and then introduce themselves. The activitiy continues for several minutes.

Keep-It-Up

Form groups of four.

Use underhand and overhand one- and two-hand striking skills to keep a ball in the air.

Groups count the number of hits they can make before the ball touches the ground.

Knots

Stand in a circle of eight people.

Extend right hand and grab someone's hand (except the person standing next to you).

Extend left hand and grab someone's hand (except the person standing next to you and the person whose hand you are already holding).

The objective is to get untangled without letting go of joined hands.

Levitation

Form groups of eight in circles with one person designated as the person to be lifted in the center of each circle.

Person to be lifted lies down on back.

Group kneels around the person.

On signal, the group lifts the person up overhead.

On signal the group returns person to the ground.

Minefield

Form groups of four.

Blindfold three people.

The member of the group not blindfolded must direct the other members around cones and polyspots (mines) to safety.

Allow verbal communication between all members, but prohibit touching.

Moon Ball

Six to eight people form a circle with one person holding a ball (preferably a fully inflated beach ball).

The goal of the game is to hit the ball as many times as possible without letting it hit the ground.

One player cannot hit the ball twice in succession.

To keep score, count the number of hits before ball hits ground.

Pharaoh's Stone

Form groups of four.

Establish a starting and ending point about 10 feet apart.

Using one rope and a foam box on top of five long cylinders, group must get each member (one member at a time) from the starting point to the ending pointing while riding on top of the foam box.

Pickle

Form groups of three.

Two play basemen, one plays the runner.

Establish two bases aboout 15 feet apart.

The runner starts on a base and tries to run to the other base.

The basemen throw the ball back and forth to one another, trying to tag the runner out.

The runner scores one point each time she reaches a base.

The players rotate positions each time a baseman tags a runner.

Prouty's Landing

Form groups of eight.

Use a swinging rope over an imaginary acid pit marked by ropes with a platform on the far side.

All members of the group must cross the acid pit without touching the ground, landing and remaining on the platform until all members are on the platform.

No one may retrieve the swinging rope by crossing the playing space.

Shark Attack

Form groups of four.

Give each group a hula hoop to hold on to while running.

On the command, "Shark!" the group puts the hula hoop down on the ground, and everyone in the group gets inside the hula hoop.

The last group to get in loses their hula hoop.

On the command, "Release!" each member of the group that lost their hula hoop must join another group.

Sherpa Walk

Form groups of eight, designating one person in each group as a leader.

Blindfold everyone who is not a leader.

The leader guides the group through an obstacle course.

The leader cannot speak or touch the group

The followers can hold hands and can speak to one another.

Spider's Web

Form groups of eight.

Make a web of rope for each group.

The objective is for the group to get all members through the web without touching any part of the webbing.

Once someone uses a web opening, it is closed to the other people.

If someone touches the web, the group must start over.

Stand Up

Pairs sit on the ground, back-to-back, knees bent, elbows linked.

The objective is to stand up together.

Switch

Form pairs.

One partner assumes one of these three positions: arms crossed, arms at right angles with left fingers touching right elbow, or right-hand salutes.

The second partner must respond with one of the other two positions.

If the second partner assumes the same position as the first, then the first partner gets to choose the exercise both will perform.

Switch roles after a set period of time.

Toss-a-Name Game

Six to eight people form a circle with one person holding a ball.

Figure C.11 Spider's Web.

Toss the ball in order from person to person as each states his or her first name.

When the ball returns to the first person, he or she calls out someone's name in the circle and tosses the ball to him or her.

The person receiving the ball calls out someone else's name and tosses the ball to him or her.

After students learn one another's names, have three or four students from each group rotate to another group.

Toss-and-Catch-a-Name Game

Six to eight people form a circle with one person holding a ball.

The person with the ball calls out someone's name in the circle and tosses the ball to him or her.

The person receiving the ball says, "Thank you," and the tosser's name.

The person receiving the ball then calls out someone else's name and tosses the ball to him or her.

After students learn one another's names, have three or four students from each group rotate to another group.

TP Shuffle

Form groups of eight divided into subgroups of four.

Each subgroup stands on a horizontal telephone pole or a raised curb facing the center.

The objective is for the two subgroups to change ends of the pole without touching the ground.

Traffic Jam

Form groups of eight divided into subgroups of four.

Place nine carpet squares in a line.

One person stands on each carpet square, facing the unoccupied middle square.

The objective is for the people on the right side of the middle square to end up on the left side of the middle square, and vice versa, only stepping on carpet squares—not the floor or ground.

A person can move onto an empty carpet square in front of him or her.

A person can move around a person facing him or her onto an empty carpet square on the other side of the person.

Trolley

Form groups of four.

Objective is for the group to all get on the trolley and walk from point A to point B. (See figure C.13.)

Trust Circle

Form groups of eight.

Seven people form a tight circle with the eighth person in the center.

Center person closes eyes and crosses arms over chest.

Center person leans back.

People in the circle pass the center person from person to person.

Switch center person until everyone has had a chance to be passed around.

Trust Fall

Form groups of thirteen.

All players must remove all jewelry and watches.

One person is the faller and twelve are the catchers.

Faller stands on a platform four to five feet off the ground with back to catchers.

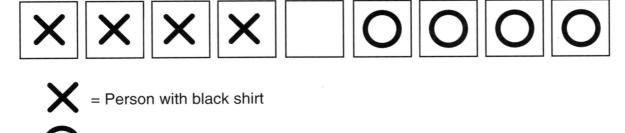

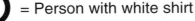 = Person with black shirt

= Person with white shirt

Figure C.12 Traffic Jam.

Figure C.13 Trolley.

Catchers stand shoulder-to-shoulder, forming two lines that face each other.

Catchers extend hands with palms up alternating arms with partner in other line to form a "bed" of arms.

Faller crosses arms over chest and closes eyes.

Faller leans backward with rigid body into arms of catchers.

Trust Walk

Form pairs and blindfold one of each pair.

The sighted partner leads the blindfolded person around the area. After a period of time, switch roles.

Turnstile

Form groups of eight.

Two people slowly turn the rope.

One person in the group runs through the rope from one side to the other followed by the other people.

The objective is for each person to get through without tripping on the rope.

Variation: Each person jumps once before exiting.

Two-Person Trust Fall

In pairs, one is the faller and one is the catcher.

Faller crosses arms over chest and announces he is ready.

Catcher announces he is ready.

Faller keeps knees and body straight while falling directly backward.

Keeping eyes on faller at all times, catcher catches the faller.

Switch roles.

Wordles

Form pairs.

Each pair gets a stack of three-by-five cards with wordles (word puzzles, see page 329 for samples).

The pair finds the solution to the puzzle.

Yeah, But

Form pairs and blindfold one of each pair.

The blindfolded partner raises arms up with palms out and jogs toward a wall or fence.

The other partner must stop the jogger before he or she runs into the wall or fence, using only verbal communication.

Bicycle:

Cycle   Cycle

Four square: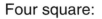

Paradise:

Dice

Dice

Figure C.14 Wordles.

Side–by–side:

Side   Side

Yurt Circle

Form a circle of eight people holding hands with feet shoulder-width apart and have them count off one-two-one-two around the circle.

All participants walk backward, expanding the circle until everyone feels their arms pulled on both sides.

Instruct the ones to lean in toward the center of the circle without bending at the waist.

Instruct the twos to lean out away from the center of the circle without bending at the waist.

After successfully accomplishing the task, switch the ones and twos.

Recommended Materials, Resources, and Reading

Music for Sixth Grade Dance Unit

- Ali pasa music from Ed Kremer's Folk Showplace (BOZ-OK 102)
- Alunelul music from Wagon Wheel Records (LSE-44 or WT 10005)
- Apat apat music from Wagon Wheel Records (*Dances Around the World* AR 572)
- Clapping dance music from Wagon Wheel Records (LSE-19 or *Folkcraft* 1523)
- Halay music from Wagon Wheel Records (*Folkcraft* 1549)
- Hora music (WT 10001) or *International Folk Dance Mixer* (GSLP 3528) from Wagon Wheel Records
- Kalvelis music from Wagon Wheel Records (*Folkcraft* 1418 or *Folk Dances From Around the World* RPT 108)
- Korobushka music from Wagon Wheel Records (WT 10005 or *Dances Around the World* AR 572)
- La raspa music from Wagon Wheel Records (EZ 716 or *Folk Dances From Near and Far* MAV 1042)
- Limbo music from Wagon Wheel Records (COL 1003 or *Children's All Time Rhythm Favorites* AR 630)
- Miserlou music from Wagon Wheel Records (WT 10001 or *International Folk Dance Mixer* GSLP 3528)
- Pata pata music from Wagon Wheel Records (OP 7500 or *International Folk Dance Mixer* GSLP 3528)
- Tanko bushi music from Wagon Wheel Records (WT 10033)
- Troika music from Wagon Wheel Records (WT 1001 or *International Folk Dance Mixer* GSLP 3528)

Music for Eighth Grade Square Dance Unit

- "Bad Bad Leroy Brown" from Wagon Wheel Records (LP1001)
- "Crawdad Song" from Wagon Wheel Records (SDR 209)

- "Engine 9" from Wagon Wheel Records (LP1001)
- "Gentle on My Mind" from Wagon Wheel Records (LP1001)
- "Hey Lei Lee Li Lee" from Wagon Wheel Records (LP1001)
- "Hey Look Me Over" from Wagon Wheel Records (BS 2172)
- "Hinky Dinky" from Educational Activities (*Get Ready to Square Dance*)
- "If They Could See Me Now" from Wagon Wheel Records (LP1001)
- "Just Because" from Wagon Wheel Records (ESP 123)
- "King of the Road" from Wagon Wheel Records (WW 922)
- "Kingston Town" from Wagon Wheel Records (H 5067)
- "Spoonful of Sugar" from Wagon Wheel Records (CW 172)
- "Tie a Yellow Ribbon" from Wagon Wheel Records (BS 2307)
- "Wheels" from Wagon Wheel Records (RB 218)

Music for Tinikling

- Kimbo KEA 8095 from Wagon Wheel Records
- RCA Victor LPM 1619 from Wagon Wheel Records

Instructional Materials

- *American Red Cross Swimming Program* available from American Red Cross
- *Longfellow's Whales Tales* available from American Red Cross
- *United States Tennis Association Schools Program Curriculum* available from the United States Tennis Association

Software for Teacher Use

- *Claris Works* from Claris Corporation
- *GradePoint* from Sunburst
- *Grady Profile* from Software for Teachers

- *Learner Profile* from Sunburst
- *Microsoft Works* from Microsoft Corporation
- *Scholastic's Electronic Portfolio* from Scholastic

Instructional Software

- *BioMachanics* from Brown & Benchmark Publishers
- *Body 'N' Mind* from Fitness Lifestyle Design, Inc.
- *DINE Healthy* from DINE Systems
- *HyperCard* from Apple
- *HyperStudio* from Roger Wagner
- *John Rae—Survival Series* from CompTech Systems Design
- *Linkway Live* from IBM
- *MacBowling Tutorial* from Bonnie's Fitware
- *MacFootball Rules Game* from Bonnie's Fitware
- *MacHealth-Related Fitness Tutorial and Portfolio* from Bonnie's Fitware
- *MacHeart Monitor Tutorial and Simulation* from Bonnie's Fitware
- *MacPortfolio* from Bonnie's Fitware
- *MacSoftball Basic Defense* from Bonnie's Fitware
- *MacSoftball Rules Game* from Bonnie's Fitware
- *MacVolleyball Complete* from Bonnie's Fitware
- *Measurement in Motion* from Learning in Motion
- *The Total Heart* from IVI Publishing

CD-ROMs

- *Interactive Soccer* from SISU
- *Interactive Volleyball* from SISU
- *Mountain Biking* from Media Mosaic
- *Rock Climbing* from Media Mosaic

Videos

- *Bowling With Holman and Petraglia* from SyberVision
- *Defend Yourself!* from SyberVision
- *Disc Video* available from Discovering the World

- *ESPN Teaching Kids Basketball* from Cambridge Physical Education and Health
- *ESPN Teaching Kids Football* from Cambridge Physical Education and Health
- *ESPN Teaching Kids Soccer* from Cambridge Physical Education and Health
- *Finding Your Way in the Wild* from Quality Video
- *Footbag Video* available from Discovering the World
- *Golf With Al Geiberger* from SyberVision
- *Home Pool Safety* from American Red Cross
- *International Unicycling Federation Achievement Skill Levels* available from the Unicycling Society of America
- *Juggle Jam* from Human Kinetics
- *Juggle Time* from Human Kinetics
- *Juggling Star* from Human Kinetics
- *The Jump Rope Primer Video* from Human Kinetics
- *Learn to Bowl* available from Young American Bowling Alliance
- *Learn to Bowl II* available from Young American Bowling Alliance
- *New Games From Around the World* from Sportime
- *New Soccer* from Sportime
- *PE-TV* from Whittle Communications
- *Rough Terrain Unicycling* available from the Unicycling Society of America
- *The Science and Myths of Tennis* from Human Kinetics
- *Slim Goodbody Presents All Fit*, a three-volume series from Human Kinetics
- *Slim Goodbody Presents Step by Step for Kids* from Human Kinetics
- *Teaching Lifetime Fitness* by David Laurie and Chuck Corbin from Audio Visual Designs of Manhattan
- *Tennis by Vic Braden* from Cambridge Physical Education and Health
- *Track and Field Techniques* from Cambridge Physical Education and Health
- *Unicycle* from the Unicycling Society of America
- *VIP Softball Series* by the Amateur Softball Association from Cambridge Physical Education and Health

- *Water, The Deceptive Power* from the American Red Cross
- *The World of Volleyball* from Human Kinetics

Addresses for Resources

- ABC News Interactive, 7 W. 66 St., 4th Floor, New York, NY 10023; 800-524-2481.
  Interactive laser disc packages
- A.D.A.M. Software, Inc., 1600 River Edge Pkwy., Suite 800, Atlanta, GA 30328; 800-755-ADAM.
  Software on human anatomy
- Amateur Athletic Foundation, address unavailable; 213-730-9696.
  General fitness and athletic information
- American Alliance for Health, Physical Education, Recreation and Dance, 1900 Association Dr., Reston, VA 22091; 800-321-0789.
  Professional organization and publications
- American Heart Association, 7272 Greenville Ave., Dallas, TX; 1-800-242-8721.
  Instructional materials on health and fitness
- American Red Cross, contact local chapter.
  Instructional materials and videos on first aid and water safety
- Apple Computer, Inc., 20525 Mariani Ave., Cupertino, CA 95014-6299; 408-996-1010.
  Macintosh hardware and software
- Association for the Advancement of Health Education, 1900 Association Dr., Reston, VA 22091; 800-321-0789.
  Professional organization and publications
- Association for Supervision and Curriculum Development, 1250 N. Pitt St., Alexandria, VA 22314-1453; 703-549-9110.
  Professional organization and publications
- Audio Visual Designs of Manhattan, 2208 Fort Riley Blvd., Manhattan, KS 66502; 913-539-1555.
  Videos on health-related fitness
- Bonnie's Fitware, 18832 Stefani Ave., Cerritos, CA 90703; 310-924-0835.
  Macintosh software for physical education
- Brown and Benchmark, 25 Kessel Ct., Madison, WI 53711; 800-338-5371.
  Software and textbooks
- BSN Sports, 12640 Moore St., Cerritos, CA 90703; 800-527-7510.
  Sporting equipment

- Cambridge Educational, P.O. Box 2153, Dept. PE 13, Charleston, WV 25328-2153; 800-468-4227.
  Instructional videos

- Cannon Sports, P.O. Box 11179, Burbank, CA 91510-1179; 800-223-0064.
  Sporting equipment

- Claris Corporation, 5201 Patrick Henry Dr., Santa Clara, CA 95054.
  Software

- CompTech Systems Design, P.O. Box 516, Hastings, MN 55033; 800-343-2406.
  Software for health education and physical education

- Cooper Institute for Aerobics Research, 12330 Preston Rd., Dallas, TX 75230; 800-635-7050.
  Prudential FITNESSGRAM materials

- Country Technology, Inc., P.O. Box 87, Gays Mills, WI 54631; 608-735-4718.
  Innovative technology devices and software

- Creative Health Products, Inc., 5130 Curtis Rd., Plymouth, MI 48170; 800-742-4478.
  Innovative technology devices and software

- DINE Systems, Inc., 586 N. French Rd., Amherst, NY 14228; 716-688-2400.
  Nutrition software

- Discovering the World, Box 911, La Mirada, CA 90637; 714-522-2202.
  New games materials

- Ed Kremer's Folk Showplace, 155 Turk St., San Francisco, CA 94102; 415-755-3444.
  Music

- Educational Activities, P.O. Box 87, Baldwin, NY 11510; 800-645-3739.
  Instructional materials

- Educational Telecommunications Network, 9300 E. Imperial Hwy., Downey, CA 90242; 310-922-6307.
  Videos on curriculum and teaching

- Electronic Arts, 1450 Fashion Island Blvd., San Mateo, CA 94403; 800-245-4525.
  Virtual reality software

- Fitness Lifestyle Design, Inc., 2317 Eastgate Way, Tallahassee, FL 32308; 800-FLD-INCL.
  Software for health-related fitness

- Flaghouse, Inc., 150 N. MacQuesten Pkwy., Mt. Vernon, NY 10550; 800-793-7900.
  Sporting equipment

- Futrex Inc., 6 Montgomery Village Ave., Suite 620, Gaithersburg, MD 20879; 800-255-4206.
  Body composition analyzer device

- GOPHER Sport, 2929 W. Park Dr., Owatonna, MN 55060; 507-451-3880.
  Sporting equipment

- Human Kinetics, P.O. Box 5076, Champaign, IL 61825-5076; 800-747-4457.
  Books and videos

- Hunter Textbooks, Inc., 823 Reynolds Rd., Winston-Salem, NC 27104; 919-725-0608.
  Student textbooks

- IBM, Bldg. 203, 3039 Cornwallis Rd., Research Triangle Park, NC 27709; 800-426-2968.
  Hardware and software

- IVI Publishing, 1380 Corporate Center Curve, Suite 305, Eagan, MN 55121; 800-952-4773.
  Software

- Kathryn Short Productions, no address available; 714-990-6075.
  Jump bands, videos, and instructional materials

- Kendall/Hunt Publishing Company, 2460 Kerper Blvd., P.O. Box 539, Dubuque, IA 52004-0539; 800-258-5622.
  Student textbooks

- Kimbo, P.O. Box 1402, Northbrook, IL 60065-1402; 800-631-2187.
  Music

- Klutz Press, P.O. Box 2992, Stanford, CA 94305; 415-857-0888.
  Books

- Learning in Motion, 500 Seabright Ave., Suite 105, Santa Cruz, CA 95062-3480; 800-560-5670.
  Software

- Macmillan Company of Australia, 107 Moray St., S. Melbourne 3205; (03) 646-6100.
  Student textbooks

- Media Mosaic, 1314 NW Irving St., Suite 713, Portland, OR 97209-2728; 800-972-3766.
  Instructional software

- Microsoft, 1 Microsoft Way, Redmond, WA 98052; 800-426-9400.
  Software

- Montebello Intermediate, 1600 Whittier Blvd., Montebello, CA 90640; 213-721-5111.
  Video showing quality middle school physical education program

- National Association for Sport and Physical Education (NASPE), 1900 Association Dr., Reston, VA 22091; 800-321-0789.
  Professional organization and publications

- National Cartographic Information Center, 507 National Center, Reston, VA 22092; 703-648-6045.
  Maps

- Orienteering Services, USA, Box 1604, Binghamton, NY 13902; 607-724-0411.
  Instructional materials for orienteering

- PickleBall Association, 801 NW 48th St., Seattle, Washington 98107; 206-784-4723.
  Instructional materials for pickleball

- PGA Foundation, P.O. Box 109601, Palm Beach Gardens, FL 33410-9601; 407-626-3600.
  Instructional materials for golf

- Polar Heart Rate Monitors, 99 Seaview Blvd., Port Washington, NY 11050; 800-227-1314.
  Heart monitors

- Project Adventure, P.O. Box 100, Hamilton, MA 01936; 508-468-7981.
  Books and materials for new games and ropes courses

- Quality Video, Inc., 7399 Bush Lake Rd., Minneapolis, MN 55439-2027; 612-893-0903.
  Fitness videos

- Roger Wagner, 1050 Pioneer Way, Suite P, El Cajon, CA 92020.
  HyperStudio software

- Scholastic, 2931 E. McCarty St., Jefferson City, MO 65101; 800-SCHOLAS.
  Software and books

- Scott, Foresman and Company, 1900 E. Lake Ave., Glenview, IL 60025; 708-729-3000.
  Student fitness textbooks

- Self-Defense Publications, no address available; 818-243-1635.
  Instructional materials for self-defense

- The Silva Company, P.O. Box 966, Binghamton, NY 13902; 800-847-1460.
  Instructional materials for orienteering

- SISU Software, Inc., P.O. Box 2305, Renton, WA 98056; 800-228-5385.
  Software

- Software for Teachers; 800-77 GRADY.
  Software

- Sport House, address unavailable; 310-695-1885.
  Heart monitors and sporting equipment

- Sportime, One Sportime Way, Atlanta, GA 30340-1402; 800-283-5700.
  Sporting equipment

- Sunburst Software, 101 Castleton St., P.O. Box 100, Pleasantville, NY 10570-0100; 800-321-7511.
  Instructional software

- SyberVision, One Sansome St., Suite 1610, San Francisco, CA 94104; 800-678-0887.
  Instructional video tapes

- Turning Points, P.O. Box 2551, Del Mar, CA 92014; 800-325-4769.
  Instructional audio tapes

- Unicycling Society of America, P.O. Box 49534, Redford, MI 48240; 800-783-2425.
  Instructional materials for unicycling

- United States Orienteering Federation, P.O. Box 1444, Forest Park, GA 33051; phone number unavailable.
  Videos and books on orienteering

- United States Team Handball Association, 1750 Boulder St., Colorado Springs, CO 80909; 303-632-5551.
  Instructional materials for team handball

- United States Tennis Association, 70 W. Red Oak Lane, White Plains, NY 10604; 914-696-7000.
  Instructional materials for tennis

- United States Volleyball Association, 4510 Executive Dr., Plaza 1, San Diego, CA 92121-3021; 619-625-8200.
  Instructional materials for volleyball

- U.S. Games, P.O. Box 117028, Carrollton, TX 75011-7028; 800-327-0484.
  Sporting equipment

- Wagon Wheels, 17191 Corbina Ln. #203, Huntington Beach, CA 92649; 714-846-8169.
  Music

- Whittle Communications, 333 Main St., Knoxville, TN 37902-1897; 310-260-0163.
  PE-TV

- Wittek Golf Supply Company, 3650 N. Avondale Ave., Chicago, IL 60618; 312-463-2636.
  Cayman golf balls

- Wolverine Sports, 745 State Circle, Ann Arbor, MI 48108; 313-761-5690.
  Sporting equipment

- Young American Bowling Alliance, Dept. BG, 5301 S. 76th St., Greendale, WI 53129; 414-421-4700.
  Instructional videos and materials

Reading to Stay Up-to-Date

- *Journal of Physical Education, Recreation and Dance.* Available from American Alliance for Health, Physical Education, Recreation and Dance, 1900 Association Dr., Reston, VA 22091; 800-213-7193.

- *Journal of Teaching in Physical Education.* Available from Human Kinetics, P.O. Box 5076, Champaign, IL 61825-5076; 800-747-4457.

- *Research Quarterly for Exercise and Sport.* Available from American Alliance for Health, Physi-

cal Education, Recreation and Dance, 1900 Association Dr., Reston, VA 22091; 800-213-7193.

- *Strategies: A Journal for Sport and Physical Education.* Available from American Alliance for Health, Physical Education, Recreation and Dance, 1900 Association Dr., Reston, VA 22091; 800-213-7193.

- *Teaching Secondary Physical Education.* Available from Human Kinetics, P.O. Box 5076, Champaign, IL 61825-5076; 800-747-4457.

- *Update.* Available from American Alliance for Health, Physical Education, Recreation and Dance, 1900 Association Dr., Reston, VA 22091; 800-213-7193. Receive as part of membership fee.

BIBLIOGRAPHY

Adams, S.H. 1990. Sport risk management for coaches: Supervision. In *Proceedings of the Third Annual Sport, Physical Education, Recreation and Law Conference.*

———. 1993. Duty to properly instruct. *Journal of Physical Education, Recreation & Dance* 64(2):22-23.

Allen, J., E. McNeill, and V. Schmidt. 1992. *Cultural awareness for children.* Menlo Park, CA: Addison-Wesley.

Amabile, T. 1989. *Growing up creative.* New York: Crown.

American Alliance for Health, Physical Education, Recreation and Dance. 1994. *New physical best educational kit.* Reston, VA: AAHPERD.

———. 1995. *Including students with disabilities in physical education.* Reston, VA: AAHPERD.

American College of Sports Medicine. 1988. Physical fitness and youth. *Medicine and Science in Sports and Exercise* 20(4):422-423.

———. 1990. The recommended quantity and quality of exercise for developing and maintaining cardiorespiratory and muscular fitness in healthy adults. *Medicine and Science in Sports and Exercise* 22(2):265-274.

———. 1993. Summary statement: Workshop on physical activity and public health. *Sports Medicine Bulletin* 28(4):7.

American Heart Association. 1986. *The corporate heart.* Needham, MA: American Heart Association.

———. 1988. *Heart facts.* Dallas: American Heart Association.

———. 1991. *Heart and stroke facts.* Dallas: American Heart Association.

———. 1995. *Heart and stroke facts: 1996 statistical supplement.* Dallas: American Heart Association.

Anglin, G.J., ed. 1991. *Instructional technology: Past, present, and future.* Englewood, CO: Libraries Unlimited.

Apple, M.W., and J.A. Beane, eds. 1995. *Democratic schools.* Alexandria, VA: Association for Supervision and Curriculum Development (ASCD).

Armstrong, T. 1994. *Multiple intelligences in the classroom.* Alexandria, VA: ASCD.

Asher, J.J. 1977. *Learning another language through actions: The complete teacher's guidebook.* Los Gatos, CA: Sky Oak Productions.

Association for Supervision and Curriculum Development (ASCD). 1975. Washington, DC: ASCD.

Aukstakalnis, S., and D. Blatner. 1992. *Silicon mirage: The art and science of virtual reality.* Berkeley, CA: Peachpit Press.

Baker, E.T., M.C. Wang, and H.J. Walberg. 1994. The effects of inclusion on learning. *Educational Leadership* 52(4):33-35.

Balan, C.M., and W.E. Davis. 1993. Ecological task analysis—An approach to teaching physical education. *Journal of Health, Physical Education, Recreation, and Dance* 64(9):54-61.

Bassin, S., D. Davidson, R. Deitrick, G.S. Morris, N. Wong, and A. Crecelius. 1989. *Montebello health and fitness research project: A three-year school-based assessment and intervention.* Paper presented at the April 19-23, 1989 AAHPERD National Convention in Boston.

Batesky, J. 1988. Teacher performance self appraisal for physical educators. *Strategies* 1(4):19-22.

Benjamin, R. 1981. *Making schools work: A reporter's journey through some of America's most remarkable classrooms.* New York: Continuum.

Benjamin, S. 1989. An ideascape for education: What futurists recommend. *Educational Leadership* 47(1):8-12.

Bensen, J. 1982. An alternative direction for middle school physical education. *Physical Educator* 39(2):75-77.

Berliner, D.C., and U. Casanova. 1993. *Putting research to work in your school.* New York: Scholastic.

Berman, P. 1994. *Mobilizing for competitiveness: Linking education and training to jobs.* San Francisco: The California Business Roundtable.

Birdwell, D. 1980. The effects of modification of teacher behavior on the academic learning time of selected students in physical education. PhD diss., Ohio State University, Columbus.

Blackall, B. 1987. *Australian physical education: Book 1.* South Melbourne: The Macmillan Company of Australia.

Blackall, B., and D. Davis. 1987. *Australian physical education: Book 2.* South Melbourne: The Macmillan Company of Australia.

Blakemore, C.L., and J.K. Rogers. 1995. Learn how middle school students think. *Strategies* February:11-14.

Block, M.E. 1994. *A teacher's guide to including students with disabilities in regular physical education.* Baltimore: Paul H. Brookes.

Bloom, B.S., ed. 1956. *Taxonomy of educational objectives, handbook I: Cognitive domain.* New York: David McKay.

Boyce, B.A. 1990. Grading practices—How do they influence students' skill performance? *Journal of Physical Education, Recreation & Dance* 61(6):46-48.

Brandt, R. 1993. On restructuring roles and relationships: A conversation with Phil Schlechty. *Educational Leadership* 51(2):9-11.

Brewer, C., and D. Campbell. 1991. *Rhythms of learning.* Tucson, AZ: Zephyr Press.

Brooks, J.G., and M.G. Brooks. 1993. *In search of understanding: The case for constructivist classrooms.* Alexandria, VA: ASCD.

Brown, J. 1995. *Tennis: Steps to success,* 2d ed. Champaign, IL: Human Kinetics.

———. 1996. *Tennis instructor guide: Steps to success.* Champaign, IL: Human Kinetics.

Brown, L., and S. Grineski. 1992. Competition in physical education: An educational contradiction. *Journal of Physical Education, Recreation & Dance* 63(1):17-19, 77.

Brown, S.C. 1993. Selecting safe equipment—What do we really know? *Journal of Physical Education, Recreation & Dance* 64(2):33-35.

Bruder, I. 1993. Alternative assessment: Putting technology to the test. *Electronic Learning* January:22-23, 26-28.

Buchanan, D. 1992. Outward Bound goes to the inner city. *Educational Leadership* 50(4):38-41.

Burrus, D. 1993. *Techno trends.* New York: HarperBusiness.

Bushweller, K. 1995. The resilient child. *The American School Board Journal* May:18-24.

Butler, L.F., and G.C. Mergardt. 1994. The many forms of administrative support. *Journal of Physical Education, Recreation & Dance* 65(7):43-47.

Caine, R.N., and G. Caine. 1990. Understanding a brain-based approach to learning and teaching. *Educational Leadership* 48(2):66-70.

———. 1991. *Making connections: Teaching and the human brain.* Alexandria, VA: ASCD.

California—Region 9. 1994. *Physical Education Curriculum.* San Diego: San Diego County Office of Education.

California Department of Education. 1986. *Handbook for physical education: Framework for developing a curriculum for California public schools.* Sacramento, CA: California Department of Education.

———. 1987. *Caught in the middle: Educational reform for young adolescents in five California public schools.* Sacramento, CA: California Department of Education.

———. 1991. *Not schools alone: Guidelines for schools and communities.* Sacramento, CA: California Department of Education.

———. 1994a. *Health framework for California public schools: Kindergarten through grade twelve.* Sacramento, CA: California Department of Education.

———. 1994b. *Physical education framework for California public schools: Kindergarten through grade twelve.* Sacramento, CA: California Department of Education.

California Department of Health Services. 1994. *Vital statistics of California 1992 (preliminary data).* Sacramento, CA: California Department of Health Services.

California Department of Health Services and UCSF Institute for Health and Aging. 1994. *Cardiovascular disease awareness survey of California adults.* Sacramento, CA: California Department of Health Services and UCSF Institute for Health and Aging.

California School Leadership Academy (CSLA). 1991a. *Structuring the school for student success.* Sacramento, CA: CSLA.

———. 1991b. *Thinking/meaning-centered curriculum module.* Sacramento, CA: CSLA.

———. 1994a. *Accountability and assessment program for improving student performance.* Sacramento, CA: CSLA.

———. 1994b. *Physical education for lifelong well being.* Sacramento, CA: CSLA.

Campbell, D. 1992. *100 Ways to improve your teaching using your voice and music.* Tucson, AZ: Zephyr Press.

Cannings, T., and L. Finkel, eds. 1993. *The technology age classroom.* Wilsonville, OR: Franklin, Beedle and Associates.

Carlson, R.P. 1984. *Ideas II for secondary school physical education.* Reston, VA: National Association for Sport and Physical Education (NASPE).

Carnegie Council on Adolescent Development. 1989. *Turning points: Preparing American youth for the 21st century.* Washington, DC: Carnegie Council on Adolescent Development.

Cassidy, J. 1982. *The hacky sack book.* Stanford, CA: Klutz Press.

Cawelti, G., ed. 1993. *Challenges and achievements of American education.* Alexandria, VA: ASCD.

Centers for Disease Control and Prevention and the American College of Sports Medicine. 1995. *Physical activity and public health—A recommendation.* Atlanta: Center for Disease Control and Prevention and the American College of Sports Medicine.

Chadwick, I., and A. Gathright. 1990. Middle school frameworks: The implications for elementary schools. *Florida Journal of Health, Physical Education, Recreation, Dance, and Driver Education* 28(1):37-38.

Chandler, G.L., and W.W. Purkey. 1986. Invitational physical education. *Physical Educator* 43(3):123-128.

Cohen, P. 1995. Schooling away from school: Some districts work with home educators. *Education Update* 37(6):1, 6, 8.

Collins, L.M. 1988. Youth problems are frightening. *Deseret News* September 13, 1988.

Cooper Institute for Aerobics Research. 1994. *The Prudential FITNESSGRAM: Test administration manual.* Dallas, TX: Cooper Institute for Aerobics Research.

Corbin, C.B. 1993a. Clues from dinosaurs, mules, and the bull snake: Our field in the 21st century. *Quest* 45(4):546-556.

———. 1993b. The field of physical education—Common goals, not common roles. *Journal of Physical Education, Recreation & Dance* 64(1):79, 84-87.

Corbin, C.B., and R. Lindsey. 1990. *Fitness for life*, 3d ed. Glenview, IL: Scott, Foresman.

———. 1990. *Fitness for life: Teacher's resource book*, 3d ed. Glenview, IL: Scott, Foresman.

Cornish, E., ed. 1994. *Outlook '95*. Bethesda, MD: World Future Society.

Costa, A.L. 1991. *Teaching for intelligent behavior: Outstanding strategies for strengthening your students' thinking skills*. Bellevue, WA: Bureau of Education and Research.

Cradler, J. 1991. Authentic assessment: Finding the right tools. *Thrust for Educational Leadership* 49(2):20-25.

Cradler, J., and M. Melendez. 1991. In with the new. *Thrust for Educational Leadership* 49(2):8-11.

Cuesta, J.G. 1981. *Team handball techniques*. Colorado Springs: United States Team Handball Federation.

Curwin, R.L., and A.N. Mendler. 1988. *Discipline with dignity*. Alexandria, VA: ASCD.

Davis, S. 1987. *Future perfect*. New York: Addison-Wesley.

Deal, T.B., and L.O. Deal. 1995. Heart to heart: Using heart rate telemetry to meet physical education outcomes. *Journal of Physical Education, Recreation & Dance* 66(3):30-35.

Dennison, P.E. 1981. *Switching on: A guide to edu-kinesthetics*. Ventura, CA: Edu-Kinesthetics.

Dennison, P.E., and G. Dennison. 1988. *Brain gym*. Ventura, CA: Edu-Kinesthetics.

Dewey, J. [1915] 1990. *The school and society*. Chicago: University of Chicago Press.

Dienstbier, R. 1989. *Periodic adrenaline arousal boosts health, coping*. Brain-Mind Bulletin 14.9A.

Diez, M.E., and C.J. Moon. 1992. What do we want students to know? . . . And other important questions. *Educational Leadership* 49(8):38-41.

Dodds, P., ed. 1987. *Basic stuff series I*. Reston, VA: AAHPERD.

Dougherty, N.J., ed. 1993. *Principles of safety in physical education and sport*. Reston, VA: NASPE.

Duffy, T.M., and D.H. Jonassen. 1992. *Constructivism and the technology of instruction: A conversation*. Hillsdale, NJ: Lawrence Erlbaum Associates.

Educational Amendment Act of 1972.

Elmore, R.F., and S.H. Fuhrman, eds. 1994. *The governance of curriculum*. Alexandria, VA: ASCD.

Evertson, C.M., E.T. Emmer, J.P. Sanford, and B.S. Clements. 1983. Improving classroom management: An experiment in elementary classrooms. *Elementary School Journal* 84(2):173-188.

Finnigan, D. 1987. *Scarf juggling*. Address unavailable: The Complete Juggler.

Fitts, P.M., and M.I. Posner. 1967. *Human performance*. Belmont, CA: Brooks/Cole.

Fleming, M., and W.H. Levie, eds. 1993. *Instructional message design: Principles from the behavioral and cognitive sciences*. Englewood Cliffs, NJ. Educational Technology Publications.

Fluegelman, A. 1976. *The new games book*. New York: Doubleday.

———. 1981. *More new games*. New York: Doubleday.

Fogarty, R. 1991a. Ten ways to integrate curriculum. *Educational Leadership* 49(2): 61-65.

———. 1991b. *The mindful school: How to integrate the curricula*. Palatine, IL: IRI/Skylight.

Fullan, M. 1993. *Change forces: Probing the depths of educational reform*. Bristol, PA: The Falmer Press.

Gagne, R.M., L.J. Briggs, and W.W. Wager. 1992. *Principles of instructional design*. Fort Worth, TX: Harcourt Brace Jovanovich College.

Gall, S.L. 1991. The fit miss less work. *Physician and Sports Medicine* 19(4):28.

Galyean, B.C. 1984. *Mindsight: Learning through imaging*. Berkeley, CA: Center for Integrative Learning.

Gamoran, A. 1992. Is ability grouping equitable? *Educational Leadership* 50(2):11-17.

Gardner, H. 1983. *Frames of mind: The theory of multiple intelligences*. New York: Basic Books.

Gaskin, L.P. 1993. Establishing, communicating, and enforcing rules and regulations. *Journal of Physical Education, Recreation & Dance* 64(2):26-27, 63-64.

Gawronski, J.D. 1991. Ready or not, assessment, here it comes. *Thrust for Educational Leadership* 49(2):12-15.

Gentile, L. 1983. *Using sports for reading and writing activities: Middle and high school years*. Phoenix, AZ: Onyx Press.

George, P.S., C. Stevenson, J. Thomason, and J. Beane. 1992. *The middle school—And beyond*. Alexandria, VA: ASCD.

Gibbs, J. 1987. *Tribes: A process for social development and cooperative learning*. Santa Rosa, CA: Center Source Publications.

Gold, R.S. 1991. *Microcomputer applications in health education*. Dubuque, IA: Brown.

Goldberger, M. 1992. The spectrum of teaching styles: A perspective for research on teaching physical education. *Journal of Physical Education, Recreation & Dance* 63(1):42-46.

Goodlad, J. 1984. *A place called school*. New York: McGraw-Hill.

Graham, G., S. Holt-Hale, and M. Parker. 1993. *Children moving: A reflective approach to teaching physical education*. Mountain View, CA: Mayfield.

Gray, G.R. 1995. Safety tips from the expert witness. *Journal of Physical Education, Recreation & Dance* 66(1):18-21.

Griss, S. 1994. Creative movement: A language for learning. *Educational Leadership* 51(5):78-80.

Gros, V. 1979. *Inside field hockey*. Chicago: Contemporary Books.

Guglielmo, C. 1994. Forecast '95. *New Media* 4(16):41-45.

Hafner, K. 1995. Wiring the ivory tower. *Newsweek* January 30: 62-63, 66.

Hall, G.E., R.C. Wallace, and W.A. Dossett. 1973. *A developmental conceptualization of the adoption process within educational institutions*. Austin, TX: Research and Development Center for Teacher Education.

Halpern, S. 1985. *Sound health*. New York: Harper and Row.

Hanvey, R.G. 1976. *An attainable global perspective*. Denver: Center for Teaching International Relations.

Harris, J.A., A.M. Pittmann, and M.S. Waller. 1988. *Dance a while*. 6th ed. Reston, VA: AAHPERD.

Harrison, J.M., and C.L. Blakemore. 1992. *Instructional strategies for secondary school physical education*. Dubuque, IA: Brown.

Hay, J.G. 1993. *The biomechanics of sports techniques*. Englewood Cliffs, NJ: Prentice-Hall.

Haywood, K.M. 1993. *Life span motor development*. Champaign, IL: Human Kinetics.

Healthy Kids Healthy California Committee. 1989. *A comprehensive approach to improving the health and well-being of California's students*. Sacramento, CA: California Department of Education.

Hellison, D.R. 1985. *Goals and strategies for teaching physical education*. Champaign, IL: Human Kinetics.

Henderson, A. 1987. *The evidence continues to grow: Parent involvement improves student achievement*. Columbia, MD: NCCE.

Herdman, P. 1994. When the wilderness becomes a classroom. *Educational Leadership* 52(3):15-19.

Hermann, D.J., and J.R. Hanwood. 1980. More evidence for the existence of the separate semantic and episodic stores in long-term memory. *Journal of Experimental Psychology: Human Learning and Memory* 6(5):467-478.

Heterick, R.C., and J. Gehl. 1995. Information technology and the year 2000. *Educom Review* January/February:23-25.

Holyoak, C., and H. Weinberg. 1986. *Meeting needs and pleasing kids: A middle school physical education curriculum*. Dubuque, IA: Kendall/Hunt.

Horowitz, J., and B. Bloom. 1987. *Frisbee: More than a game of catch*. La Mirada, CA: Discovering the World.

Housner, L.D. 1995. Physical education: Visions for the future. *Proceedings of the AAHPERD Southwest District/Hawaii Convention*, pp. 93-94.

Housner, L.D., and D.C. Griffey. 1994. Wax on, wax off. *Journal of Physical Education, Recreation & Dance* 65(2):63-68.

Houston, J. 1982. *The possible human: A course in enhancing your physical, mental and creative abilities*. Los Angeles: Jeremy Tarcher.

Humberstone, B. 1990. Warriors or wimps? Creating alternative forms of physical education. In *Sport, men, and the gender order: Critical feminist perspectives*, ed. M.A. Messner and D.F. Sabo, 201-210, Champaign, IL: Human Kinetics.

Hunter, M. 1982. *Mastery teaching*. El Segundo, CA: TIP Publications.

Hutchinson, G.E. 1995. Gender-fair teaching in physical education. *Journal of Physical Education, Recreation & Dance* 66(1):42-47.

Issacs, K.R. 1992. Exercise and the brain: Angiogenesis in the adult rate cerebellum after vigorous physical activity and motor skill learning. *Journal of Cerebral Blood Flow and Metabolism* 12(1):110-119.

Jacobs, H.H. 1991. Planning for curriculum integration. *Educational Leadership* 49(2):27-28.

———, ed. 1989. *Interdisciplinary curriculum: Design and implementation*. Alexandria, VA: ASCD.

Jambor, E.A., and E.M. Weekes. 1995. Videotape feedback: Make it more effective. *Journal of Physical Education, Recreation & Dance* 66(2):48-50.

Jensen, E. 1994. *The learning brain*. Del Mar, CA: Turning Point.

———. 1995. *Brain-based learning and teaching*. Del Mar, CA: Turning Point.

Jewett, A.E., L.L. Bain, and C.D. Ennis. 1995. *The curriculum process in physical education*. Dubuque, IA: Brown.

Johnson Camping. 1991. *Teaching orienteering*. Binghamton, NY: Johnson Camping.

Johnson, D.W., and R.T. Johnson. 1975. *Learning together: Cooperation, competition, and individualization*. Englewood Cliffs, NJ: Prentice-Hall.

———. 1991. *Teach students to be peacemakers*. Edina, MN: Interaction Book Company.

Joint Committee on National Health Education Standards. 1995. *National Health Education Standards*. Reston, VA: Association for the Advancement of Health Education.

Joyce, B., and B. Showers. 1988. *Student achievement through staff development*. New York: Longman.

Joyce, B., ed. 1990. *Changing school culture through staff development*. Alexandria, VA: ASCD.

Kagan, S. 1985. *Cooperative learning workshops for teachers*. Laguna Niguel, CA: Resources for Teachers.

———. 1989. *Cooperative learning: Resources for teachers*. Laguna Niguel, CA: Resources for Teachers.

Kentucky Education Reform Act of 1990, House Bill 940.

Kerman, S. 1979. Teacher expectations and student achievement. *Phi Delta Kappa* 36(2):14-15.

Kimiecik, S.J., K.R. Demas, and C.B. Demas. 1994. Establishing credibility: Proactive approaches. *Journal of Physical Education, Recreation & Dance* 65(7):38-42.

Kirchner, G. 1991. *Children's games from around the world*. Dubuque, IA: Brown.

Kirchner, G., and G.J. Fishburne. 1995. *Physical education for elementary school children*. Dubuque, IA: Brown and Benchmark.

Kirkpatrick, B. 1987. Ultra physical education in middle schools. *Journal of Physical Education, Recreation & Dance* 58(6):46-49.

Kirkpatrick, B., and M.M. Buck. 1995. Heart Adventures Challenge Course: A lifestyle education activity. *Journal of Physical Education, Recreation & Dance* 66(2):17-24.

Kittleson, S. 1992. *Racquetball: Steps to success*. Champaign, IL: Human Kinetics.

———. 1993. *Teaching racquetball: Steps to success*. Champaign, IL: Human Kinetics.

Knudson, D. 1993. Biomechanics of the basketball jump shot—Six key teaching points. *Journal of Physical Education, Recreation & Dance* 64(2):67-73.

Kohn, A. 1987. *No contest: The case again competition*. New York: Houghton Mifflin.

———. 1991a. Caring kids: The role of the schools. *Phi Delta Kappa* 48(1):498-506.

———. 1991b. Don't spoil the promise of cooperative learning. *Educational Leadership* 48(5):93-94.

———. 1991c. Group grade grubbing versus cooperative learning. *Educational Leadership* 48(5):83-87.

———. 1993. *Punished by rewards*. New York: Houghton Mifflin.

———. 1994. Grading: The issue is not how but why. *Educational Leadership* 52(2):38-41.

Kounin, J. 1977. *Discipline and group management in classrooms*. Melbourne, FL: RE Krieger Publishing.

Kuykendall, C. 1992. *From rage to hope: Strategies for reclaiming black and Hispanic students*. Bloomington, IN: National Educational Service.

Lauffenburger, S.K. 1992. Efficient warm-ups: Creating a warm-up that works. *Journal of Physical Education, Recreation & Dance* 63(4):21-25.

Laughlin, N., and S. Laughlin. 1992. The myth of measurement in physical education. *Journal of Physical Education, Recreation & Dance* 63(4):83-85.

Lavroff, N. 1992. *Virtual reality playhouse*. Corte Madera, CA: The Waite Group.

Lebow, D., and D. Johnson. 1993. Integrating emerging technologies into fitness education. *Florida Journal of Health, Physical Education, Recreation, Dance, and Driver Education* 31(3):38-45.

Lemaster, K.J., and A.C. Lacy. 1993. Relationship of teacher behaviors to ALT-PE in junior high school physical education. *Journal of Classroom Interaction* 28(1):21-25.

Lepper, M., and D. Green, eds. 1978. *The hidden cost of rewards: New perspectives on the psychology of human motivation*. New York: Erlbaum.

Levy, J.R., and H. Bjellan. 1995. *Create your own virtual reality system*. New York: Windcrest/McGraw-Hill.

Los Angeles Unified School District and the Office of the

Los Angeles County Superintendent of Schools. 1983. *Multicultural games for elementary school children*. Los Angeles: Los Angeles Unified School District and the Office of the Los Angeles County Superintendent of Schools.

Luxbacher, J. 1996. *Soccer instructor guide: Steps to success*. Champaign, IL: Human Kinetics.

———. 1996. *Soccer: Steps to success*, 2d ed. Champaign, IL: Human Kinetics.

Magill, R.A. 1993. *Motor learning: Concepts and applications*. Madison, WI: Brown and Benchmark.

Maloy, B.P. 1993. Legal obligations related to facilities. *Journal of Physical Education, Recreation & Dance* 64(2):28-30, 64.

Martin, R.M. 1975. *Gravity guiding system*. San Marino, CA: Essential.

Martinek, T.J., and J.B. Griffith. 1993. Working with the learned helpless child. *Journal of Physical Education, Recreation & Dance* 64(6):17-20.

Martinek, T.J., P.B. Crowe, and W.J. Rejeski. 1982. *Pygmalion in the gym: Causes and effects of expectations in teaching and coaching*. West Point, NY: Leisure Press.

Maryland State Department of Education. 1989. *Better physical education*. Maryland: Maryland State Department of Education.

Marzano, R.J. 1992. *A different kind of classroom: Teaching with dimensions of learning*. Alexandria, VA: ASCD.

Marzano, R.J., D. Pickering, and J. McTighe. 1993. *Assessing student outcomes: Performance assessment using the dimensions of learning model*. Alexandria, VA: ASCD.

McDonald, J.P., S. Smith, D. Turner, M. Finney, and E. Barton. 1993. *Graduation by exhibition: Assessing genuine achievement*. Alexandria, VA: ASCD.

Mechikoff, R., and S. Estes. 1993. *A history and philosophy of sport and physical education*. Madison, WI: Brown and Benchmark.

Melograno, V. 1985. *Designing the physical education curriculum: A self-directed approach*. Dubuque, IA: Kendall/Hunt.

Melograno, V.J. 1994. Portfolio assessment: Documenting authentic student learning. *Journal of Physical Education, Recreation & Dance* 65(8):50-55, 58-61.

Mendon, K. 1994. Outstanding middle school physical education program. *CAHPERD Journal/Times* 56(8):10, 34.

Mercier, R. 1992. Beyond class management—Teaching social skills through physical education. *Journal of Physical Education, Recreation & Dance* 63(6):83-87.

———. 1993. Student-center physical education—Strategies for teaching social skills. *Journal of Physical Education, Recreation & Dance* 64(5):60-65.

Merriman, J. 1993. Supervision in sport and physical activity. *Journal of Physical Education, Recreation & Dance* 64(2):20-21, 23.

Mesenbrink, R. 1974. National Association of Secondary School Principals. *Curriculum Report* 4(2).

Miller, B., B. Lord, and J. Dorney. 1994. *Summary report. Staff development for teachers. A study of configurations and costs in four districts.* Newton, MA: Education Development Center.

Mohnsen, B.S. 1987. *Physical education playground and field safety for grades K-12.* Downey, CA: Los Angeles County Office of Education.

———. 1990a. Physical education: Caught in the middle and forgotten. *Journal of Supervision and Curriculum Improvement* 3(3):10-16.

———. 1990b. Quality physical education: A three-part series. *CAHPERD Journal* 53(2):7-8.

———. 1991. Quality physical education: Part 2. *CAHPERD Journal* 53(4):3-4.

———. 1994. *Using technology in physical education.* Champaign, IL: Human Kinetics.

———. 1995. *Building a quality physical education program (Grades 6-12).* Medina, WA: Institute for Educational Development.

Mohnsen, B.S., and B. Hennessy. 1991. Quality physical education: Part 3. *CAHPERD Journal* 53(6):3-4, 6.

Mohnsen, B.S., and C. Thompson. 1995. Authentic assessment in physical education. *Teaching High School Physical Education* 1(1):6-8.

Morford, L. 1996. Can you believe this? *Teaching Secondary Physical Education* 2(2):2.

Morris, G., and J. Stiehl. 1989. *Changing kids' games.* Champaign, IL: Human Kinetics.

Mosston, M., and S. Ashworth. 1994. *Teaching physical education.* New York: Macmillan College.

Mustain, W.C. 1996. Navigating with assessment. *Teaching Secondary Physical Education* 2(2):4-6.

Naisbitt, J. 1984. *Megatrends: Ten new directions transforming our lives.* New York: Warner Books.

Naisbitt, J., and P. Aburdene. 1985. *Re-inventing the corporation.* New York: Warner Books.

National Association for Sport and Physical Education. 1990. *Definition of the physically educated person: Outcomes of quality physical education programs.* Reston, VA: NASPE.

———. 1994. *NASPE Sport and Physical Education Advocacy Kit.* Reston, VA: NASPE.

———. 1995a. *Appropriate practices for middle school physical education.* Reston, VA: NASPE.

———. 1995b. *National physical education standards: A guide to content and assessment.* Reston, VA: NASPE.

National Association of School Nurses. 1990. *Resolutions and policy statements.* Scarborough, ME: National Association of School Nurses.

National Staff Development Council. 1994. *Standards for staff development.* Oxford, OH: National Staff Development Council.

Negroponte, N. 1995. *Being digital.* New York: Knopf.

Neil, G. 1976. *Modern team handball: Beginner to expert.* Montreal, Canada: McGill University.

Nelson, J., J. Moore, and J. Dorociak. 1983. A survey of grading practices in physical education in Louisiana. *Louisiana Journal for Health, Physical Education, Recreation, and Dance* 28:18-21.

Nelson, J.M. 1991. *Self-defense: Steps to success.* Champaign, IL: Human Kinetics.

———. 1994. *Teaching self-defense: Steps to success.* Champaign, IL: Human Kinetics.

Nelson, W.E., and H. Glass. 1992. *International playtime: Classroom games and dances from around the world.* Carthage, IL: Fearon Teacher Aids.

Newmann, F.M. 1991. Linking restructuring to authentic student achievement. *Phi Delta Kappa* 48(1):35-40.

Nichols, B. 1994. *Moving and learning: The elementary school physical education experience.* St. Louis: Mosby.

Nieto, S. 1992. *Affirming diversity: The sociopolitical context of multicultural education.* White Plains, NY: Longman.

Orlick, T. 1978. *The cooperative sports and games book.* New York: Pantheon Books.

———. 1982. *The second cooperative sports and games book.* New York: Pantheon Books.

Ostrow, A.C. 1990. *Directory of psychological tests in the sport and exercise sciences.* Morgantown, WV: Fitness Information Technology.

Owens, D., and L.K. Bunker. 1995. *Golf: Steps to success,* 2d. ed. Champaign, IL: Human Kinetics.

———. 1996. *Golf instructor guide: Steps to success.* Champaign, IL: Human Kinetics.

Palmer, J.M. 1991. Planning wheels turn curriculum around. *Educational Leadership* 49(2):57-60.

Pangrazi, R., and C. Corbin. 1994. *Teaching strategies for improving youth fitness.* Reston, VA: AAHPERD.

Patterson, J.L. 1993. *Leadership for tomorrow's schools.* Alexandria, VA: ASCD.

Paulson, F.L., P.R. Paulson, and C.A. Meyer. 1991. What makes a portfolio a portfolio? *Educational Leadership* 48(5):60-63.

Peddiwell, J.A. 1939. *The saber-tooth curriculum.* New York: McGraw-Hill.

Pellett, T.L., H.A. Henschel-Pellet, and J.M. Harrison. 1994. Feedback effects: Field-based findings. *Journal of Physical Education, Recreation & Dance* 65(9):75-78.

Perelman, L.J. 1992. *School's out: Hyperlearning, the new technology, and the end of education.* New York: Morrow.

Petersen, S.C., V.L. Allen, and V.L. Minotti. 1994. Teacher knowledge and reflection. *Journal of Physical Education, Recreation & Dance* 65(7): 31-37.

Petray, C.K., and S.L. Blazer. 1986. *Health-related physical fitness: Concepts and activities for elementary school children.* Edina, MN: Bellwether Press.

Philipp, J.A., and J.D. Wilkerson. 1990. *Teaching team sports: A coeducational approach.* Champaign, IL: Human Kinetics.

Pickle-Ball, Inc. 1972. *Pickle-Ball.* Seattle, WA: Pickle-Ball.

Pimentel, K., and K. Teixeira. 1993. *Virtual reality: Through the new looking glass.* Carlsbad, CA: Windcrest Books.

Placek, J. 1983. Conceptions of success in teaching: Busy, happy, and good? In *Research on Teaching in Physical Education.* Champaign, IL: Human Kinetics, 46-56.

———. 1992. Rethinking middle school physical education curriculum: An integrated thematic approach. *Quest* 44(3):330-341.

Polin, L. 1991. Portfolio assessment. *The Writing Notebook* January/February:25-27, 42.

Poplin, M.S. 1988. Holistic/constructivist principles of the teaching/learning process: Implications for the field of learning disabilities. *Journal of Learning Disabilities* 21(7):402-416.

Potter, D.L., and G. Brockmeyer. 1989. *Softball: Steps to success.* Champaign, IL: Human Kinetics.

———. 1989. *Teaching softball: Steps to success.* Champaign, IL: Human Kinetics.

Professional Golfers' Association of America Junior Golf Foundation. 1987. *First swing manual.* Palm Beach Gardens, FL: National Golf Foundation.

Randall, L.E. 1992a. *The student teacher's handbook for physical education.* Champaign, IL: Human Kinetics.

———. 1992b. *Systematic supervision for physical education.* Champaign, IL: Human Kinetics.

Ray, O.M. 1992. *Encyclopedia of line dances: The steps that came and stayed.* Reston, VA: AAHPERD.

Reauthorized U.S. Public Law 99-057, 1986. Section 504 of the *Rehabilitation Act of 1973.*

Redican, K.J., L.K. Olsen, and C.R. Baffi. 1986. *Organization of school health programs.* New York: Macmillan.

Richard-Amato, P.A., and M.A. Snow. 1992. *The multicultural classroom: Reading for content-area teachers.* White Plains, NY: Longman.

Rink, J.E. 1993. *Teaching physical education for learning.* St. Louis: Mosby.

———, ed. 1993. *Critical crossroads: Middle and secondary school physical education.* Reston, VA: NASPE.

Rohnke, K. 1989a. *Cowstails and cobras II.* Hamilton, MA: Project Adventure.

———. 1989b. *Silver bullets.* Hamilton, MA: Project Adventure.

———. 1989c. *The bottomless bag: This one.* Dubuque, IA: Kendall/Hunt.

———. 1991. *The bottomless bag: That one.* Dubuque, IA: Kendall/Hunt.

Rosenshine, B. 1983. Teaching functions in instructional programs. *Elementary School Journal* 83:335-351.

Ross, J.G., and R.P. Pate. 1987. The national children and youth fitness study: A summary of findings. *Journal of Physical Education, Recreation & Dance* 58(9):51-56.

Ryser, O.E., and J.R. Brown. 1980. *A manual for tumbling and apparatus stunts.* Dubuque, IA: Brown.

Sander, A.N., M. Harageones, T. Ratliffe, and D. Pizzaro. 1993. Florida's fit to achieve program. *Journal of Physical Education, Recreation & Dance* 64(7):26-28.

Schmidt, R.A. 1991. *Motor learning and performance: From principles to practice.* Champaign, IL: Human Kinetics.

Schneider, R.E. 1992. Don't just promote your profession—Market it! *Journal of Physical Education, Recreation & Dance* 63(5):70-73.

Schnitzer, S. 1993. Designing an authentic assessment. *Educational Leadership* 50(7):32-35.

School Improvement Office, California Department of Education. 1994. *Guide and criteria for program quality review middle level.* Sacramento, CA: School Improvement Office, California Department of Education.

Sebren, A. 1994. Reflective thinking—Integrating theory and practice in teacher preparation. *Journal of Physical Education, Recreation & Dance* 65(6):23-24, 57-59.

Secretary's Commission on Achieving Necessary Skills (SCANS). 1991. *What work requires of schools: A scans report for America 2000.* Washington, DC: U.S. Department of Labor.

Seefeldt, V., and P. Vogel. 1986. *The value of physical activity.* Reston, VA: AAHPERD.

Shakarian, D.C. 1995. Beyond lecture: Active learning strategies that work. *Journal of Physical Education, Recreation & Dance* 66(5):21-24.

Shulman, L.S. 1987. Knowledge and teaching: Foundations of the new reform. *Harvard Educational Review* 57(1):1-22.

Siedentop, D. 1983. *Developing teaching skills in physical education.* Mountain View, CA: Mayfield Company.

———. 1991. *Developing teaching skills in physical education.* 2nd ed. Mountain View, CA: Mayfield Company.

Siedentop, D., J. Herkowitz, and J. Rink. 1984. *Elementary physical education methods.* Englewood Cliffs, NJ: Prentice-Hall.

Siedentop, D., C. Mand, and A. Taggart. 1986. *Physical education: Teaching and curriculum strategies for grades 5-12.* Mountain View, CA: Mayfield.

Silverman, S. 1991. Research on teaching in physical education: Review and commentary. *Research Quarterly for Exercise and Sport* 62(4):352-364.

Sizer, T.R., and B. Rogers. 1993. Designing standards: Achieving the delicate balance. *Educational Leadership* 50(5):24-26.

Slavin, R.E. 1990. Achievement effects of ability grouping in secondary schools: A best-evidence synthesis. *Review of Educational Research* 60:471-499.

———. 1991. Synthesis of research on cooperative learning. *Educational Leadership* 48(5):71-82.

Smith, M.D. 1993. Physical education in the British national curriculum. *Journal of Physical Education, Recreation & Dance* 64(9):21-32.

Solipaz. Undated. *Basic circus skills*. Lodi, CA: Solipaz.

———. Undated. *How to ride a unicycle*. Lodi, CA: Solipaz.

Spady, W.G. 1994. Choosing outcomes of significance. *Educational Leadership* 51(6):19-22.

Spickelmier, D., T. Sharpe, C. Deibler, C. Golden, and B. Krueger. 1995. Use positive discipline for middle school students. *Strategies* 8(8):5-8.

Spindt, G.B., W.H. Monti, and B. Hennessy. 1992a. *Moving as a team*. Dubuque, IA: Kendall/Hunt.

———. 1992b. *Moving as a team physical education portfolio*. Dubuque, IA: Kendall/Hunt.

———. 1992c. *Moving with confidence*. Dubuque, IA: Kendall/Hunt.

———. 1992d. *Moving with confidence physical education portfolio*. Dubuque, IA: Kendall/Hunt.

———. 1992e. *Moving with skill*. Dubuque, IA: Kendall/Hunt.

———. 1992f. *Moving with skill physical education portfolio*. Dubuque, IA: Kendall/Hunt.

Staff. 1990. White House document outlines President's education goals. *Education Daily Bulletin* 23(14).

Stevenson, H.W., and J.W. Stigler. 1992. *The learning gap: Why our schools are failing and what we can learn from Japanese and Chinese education*. New York: Touchstone.

Stiehl, J. 1993. Becoming responsible—Theoretical and practical considerations. *Journal of Physical Education, Recreation & Dance* 64(5):38-40, 57-59, 70-71.

Stokes, R., C. Moore, and S.L. Schultz. 1993. *Personal fitness and you*. Winston-Salem, NC: Hunter Textbooks.

Strand, B., and S. Reeder. 1993. P.E. with a heartbeat—Hi-tech physical education. *Journal of Physical Education, Recreation & Dance* 64(3):81-84.

Strand, B.N., and R. Wilson. 1993. *Assessing sport skills*. Champaign, IL: Human Kinetics.

Strickland, R.H. 1996. *Bowling instructor guide: Steps to success*. Champaign, IL: Human Kinetics.

———. 1996. *Bowling: Steps to success*, 2d. ed. Champaign, IL: Human Kinetics.

Superintendent Bill Honig's Middle Grade Task Force. 1987. *Caught in the middle: Educational reform for young adolescents in California public schools*. Sacramento, CA: California State Department of Education.

Sutliff, M. 1996. The duty to warn of inherent dangers. *Teaching Secondary Physical Education* 2(2):18-19.

Sylvester, R. 1993. What the biology of the brain tells us about learning. *Educational Leadership* 51(4):46-51.

Tannehill, D., and D. Zakrajsek. 1993. Student attitudes towards physical education: A multicultural study. *Journal of Teaching in Physical Education* 13(1):78-84.

The Juggle Bug. 1979. *The joy of juggling*. Champaign, IL: Human Kinetics.

Thomas, D.G. 1996. *Swimming instructor guide: Steps to success*. Champaign, IL: Human Kinetics.

———. 1996. *Swimming: Steps to success*, 2d. ed. Champaign, IL: Human Kinetics.

Thornburg, D.D. 1992. *Edutrends 2010: Restructuring, technology, and the future of education*. San Francisco: Starson Publications.

Tip, C., and D. Roddick. 1985. *Frisbee games*. La Mirada, CA: Discovering the World.

Toch, T. 1991. In the name of excellence: The struggle to reform the nation's schools, why it's failing, and what should be done. *Oxford University Press* 63(7):80-87.

Toffler, A. 1968. *The schoolhouse in the city*. New York: Praeger.

Tye, K.A., ed. 1990. *Global education: From thought to action*. Alexandria, VA: ASCD.

United States Consumer Product Safety Commission. 1990. *Public playground handbook for safety*. Washington, DC: United States Consumer Product Safety Commission.

United States Department of Health and Human Services. 1990. *Healthy people 2000: National health promotion and disease prevention objectives*. Washington, DC: United States Department of Health and Human Services.

United States Department of Health and Human Services. 1996. *Physical activity and health: A report of the Surgeon General*. Atlanta, GA: USDHHS.

United States Team Handball Federation. 1981. *Team handball—Official rules of the game*. Colorado Springs: United States Team Handball Federation.

United States Tennis Association Schools Program. 1993. *United States Tennis Association schools program curriculum*. White Plains, NY: United States Tennis Association Schools Program.

U.S. Public Law 94-142. *Education for All Handicapped Children Act of 1975*.

Valentine, B., and B. Valentine, 1991. *Self-defense for life*. Glendale, CA: Self-Defense Publications.

van der Smissen, B. 1990. *Legal liability and risk management for public and private entities*. Cincinnatti: Anderson.

Viera, B.J., and B.J. Ferguson. 1996. *Volleyball instructor guide: Steps to success*. Champaign, IL: Human Kinetics.

———. 1996. *Volleyball: Steps to success*, 2d. ed. Champaign, IL: Human Kinetics.

Vogel, P., and V. Seefeldt. 1988. *Program design in physical education*. Indianapolis: Benchmark Press.

Wang, M.C., G.D. Haertel, and H.J. Walberg. 1993. What helps students learn? *Educational Leadership* 51(4):46-51.

Weidel, B.L., F.R. Biles, G.E. Figley, and B.J. Neuman. 1980. *Sports skills: A conceptual approach to meaningful movement*. Dubuque, IA: Brown.

Wheatley, M.J. 1994. *Leadership and new science: Learning about organization from an orderly universe.* San Francisco: Berrett-Koehler.

Wiburg, K. 1995. Becoming critical users of multimedia. *The Computing Teacher* 22(7):59-61.

Wiggins, G. 1994. Toward better report cards. *Educational Leadership* 52(2):28-37.

Wikgren, S. 1995. Coeducational physical education: Seeking quality and equity for all students. *Teaching Middle School Physical Education* 1(4):1, 4-5.

———. 1996. Are you a "C"? *Teaching Secondary Physical Education* 2(2):7.

Wiley, J. Undated. *Complete book of unicycling.* Lodi, CA: Solipaz.

———. Undated. *Unicycling society of America.* Lodi, CA: Solipaz.

Williamson, K.M. 1993. Is your inequity showing? Ideas and strategies for creating a more equitable learning environment. *Journal of Physical Education, Recreation & Dance* 64(8):15-23.

Wilmore, J.H., and D.L. Costill. 1994. *Physiology of sport and exercise.* Champaign, IL: Human Kinetics.

Wissel, H. 1994. *Basketball: Steps to Success.* Champaign, IL: Human Kinetics.

———. 1996. *Basketball instructor guide: Steps to Success.* Champaign, IL: Human Kinetics.

Wlodkowski, R. 1985. *Enhancing adult motivation to learn.* San Francisco: Jossey-Bass.

Wolk, S. 1994. Project-based learning: Pursuits with a purpose. *Educational Leadership* 52(3):42-45.

Wong-Fillmore, L. 1980. *Language learning through bilingual instruction.* Berkeley, CA: University of California, Berkeley.

Wood, K., C. Fisher, T. Huth, and P. Graham. 1995. Opening the door to tomorrow's classroom. *Teaching Middle School Physical Education* 1(1):1, 4-5, 8.

Wuest, D.A., and B.J. Lombardo. 1994. *Curriculum and instruction: The secondary school physical education experience.* St. Louis: Mosby.

Zakrajsek, D., and L.A. Carnes. 1986. *Individualizing physical education: Criterion materials.* Champaign, IL: Human Kinetics.

INDEX

Note: Information in boxes is indexed as "Inventions, 5 (box)," except where information in a box amplifies information in the text, in which case the box is not identified separately. Page numbers in italics refer to illustrations.

Activities that emphasize teamwork and group problem solving

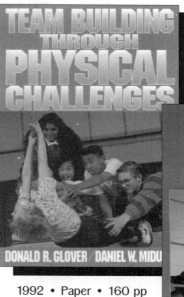

1992 • Paper • 160 pp
Item BGLOO359
ISBN 0-87322-359-4
$16.95 ($23.95 Canadian)

1995 • Paper • 120 pp
Item BMID0785
ISBN 0-87322-785-9
$14.95 ($20.95 Canadian)

Looking for ways to challenge participants, promote teamwork, and initiate problem-solving? These fun activities—22 in *Team Building Through Physical Challenges,* 15 in *More Team Building Challenges*—help your students build self-confidence and improve interpersonal relationships while they improve their motor skills.

Each book gives you specific techniques and strategies to incorporate problem-solving activities into your curriculum. Participants interact verbally and physically, struggle, deal with failure, persevere, and work together to master problems while learning to value teamwork, practice leadership skills, improve listening skills, and appreciate individual differences.

Each member of the group is important, because everyone must meet the challenge before the team can succeed. Team members take turns filling the roles of organizer, praiser, encourager, summarizer, and recorder.

Easy-to-use introductory, intermediate, and advanced challenges make the books ideal for most participants.

Prices subject to change.

To request more information or to place your order, U.S. customers call **TOLL-FREE 1-800-747-4457.** Customers outside the U.S. use appropriate telephone number/address shown in the front of this book.

"Remarkably motivating for students of all ages! These innovative activities create an excellent learning environment for the gym. They allow all students an opportunity to experience a multitude of challenges to enhance their physical, mental, and social development. The examples are well-written and teacher-friendly. Great for integration across the curriculum—a must for all teachers."

Kathleen F. Engle, BS, MA
Wyoming Middle School Teacher of the Year, 1994
NASPE Central District Middle School PE Teacher of the Year, 1995
Honoree in Disney Channel Salutes the American Teacher, 1995-96

30-day money-back guarantee!

Human Kinetics
The Information Leader in Physical Activity
http://www.humankinetics.com/

ABOUT THE AUTHOR

With 13 years of middle school physical education teaching experience, Bonnie Mohnsen is no stranger to the needs of middle school students and teachers. She has been recognized many times for her outstanding achievements in the field of physical education; her numerous honors include being named the California Association for Health, Physical Education, Recreation and Dance (CAHPERD) Southern District Outstanding Physical Education Teacher (1989) and receiving the CAHPERD State Honor Award (1995). A highly sought after consultant and speaker, Dr. Mohnsen has helped countless physical educators across the United States improve the quality of their programs.

An outspoken proponent of using technology in physical education, Dr. Mohnsen is the coordinator of physical education and integrated technology for the Orange County Department of Education. She is a member of the technology task force for the National Association for Sport and Physical Education and the author of *Using Technology in Physical Education* (Human Kinetics, 1995). She is also the owner of and a programmer for Bonnie's Fitware, which develops affordable software for use in physical education.

Dr. Mohnsen belongs to several professional organizations, including the American Alliance for Health, Physical Education, Recreation and Dance; CAHPERD; and the Association for Supervision and Curriculum Development. She earned her doctoral degree from the University of Southern California in 1984. She lives in Cerritos, California, where she enjoys reading, jogging, and playing on her computer.